Immigrants Out!

CRITICAL AMERICA

General Editors: RICHARD DELGADO and JEAN STEFANCIC

White by Law:
The Legal Construction of Race
Ian Haney López

Cultivating Intelligence:
Power, Law, and the Politics of Teaching
Louise Harmon and Deborah W. Post

Privilege Revealed:
How Invisible Privilege Undermines America
Stephanie M. Wildman
with Margalynne Armstrong, Adrienne D. Davis, and Trina Grillo

Does the Law Morally Bind the Poor?
or What Good's the Constitution When You Can't Afford a Loaf of Bread?
R. George Wright

Hybrid:
Bisexuals, Multiracials, and Other Misfits Under American Law
Ruth Colker

Critical Race Feminism:
A Reader
Edited by Adrien Katherine Wing

Immigrants Out!
The New Nativism and the Anti-Immigrant Impulse in the United States
Edited by Juan F. Perea

Immigrants

Out!

The New Nativism and the Anti-Immigrant Impulse in the United States

Edited by Juan F. Perea

NEW YORK UNIVERSITY PRESS

New York and London

BHT 5757 - 5/3

NEW YORK UNIVERSITY PRESS
New York and London

© 1997 by New York University

A previous version of chapter 18 was published in the *Hastings Constitutional Law Quarterly,* Vol. 22, No. 4, pp. 915-24. © 1995 by University of California, Hastings College of the Law.

Library of Congress Cataloging-in-Publication Data
Immigrants out! : the new nativism and the anti-immigrant impulse in
the United States / edited by Juan F. Perea.
p.   cm.—(Critical America)
Includes bibliographical references (p.) and index.
ISBN 0-8147-6627-7 (cloth : alk. paper).—ISBN 0-8147-6642-0
(pbk. : alk. paper)
1. Nativism. 2. Immigrants—United States. 3. United States—
Emigration and immigration.   I. Perea, Juan F., 1952– .
II. Series.
E184.A1I4355 1997
305.8'00973—dc20   96-25258
                              CIP

New York University Press books are printed on acid-free paper,
and their binding materials are chosen for strength and durability.

Manufactured in the United States of America
10 9 8 7 6 5 4 3 2 1

I dedicate this book to my spouse, Jan, and to my sons Alexander and Daniel. With hope that this nation will recognize the beauty in their brown hair, and their beautiful hazel, brown, and blue eyes. And with hope that they shall be fair children, of full fairness and decency. May their fairness and compassion not be limited to those who are fair only in complexion.

CONTENTS

Acknowledgments   xi
Contributors   xiii

1   Introduction   1
Juan F. Perea

PART I   HISTORICAL THEMES:
Nativism in American History and the Meaning of
the Statue of Liberty

2   Old Poison in New Bottles:
The Deep Roots of Modern Nativism   13
Joe R. Feagin

3   The Statue of Liberty:
Notes from Behind the Gilded Door   44
Juan F. Perea

PART II   IDENTIFYING THE NEW NATIVISM:
Its Ways and Means

4   Immigration Reform and Nativism:
The Nationalist Response to the
Transnationalist Challenge   61
Leo R. Chavez

5   Official English as Nativist Backlash   78
Raymond Tatalovich

PART III CAUSATION OF THE NEW NATIVISM:
Why Is It Happening Now?

6 Nativism in the Mid-1990s: Why Now?   105
Thomas Muller

7 Funding the Nativist Agenda   119
Jean Stefancic

8 The Tables Are Turned: Immigration, Poverty, and Social
Conflict in California Communities   136
Patricia Zavella

PART IV NATIVISM PAST:
Historical Context and the New Nativism

9 The New Nativism: Something Old, Something New,
Something Borrowed, Something Blue   165
Kevin R. Johnson

10 Latinos in the United States: Invitation and Exile   190
Gilbert Paul Carrasco

11 Who May Give Birth to Citizens?
Reproduction, Eugenics, and Immigration   205
Dorothy E. Roberts

PART V BORDER CROSSINGS:
Critical Views of the Border

12 The Social Construction of the U.S.-Mexico Border   223
Néstor P. Rodríguez

13 A Meditation on Borders   244
Robert S. Chang

14 Reconciling Rights in Collision:
An International Human Rights Strategy   254
Berta Esperanza Hernández-Truyol

PART VI ANALYZING THE DISCOURSE OF IMMIGRATION
AND CITIZENSHIP

15 "Nativism" the Concept: Some Reflections   279
Linda S. Bosniak

16 Dangerous Undertones of the New Nativism:
Peter Brimelow and the Decline of the West 300
Daniel Kanstroom

17 Citizenship 318
Richard Delgado

18 The Tightening Circle of Membership 324
T. Alexander Aleinikoff

Index 333

ACKNOWLEDGMENTS

It is said that it takes an entire village to raise a child. It takes at least a small village to produce a book. My thanks to all who have fueled my impulse to write. Special thanks to Richard Delgado and Jean Stefancic for inviting me to do this project, for supporting me in the endeavor, and for the shining examples of scholarly brilliance and achievement that they have provided for an entire generation of writers. Special thanks also to Niko Pfund, editor-in-chief of New York University Press, and his staff, who have diligently and compassionately helped me when I asked and who have assisted enormously in producing this book.

I must express my appreciation to the contributors to this volume. It has been a genuine pleasure to have the opportunity to work with each of them. I have learned much from them all. Their dedication, knowledge, and insight have made a book of this kind and quality both possible and worthwhile.

My thanks also for the generous financial support that has made this book possible. My sincere thanks to Dean Jeffrey E. Lewis and Associate Dean Barry A. Currier of the University of Florida College of Law for their continuous support of my research for many years now, and especially during the two years I have spent working on this book. Thanks, too, to Dean Avi Soifer of Boston College Law School for his intellectual encouragement of my scholarship generally and for helpful financial support during my visit to Boston College Law School during the Fall Semester, 1995. I am grateful for the excellent research assistance of three outstanding former law students, Mr. Lew Minsky and Mr. John Marshall, graduates of the University of Florida College of Law, and Ms. Virginia Wei, graduate of the Boston College Law School.

And last, but never least, my thanks to the most important people in my life, my family. My spouse, Dr. Jan Snyder Perea, breaks through occasionally dense walls of character and habit and helps me appreciate what really matters, which she knows so well. My sons Alex and Daniel also teach me precious truths, with humor and surprise and delight, about what really matters. I count myself fortunate to be surrounded by special people who make knowledge, insight, and learning possible.

CONTRIBUTORS

T. ALEXANDER ALEINIKOFF is Executive Associate Commissioner for Programs, Immigration and Naturalization Service. He is currently on leave from his position as Professor of Law at the University of Michigan. He has published a leading textbook on immigration law, and is the author of articles on immigration and refugee law, constitutional law, and race discrimination law.

LINDA S. BOSNIAK is Associate Professor of Law at the Rutgers School of Law, Camden. She has written extensively on issues concerning immigration policy, the status of aliens, and nationalism.

GILBERT P. CARRASCO is Professor of Law at the Villanova University School of Law. Professor Carrasco has authored casebooks on immigration law and civil rights and specializes in constitutional law and immigration law.

ROBERT S. CHANG is Associate Professor of Law at the California Western School of Law. His scholarship has focused on the construction and understanding of Asian Americans in legal and racial discourse. He is the author of *Dis-Oriented: Asian Americans, Law, and the Nation-State* (New York University Press, forthcoming).

LEO R. CHAVEZ is Professor and Chair of the Department of Anthropology at the University of California, Irvine. Professor Chavez has written extensively on issues of immigration, particularly undocumented immigration, including families and household structure, factors of settlement, community membership, labor force participation, and the use of medical services. He is the author of *Shadowed Lives: Undocumented Immigrants in American Society* (Harcourt Brace Jovanovich College Publishers, 1992).

RICHARD DELGADO is Charles Inglis Thomson Professor of Law at the University of Colorado School of Law. He is the author of several highly regarded books, including *The Rodrigo Chronicles* (New York University Press, 1995). He is widely known as one of the most influential critical legal scholars in the nation.

JOE R. FEAGIN is Graduate Research Professor in the Department of Sociology at the University of Florida. He is the author of many books and is widely recognized as one of the nation's foremost scholars of racial and ethnic relations in the United States. He received a Pulitzer Prize nomination for his book *Ghetto Revolts* (Macmillan, 1973). He has recently published *White Racism: The Basics* (Routledge, 1995) with Herman Vera and *Racial and Ethnic Relations* (Prentice-Hall, 1995) with Clairece Feagin.

BERTA ESPERANZA HERNÁNDEZ-TRUYOL is Professor of Law at St. John's University School of Law. She has published extensively in the areas of women's rights and international law.

KEVIN R. JOHNSON is Professor of Law at the University of California at Davis School of Law. Professor Johnson has published many articles on issues of immigration law and policy, including significant work on California's Proposition 187. His work has focused on the influence of race on U.S. immigration laws.

DANIEL KANSTROOM is Assistant Clinical Professor of Law at Boston College Law School, specializing in immigration and criminal law, and is the Director of the Boston College Immigration and Asylum Project. He has published articles about immigration and citizenship law in the United States and Germany.

THOMAS MULLER is an economist and consultant in private practice. He is the author of many articles and books, including *Immigrants and the American City* (New York University Press, 1993).

JUAN F. PEREA is Professor of Law at the University of Florida College of Law. He has written extensively on American multilingualism and language policy, nativism, and ethnic identity and American law.

DOROTHY E. ROBERTS is Professor of Law at Rutgers University School of Law in Newark, New Jersey. She has written many leading articles on race, reproduction, welfare, and the criminal justice system and co-authored a forthcoming casebook on constitutional law. She is currently working on a book tentatively entitled *Race, Reproduction, and the Meaning of Liberty*.

NÉSTOR P. RODRÍGUEZ is Professor in the Department of Sociology at the University of Houston. He has written on the subjects of the social construction of the border and transnational communities.

JEAN STEFANCIC is Research Associate at the University of Colorado School of Law. She has written several articles on civil rights and legal scholarship, and is the author of *No Mercy: How Conservative Think Tanks and Foundations Changed America's Social Agenda* (Temple University Press, 1996).

RAYMOND TATALOVICH is a Professor of Political Science at Loyola University, Chicago. He specializes in public policy analysis, particularly moral conflicts, and recently authored *Nativism Reborn? The Official English Movement and the American States,* a sophisticated and systematic study of the politics behind the current agitation to establish English as the official language of the United States.

PATRICIA ZAVELLA is an anthropologist and Professor of Community Studies at the University of California at Santa Cruz. She is the author of two books on working-class Mexican-American women, *Women's Work and Chicano Families: Cannery Workers of the Santa Clara Valley* (Cornell University Press, 1987), and with Louise Lamphere, Felipe Gonzales, and Peter B. Evans, *Sunbelt Working Mothers: Reconciling Family and Factory* (Cornell University Press, 1993).

1. INTRODUCTION
Juan F. Perea

One of the pivotal dimensions of any human world is the enemy, that
which is held responsible for the bad things in life.
—James Aho, *This Thing of Darkness*

A book on nativism, old and new, must begin with a definition
of its subject:

intense opposition to an internal minority on the grounds of
its foreign (i.e. "un-American") connections. Specific nativistic antagonisms may,
and do, vary widely in response to the changing character of minority irritants
and the shifting conditions of the day; but through each separate hostility runs
the connecting, energizing force of modern nationalism. While drawing on much
broader cultural antipathies and ethnocentric judgements, nativism translates
them into a zeal to destroy the enemies of a distinctively American way of life.[1]

The word *nativism* also suggests some part of its meaning: a preference for
those deemed natives; simultaneous and intense opposition to those deemed
strangers, foreigners.

During nativist times in the United States, democratic processes are turned
against internal minorities deemed foreign or "un-American," resulting in
discriminatory legislation and immigration restrictions. Nativist movements,
and the legislation they spawn, seek to rid the nation of perceived enemies of
the American way of life. The social sanction given to majoritarian legislative
action is crucial in the creation of such enemies.[2] Through legislative rejection
of some perceived enemy in our midst, nativism seeks the ritual purification
of American society, the separation of those who belong from those who do
not. The majority enhances its status as the "real" Americans, those who
belong, and rejects those currently deemed threatening to American values.

We have been through all of this before. During the controversy over the
Alien and Sedition Acts in 1798, the enemy took the form of French ethnicity
and ideology, and Americans associated with that ideology.[3] The 1850s saw

the vilification of the Irish "savages" who, for the first time, had migrated in substantial numbers to the United States.[4] The years during and after World War I yielded intense hatred of the Germans and German Americans among us.[5] During World War II, the hatred of the Japanese enemy, and of loyal Americans of Japanese ancestry who looked like the enemy, resulted in the forced incarceration of seventy thousand Japanese American *citizens* and between thirty and forty thousand Japanese aliens in domestic internment camps.[6] During the 1950s, fear of the Communist enemy was played out in the frequent interrogation of immigrants from Southeastern European Countries, in suspicions regarding their ethnicity, and in the blacklisting of Jews.[7]

The targets of today's nativism wear Mexican, Central American, and Asian faces. Indeed, the public identification of "illegal aliens" with persons of Mexican ancestry is so strong that many Mexican Americans and other Latino citizens are presumed foreign and illegal.[8] When citizens and aliens look alike, then all are presumed to be alien and foreign and undermining of the national character. This is an old theme in American politics.

As a society, we have declared legislative and border war on both undocumented and legal aliens. California's Proposition 187 and its progeny deny to undocumented aliens medical services in public hospitals and education in public schools.[9] Federal legislation has been proposed to deny benefits to undocumented aliens, and to reduce levels of legal immigration. Even the Fourteenth Amendment is under attack. Several resolutions introduced in Congress have sought an unprecedented amendment to the first sentence of the Fourteenth Amendment, to change entitlement to birthright citizenship, denying citizenship to the U.S.-born children of undocumented aliens.[10] Undocumented persons, and increasingly the broader class of noncitizens, are the new enemy, the new objects of legislative war.

Undocumented aliens have been a most useful and productive enemy. As several of the chapters in this book make clear, upper and middle class Americans benefit from lower-priced goods and services produced by undocumented persons.[11] Zoe Baird, former candidate for Attorney General, hired illegal aliens while earning over five hundred thousand dollars a year.[12] Even Governor Pete Wilson of California, self-declared guardian and savior of his state from the alien peril he first identified, saw fit to hire an undocumented person as his housekeeper.[13]

For a chance at a better life, the undocumented are willing to work hard for much less than they deserve, and often for less than they would be entitled to under United States law.[14] Because it is in the financial interest of those hiring undocumented persons to pay less, there is a substantial demand for their underpriced services. If there were no demand for their services, it would make no sense for them to come. But time and time again, employers ignore immigration laws and hire undocumented workers in order to lower their labor costs and increase their profits.[15]

Governor Wilson of California enjoyed great political success blaming the economic atrophy in his state on undocumented persons. Conservative Republican politicians make use of immigration reform as one of their most prominent political issues. The undocumented make easy targets: they lack the power to vote and so they lack political legitimacy, clout, and voice. Beyond their inability to vote, they are extraordinarily vulnerable to exploitation. They dare not assert any rights they may have publicly out of fear that identification will result in their deportation from the country. The basis for this fear is well illustrated by the recent case of undocumented aliens from Thailand who were required to work in near-imprisonment in textile sweat-shops as a condition of their entry to the United States.[16] Ironically, as soon as their plight was publicized, and their treatment condemned and deplored, the Thai immigrants were promptly re-imprisoned in INS detention centers.[17]

The new nativism cannot be understood adequately in isolation from other current social phenomena. The deteriorating treatment and scapegoating of undocumented persons is vitally linked to the deteriorating treatment and scapegoating of persons of color, minorities, and women. One of the most powerful insights into the treatment of persons of color in the United States is Derrick Bell's theory of interest-convergence.[18] Briefly stated, the theory holds that the treatment of African Americans, and by extension other peoples of color, will improve only when it is in the interest of the white majority.[19] During the cold war, American embarrassment at the United States' mistreatment of its peoples of color, and Soviet advertisement of this mistreatment, was a major motivating factor in the proposal and subsequent enactment of civil rights legislation intended to promote equal treatment of blacks and whites.[20] American embarrassment about its mistreatment of blacks may also have played some role in the pivotal decision in *Brown v. Board of Education.*[21] When it was in the political interest of the white majority to promote racial equality and to prohibit race discrimination, these events happened.

There is a powerful corollary to the interest-convergence theory, which may explain, at least in part, both the new nativism and the broad deterioration in support for racial equality. The corollary is that in the absence of an external moral imperative such as cold-war competition, when it is no longer perceived to be in the interests of whites to support equality goals, then there will be a deterioration in concern about the condition of America's racial and ethnic minorities. This deterioration is apparent in many recent events: the widespread legislative[22] and judicial attack on affirmative action;[23] the judicial attack on enforcement, in ways calculated to increase the numbers of minority representatives, of the Voting Rights Act;[24] the renascent presence of the Official English movement;[25] and the punitive restrictions on immigration and citizenship that form the cold heart of the new nativism. All of these developments can be interpreted as parts of an elaborate ritual of purification designed, as nativist rituals always seem to be, to ease internal insecurities by creating enemies, internal and external, to whom we assign blame for the problems of our own making.

Among the most visible events signaling the flaring of new nativism is California's Proposition 187. It was in the wake of Proposition 187 that the idea for this book was first suggested to me by Richard Delgado and Jean Stefancic, two of the distinguished contributors to this volume and coeditors of the Critical America series. California voters had just enacted the law. While I was generally aware of Proposition 187 and the heated, emotional rhetoric generated on both sides of the debate about it, I had yet to study and consider it carefully.

I began with vague apprehensions and unease about this law. My first impressions were that the law was anti-Latino, since its rhetoric concerned only undocumented Latinos, principally Mexicans and Central Americans, and not other persons illegally within the country. It seemed unconstitutional, at least in part, in light of the Supreme Court's decision in *Plyler v. Doe,* which guaranteed the right of children of undocumented immigrants to receive a public-school education.[26] This law was also highly charged politically; it had generated an intense and acrimonious debate, with charges of racism, nativism, and out-of-control borders flung far and wide, daily, through the newspapers.

On the other hand, I wondered about the strength of the moral claim that undocumented people could make upon a government's resources. If it was true that undocumented persons were generating excessive costs in California and other states, were states unable to do anything to curtail these costs? *Plyler v. Doe* had been decided over twenty years ago by a Supreme Court very differently constituted and very differently disposed towards civil rights than the current court. Will the current court deny state power to curtail benefits to undocumented people, or even legal aliens, during times of economic hardship? At a more general level, if all persons, regardless of immigration status within the United States, were entitled to roughly the same rights and benefits, then was there any meaningful difference between the status of citizen, the status of legal alien, and the status of undocumented alien? Should such differences in citizenship status justify differences in entitlement to social benefits?

I began this book, therefore, with many difficult questions which I had not answered for myself and some of which must remain unanswered for the time being. However, as I studied Proposition 187 and other laws restricting immigrants that had been proposed at about the same time, I was struck by parallels between the present and the past. Although aspects of some of these proposals seemed unprecedented, the anti-immigrant rhetoric used to defend them sounded very familiar to me. The rhetoric sounded very similar to the rhetoric used between 1890 and 1924, a period of intense anti-immigrant feeling that culminated in the highly restrictive national origin quota restrictions of 1924. There also seemed to be parallels with the movement against German-speaking peoples in the United States during the era of World War I, which resulted in prohibitions on the teaching and use of the German language, among other restrictions. One observer described the anti-German movement as "the most strenuous nationalism *and* the most pervasive nativism that the United States had ever known."[27]

The outlines of a present-day nativist movement seemed clear enough in Proposition 187, in proposed legislation that would deny citizenship to the U.S.-born children of undocumented persons, and in the increasing legislative success of the Official English movement. But while these outlines seem clear, more rigorous analysis and inquiry is necessary to establish or disprove the connections between past and present nativism. The principal works on nativism have always reflected upon, and generally condemned, long-past nativism. While the passage of time facilitates historical inquiry, making a focus on past nativism understandable, to write solely about past nativism and to ignore unmistakable signs of present nativism makes much writing on nativism of limited usefulness in identifying, understanding, and intervening in current political developments. Passive hand-wringing about past wrongs is of little use in confronting serious questions of public policy raised by present nativism.

In the midst of an era of recognizable nativism, the time for this book is *right now*. The essays in this book take an unflinching critical look at a series of contemporary political developments that may accurately be labeled nativist. The purpose of the book is to put this new nativism into full interdisciplinary context so that we might convincingly identify our era as nativist. Through the varied perspectives of an interdisciplinary collection of writers, this volume provides the intellectual tools with which to use the nativism in our national past to analyze and confront the nativism presently in our midst.

This book is thus a very conscious attempt to avoid the often-posed conundrum regarding whether, without confronting our past, we can avoid repeating it. Here, we can confront the past: the stories and methods of past nativism supply necessary context and ample links to present nativism. Anyone who reads this book will become conscious of the many parallels between this historical moment and past moments that we have come to regret. And we *can* avoid repeating this past: consciousness of our present repetition of the past enables a choice. We can choose to repeat the past, or we can choose to avoid those parts of the past that we may later regret. We need not be swept by strong political currents, for knowledge makes the choice ours.

This book is thus unique and important in several ways. Its purpose is to provide interdisciplinary frameworks within which we can recognize and analyze current nativism, immigration policy, and citizenship in light of our past and present. It is a unique commentary upon and intervention into evolving events of historical significance. It is truly an interdisciplinary book, bringing together the varying viewpoints of very distinguished scholars and policymakers: sociologists, anthropologists, legal scholars, a political scientist, an economist, and a national policymaker on immigration. Taken together, the essays provide both unprecedented analytical depth and remarkable subtlety and insight into the manifold issues raised by current nativism and immigration policy.

I am grateful to each of the extraordinary scholars who have contributed their time and expertise to fulfill this book's unique purpose. Each scholar is a recognized expert in his or her field, and each was chosen to write on particular topics within his or her expertise. The book is organized into several parts, each covering a different aspect of nativism.

Part I introduces the twin themes developed throughout this book, the historical context that enables an understanding of present nativism, and the critical assessment of the symbolism and language of our discourse on nativism, immigration, and citizenship. Sociologist Joe R. Feagin begins with a sweeping history of American nativism, discussing its past and present rhetorical construction by ruling elites. My chapter on the Statue of Liberty describes its history and the evolution of conflicting meanings attributed to our preeminent symbol of immigration. As revealed in many mostly contemporaneous writings, the Statue of Liberty provided a benchmark against which many Americans—particularly people of color and women—could measure and protest their lack of freedom.

Part II identifies the new nativism, its features and effects. Anthropologist Leo R. Chavez describes and interprets some of the most interesting aspects and effects of anti-immigrant legislation, particularly its reproduction of a low-cost, non-citizen Mexican work force. Political scientist Raymond Tatalovich then discusses the development of the Official English movement and concludes that it is primarily a guise for a conservative politics of nativism.

Part III discusses the complex causation of the new nativism. Economist Thomas Muller provides an analysis of possible economic and political factors that encourage nativism. Legal scholar Jean Stefancic discusses causation from a different angle: the organized financing and production of nativism by conservative think tanks and politicians. Stefancic also demonstrates the extensive links between the principal activists for immigration reform and those sponsoring the Official English movement. Anthropologist Patricia Zavella describes California, spawning ground for the new nativism, as a "paradise lost" for whites, who feel they have surrendered control over their affairs and who blame mostly Latino immigrants for their loss. Zavella studies the resultant tensions through case studies of two low income families—a family of Mexican farm workers and a family headed by a white female single parent.

Part IV places the new nativism in historical context, enabling striking comparisons between what we know to have been nativism before and what we can confidently identify as nativism now. Legal scholar Kevin R. Johnson describes historical images of the alien in legal history, images created and promulgated by our courts and legislatures, which form an important part of the context for evaluating our current images of undocumented persons. Gilbert Paul Carrasco's chapter places current anti-immigrant initiatives, which seem directed mostly at Mexicans and other Latino people, into the lengthy historical relationship between the United States and Mexican labor. Since around the time of World War I, the United States government has encouraged the presence and use of Mexican labor during times of labor shortages. When the labor shortages end, the United States government is quick to expel Mexican laborers, and to expel Mexican American citizens along with them. Mexicans, and Mexican Americans, then, historically have constituted a kind of disposable labor force, easily discarded at the whim of the government. Dorothy E. Roberts then links aspects of our new nativism to the era of discredited but renascent eugenics. Roberts argues that current legislation, enacted and proposed, seeks to control reproduction and also communicates a powerful message about who among us are entitled to produce, and reproduce, citizens of the United States.

Part V discusses the new nativism and the significance of borders, national and ideological. Despite tacit acceptance of the border as a rigid geopolitical boundary with fixed meaning, the essays in this section demonstrate the much more fluid and contingent nature of the idea of *border*. Sociologist Néstor P. Rodríguez explains the social construction and interpretation of the border and subtly derives the border's meanings from the metaphors commonly used in its description. Robert S. Chang's meditation on borders demonstrates, unforgettably, that people of color always carry the border with them: they can never leave it behind nor escape it, regardless of legality or documentation. Berta Esperanza Hernández-Truyol then places the new nativism in the United States in international legal context. She argues that legislation like Proposition 187 and its progeny violate accepted and binding norms of international human rights law, which apply to all "persons," regardless of national borders and citizenship status. Hernández-Truyol argues forcefully that norms of international human rights should be enforced as domestic U.S. law. She also raises the troubling question of why the United States, self-proclaimed remaining superpower, falls short of compliance with well-accepted norms of human rights.

The final part analyzes the discourse of nativism, citizenship, and community membership in the United States. Professor Linda S. Bosniak analyzes the term *nativism* itself, providing a subtle, nuanced reading of its significance as the term we use to define boundaries of propriety in discourse about immigration policy. Daniel Kanstroom analyzes the rhetoric of one of the most prominent immigration restrictionists, Peter Brimelow, and its implications. Comparing Brimelow's rhetoric to that of Oswald Spengler, whose *The Decline of the West* preceded and helped produce the ascendancy of the National Socialist Party in Germany in the 1930s, Kanstroom illustrates the potential dangers of race and ethnicity-based discourse about citizenship and community membership. Richard Delgado then analyzes several recent proposals, statutory and constitutional, that may change the way this country defines citizenship. He argues that these proposed changes rest on an incorrect and dangerous misunderstanding of communitarian philosophy and should be resisted. Finally, legal scholar T. Alexander Aleinikoff describes "the tightening circle of membership" from his unique vantage point as both an academic and a policymaker. Aleinikoff warns that, as society considers restricting its membership, the circle must not be closed too tightly.

So I invite you to read these chapters, diverse commentaries by experts in many fields, and to draw your own conclusions about our new nativism. As you read these chapters, and as you consider the new nativism, its parallels in the past and its ramifications for the future, you will become a much more informed and sophisticated participant in one of this country's most important and recurrent political debates. It is the debate over who and what we are as a country and over what we should become. It is no less than the debate over the proper identity of the United States and its people.

NOTES

1. John Higham, *Strangers in the Land* at 4 (2d ed.; New Brunswick, N.J.: Rutgers University Press, 1988).

2. James Aho, *This Thing of Darkness: A Sociology of the Enemy* 6 (Seattle: University of Washington Press, 1994).

3. See James Morton Smith, *Freedom's Fetters* 12, 20–21 (Ithaca, N.Y.: Cornell University Press, 1956).

4. See Joe R. Feagin, "Old Poison in New Bottles: The Deep Roots of Modern Nativism," this volume, chapter 2.

5. See Higham, *Strangers in the Land*.

6. See Ronald Takaki, *A Different Mirror* 378–85 (Boston: Little, Brown, 1993);

Allan R. Bosworth, *America's Concentration Camps* 18 (New York: W. W. Norton, 1967).

7. See, e.g., Juan F. Perea, "Demography and Distrust: An Essay on American Languages, Cultural Pluralism, and Official English," 77 *Minnesota Law Review* 269, 337–40 (1992).

8. See generally, David G. Gutierrez, *Walls and Mirrors* 1–11, 211–16 (Berkeley: University of California Press, 1995). Although Mexican American attitudes toward immigration are varied, as among the rest of the population, some Mexican Americans sense vital links between them and their immigrant counterparts: "Noting that Americans seem to discriminate against Mexicans whether they are U.S. citizens or not, Mexican Americans oriented in this way can see little difference between their position in American society and that of more recent immigrants. From their point of view, as one elderly Mexican American woman put it to the historian Albert Camarillo, 'We were all poor. We were all in the same situation,' " (citation omitted).

9. See Leo R. Chavez, chapter 4 in this volume. See also Ann Davis, "The Return of the Nativists," *National Law Journal,* June 19, 1995, p. A1.

10. See Dorothy E. Roberts, "Who May Give Birth to Citizens," and Richard Delgado, "Citizenship," chapters 11 and 17, respectively, in this volume.

11. See, e.g., Chavez, chapter 4 of this volume, and Thomas Muller, "Nativism in the mid-1990s: Why Now?" chapter 6 of this volume.

12. See Thomas L. Friedman, "Settling In: The Overview; Clinton Concedes He Erred on Baird Nomination," *New York Times,* January 23, 1993, p. 1.

13. Peter A. Brown, "Illegal Alien Admission Hurts Gov. Wilson for '96," *Plain Dealer,* May 5, 1995, p. 13A.

14. For example, under the Fair Labor Standards Act, covered employers are required to pay employees the minimum wage and to pay for overtime labor. Employers are also required to pay social security taxes for their employees.

15. See Robert Pear, "Clinton Will Seek Spending to Curb Aliens, Aides Say," *New York Times,* January 22, 1995, p. 1.

16. William Branigin, "Sweatshop instead of Paradise; Thais Lived in Fear as Slaves at L.A. Garment Factories," *Washington Post,* September 10, 1995, p. A1.

17. Kenneth B. Noble, "Workers in Sweatshop Raid Start Leaving Detention Site," *New York Times,* August 12, 1995, p. 6. Some of the Thai workers have been released from detention but most still await deportation.

18. See Derrick A. Bell, Jr., "*Brown v. Board of Education* and the Interest-Convergence Dilemma," 93 *Harvard Law Review* 518, 523 (1980).

19. Ibid. at 523 ("this principle of 'interest convergence' provides: The interest of blacks in achieving racial equality will be accommodated only when it converges with the interests of whites").

20. See William C. Berman, *The Politics of Civil Rights in the Truman Administration* 83–85 (Columbus: Ohio State University Press, 1970) (describing Truman's view that foreign policy requirements required congressional action on his ten-point program for civil rights reform).

21. See Bell, "*Brown v. Board of Education*" at 518. See also Mary L. Dudziak, "Desegregation as a Cold War Imperative," 41 *Stanford Law Review* 61 (1988).

22. See Steven A. Holmes, "GOP Lawmakers Offer a Ban on Federal Affirmative Action," *New York Times,* July 28, 1995, p. A17; Steven A. Holmes, "As Affirmative Action Ebbs, a Sense of Uncertainty Rises," *New York Times,* July 6, 1995, p. A1.

23. See *Adarand Constructors, Inc. v. Pena,* 115 S. Ct. 2097 (1995) (striking down Federal affirmative action program and subjecting other such Federal programs to strict judicial scrutiny).

24. See *Miller v. Johnson,* 115 S. Ct. 2475 (1995); *Shaw v. Reno,* 113 S. Ct. 2816 (1993).

25. See Raymond Tatalovich, chapter 5 in this volume. See also Raymond Tatalovich, *Nativism Reborn* (Lexington: University Press of Kentucky, 1995).

26. See *Plyler v. Doe,* 457 U.S. 202 (1982).

27. Higham, *Strangers in the Land* at 195.

HISTORICAL THEMES
Nativism in American History and the
Meaning of the Statue of Liberty

The chapters in this part introduce the two principal themes of this book: the connections between past and present nativism and critical analysis of the symbols and language of our discourse regarding nativism, immigration, and citizenship. Joe R. Feagin's chapter provides a comprehensive history of American nativism, setting the stage for comparisons between historical expressions of nativism and today's expressions that may be labeled nativist. My chapter on the history of the Statue of Liberty and the unsuspected complexity and evolution of its meanings suggests the importance of critical evaluation of the symbols and language of our discourse on immigration. Through critical analysis and historical context, commonly accepted meanings of our symbols and language give way to much deeper and more nuanced understanding.

2. OLD POISON IN NEW BOTTLES

The Deep Roots of Modern Nativism

Joe R. Feagin

Recently, white students attacked the home of Asian Indian immigrants on Staten Island. They broke windows, smeared the house with paint, and left a statement on the drive: "Indians go home. Leave or die." Across the country in Houston white skinheads beat and killed a Vietnamese teenager. The Vietnamese boy, according to one of the murderers, cried out: "God forgive me for coming to this country."[1] Contemporary nativism, the desire of many Americans to restrict, exclude, or attack immigrants, has taken many forms, ranging from verbal epithets against "foreigners" and restrictive legislation to vandalism of property and murder.

Contemporary attacks on immigrants do not represent a new social phenomenon with no connection to past events. Anti-immigrant nativism in North America is at least two centuries old. In this chapter, I will examine the deep roots of modern nativism. Historically, and on the present scene, nativists have stressed to varying degrees four major themes. One common complaint is that certain "races" are intellectually and culturally inferior and should not be allowed into the country, at least not in substantial numbers. Nativists have often regarded immigrant groups as racial "others" quite different from the Euro-American majority. A second and related theme views those who have immigrated from racially and culturally inferior groups as problematical in terms of their complete assimilation to the dominant Anglo culture. A third theme, articulated most often in troubled economic times, is that "inferior" immigrants are taking the jobs and disrupting the economic conditions of native-born Americans. A fourth notion, also heard most often in times of fiscal crisis, is that immigrants are creating serious government crises, such as by corrupting the voting system or overloading school and welfare systems.

These nativistic arguments and movements date back at least to the late 1700s and early 1800s. Moreover, the consequences and impact of the nativistic movements, restrictions, and laws of the first two centuries of American development are serious. These movements and laws have had profound consequences for the history and present demography of this nation. For instance, the 1990 census revealed that *only twelve* of the world's nearly two hundred countries were checked off by as much as 1 percent of Americans as countries of national origin: Britain, Ireland, Canada, Italy, Russia, Poland, France, Netherlands, Sweden, Germany, Norway, and Mexico. In assessing major population sources, one would need to add Native Americans and African Americans to this list, although the latter could only check off a continent (Africa), not a country of origin. Dozens of other countries of ancestry are represented in the U.S. population, but at proportions of less (or far less) than 1 percent. This list demonstrates that from 1607 to 1990 the major infusions of immigrants to this country originated in Great Britain and certain other European countries (all but one in northern Europe), and in Africa and Mexico. Conspicuously absent from the list are *any* countries in the Middle East, Asia, South America, or postcolonial Africa.[2]

Whether in the past or in the present, significant human migration across national boundaries is much more than a question of the individual decisions of migrating individuals seeking opportunities in a new country. As a rule, international migration is shaped at its base by broad political-economic conditions and institutions. For the most part, both immigration and the shape of the U.S. population reflect the desires, interests, and purposes of Americans of European descent. As we will see, a certain variability, if not schizophrenia, characterizes American thought about immigration. While there has been much anti-immigrant sentiment in the United States, in most periods some immigration has been viewed as desirable, at least when immigrants come from certain areas of the globe. Indeed, between 1820 (the date of the first records) and the mid-1990s more than *52 million* legal immigrants entered the United States. In addition, a large number of legal immigrants came prior to 1820, and since 1820 millions of undocumented immigrants have come from Europe, Latin America, and other areas of the globe. In addition, nearly half a million Africans came in chains. It is with good reason that one can call the United States a "nation of immigrants."

However, as the aforementioned data on countries of origin suggest, this immigration has been highly focused in terms of its points of origin. Historically, most immigrants to this nation have come from Europe, and relatively few immigrants have come from Asia, the Middle East, or, since 1865, Africa. This fact suggests the national-origin bias in U.S. immigration policy.

Indeed, if the United States had not had a Euro-American nativist movement from the 1880s to 1920s, there would not have been a Chinese Exclusion Act (1882), an anti-Japanese "Gentleman's Agreement" (1907–8), or a series of immigration acts from 1917 to 1924 designed to keep out southern and eastern Europeans. In addition, there would not have been a 1924 Immigration Act sharply reducing the number of Catholic immigrants from countries like Italy and Poland and the number of Jewish immigrants from eastern Europe—and excluding Asian immigrants. If these biased regulations and laws had not been in effect, the current U.S. population would likely include far more Asian Americans and have a majority composed of Catholic and Jewish Americans.

Clearly, then, battles over immigration have more than temporary effects. Indeed, they are struggles over the composition and character of the nation. Today, many native-born Americans are rising to assert their desire to shape the U.S. population, once again in narrow cultural or racial terms. As in the past, most of the new American nativists wish to keep the nation predominantly white and European.

THE COLONIES: DEFINING "SAVAGES" AND "FOREIGNERS"

A full understanding of contemporary nativism requires some comprehension of the deep historical background. The foundation for aggressive nativism in North America begins in the expansion of European capitalism. By the sixteenth and seventeenth centuries, several European nations, especially the Netherlands, France, and England, had spurred the globalization of capitalism. In the process, they created a type of colonialism with fundamental inequalities between colonizers and the newly colonized. Beginning in the 1600s, English immigrants began a major colonization of North America, taking over Native American lands in four distinctive waves. The first to come were English Puritans, who settled in New England and brought dissenting Protestant churches. A second wave, a few Royalists and many indentured servants, came to Virginia in the mid-seventeenth century and established a hierarchical colony with Anglican churches. A third wave of English Quakers came to the Delaware Valley between 1675 and 1725 and established a pluralistic system based on spiritual and social equality and an intense work ethic. The fourth wave came to the Appalachian backcountry from the borderlands of Britain between 1718 and 1775; this group represented English, Scotch, and Scotch-Irish ancestries and was mostly Protestant. While each group had a distinctive type of English or Scottish culture, for the most part they shared a commitment to an Anglo-Protestant culture, central to which were variants of the English language.[3]

This fierce commitment to the English norms, values, and ways of operating begins the trail to modern nativism. In particular, the famous Puritans built a base for the ethnocentrism and parochialism of the newly emerging U.S. republic. They developed, as Joel Kovel has noted, "a powerful tradition of hating strangers, foreigners, and subversives."[4] This tradition was honed in the bloody attacks by Puritans on the native population. The Puritan immigrants created the first colonial settler-society, one animated by the arrogant notion that these English settlers would make better use of what they saw as undeveloped "wilderness" than "wild savages" who were the present occupants. Commenting on this English settler perspective, Kovel has noted that "the land wasn't densely settled, but it was settled everywhere, and everywhere the whites went they had to get rid of highly developed and very profoundly interesting cultures that had achieved a kind of equilibrium with the land over millennia."[5] English immigrants' destruction or oppression of highly civilized Native American communities was soon coupled with the importation and oppression of Africans brought to the new immigrant colonies in the slave trade.

Genocide against Native Americans and enslavement of Africans were part of the original foundation of this nation. These oppressions gave the lie to the idealized notions of liberty and democracy freely espoused in the struggle between British Americans and the British Crown called the Revolutionary War. For most Americans of British ancestry, these ideals did not encompass African Americans and Native Americans, who were viewed as cultural "others," as aliens, strangers, and uncivilized savages. Among the English invaders the anti-other images increasingly accented not only cultural differences but also physical and racial characteristics. From the seventeenth century to the late twentieth century this racialized framework of otherness has shaped Euro-American attempts to exclude or oppress subsequent non-European groups, such as the Chinese and Japanese immigrants brought in for cheap labor in the nineteenth and early twentieth centuries or the Mexican immigrants brought in for cheap labor since the early 1900s. Over four centuries, many non-European groups have been defined by Euro-Americans as sub-human "others," as non-citizens without rights or as citizens with only limited rights.

Early European interpretations of the colonial enterprise could be found both in popular sentiment and in the systematic perspectives developed by intellectuals and political leaders. From the fifteenth century onward, European and Euro-American intellectual and political elites defended the racism and exploitation of the imperialist enterprises. Scholars, theologians, and politicians in European and the new American colonies developed theories of the superiority of white Europeans and of the animal-like inferiority of peoples exploited in the expansion of colonialism. These views buttressed popular feelings about certain outgroups. Common to most societies is ethnocentrism—the perspective that sees one's own group as the center and evaluates outgroups with reference to that center. However, a distinctively negative ethnocentrism in regard to outsiders developed in the American colonies and, later, the United States. Europeans distinguished themselves from the "savages," and colonized peoples were demonized as replete with vices Europeans feared in themselves: wildness, brutishness, cruelty, laziness, and heathenism. "Far from English civilization, [the Europeans] had to remind themselves constantly what it meant to be civilized—Christian, rational, sexually controlled, and white. And they tried to impute to peoples they called 'savages' the instinctual forces they had within themselves."[6] By the 1700s and 1800s well-developed theories of the cultural and racial inferiority of the "uncivilized savages" were common in both England and the new United States.

IMMIGRANTS AS SAVAGES: NATIVISM IN THE 1800S

From the 1700s onward Euro-American views of savage outsiders were directed not only at Americans of color but also at certain new immigrants of European origin. By the 1830s and 1840s, negative ethnocentrism took on a distinctive American form that was given the name *nativism*. Many English American leaders, as well as many in the English American public, had negative or mixed feelings about new European immigrants who were not Protestants. Then, as now, we glimpse the schizophrenia in regard to immigrants. The new immigrants were often needed to meet the labor needs of U.S. employers, and many native-born Americans profited from the economic impact of immigration. At the same time, many Americans viewed the new immigrants as a major threat to the nation's Anglo culture and institutions.

By the late eighteenth century, well-established English Americans often viewed themselves as liberty-loving "republicans" who were concerned with protecting the new nation, as some said, for the "worthy part of mankind."[7] Before the revolution, nativistic concern about new immigrants was centered in the latter's religious and moral traits. Certain religious groups (particularly Catholics), the very poor, and convicts were discouraged from entering the colonies. Anti-foreign sentiment was directed primarily at non-English immigrant groups. English American colonists and their descendants increasingly resented the intrusion of new peoples onto what was seen as English soil. This anti-immigrant sentiment took the form of law by the late 1700s. The dominant Federalist party was concerned about the support of non-British immigrants for Jeffersonianism. Thus, a 1798 Alien Act empowered the English American president to deport immigrants considered a threat, and the period of residence for citizenship was raised significantly in 1798.

If immigrants could not be excluded, restricted, or discouraged, the next best thing was to assimilate them, in a one-way adaptation pattern, to the dominant Anglo-Protestant culture. From the 1700s to the present, the assimilation of immigrants to the dominant Anglo culture has been a central feature of much nativist thought. Immigrant assimilation has been seen as one-way, as conformity to the Anglo-Protestant culture: "If there is anything in American life which can be described as an overall American culture which serves as a reference point for immigrants and their children, it can best be described, it seems to us, as the middle-class cultural patterns of, largely, white Protestant, Anglo-Saxon origins."[8]

Nativists have long used forced or pressured assimilation as an essential weapon in insuring the hegemony of whiteness and the Anglo culture over the immigrants who reside in the United States. From the dominant perspective, the impact of new immigrants is reduced if they assimilate culturally to Anglo ways and institutions. For example, when Benjamin Franklin set up a Pennsylvania school in the 1740s, he was greatly concerned that many non-English immigrants did not know the English language or customs.[9] Like many of his fellow English Americans, Franklin had strong prejudices about the new German immigrants to the colonies and feared these uncivilized immigrants would "shortly be so numerous as to Germanize us instead of us Anglifying them."[10] Ethnic homogeneity was a proclaimed goal of prominent English American leaders. Indeed, George Washington believed in a homogeneous citizenry, and both Thomas Jefferson and Benjamin Rush wished immigrants to be Anglo-assimilated.[11]

In the first decades of the nineteenth century, nativists honed their anti-foreign perspective further, with increasing emphasis on anti-Catholicism and white supremacy. Many nativists targeted Irish Catholic immigrants and their children. In the early nineteenth century, industrial capitalists faced a shortage of labor. Native-born workers resisted the oppressive conditions of the new industrial enterprises, and capitalists increasingly recruited workers for building transportation projects and manufacturing mills from overseas. By the mid-nineteenth century, Irish and German immigrants were critical to many new industrial enterprises, including textile mills, railroad lines and shops, and foundries. The ability of a capitalist system to "expand successfully is a function both of the ability to maintain relative social solidarity at home and the arrangements that can be made to use cheap labor far away."[12] In this case, major capitalists aggressively sought the new immigrant workers, while other Americans wished to see this immigration reduced if not curtailed. Over the course of U.S. history, capitalists and exclusionary nativists have periodically found themselves at odds on the matter of immigration. Indeed, every time that nativists have succeeded in getting restrictive legislation, business interests needing cheap labor have found ways around the laws. Laws have never stopped immigration because powerful interests desire it, at least in times of labor shortage.[13]

English American resistance to Irish immigrants dates from the seventeenth century, but it was the nineteenth-century Catholic immigrants from famine-ridden Ireland who were attacked viciously under the new banners of nativism. Anglo-Protestant nativist organizations played a major role in verbal and physical attacks on the Irish Americans. Catholics were hated not only because they were "foreign" immigrants but because of Protestant stereotypes of Catholic "popery." The large number of Catholic immigrants from Ireland (and to a lesser extent Germany) in the mid-nineteenth century brought new targets for the anti-immigrant nativists among Anglo-Protestant Americans.

THE RISE OF RACIST NATIVISM

By the mid-nineteenth century a racist perspective joined anti-Catholicism at the heart of much Anglo-American thought and action in regard to immigrants. Initially, the racial supremacy perspective took the form of accenting the superiority of those Americans whose ancestors came from the dominant "race" of northern Europe. This perspective defined the dominant core of the U.S. population in positive terms, by accenting the achievements and culture of the so-called Anglo-Saxon race. It was common in England and the United States in the early nineteenth century. Other north European Protestants often joined together with British Americans to celebrate a "superior Anglo-Saxon race." By the 1840s and 1850s, Anglo-Saxonism could be found in many nooks and crannies of the new nation. Sometimes it targeted white immigrants; in other cases, it targeted people of color, whose lands were still coveted by white colonizers. It was adopted by Euro-American expansionists who lusted after Mexican land in California and Texas. The vigorous thrust into those areas was seen as legitimated by a racial mandate to colonize, as one expansionist proclaimed: "The Mexican race now see in the fate of the aborigines of the north, their own inevitable destiny. They must amalgamate or be lost in the superior vigor of the Anglo-Saxon race, or they must utterly perish."[14]

In the eighteenth and nineteenth centuries, the "white race" emerged as a constructed social group for the first time in history. As we noted above, the early English invaders and their descendants saw themselves as culturally and physically different from Native and African Americans, the stereotyped "uncivilized savages." Moreover, by the early 1800s the importance of Southern cotton plantations for the U.S. economy had brought a growing demand for Native American land and for African and African American slaves. Slavery was being abolished in the North, and the number of free black men and women was growing. In this period, the Anglo-Protestant ruling elite developed the ideology of a superior "white race" as one way of providing racial privileges for poorer European Americans and keeping the latter from joining with black Americans in worker organizations. White nationalism grew dramatically. By the mid-nineteenth century, not only later English immigrants but also immigrants from Scotland and Scandinavia, Ireland, and Germany had come to accept a place in this socially constructed "white race," whose special racial privileges included the rights of personal liberty, travel, and voting.[15]

The dominant economic and political elites, still entirely north European in ancestry, became bastions of a racialized nativism after the Civil War. They were influenced by English and U.S. historians who argued for the superiority of the Anglo-Saxon background and its role in English and U.S. greatness. Convinced that "Anglo-Saxon institutions" were the most civilized, many English and U.S. intellectuals adopted a social Darwinist viewpoint with racist notions accenting the "survival of the fittest" nations on the world scene. Popular U.S. writers like Josiah Strong, whose book *Our Country* sold thousands of copies in the last years of the nineteenth century, parroted racial myths of Anglo-Saxon superiority in attacks on non-British immigrants. The English peoples were rapidly multiplying and the United States was destined to be the seat of an "Anglo-Saxon race" whose numbers, Strong asserted, would reach a billion by the 1980s. This survival of the racially fittest dictated the ultimate superiority of the "Anglo-Saxon race" throughout the world.[16] Vigorous Anglo-Saxonism was initially developed in patrician circles and was centered on the superiority of English traditions and culture. Gradually, however, it came to target in a negative way the new immigrants from southern and eastern Europe. Racist thinkers like Strong saw these immigrants not only as culturally deviant but also as racially inferior.

Still, racialized immigrant-bashing was countered in part by the needs of the ever expanding U.S. economy. Over the course of U.S. history, immigration flows have usually reflected the labor needs of U.S. capitalists—an important aspect of immigration often ignored by U.S. nativists. "In times of great labor shortage the state imposes few obstacles on immigration."[17] In addition, native-born workers worry less about labor competition from immigrants in such periods. This was the case during most of the nineteenth century; after the U.S. Civil War, the federal government generally encouraged immigration, particularly from Europe. There were overseas recruitment campaigns; periodically, industrial employers and land companies sent agents to Europe and Asia to recruit labor. As of 1900, the major source of new labor for expanding industries was southern and eastern European immigrants. Indeed, between 1881 and 1920 the majority of the twenty-one million immigrants emigrated from southern and eastern Europe.[18]

In spite of the fact that U.S. business interests had played a crucial role in generating much of this migration, many Americans at all class levels were becoming opposed to these new immigrants, an opposition that intensified during and after World War I. The renewed nativism of the late 1910s and 1920s made use of the sciences of biology, anthropology, and psychology. Racial eugenics thinking spread from European intellectuals to U.S. leaders. Promulgated in many articles in the media, this eugenics perspective accented the importance of breeding the right racial groups. For most U.S. nativists, immigrants from southern and eastern Europe did not represent the "superior races." Madison Grant, an influential ideologue of racism, argued that the "Nordic race" (for him the "white man par excellence") was being destroyed by the millions of immigrants from southern and eastern Europe, the "inferior races."[19] In Grant's view, the Nordic race, seen as the original white race in North America, was intellectually, culturally, and politically superior to all others. In the early 1900s, many Americans of northern European descent described themselves as "white men," taking this substantially to mean that they were completely different in racial terms from the southern and eastern Europeans. Others, however, saw the southern and eastern Europeans as "inferior" races within the white race. A great fear among native-born Euro-Americans was that the mixing of the Nordic race with the inferior white races would "mongrelize" and destroy the true white race.

Popular writers, scholars, and members of Congress spread the alarm. They warned of the disaster that would come from allowing inferior racial stocks from Europe into the United States. Prominent journalist Kenneth L. Roberts wrote of the dangers of the immigrants: "Races can not be cross-bred without mongrelization, any more than breeds of dogs can be cross-bred without mongrelization. The American nation was founded and developed by the Nordic race, but if a few more million members of the Alpine, Mediterranean, and Semitic races are poured among us, the result must inevitably be a hybrid race of people as worthless and futile as the good-for-nothing mongrels of Central America and southeastern Europe."[20] The "Alpine, Mediterranean, and Semitic races" generally covered countries of heavy emigration other than those of northern Europe; Italians and European Jews were seen as examples. At the heart of this racist attack was a great fear that the immigrants would damage the U.S. economic and political systems. One writer warned in a 1913 magazine article that "unless Americans are careful, they will take over."[21]

Among the favorite targets of these nativists were Italian Catholic immigrants. Nativists saw the "Italian race stock" as "inferior and degraded." They also accented an old nativist theme, that the new "racial stock" will "not assimilate naturally or readily with the prevailing 'Anglo-Saxon' race stock of this country; that intermixture, if practicable, will be detrimental; that servility, filthy habits of life, and a hopelessly degraded standard of needs and ambitions have been ingrained in Italians by centuries of oppression and abject poverty." [22] Racial indictments of Italian Americans appeared in national magazines. In the 1888 *North American Review,* labor activist T. V. Powderly alleged that southern Europeans were an inferior stock that lived immoral lives centered in liquor. [23] Like poor immigrants before and after them, the Italians were blamed for destroying the moral fabric of the nation and for accelerating the costs of government, particularly in relation to crime and poverty.

For many of the same reasons, Jewish immigrants from eastern Europe were also major targets by the early 1900s. Widely accepted racial stereotypes caricatured Jewish immigrants in the national and local media. Jews were seen as immoral and as unscrupulous business competitors. They were accused of taking the jobs of "Americans." By the early 1900s, riots erupted among Gentile workers against Jewish American workers brought into factories. In Georgia, the Jewish part-owner of a pencil factory was convicted of killing a girl employee, though evidence pointed elsewhere. After being beaten up in prison, he was lynched by a white Gentile mob. Moreover, by the 1920s a revived Ku Klux Klan waged violence against both Jewish and Catholic immigrants and their children. Crosses were burned on Jewish property, and synagogues were desecrated and vandalized. [24]

In the early decades of the twentieth century, Anglo-Protestant stereotypes of the immigrants' intellectual inferiority were based in part on misreadings of the results of new psychological tests inaccurately labeled intelligence tests. (The new tests actually measured only a limited range of learned skills not a global intelligence called IQ.) With the coming of World War I, psychologists developed verbal and performance tests for large-scale testing of draftees. In the early 1900s, prominent psychologists and other professionals, as well as north European political leaders, used the new test results to defend racist views of southern and eastern European immigrants. Detailed statistical analyses gained public and congressional attention because of the racial inferiority interpretation placed on the test results of southern and eastern European draftees. Indeed, in the early 1920s, Carl Brigham, a Princeton psychologist, published a detailed analysis of the alleged intellectual inferiority of white immigrant groups, drawing on data from army tests. The average scores for foreign-born draftees ranged from a high of 14.87 for English draftees to lows of 10.74 for Polish American draftees and 11.01 for Italian American draftees. The lower test scores of these white groups "proved" they were "inferior" racial stocks. [25] Major psychologists, such as Brigham and Robert M. Yerkes, the army's chief psychologist and one of the nation's prominent scientists, interpreted these "scientific" results to support the ideology of

Nordic racial superiority. The arguments of scientific racism permeated the debates leading to the anti-immigrant legislation discussed in the next section. Interestingly, these debates over the IQ inferiority of "racial" groups among white Americans now seem an absurd historical curiosity, but this is not the case for similar debates over the intelligence levels of African Americans and recent Latino and Asian immigrants.

In the nativistic attacks on the southern and eastern European immigrants, we see all four aspects of nativism suggested earlier. Not only are these immigrants viewed as racially and intellectually inferior but they are also accused of being incapable of assimilation to the Anglo culture. Periodically, they are also blamed for problems of unemployment and for increasing societal crises, such as poverty, disease, and crime, that must be dealt with by burgeoning governments at the federal, state, and local levels.

NATIVISTIC ACTION AGAINST IMMIGRANTS: THE 1920S

Nativistic Organization and Anti-Immigrant Laws

At the turn of the twentieth century, large-scale immigration from southern and eastern Europe and the modest immigration from Asia became the target of much anti-immigration action. Many in the political elites were vigorously questioning the new immigrants and immigration regulation. Henry Cabot Lodge, an English American aristocrat from New England and a powerful political figure, was determined to use politics and the law to defend the nation against what he saw as immigrant threats. Some British Americans in Boston formed the Immigration Restriction League to try to curtail immigration. Working in several different arenas, the League pressed the U.S. Congress to pass literacy restrictions on immigrants. Some of the League's members were enamored of the eugenics philosophy spreading from England to the United States. American eugenicists were obsessed with racial miscegenation and feared that allowing racially inferior southern and eastern Europeans into the country would destroy the "superior Nordic race."[26]

Southern and eastern Europeans faced other anti-immigrant organizations as well. Oddly enough, these organizations were made up of the descendants of earlier immigrants. In the late nineteenth century, the American Protective Association (APA) and a revived Ku Klux Klan were working aggressively against immigration of the southern and eastern European and Asian workers. The membership of these groups included many business people, white-collar workers, and fundamentalist Protestants. The often racist anti-immigrant agitation led to restrictive laws; between 1875 and 1917, the U.S. Congress passed laws excluding "immoral" aliens, those with diseases, political radicals, and the illiterate. Congress overrode a presidential veto to enact a law excluding persons of "psychopathic inferiority," vagrants, and illiterate adults. In addition, one 1917 Act created an Asiatic barred zone, from which no immigrants could enter. Such laws reflected the northern European prejudices against immigrants from Asia and southern and eastern Europe.[27]

By the 1920s, the anti-immigrant hysteria had taken on major proportions, and in many areas aliens were prohibited from practicing certain jobs or professions, including medicine, engineering, and law. In the heat of postwar fears of "foreigners" taking jobs from demobilized soldiers, and of the United States being inundated by inferior races, the first major law restricting immigration across the board was passed. While temporary, it was the first to impose numerical limits on immigrants by means of a nationality quota system. It limited European immigrants to about 3 percent of the number of foreign-born from each country present in the United States in 1910. The total limit was about 350,000, with most slots reserved for northern Europeans. This law was in effect until the more restrictive 1924 law was set into motion in the late 1920s. However, there was nativist opposition even to this act, as many northern European Americans wished to exclude all immigrants, and others wanted to restrict the number of southern and eastern Europeans even further.[28]

The chair of the House committee dealing with immigration laws, Albert Johnson, a high school dropout who was semiliterate himself, was closely linked to the nation's racist intellectuals and anti-immigrant activists. He shared in the arguments about immigration being generated by some of nation's Ivy League scientists, like Carl Brigham, and by racist advocates of Nordic supremacy like Madison Grant and Kenneth Roberts. As a result, the 1924 Immigration Act crafted under Johnson's leadership sharply limited immigration; it specified the baseline year to be 1890, when there were few southern and eastern Europeans in the United States, and reduced the percentage allowed from 3 to 2 percent.[29] This overtly racist law established small discriminatory quotas for southern and eastern Europeans. For example, the annual quota for Italian immigrants was about 5,800, compared with nearly 66,000 for Great Britain and nearly 26,000 for Germany. The British, Germans, Irish, and Scandinavians got most of the total allowance. As a result of these skewed quotas, Allan Chase estimates, about six million people from southern and eastern Europe, including many who would die in Adolf Hitler's concentration camps, were excluded.[30] The nativists' greatest victory, a racist immigration law, would stay in effect until the mid-1960s.

These discriminatory quotas were defended as maintaining the "racial balance" that had existed in the country as of 1890, a balance that of course heavily favored those from northern Europe. The year 1910 could not be used as the baseline for quotas, the nativists argued, because it would favor southern and eastern Europeans by making them more important than they had been "historically" in forming the United States. The new law explicitly relied on the views of contemporary pundits and experts who spoke of the necessity of maintaining the "racial preponderance" of the "basic strain of our population." [31] Clearly, racist nativism had reached its peak of power and influence in the United States. The 1924 Immigration Act was widely seen as a victory for the Nordic race, as in this April 13, 1924 headline of the *Los Angeles Times:* "Nordic victory is seen in Drastic Restrictions." [32] Nativists were overjoyed that immigrants at Ellis Island now looked like real "Americans." The discriminatory law even got support at the highest political levels. It was approved of by the new president, Calvin Coolidge, who had earlier written in a 1921 *Good Housekeeping Magazine* article that the Nordic population propagates itself successfully but will deteriorate if it is mixed with other racial groups. Coolidge even argued that this was a basic "ethnic law." [33] The history of early nativism makes it clear that it was not the invention of poor or working-class white Americans, as it has often been portrayed.

Forcing One-Way Assimilation

Nativist pressures do not stop at excluding immigrants. There was growing concern about those immigrants who were already here, as well as immigrants' children. As we noted above, non-British immigrants have long faced great pressure to assimilate rapidly to the dominant Anglo-Protestant culture. One of the first great conflicts took place when Anglo nativists became obsessively concerned with the Irish immigrants of the 1830s and 1840s and with their Catholicism. Maintaining a significant Irish ethnicity was important for these new immigrants, a way of asserting their own identity against Anglo-Protestant assimilation pressures.[34] The Irish, however, did share certain cultural mores with the English and most did assimilate relatively easily to many aspects of the dominant culture.

This was not the case for immigrants at the turn of the twentieth century. They usually came from cultures quite different from that of the English Americans. As a result, the assimilation pressures were heated up to blast-furnace levels. In this regard, it should be noted that not all U.S. nativists are alike. While some nativists wished to exclude all or most immigrants who were not English, other influential Americans wanted the immigrants to be allowed in, but only on anglocentric terms. Indeed, the view that immigrants must quickly "Americanize" was widely shared by powerful U.S. capitalists. The nation's most famous capitalist, Henry Ford, pressed strongly for immigrant Americanization. Working with his firm's executives, Henry Ford recruited southern and eastern European immigrants for his auto plants. The company set up a "Sociological Department" with investigators who visited workers' homes, providing strong advice on family matters and personal morality. In addition, the immigrant workers had to attend a "melting pot school," where they learned English and certain Anglo-Protestant values of great concern to men like Ford. Remarkably, during graduation ceremonies Ford's employees, at first dressed as in their home countries, walked through a big pot labeled "melting pot" and emerged in business suits holding American flags.[35] Although this process was labeled "melting pot" assimilation, the actual model is one-way assimilation to the dominant culture.

From the mid-nineteenth century to the early twentieth century, new public school systems grew hand in hand with the expansion of industrial capitalism. Homer Bartlett, a representative of the Massachusetts Cotton Mills, argued that the "owners of manufacturing property have a deep pecuniary interest in the education and morals of their help." For these industrialists one of education's major goals was assimilating immigrants by teaching them the Anglo culture's values of discipline, obedience, and respect for economic and political authorities. In the mid-nineteenth century one urban school board complained that many youngsters "have to receive their first lessons of subordination and obedience in the school room."[36] From the capitalists' point of view, properly trained and educated immigrant workers would abide by the Protestant work ethic and would be less likely to join unions or to protest substandard working conditions. Typically, the nativism of corporate capitalists accented one-way assimilation rather than exclusion of immigrants.

NATIVISM: FROM THE 1930S TO THE 1960S

Changes in economic conditions in the United States have often affected the surges of anti-immigrant thought and movements. Nativism took a particularly ugly form in the economically troubled years between the late 1920s and the mid-1940s. The racist 1924 immigration law significantly reduced the numbers of immigrants, including Jewish immigrants in countries where genocide against the Jews was becoming public policy. Franklin Roosevelt's administration, particularly his State Department, did much less than it could have to allow Jews to flee the Nazi Holocaust. At first, the State Department adopted callous immigration restrictions to reduce the flow of refugees fleeing Hitler's reign of terror, then in mid-1940 it put an end to most immigration from central Europe. More than 400,000 slots within U.S. immigration quotas for refugees from countries under Nazi control were left unused.[37]

Moreover, with immigration limited by these special restrictions and the older nativistic immigration laws (as well as the Great Depression and World War II) the primary targets of nativist groups were now the immigrants already in the United States, together with their children. The number of openly anti-Semitic organizations was increasing dramatically, from only one in the early 1930s to well over a hundred just a few years later. Many of these were large-scale enterprises that sponsored large anti-Jewish rallies and distributed millions of anti-Jewish pamphlets and newspapers. Prominent groups included the German-American Bund, the Silver Shirts, and the Christian Front. By 1941, hatred of Jewish immigrants and their children was growing in the United States, even as the nation went to war against Nazi Germany. Radical organizations like the Ku Klux Klan created new outlets for white Americans desiring to attack Catholic and Jewish Americans, who were often immigrants or their children, and thereby preserve, as they said, the "Anglo-Saxon race." [38]

The end of World War II did not curtail this outburst of nativism. Opposition to immigration continued after World War II, when various members of Congress and various northern European organizations even opposed legislation permitting displaced persons, such as European Jews and Catholics, to migrate in significant numbers to the United States. In addition, anti-Semitism continued. Attacks on Jewish Americans, their property, and their synagogues have been common since 1945.[39]

As we will see in later sections, most contemporary nativism targets immigrants of color. This and much media discussion of current racial troubles may give the false impression that the old antagonisms directed at southern and eastern European Americans is dead. This is not the case. Once developed, the harsh stereotypes and prejudices central to nativistic thought have a certain inertia. Today there are lingering traces of the earlier prejudices and practices. Sometimes this nativism takes the form of stereotyping and harassing those not of north European ancestry. In recent presidential campaigns, for example, Democratic party candidates have been targeted because of their ancestry. In the 1984 election, the Italian ancestry of vice-presidential candidate, Geraldine Ferraro, was attacked. Republicans (many of north European ancestry) alleged that she and her Italian American husband had major connections to organized crime (the "Mafia"). Moreover, in the 1990s a number of Italian Americans, such as Governor Mario Cuomo of New York, have been forced to change their political plans because of "Mafia" stereotyping directed at them or their families. In the 1988 election, supporters of Republican candidate George Bush, an English American, poked fun at the Greek ancestry and name of Democratic candidate Michael Dukakis.[40]

Americans of south European ancestry are still not viewed by many northern Europeans as fully "American." In the United States there is still much anti-Semitic vandalism and violence directed at Jewish Americans. For example, in the half decade between 1979 and 1984 nearly 3,700 anti-Jewish incidents were reported, including arson and the painting of swastikas on tombstones or synagogues. These numbers had increased by 1991, when a record number of 1,897 incidents were recorded.[41] Among the most serious contemporary manifestations of the old nativism are these attacks on the property and persons of Jewish immigrants and their descendants.

MODERN NATIVISM: THE 1980S AND 1990S

By the late 1950s, discontent over nativism, racism, and other oppressive social conditions was growing, and large numbers of protest organizations were springing up in the communities of color across the nation—from Atlanta and Birmingham to New York to Los Angeles. In particular, African Americans and Latinos organized many protest organizations and rallies, as well as civil disobedience. In addition, by the late 1950s the earlier immigrants from southern and eastern Europe and their adult children, now central to the Democratic party, had increased their political clout and pressed for changes in the racist quota system.[42] Finally, the new liberal Democratic politics of the 1960s brought an end to the racist immigration law that had dominated the United States since the 1920s. A pathbreaking 1965 Immigration Act eliminated the racist immigration quotas and opened up immigration to Asians and other formerly excluded or restricted immigrants, including southern and eastern Europeans.

Shifting Patterns of Immigration

Not surprisingly, immigrants of color took advantage of the end of racist quotas. Between 1970 and 1990, the U.S. population grew by a fifth, while the Asian American and Latino populations grew at 385 percent and 141 percent respectively. In this period about nine million new Americans were added from countries in Asia and Latin America. Asian Americans and Latinos now make 3 percent and 9 percent of the total population, with much of the growth coming from immigration.[43]

These Asian and Latino immigrants are viewed as a "problem" by many native-born Americans, some of whom have joined new nativist organizations. Interestingly, these nativists seem to view the immigrants as dropping like unwanted sky hooks into the body politic, with no connection to the past history of the United States. Yet recent immigrants have mostly come from countries that have been substantially influenced by imperialistic efforts by U.S. corporations and by the U.S. government around the globe. As we saw earlier, human migration across national boundaries is more than a matter of individuals seeking opportunities, for international migration is greatly shaped by broader social conditions. Beginning in the 1940s, the U.S. government, its military forces, and multinational corporations came to dominate not only the U.S. economy and politics but increasingly the world economy and politics overseas. Large corporations have moved capital investments from the central cities to the suburbs and from U.S. cities to cities and rural areas in many countries around the globe. This capital "flight" has resulted in fewer well-paying jobs in central cities of large U.S. metropolitan areas. As a result, many ordinary Americans have lost their jobs, and, not surprisingly, view immigrants as a job threat. Yet few commentators in the mainstream media, and no one in the U.S. Congress, help native-born U.S. workers understand the linkage between corporate investments overseas and the loss of well-paying jobs in the United States. Instead, they often encourage immigrant-bashing.

In addition, U.S. corporations and the U.S. government are directly implicated in generating much out-migration from key sending countries, a point also missed by most commentators on immigration. For example, large numbers of Latino immigrant workers have come to U.S. cities and rural areas from Mexico, Central America, and South America. Some have migrated for economic "pull" reasons, and they have often been recruited by U.S. employers, particularly those in the agribusiness and garment manufacturing sectors. In addition, U.S. corporations have played a major role in pushing poor Mexican and Central American workers out of their countries. For several decades, U.S. agribusinesses operating in Mexico have stimulated the development of export-oriented agriculture there, thereby driving many peasant farmers and their families off their land and reducing the crops grown for local consumption. Many agricultural workers and small farmers have left rural areas and gone to Mexican cities, enlarging the number of unemployed workers, many of whom have come to the United States to earn money to support families. They mostly take low-wage jobs in textile, construction, agriculture, and service firms, and, as happened in earlier decades, the competitive job situation causes resentment from native-born workers. This is the case even though most immigrants have little effect on the employment situation of native-born workers, because they mostly fill low-wage jobs that would not otherwise have been created or filled by employers seeking to pay very low wages.[44]

In addition, many Latino immigrants have come to the United States to flee political oppression. Large U.S. corporations have played a dominant role in the economies and politics of numerous Central American countries since 1900. For instance, the United Fruit Company became so strong in Guatemala that the threat, by a democratically elected government, to nationalize the company's lands led to intervention by the U.S. Central Intelligence Agency, and many Guatemalans were forced to flee the brutal U.S.-backed dictatorship that was established. U.S. corporations and the U.S. government have played a major role in generating emigration from Nicaragua and El Salvador. Similarly, since the 1970s there has been a great increase in the Taiwanese (Chinese), Koreans, and Vietnamese coming to the United States. These migrations were triggered for the most part by U.S. involvement in supporting Taiwan against mainland China, in the Korean War of the 1950s, and in the Vietnam War. U.S. participation in these struggles has created a significant group of Asians politically oriented to, or economically dependent on, the United States. In addition, the U.S. government long supported the corrupt Fulgencio Batista dictatorship in Cuba, whose oppressiveness generated the guerrilla movement led by Fidel Castro. When Castro took power, many Cubans who had prospered under the dictatorship fled to the United States.

Here we do not have the space to probe further the implications of the widespread and aggressive U.S. involvement overseas for recent patterns of immigration to the United States, but it is clear from this brief review that this immigration is not something that "just happens" without any input from or generation by U.S. corporate or governmental actions abroad. Neither U.S. schools and colleges nor the mass media recount these intimate economic and political connections between U.S. intervention in other countries and the streams of migration to the United States, historical connections that began in the nineteenth century and persist today. If critics of immigration really want to reduce immigration, it would seem, they might well turn their attention to eradicating U.S. imperialism, both economic and military imperialism, overseas.

Nativist Reactions to Recent Immigrants

The four historic themes of nativism can all be seen in recent opposition to immigration from native-born Americans and others, including some long-term resident immigrants who have picked up the nativist cause. For example, the theme of immigrants taking good "American" jobs is obvious in much recent debate over immigration. Recent opposition to immigrants by many native-born workers is linked not only to the selling of anti-immigrant messages to these workers by the media and politicians seeking votes, but also to the increasingly troubled character of the U.S. economy. Significantly, the problems of the U.S. economy are substantially due to the failure of top corporate executives to invest adequately in creating decent-paying jobs in the United States. Worker opposition to immigration would doubtless decrease if this major corporate disinvestment were to be reversed.

Polls show mixed public reactions to immigrants. A 1993 national opinion poll found that two-thirds of Americans believed immigrants today are hard-working and productive. In addition, the majority felt immigrants "take jobs away from Americans."[45] This public opinion is greatly shaped by anti-immigrant advocates in the mass media and in politics, as well as by the ever-present intellectuals and pundits who, like Madison Grant and Kenneth Roberts in the early twentieth century, try to sell a new version of nativism to U.S. workers and their families. For example, Dan Stein, who heads the

Federation for American Immigration Reform, has argued that new immigrants are "driving Americans" out of certain places like southern California and New York and are "eroding jobs for native Americans, especially the unskilled."[46] Similarly, *Forbes* editor Peter Brimelow, a member of the Anglo-American elite, has articulated a strong anti-immigrant perspective. In a recent book, *Alien Nation,* Brimelow worries that immigrants are, or soon will be, taking many jobs from U.S. workers, particularly from low-wage workers.[47] Interestingly, Brimelow's best-selling book echoes the title of a famous collection, *The Alien in Our Midst,* that was put out more than sixty-five years ago under the editorship of the arch nativist Madison Grant.[48]

However, most research studies show that immigrants do not take away more jobs than they create. Drawing on several studies, a report of the Council of Economic Advisors concluded that the low-wage jobs "taken by immigrants in years past have . . . increased employment and income for the population as a whole."[49] On the whole, immigrants create jobs, as well as take them; they create new jobs by their demands for housing and other consumer goods. In addition, it is the lowest-wage native-born workers who are likely to be affected by immigrants, and yet they play little or no part in the ideological or political debates over immigration.[50]

Since the truth about U.S. corporate and government interventions overseas and their link to immigration are not discussed much in the United States, alternative explanations for the troubled U.S. economy and government are developed. Much of the anti-immigrant diatribe is socially constructed by political, business, and media leaders, as well as the white-collar whites who have organized anti-immigrant groups. These elites and groups intentionally, according to immigration scholar Wayne Cornelius, "prey upon the fears and lack of knowledge of the average citizen, creating doomsday 'Third World-ization' scenarios out of a jumble of unrelated facts and unsubstantiated assertions."[51] As a result of biased media coverage, many Americans do not understand the character of contemporary immigration. For instance, a 1993 survey revealed that most respondents vastly overestimated the percentage of immigrants who enter the United States illegally. Almost two-thirds believed that *most* immigrants enter illegally, although official estimates put the proportion at just under one-quarter of all immigrants. Such myths have fuelled anti-immigrant organizations and efforts.[52] Indeed, the concern with illegal immigration is often a mask for other interests. Anti-immigrant groups like the Forum for American Immigration Reform harp on the number of illegal immigrants, some argue, as a way of getting the public to accept major cutbacks in legal immigration.[53]

As we have seen, nativists have often questioned the racial inferiority and the character or culture of immigrants. Like their counterparts in the late nineteenth and early twentieth centuries, many native-born civic and political leaders, as well as many in the general public, today question the intelligence of the Latino and Asian immigrants who constitute the majority of recent newcomers. For example, the most prominent contemporary advocate of racial differences in intelligence, the late Richard Herrnstein, let his ideological concerns over immigrants of color affect his scholarly analyses. In his best-selling *The Bell Curve* Herrnstein, and coauthor Charles Murray, argue that white immigrants at the turn of the century, the southern and eastern Europeans, were different from today's immigrants, for they were likely to be "brave, hard-working, imaginative, self-starting—and probably smart."[54]

What is remarkable here, in addition to the revisionist view of these earlier immigrants, is that the most important early study of so-called IQ differentials, the aforementioned study of Carl Brigham, has test figures relevant to this point, but Herrnstein does not cite the earlier study in his discussion of these white immigrants. Interestingly, the Brigham book is noted in the opening of *The Bell Curve,* and Brigham's test statistics are similar to those Herrnstein lauds throughout his book. Yet, the Brigham data are *not* cited on this question of how "smart" the early immigrants were. The reason doubtless lies in the fact that Brigham reports southern and eastern European immigrants to have had very low IQ scores, some 25 percent lower than those of English immigrants and well below the average for native-born whites. However, not long after commenting on how brave and smart earlier white immigrants were, Herrnstein and Murray make use of the 9 percent lower (than whites) average IQ test scores for Latinos in a negative assessment of the future of the overall intelligence of the U.S. population. The allegedly declining level of intelligence that stems from the "lesser intelligence" of immigrants of color is, in their view, very serious, and they suggest it may lead to increasing social problems like single-parent households, women on welfare, and crime.[55] It seems likely that Herrnstein does not deal with the earlier Brigham study because it would contradict his major point about recent immigrants. Of course, in both cases, the so-called IQ tests do not measure a general "intelligence" but, mostly, a limited range of verbal skills (in the English language).

The image of immigrants as a problem group with character and morality problems greater than those of the native-born population is an old nativistic canard. Today, as in the past, the reality of immigrants is different from the nativistic fictions. As a group, to quote a prominent social demographer, immigrants are still "upwardly mobile, ambitious, saving; they have traditional values, care about their children, all that sort of stuff. They've done something very dramatic to upgrade themselves."[56] There is no evidence that immigrants as a group are not as hardworking or honest as native-born Americans. Almost all are here to make a better life for their families. Today, as in the past, immigrants make mostly positive contributions. Data from the

1990 census on immigrants' financial status underscore this point. Even though the median family income of foreign-born Americans was well below that of native-born Americans, the per capita income of the foreign-born was higher than that of the native-born, reflecting in part a greater number of workers per family among the foreign-born. In addition, immigrant incomes rise dramatically with length of residence in the United States.[57]

Moreover, just as in earlier decades, contemporary nativists blame certain governmental problems on the new immigrants from Asia and Latin America. This can be most clearly seen in the attacks on immigration by California politicians and citizen groups. As Wayne Cornelius has put it, "In illegal immigrants (or immigrants in general), they find convenient scapegoats for virtually every ill afflicting California today, from the crisis in public finance to rising crime rates to environmental hazards."[58] Some nativistic intellectuals, such as *Forbes* editor Brimelow, also complain that immigrants are consuming the taxes of ordinary working Americans by becoming public charges and rely much too heavily on government, an argument made by anti-immigrant advocates in the nineteenth and early twentieth centuries against southern and eastern Europeans.[59] However, the data suggest such perspectives are exaggerated. Jeffrey Passel, an immigration specialist, has argued on the basis of Urban Institute research that immigrants likely pay far more in government taxes than they get back, "with a $25 billion to $30 billion annual surplus from recent post-1970 immigrants."[60]

Another nativist concern focuses on the number of immigrants coming to the United States. These numbers are heralded, often with fanfare, as unprecedented. Brimelow, for example, argues that today the United States is "engulfed by what seems likely to be the greatest wave of immigration it has ever faced."[61] Like earlier nativists, modern opponents of immigration doubt the United States can absorb the "huge numbers" of new immigrants. Contrary to popular images, however, the recent immigration is not the greatest faced by this nation, nor is it fueling a huge population expansion. Indeed, the 1980s saw a population increase of only 10 percent, the second-lowest rate of increase for any decade in U.S. history. Moreover, the ratio of immigrants to the native-born population is much lower today than in earlier decades of the twentieth century. In 1910, the foreign-born constituted nearly 15 percent of the population, yet in the mid-1990s the figure was still just 8 percent. Indeed, the United States now has a smaller percentage of foreign-born citizens than many other nations, including England, Germany, Switzerland, Australia, Canada, and New Zealand.[62]

In recent years, popular magazines have run major stories asking "What will America be like when whites are no longer the majority?" However, one can ask what the predominance of whites has to do with the future of the nation, unless one has racist proclivities? As with earlier anti-immigrant perspectives, the views of nativists today include a worry about immigrants' physical and cultural characteristics. Earlier in the century it was the southern and eastern European immigrants who were seen as racially and culturally inferior. Today, it is the Latino and Asian immigrants. Some anti-immigrant advocates like Brimelow have developed explicitly racial arguments directed at the character and provenance of new immigrants. As Brimelow sees it, "the American nation has always had a specific ethnic core. And that core has been white." [63] Later, he notes that as late as 1950 some 90 percent of Americans "looked like me. That is, they were of European stock. And in those days, they had another name for this thing dismissed so contemptuously as 'the racial hegemony of white Americans.' They called it 'America.' " [64]

Representing some in the ruling elite, analysts like Brimelow take the position that public policy should insist on the speedy Americanization of all immigrants, an assimilation policy often explicitly modelled on that for turn-of-the-century immigration. [65] These analysts often insist that all money spent on cultural diversity and foreign-language retention be cut off, because these programs forestall the anglicization of immigrants. The old theme of pressured one-way assimilation is common among modern nativists, who feel that the cultures of the immigrants of color are not compatible with the dominant Anglo culture.

TAKING ACTION AGAINST IMMIGRANTS

Modern nativists, like their predecessors, are not content with developing anti-immigrant ideologies. Many are organizing and pressuring political leaders to take action to restrict or exclude immigrants. Language is now one focus of this new parochialism. About one in ten Americans, some 25 million people, live in homes where a language other than English is spoken. Many of these Americans are immigrants or their children. Recent organizing by nativists targets the language and culture of these Americans, particularly those who are Spanish speakers. For instance, an amendment to the Arizona state constitution went so far as to make English the language "of all government functions and actions," but as of this writing, the federal courts have ruled this violated the constitution. [66] The intensity of this anti-Latino sentiment can be seen in a quote from a Council on Interamerican Security paper: "Hispanics in America today represent a very dangerous and subversive force that is bent on taking over our nation's political institutions for the purposes of imposing Spanish as the official language of the U.S. and indeed of the entire Western Hemisphere. . . . If we desire to preserve our unique culture and the primacy of the English language, then we must so declare rather than sitting idly by as a de facto nation evolves." [67]

On the contemporary scene, xenophobic nativists view English-Only policies as a way to promote Anglocentric values. These efforts are a type of colonial "hegemony that threatens to silence the less powerful."[68] One result of lobbying by nativist organizations is the introduction of legislation to make English the official language. In 1986, California passed a ballot proposition declaring English to be the official language there, and by the mid-1990s such legislation was passed in seventeen states. In addition, from the early 1980s to the 1990s an English Language Amendment to the U.S. Constitution has regularly been introduced in the U.S. Congress. Today anti-immigrant advocates still vigorously argue for a constitutional amendment making English the official language.[69]

Leaders of contemporary nativist organizations such as the California English Campaign and the national group U.S. English argue that they are not trying to discriminate against immigrants, but that they wish immigrants to quickly become part of the mainstream by adopting English and the Anglo culture. However, until the late 1980s U.S. English was linked to an organization pressing for immigration restrictions. Moreover, many pro-English advocates favor discrimination such as prohibiting Spanish as a language in government agencies and cutting off bilingual programs in schools.[70]

Nativist campaigns to promote the English language underscore the uneasiness that descendants of earlier immigrants feel in the presence of languages and cultures brought by relative newcomers. As Juan F. Perea notes, their "first myth is that our national unity somehow depends solely on the English language, ergo we must protect the language through constitutional amendment or legislation. A corollary is that the only language of true American identity is the English language."[71]

A number of citizen organizations, such as Americans for Immigration Control (AIC), are openly pressing for immigration policies favoring immigrants from Western Europe. In this manner, the anti-immigrant viewpoint is racialized. A few prominent politicians are beginning to take the same perspective. For example, the 1992 elections signaled the beginning of a major political attack on Latino and Asian immigrants. In 1992, both Patrick Buchanan and David Duke used hoary nativistic appeals as part of their campaigns. A former leader of the Ku Klux Klan, David Duke put his hat in the ring for the 1992 Republican presidential nomination. Duke echoed Madison Grant and other early-twentieth-century nativists in his assertion that immigrants are destroying the dominant Anglo culture and its values: "We've got to begin to protect our values. We've got to begin to realize that we're a Christian society. We're part of Western Christian civilization."[72]

Moreover, in 1992 Pat Buchanan challenged President George Bush for the Republican nomination, and in 1996 he made another run for the presidency. In his comments, articles, and interviews since the early 1990s, Buchanan has strongly articulated the classic nativists' concern with unassimilable immigrants of color. In his announcement for the 1992 presidential race, Buchanan signaled he was worried about the racial mix of the U.S. population: "Our Judeo-Christian values are going to be preserved and our Western heritage is going to be handed down to future generations and not dumped on some landfill called multiculturalism."[73] The caustic landfill comment targeted immigrants of color. Commenting in a similar vein, Buchanan told an ABC interviewer that "if we had to take a million immigrants in, say, Zulus next year or Englishmen, and put them in Virginia, what group would be easier to assimilate and would cause less problems for the people of Virginia? There is nothing wrong with us sitting down and arguing that issue that we are a European country, English-speaking country."[74] In Buchanan's view, the new immigrants of color cannot be easily assimilated and the dominant European American culture is being watered down seriously by immigration.[75] Buchanan represents the nativist position that there is one "true" culture, that of European Americans, and those who are not European are not really "American." Commenting on why Americans are more shocked at massacres in the former Yugoslavia than in Africa, Buchanan says it is because the former "are white people. That's who we are. That's where America comes from."[76] This paean to whiteness may not be surprising in light of his previous opinion about white fascist leaders, as in his famous comment some years back that, while Adolf Hitler was a villain, he was "an individual of great courage" who had "extraordinary gifts."[77] Modern nativism can be as autocratic and racial as the old nativism of the nineteenth and early-twentieth centuries.

In the mid-1990s, not only Duke and Buchanan but a number of formerly moderate politicians took up the nativist rant. These included California Governor Pete Wilson, a candidate for the 1996 Republican party presidential nomination, who moved away from a pro-immigration stance to a more nativist approach. He emphasized the large number of illegal immigrants in California as a major source of the state's fiscal problems.[78]

Nativists have scored important legislative victories. Nativist concern over the presence of undocumented immigrants was one source of support for the 1986 Immigration Reform and Control Act (IRCA). The congressional and public debate over this 1986 legislation conjured up anti-immigrant arguments of the early twentieth century, including concerns that the new immigrants were taking jobs from "Americans" and that many Latinos and Asians were not really interested in assimilating to the dominant culture. We should note that this argument was, and is, nativistic and inaccurate, for many Latino immigrants come to the United States partially assimilated because of the dominance of U.S. culture and corporations in their countries.[79] In addition, the majority assimilate relatively rapidly to the English language and other aspects of Euro-American culture. Surveys have found that most Mexican Americans are bilingual and that almost all Latino adults feel it is very important for their children to be fluent in English. They do not need nativists to tell them that they and their children will do better socially and economically if they learn English.[80]

Many Latino Americans are troubled by provisions of the IRCA law, including intrusive government documentation of legal work status, sanctions for businesses that employ undocumented aliens, and a program screening welfare applicants for migration status. In 1990, nativists were again successful in reducing the number of immigrants. This new limit most affects immigrants from those countries in Asia and Latin America from which many people wish to enter the United States. This contrasts with the generally unlimited immigration allowed before the 1910s, when most potential immigrants were European.[81]

In 1994, anti-immigrant groups scored an important political success in California. Citizen groups forced Proposition 187 onto the California ballot, which passed with a substantial majority in the fall of 1994. Proposition 187 severely restricts access of undocumented immigrants to public services, including schools and hospitals, and requires public employees to report undocumented immigrants. Immigrant-bashing was common among white political candidates during the 1994 election campaign in California, and a number of anti-immigrant groups aggressively supported the proposition. These political victories are the modern parallels to the 1924 Immigration Act and may signal the beginning of a string of anti-immigrant actions by citizens' groups and state and federal legislatures.

Nativism has waxed and waned over the course of U.S. history, but it remains an important perspective that many native-born Americans use to construct and interpret hard economic times. Certain essential components of nativism remain more or less constant: the accent on the racial or cultural inferiority of immigrants, the problematizing of assimilation of immigrants, the idea that immigrants are a serious threat to the U.S. economy, and the notion that immigrants are responsible for government crises. These images of immigrants remain a critical part of the "cultural shelves" in the minds of a majority of native-born (and even many long-term resident) Americans. The development of U.S. society has been such that few alternative explanations have ever been allowed on those cultural shelves, so immigrants, together with Jewish Americans and black Americans, are often the scapegoats for the political-economic difficulties that this capitalist society routinely faces. These naive, stereotyped, often racist explanations help many Americans explain what seems to them inexplicable, and in the process leave many other

Americans, especially the newcomers who face many adjustment problems anyway, hurting from the nativistic attacks.

The cultural explanations have a folk component and are to some degree rooted in the ancient folkways of the dominant racial-ethnic groups in this society. However, today as in the past, crises over immigration are often *manufactured* by the nation's ruling elite, both through capitalists' investment decisions that reduce job opportunities and through the creation of immigrant bogeymen that native-born citizens can use as scapegoats. Immigrant myths and fictions are frequently created in the speeches of prominent politicians, the writings of establishment pundits, and the journalistic commentaries in the mass media. In particular, anti-immigrant advocates and nativist leaders often suggest that native-born Americans are strongly opposed to immigration and want it to be curtailed sharply or ended.

However, in spite of certain folk interpretations of immigration and the elite efforts to create myths about immigrants, even today a majority of Americans are not as anti-immigrant and exclusionist as many national leaders, and especially leaders of nativist organizations, often suggest. Indeed, how strongly Americans feel about limiting immigration depends on how it is presented to them. In some national surveys three-quarters of those polled favor limiting immigration. However, this does not mean all favor major cutbacks in the number of immigrants. Indeed, in a 1994 National Opinion Research Center poll considerably less than half (34 percent) the respondents thought immigration should be decreased a lot. Another 28 percent felt it should be decreased only a little, while one third felt immigration should actually be increased or stay about the same. A clear *majority* of those Americans polled did not wish to see major changes in immigration flows.[82] In addition, there were no large variations in opinions about immigration by region or income group, although the most affluent respondents were a little less inclined to support major cuts in immigration than others. Black and white Americans had similar levels of concern about immigration.[83] There is no evidence that the majority of Americans favor significant cutbacks in immigration or that those native-born Americans who see the most new immigrants, those on the West Coast or in New York, are the most opposed to continuing immigration.

Today nativists face a major demographic problem. The dominance of people of color is coming to the United States whether white and other nativistic Americans like it or not. Even if some immigration restrictions are imposed, current demographic trends are likely to persist, and the United States will have a population where the majority is composed of people of color sometime in the middle of the twenty-first century. Around 2050–60 a.d. the majority of Americans will be of African, Asian, Latin American,

Middle Eastern, or Native American ancestry. Moreover, long before that date more than half of all young Americans will be people of color, and large cities in several states will have populations that are mostly people of color.[84] By the year 2002, it is estimated, whites will be the minority in the largest state in the union, California. Latinos, Africans, Asians, and Middle Eastern Americans will be the majority there.[85] By approximately these dates European Americans will, as in the 1700s, be a minority population.

As a result, there will be major social and political changes. Over the next several decades these changes in demographic composition will force actions to be taken against the racist aspects of the nativistic ideologies. People of color will not tolerate their inferiorization in racial and cultural terms. In addition, those Americans with political and economic power, mostly white Americans today, will have to cease the now common discriminatory practices targeting people of color in most sectors of U.S. society. Over the next few decades, as they increase in political and economic power, people of color will refuse to accept inferior treatment and subordinate positions in the institutions of U.S. society.

In my judgment now is the time for European Americans, who are themselves all descendants of immigrants, to return to the inclusionist philosophy celebrated in the inscription on the Statue of Liberty. They might well remember the inscription by Jewish American poet Emma Lazarus: "Give me your tired, your poor, Your huddled masses, yearning to breathe free, The wretched refuse of your teeming shore, Send these, the homeless, tempest-tost to me, I lift my lamp beside the golden door."

NOTES

Portions of this article draw on and extend some arguments made in Joe R. Feagin and Clairece B. Feagin, *Racial and Ethnic Relations,* 5th ed. (Englewood Cliffs, N.J.: Prentice-Hall, 1995), chapters 1–3, 5–6, and 13. These materials are used by permission.

1. Deborah Sontag, "Across the U.S., Immigrants Find the Land of Resentment," *New York Times,* December 11, 1992, p. A1.

2. U.S. Bureau of the Census, *1990 Census of Population: Social and Economic Characteristics: United States,* CP-2–1 (Washington, D.C.: U.S. Government Printing Office, 1993), p. 166.

3. David Hackett Fischer, *Albion's Seed: Four British Folkways in America* (New York: Oxford University Press, 1989), pp. 6, 13–205, 785–86, and passim.

4. Quoted in Gerry O'Sullivan, "Mythmaking in the Promised Land; An Interview with Joel Kovel," *Humanist,* September 1994, p. 18.

5. Ibid., p. 18.

6. Ronald Takaki, *Iron Cages* (New York: Oxford University Press, 1990), p. 12.

7. Ibid., pp. 12–14.

8. Milton M. Gordon, *Assimilation in American Life* (New York: Oxford University Press, 1964), pp. 72–73.

9. Michael Kammen, *People of Paradox* (New York: Knopf, 1972), p. 66.

10. Quoted in Nancy F. Conklin and Margaret A. Lourie, *A Host of Tongues* (New York: Free Press, 1983), p. 69.

11. See Kammen, *People of Paradox*, p. 74.

12. Immanuel Wallerstein, *The Modern World-System* (New York: Academic Press, 1974), pp. 85–86.

13. See Aristide R. Zolberg, "Reforming the Back Door: The Immigration Reform and Control Act of 1986 in Historical Perspective," in *Immigration Reconsidered,* ed. Virginia Yans-McLaughlin (New York: Oxford University Press, 1990), pp. 315–35.

14. Quoted in Richard Hofstadter, *Social Darwinism in American Thought,* rev. ed. (Boston: Beacon Press, 1955), pp. 171–72.

15. Theodore W. Allen, *The Invention of the White Race* (New York: Verso, 1994), pp. 21, 184.

16. Lewis H. Carlson and George A. Colburn, *In Their Place* (New York: John Wiley, 1972), pp. 305–8.

17. Albert Szymanski, *The Capitalist State and the Politics of Class* (Cambridge, Mass.: Winthrop, 1978), pp. 187–88.

18. Douglas F. Dowd, *The Twisted Dream* (Cambridge, Mass.: Winthrop, 1977), pp. 146–47.

19. John Higham, *Strangers in the Land* (New York: Atheneum, 1963), p. 156.

20. Kenneth L. Roberts, *Why Europe Leaves Home,* excerpted in "Kenneth L. Roberts and the Threat of Mongrelization in America, 1922," in *In Their Place,* ed. Lewis H. Carlson and George A. Colburn (New York: John Wiley, 1972), p. 312.

21. In *Scribner's,* April 1913, quoted in Rita J. Simon and Susan H. Alexander, *The Ambivalent Welcome: Print Media, Public Opinion, and Immigration* (Westport, Conn.: Praeger, 1993), p. 123.

22. Eliot Lord, John J. D. Trenor, and Samuel J. Barrows, *The Italian in America,* reprint ed. (San Francisco: R & E Associates, 1970), pp. 17–18.

23. Quoted in Luciano J. Iorizzo and Salvatore Mondello, *The Italian-Americans* (New York: Twayne, 1971), p. 64.

24. See Henry L. Feingold, *Zion in America* (New York: Twayne, 1974), pp. 143–44; C. Vann Woodward, *Tom Watson* (New York: Oxford University Press, 1963), pp. 435–45.

25. Carl C. Brigham, *A Study of American Intelligence* (Princeton, N.J.: Princeton University Press, 1923), pp. 124–25, 177–210. Later Brigham recanted.

26. Allan Chase, *The Legacy of Malthus: The Social Costs of the New Scientific Racism* (New York: Knopf, 1977), pp. 111–13; E. Digby Baltzell, *The Protestant Establishment* (New York: Vintage Books, 1966), pp. 96–100.

27. See Rufus Learski, *The Jews in America* (New York: KTAV Publishing House, 1972), pp. 290–93.

28. Higham, *Strangers in the Land,* pp. 301–13.

29. Chase, *The Legacy of Malthus,* pp. 270–90.

30. These are extrapolations from the rates of migration before the 1924 immigration act. Ibid., pp. 300–301.

31. Higham, *Strangers in the Land,* p. 321.

32. Cited in ibid., p. 300.

33. Chase, *The Legacy of Malthus,* pp. 174–75.

34. See Feagin and Feagin, *Racial and Ethnic Relations,* chapter 4.

35. James J. Fink, *The Car Culture* (Cambridge: MIT Press, 1975), pp. 88–90.

36. The quotations are from Samuel Bowles and Herbert Gintis, *Schooling in Capitalist America* (New York: Basic Books, 1976), p. 162.

37. Milton Meltzer, *Never to Forget: The Jews of the Holocaust* (New York: Harper and Row, 1976), p. 45.

38. Milton R. Konvitz, "Inter-group Relations," in *The American Jew,* ed. O. I. Janowsky (Philadelphia: Jewish Publication Society of America, 1964), pp. 78–79; Donald S. Strong, *Organized Anti-Semitism in America* (Washington, D.C.: American Council on Public Affairs, 1941), pp. 14–20.

39. See Feagin and Feagin, *Racial and Ethnic Relations,* chapter 6.

40. See Richard Alba, *Ethnic Identity: The Transformation of White America* (New Haven: Yale University Press, 1990), pp. 364–66.

41. Lenni Brenner, *Jews in America Today* (Secaucus, N.J.: Lyle Stuart, 1986), pp. 205–9; Stephanie Chavez, "Anti-Semitic Incidents Reported Rising," *Los Angeles Times,* February 7, 1992, p. A3.

42. They were particularly concerned with family reunion. See Zolberg, "Reforming the Back Door," pp. 319–20.

43. U.S. Bureau of the Census, *1970 Census of Population: Detailed Characteristics—United States Summary* (Washington, D.C.: U.S. Government Printing Office, 1973), p. 591; U.S. Bureau of the Census, *1990 Census of Population and Housing: Summary Population and Housing Characteristics-United States* (Washington, D.C.: U.S. Government Printing Office, 1992), p. 59. I draw on the summary in Bill Ong Hing, "Beyond the Rhetoric of Assimilation and Cultural Pluralism: Addressing the Tension of Separatism and Conflict in an Immigration-Driven Multiracial Society," *California Law Review,* vol. 81 (July 1993): 863.

44. Michael Fix and Jeffrey S. Passel, *Immigration and Immigrants: Setting the Record Straight* (Washington, D.C.: Urban Institute, 1994), p. 24; David Cole, "Five Myths about Immigration," *Nation,* October 7, 1994, p. 410.

45. Bruce W. Nelan, "Not Quite So Welcome Anymore," *Time,* Special Issue, Fall 1993, pp. 10–12.

46. Spencer Rich, "U.S. Immigrant Population at Postwar High," *Washington Post,* August 29, 1995, p. A1.

47. Peter Brimelow, *Alien Nation: Common Sense about America's Immigration Disaster* (New York: Random House, 1995), pp. 137–57.

48. Madison Grant and Charles Stewart Davison, *The Alien in Our Midst or "Selling Our Birthright for a Mess of Pottage": The Written Views of a Number of Americans (Present and Former) on Immigration and Its Results* (New York: Galton Publishing Co., 1930).

49. Cited in Shawn Foster, "Immigrants: Blessing or Curse for Utah?" *Salt Lake Tribune,* November 10, 1994, p. A1.

50. Immigrants do sometimes displace significant numbers of workers from low-wage jobs, and thus they may have the greatest effect on poorer Americans.

51. Wayne A. Cornelius, "Perspective on Immigration; Neo-nativists Feed on Myopic Fears; No Industrial Country Is Able to Keep Foreign Workers from Settling In; Once Here, They Become 'Our Own,' " *Los Angeles Times,* July 12, 1993, Metro, p. B7.

52. Nelan, "Not Quite So Welcome Anymore," pp. 10–12.

53. Joel Kotkin, "Whatever Happened to the Ideal of Citizenship for Immigrants?" *Houston Chronicle,* July 18, 1993, Outlook Section, p. 1.

54. Richard J. Herrnstein and Charles Murray, *The Bell Curve: Intelligence and Class Structure in American Life* (New York: Free Press, 1994), p. 361.

55. Ibid., pp. 362–65.

56. Ben Wattenberg, as quoted in Keith Henderson, "Immigration as an Economic Engine," *Christian Science Monitor,* March 27, 1992, p. 9. See also Ben Wattenberg, *The First Universal Nation* (New York: Free Press, 1990).

57. U.S. Bureau of the Census, *1990 Census of Population: Ancestry of the Population in the United States* (Washington, D.C.: U.S. Government Printing Office, 1993), pp. 307, 409.

58. Cornelius, "Perspective on Immigration," p. B7.

59. Brimelow, *Alien Nation,* pp. 146–51.

60. Quoted in Rich, "U.S. Immigrant Population at Postwar High," p. A1.

61. Brimelow, *Alien Nation,* p. 5.

62. Bureau of the Census, *1990 Census of the Population: Ancestry of the Population in the United States,* p. 1; Karen A. Woodrow and Jeffrey S. Passel, "Post-IRCA Undocumented Immigration to the United States," in *Undocumented Migration to the United States,* ed. Frank Bean, Barry Edmonston, and Jeffrey Passel (Santa Monica, Calif.: Rand Corporation, 1990), p. 42.

63. Brimelow, *Alien Nation,* p. 10.

64. Ibid., p. 59. Ironically, Brimelow himself is a British immigrant to the United States.

65. Ibid., p. 264.

66. Catherine E. Walsh, *Pedagogy and the Struggle for Voice* (New York: Bergin and Garvey, 1991), pp. 101, 127.

67. Rusty Butler, *On Creating a Hispanic America: A Nation within a Nation?* (Washington, D.C.: Council for Interamerican Security, 1985), as quoted in Walsh, *Pedagogy and the Struggle for Voice,* p. 100.

68. Walsh, *Pedagogy and the Struggle for Voice,* p. ix.

69. Brimelow, *Alien Nation,* p. 265.

70. Bill Piatt, *Only English? Law and Language Policy in the United States* (Albuquerque: University of New Mexico Press, 1990), p. 159.

71. Juan F. Perea, "Demography and Distrust: An Essay on American Languages, Cultural Pluralism and Official English," 77 *Minnesota Law Review* (1992): 269–373.

72. Quoted in Clarence Page, "U.S. Media Should Stop Abetting Intolerance," *Toronto Star,* December 27, 1991, p. A27.

73. Quoted in ibid., p. A27.

74. Quoted in John Dillin, "Immigration Joins List of '92 Issues," *Christian Science Monitor,* December 17, 1991, p. 6.

75. Sontag, "Across the U.S., Immigrants Find the Land of Resentment," p. A1.

76. Quoted in Tom Mathews, Howard Fineman, and Eleanor Clift, "Why Is Buchanan So Angry?" *Newsweek,* January 27, 1992, p. 22.

77. Quoted in ibid., p. 22.

78. Hearst News Service, "California Chief Defends Tough Stand on Illegals," *Arizona Republic,* May 27, 1994, p. A8.

79. See Alejandro Portes, "From South of the Border: Hispanic Minorities in the

United States," in *Immigration Reconsidered,* ed. Virginia Yans-McLaughlin (New York: Oxford University Press, 1990), pp. 160–80.

80. See Strategy Research Corporation, *1991 U.S. Hispanic Market* (Miami, 1991), especially pp. 78–129.

81. See Stephen Koepp, "Rotten Shame: Who Will Pick the Crops?" *Time,* June 22, 1987, p. 49; Feagin and Feagin, *Racial and Ethnic Relations,* pp. 295–96.

82. National Opinion Research Center, *1994 General Social Survey.* Tabulation by author.

83. The greatest concern about reducing immigrants was expressed in the old South where there are in fact few immigrants; the least concern was expressed in the New York, New Jersey, Pennsylvania area (26 percent). There was some variation by racial group and ethnicity, with Canadian Americans showing the greatest anti-immigrant views (58 percent for decreasing it a lot), and Asian Americans and Latin Americans showing the least concern, at 12 percent and 18 percent for major restrictions respectively. National Opinion Research Center, *1994 General Social Survey.* Tabulation by author.

84. See Joe R. Feagin, Hernan Vera, and Barbara A. Zsembik, "Multiculturalism: A Democratic Basis for American Society," in *Primis* (New York: McGraw-Hill, 1995).

85. Nancy Rivera Brooks, "A Los Angeles Times-Financial Times Special Report; The Next California—The State's Economy in the Year 2000; the Next California/ Immigration and Diversity; the State in 2000," *Los Angeles Times,* September 12, 1995, Special Section, p. J5.

3. THE STATUE OF LIBERTY
Notes from Behind the Gilded Door
Juan F. Perea

The man on lookout shouted down the companion way to the pilots that he thought it was a tramp. The vessel was hailed and a voice asked, "What ship?"

"Isère, from Rouen," came back through the darkness, in broken English.

"It's all right," said Pilot Henderson, getting into a small boat and heading for the vessel; "she's got that big Liberty aboard."

—*New York Times,* June 18, 1885

From the beginning she was a boat person, possible tramp, French import. She was an immigrant arriving under cover of darkness and shrouded meaning. In time, she became the preeminent symbol of the United States, "the premier monumental icon of modern times."[1]

It is the way of a symbol to be endowed with meaning by its creators, its observers, and its interpreters.[2] In this chapter, I want to identify some of the principal meanings associated with the Statue of Liberty and to explore their evolution. These meanings include those intended by its French creators and donors, those understood by its American recipients, and the meaning attributed principally by European immigrants to the United States. This overly simple and short list hints at the complexity in deciphering what the Statue "means" in any definitive way. I also want to evaluate critically these meanings in light of the historical context surrounding the Statue and in light of mostly contemporaneous writings of observers of the Statue. The historical context reveals enormous tension between ideals symbolized by the Statue and the lived experience of people of color and women.

The Statue was a gift from the French people to the United States. Its idea was conceived in 1865 by Edouard de Laboulaye and other liberal French intellectuals, including sculptor Auguste Bartholdi. In 1875, Laboulaye formed the Franco-American Union, to raise funds for the construction of the Statue.[3] Later in 1875, Laboulaye made a formal request for Bedloe's Island in New York harbor as the site for the Statue of Liberty. Congress passed a resolution authorizing the use of Bedloe's island and providing for the maintenance of the Statue (as a lighthouse) in 1877.[4] Auguste Bartholdi completed the Statue in 1884, and it was presented to and accepted officially by the United States, in France, on July 4, 1884.[5] The Statue arrived in the United States aboard the Isère in 1885, where it was unloaded on Bedloe's Island.

The French had agreed to give the huge statue if the United States would provide an appropriate site and a pedestal for it. The Statue, however, lay in pieces on Bedloe's island in its 210 shipping crates, its construction uncertain, for nearly one year because of insufficient funds for completion of the pedestal.[6] The pedestal on Bedloe's Island might never have been constructed except for the contributions and fundraising efforts of immigrants. Largely due to the intensive efforts of Joseph Pulitzer, a Hungarian immigrant who published the *New York World* and other newspapers, sufficient funds were collected.[7] Pulitzer published the name of every person who made a contribution to finance the pedestal. Approximately 120,000 persons from all over the country contributed whatever they could to finance the construction of the pedestal on which the statue rests.[8] Ultimately the pedestal was completed and the Statue was constructed upon it. The Statue was dedicated officially and unveiled with much fanfare in October 1886.

To understand the Statue more fully, we begin by considering what the Statue, and its donation to the United States, meant to its French creators. The Statue was conceived as a way to immortalize ideals of liberty and Republicanism at a time when these ideals were vulnerable in France.[9] The Statue was intended to symbolize values repressed by Emperor Napoleon III.[10] The United States was seen by these Frenchmen as the best embodiment of the liberty they wished for themselves.[11]

Interestingly, the history of the Statue of Liberty is inextricably intertwined with the abolition of American slavery.[12] Silenced by Napoleon, Laboulaye aspired to his conception of American-style freedoms and liberalism.[13] American slavery, however, was the most glaring exception to liberalism.[14] Chairman of the French Anti-Slavery Society, Laboulaye commented that "[a]lthough forbidden to talk to my fellow citizens about their concerns, I was allowed to interest myself in the American Negroes. . . . To serve the freedom of the blacks was still a way to serve the freedom of the whites."[15] Laboulaye celebrated Abraham Lincoln's reelection in 1864 as "the salvation of the American republic and of the liberty which is of interest to the whole world. With the eradication of slavery America had matured."[16] The formal abolition of slavery in America was greeted with great enthusiasm by French liberals.[17]

In a speech given in 1876, Laboulaye commented on the meaning of the

Statue: "This statue, symbol of liberty, tells us . . . that Liberty lives only through Truth and Justice, Light and Law. This is the Liberty that we desire."[18] Laboulaye's statement makes explicit his wish that the Statue embody French aspirations for liberty. By exporting a symbol of French liberty to the United States, its creators hoped at least for a permanent symbol of their aspirations for French republicanism. By exporting it beyond French borders and beyond the reach of French politics, their symbol would last regardless of anticipated reversals and antipathy in France.

Thus the Statue was intended by its creators to symbolize a French conception of liberty. The French had provided vital assistance in the American colonies' struggle for independence from British monarchist oppression. So the French conception of liberty as freedom from monarchist oppression converged historically and ideologically with American independence.[19] This convergence provided one of the rationales for the Statue of Liberty, a French commemoration of the centennial of American independence.

The French also equated liberty with equality much more readily than Americans. Liberty and equality were firmly linked in the mind of Laboulaye, for example, who celebrated the abolition of slavery as testament to the maturation of American liberty. According to historian Michael Kammen, "since the French Revolution of 1789, Liberty and Equality has been regarded as a concept especially meaningful to the French."[20] Interestingly, the correlation between liberty and equality arises in the United States prominently only much later, during the twentieth century.[21] And this correlation in the United States, unlike other meanings of the term liberty, has "neither deep historical roots nor particularly strong parallels (until well into the twentieth century) in Great Britain."[22]

The people and government of the United States were ambivalent and weak in their acceptance and support for the Statue. Many Americans were suspicious of the gift Statue and the motives of its French donors. As one anonymous American commented in the *New York Times,* "It is ridiculous for Frenchmen to continue to impose on Americans a present they refuse to accept, to worry them with a souvenir that offends them, to humiliate them with a generous idea they do not comprehend, and to beg for thanks that they will not give."[23] Clergymen expressed concern about pagan values they saw embodied in the Statue and feared for the idolatry it might spawn. And many in the South objected to a symbol which represented the racial equality so many Southerners had fought to repel: "At first it was mostly in the South (where it was twice confounded, as unchristian and as the embodied slogan against which the South had fought in vain) that the Statue was denounced as pagan and idolatrous, by Protestants."[24]

To many observers, however, the Statue represented the United States as the fullest embodiment of the ideal that free people, living in liberty, would be capable of the greatest achievements and the most perfect form of government that would enable their freedom. This liberty, and the renewed alliance between France and the United States engendered by the gift of the Statue, inspired many of the speakers who spoke at ceremonies dedicating the Statue in October 1886. Several speakers described the liberty that "enlightens the world."[25] President Grover Cleveland vowed that "[w]e will not forget that Liberty has here made her home, nor shall her chosen altar be neglected. . . . [A] stream of light shall pierce the darkness of ignorance and men's oppression until liberty shall enlighten the world."[26] Speakers also celebrated the renewed alliance between the French and American peoples and the role of the French in assisting victory in the Revolutionary War. Noticeably absent from the speeches was much mention of the Statue as a symbol welcoming new immigrants.[27]

It is clear that the pro-immigrant, welcoming meanings of the Statue of Liberty were neither intended by its creators nor perceived by most persons at the time of its dedication. A principal source of pro-immigrant meanings associated with the Statue is Emma Lazarus's famous poem, "The New Colossus," written around 1883.[28] While the fundraising campaign for the Statue's pedestal languished, an auction of art and letters was held in 1883 to raise additional money. Lazarus, primarily a poet and writer of Jewish history and culture, contributed "The New Colossus" for the auction.[29]

Lazarus's poem renamed the Statue "Mother of Exiles," and asserted a duty for its new guardian land:

> Not like the brazen giant of Greek fame,
> With conquering limbs astride from land to land;
> Here at our sea-washed, sunset gates shall stand
> A mighty woman with a torch, whose flame
> Is the imprisoned lightning, and her name
> Mother of Exiles. From her beacon-hand
> Glows world-wide welcome; her mild eyes command
> The air-bridged harbor that twin cities frame.
> "Keep, ancient lands, your storied pomp!" cries she
> With silent lips. "Give me your tired, your poor,
> Your huddled masses yearning to breathe free,
> The wretched refuse of your teeming shore.
> Send these, the homeless, tempest-tost to me,
> I lift my lamp beside the golden door!"[30]

It took the United States many years to acknowledge and later to embrace (to whatever extent this has occurred) Lazarus's pro-immigrant view of the Statue. Poet James Russell Lowell sent Lazarus a note, stating "I must write you again to say how much I liked your sonnet about the Statue. Much better than I like the Statue itself. But your sonnet gives its subject a raison d'etre which it wanted before, quite as much as it wants a pedestal."[31] It was obvious, at least to Lowell, that the Statue lacked an American meaning, an American reason for its existence.

Notwithstanding Lowell's praise, after the auction Lazarus's poem slipped quickly into obscurity. She took no further interest in the Statue. When Lazarus died, obituaries did not mention "The New Colossus." The poem was generally ignored by literary critics and was not included in literary anthologies which included her other poems.[32] In 1903, as a memorial to Lazarus, Georgina Schuyler arranged for and financed a bronze plaque containing the poem, which was placed on an interior wall of the statue.[33] Finally, in the 1930s, Lazarus's interpretation of the Statue began to gain more public acceptance. Ironically, this occurred after immigration had been drastically curtailed by the National Origins Quotas of 1924. Lazarus's poem was revived after increasing numbers of Jewish refugees from Nazism created a need to renew the United States' image as a bastion of liberty.[34]

Interestingly, Lazarus's immigrant-welcoming reinterpretation of the Statue, while not widely shared at the time, was consistent with the views of some early American leaders, who saw America as a haven for oppressed peoples.[35] George Washington, for example, in a speech given in 1783 to recent Irish immigrants, stated that "the Bosom of America is open to receive not only the opulent and respectable stranger but the oppressed and persecuted of all Nations and Religions."[36]

But it was the immigrants themselves, mostly from eastern and southeastern Europe, who were largely responsible for the pro-immigrant, welcoming interpretation of the Statue of Liberty.[37] Immigrants made the Statue a celebration of their own arrival in the United States. Jose Marti, leader of Cuban independence, reported on the Statue's unveiling for the Argentinean newspaper *La Nación.*[38] Marti noticed the apparent importance of the Statue to the lower classes and immigrants:

Behold how they run towards the wharves from which the statue can be seen, elated as shipwrecked people who descry a hopeful sail! These are the humblest, those who fear the main streets and the clean people: pale tobacco workers, humpbacked stevedores, Italian women with their colored shawls. . . . They come from the east side, the west side, the congested alleys of the poor neighborhoods.[39]

"Behold," Marti observed, "they all reveal the exhilaration of being reborn! . . . [A]ll these luckless Irishmen, Poles, Italians, Bohemians, Germans redeemed from oppression or misery, hail the monument to Liberty because they feel that through it they themselves are uplifted and restored."[40]

In contrast to the self-celebration of these immigrants, American leaders who spoke during the unveiling ceremony hardly mentioned immigration and spoke few words to encourage it. Indeed, the image of the statue as a watchful "guardian of the gates" was revealed as one of the prominent American interpretations of the Statue. President Grover Cleveland suggested this meaning in his brief speech accepting the Statue on behalf of the United States. After expressing his gratitude and his recognition of France as a steadfast ally, Cleveland described the Statue as "our own peaceful deity keeping watch before the open gates of America."[41] Although the threat against which Cleveland urged the Statue to "keep watch" may not have been clear from his remarks, later nativists developed more fully the image of the Statue as a guardian of America's gates.

Only one of the speakers at the dedication ceremony made any reference at all to immigration. Chauncey M. Depew's address contained words both of welcome and of warning:

The rays from this beacon, lighting this gateway to the continent, will welcome the poor and the persecuted with the hope and promise of homes and citizenship. It will teach them that there is room and brotherhood for all who will support our institutions and aid in our development, but that those who come to disturb our peace and dethrone our laws are aliens and enemies forever.[42]

According to Depew, the price of belonging to America was unquestioning loyalty, utility, and conformity.

When it was initially received, then, the Statue had little formal association with, and even less encouragement of, immigration. American liberty also had little association with equality. In the United States, liberty was associated with the American struggle for independence and its most fundamental and eloquent documentary exposition, the Declaration of Independence. Liberty in the United States has often been linked, however, to the Declaration and its first self-evident truth: "that all men are created equal."[43]

Notwithstanding the words of the Declaration, the embrace of equality as an American value symbolized by the Statue of Liberty developed slowly. The ideal of equality did not even become a part of our Constitution until the enactment of the Fourteenth Amendment, containing its equal protection clause, in 1868. It is the problem of persistent inequality, living in the shadows cast by the symbols and language of liberty and equality which poses one of our most profound problems and paradoxes.[44]

Perhaps the Statue's most interesting meanings lie in these paradoxes, the many contradictions between values it symbolizes and the lived reality of many persons within our borders. The presence of a powerful and enduring symbol of liberty has led many observers, both inside and outside the country, to assume that life corresponded, in some large degree, with the values represented by the Statue. The Statue has frequently symbolized American exceptionality in personal freedom and human liberty. Immigrants have left their homes and families pursuing this freedom and liberty. Yet the lived experience of many Americans and immigrants, their stories contrapuntal narratives surrounding and intersecting the story of the Statue and its liberty, yielded a more complex and tempered view of the mythology and reality of American liberty. Both before and after the Statue of Liberty, many Americans have lived unfree, posing the basic paradox between the symbolism of Liberty and conditions of life within the United States. Perhaps one of the most important American roles of the Statue is that it provided a locus for calling attention to the betrayal of the values it purported to represent.

The broader historical and cultural context surrounding the delivery and acceptance of the Statue of Liberty begins to define the contours of contradiction between the mythology of liberty and the reality of inequality and restriction. The late nineteenth century was a time of great ambivalence and hostility toward immigration. The late nineteenth century was the beginning of an era of increasing nativism and anxiety about immigration that led ultimately to severe restrictions curtailing immigration. In 1894, for example, the Immigration Restriction League was formed and began lobbying for a literacy test, intended to exclude immigrants arriving from unaccustomed places, such as Southeastern Europe.[45] Although ultimately unsuccessful in excluding these undesired immigrants, a literacy requirement was enacted in 1917.[46]

Thomas Bailey Aldrich, American poet and editor of the *Atlantic Monthly,* expressed the prevailing fear of these new immigrants in his poem "Unguarded Gates."[47] In an excerpt from the poem, Aldrich wrote:

> Wide open and unguarded stand our gates . . .
> Portals that lead to an enchanted land . . .
> A later Eden planted in the wilds,
> With not an inch of earth within its bound
> But if a slave's foot press it sets him free. . . .
>
> Wide open and unguarded stand our gates,
> And through them presses a wild motley throng—
> Featureless figures of the Hoang-Ho,
> Malayan, Scythian, Teuton, Kelt, and Slav,
> Flying the Old World's poverty and scorn;
> These bringing with them unknown gods and rites,
> Those, tiger passions, here to stretch their claws.
> In street and alley what strange tongues are loud,
> Accents of menace alien to our air,
> Voices that once the Tower of Babel knew!

O Liberty, white Goddess! is it well
to leave the gates unguarded? On thy breast
Fold Sorrow's children, soothe the hurts of fate,
Lift the down-trodden, but with hand of steel
Stay those who to thy scared portals come
To waste the gifts of freedom. Have a care
Lest from thy brow the clustered stars be torn
And trampled in the dust. For so of old
The thronging Goth and Vandal trampled Rome,
And where the temples of the Caesars stood
The lean wolf unmolested made her lair.[48]

Fully contradicting Lazarus's image of the Statue as a welcoming "Mother of Exiles," Aldrich construes the Statue as warlike symbol of restriction, a guardian against unwelcome invasion. Aldrich's narrator celebrates the freedom of persons within the gates, describing the United States as an "Eden," "With not an inch of earth within its bound / But if a slave's foot press it sets him free." But the freedom within must be withheld and protected from those outside the gates. In telling racial imagery, the Statue of Liberty is a "white Goddess," whose "hand of steel" must guard the gates to prevent the entry of the "wild motley throng" of "featureless figures." The narrator fears that this new and unwanted immigration, the perceived nonwhite "wild motley throng," threatens the end of American democracy, as foreseeable as the disappearance of the Roman and Greek empires.

The fear of immigrants from southeastern Europe, at that time considered nonwhite, culminated in the enactment of the National Origins Act of 1924, which curtailed immigration from these nations severely. Ironically, President Calvin Coolidge, who signed into law these immigration restrictions, declared the Statue of Liberty a national monument that same year.[49] One can fairly ask, a national monument to what? To Emma Lazarus's "Mother of Exiles," welcoming immigrants to the United States? Or to the "white Goddess," the guardian of the gates as portrayed by Aldrich?

Majoritarian fear and hostility were not, of course, limited to immigrants during the late nineteenth and early twentieth centuries. They also targeted nonwhite Americans. Reconstruction of the South after the Civil War had ended just nine years before the dedication of the Statue, in 1877. The era of Jim Crow laws, recreating near-slave status for black Americans, was in full force in the Southern United States.[50] As Frederick Douglass observed, the Reconstruction Amendments had expressed equality "on paper and parchment."[51] Douglass expressed bitterly the stark difference between "paper and parchment" rights and the bleak lives of newly enfranchised African *Americans:*

But to-day, in most of the Southern States, the fourteenth and fifteenth amendments are virtually nullified. The rights which they were intended to guarantee are denied and held in contempt. The citizenship granted in the fourteenth amendment is practically a mockery, and the right to vote, provided for in the fifteenth amendment, is literally stamped out in face of government. The old master class is to-day triumphant, and the newly enfranchised class in a condition but little above that in which they were found before the rebellion.[52]

One of the final acts of the Radical Reconstruction Congress was the Civil Rights Act of 1875, which guaranteed to all citizens rights to "equal and impartial facilities and accommodations from common carriers, innkeepers, managers of theaters and other places of public amusement, the officers of common schools and other institutions of learning." This legislation ostensibly abolished much segregation. In *The Civil Rights Cases* of 1883, however, a hostile Supreme Court decided that Congress lacked power under the Thirteenth and Fourteenth Amendments to enact such legislation, so the Civil Rights Act was declared invalid.[53] Shortly, the Supreme Court would find constitutional the "separate but equal" doctrine in *Plessy v. Ferguson*, and so uphold the massive systems of segregation that existed most overtly in the South.[54] At the time of the Statue of Liberty, liberty and equality for blacks was no more than a "paper and parchment" promise overwhelmed by white hostility and supported by Supreme Court and state-enforced inequality and segregation.

The oppressed condition of American blacks posed a severe challenge and rebuke to the credibility of the liberty mythology. And there were other contradictions, other rebukes. The mid-1870s were the beginning of an intense period of anti-Chinese hatred and violence, particularly on the West Coast. The hatred culminated in the federal Chinese exclusion laws of 1882, which excluded all Chinese laborers from the country for ten years and prohibited Chinese persons from obtaining citizenship.[55] President Grover Cleveland, who, at its unveiling, saw emanating from the Statue "a stream of light [that] shall pierce the darkness of ignorance and men's oppression," signed legislation which broadened the class of excluded Chinese laborers and made their entry or reentry to the United States far more difficult.[56] In 1892, Congress excluded Chinese laborers for ten more years.[57] The Supreme Court pronounced the constitutionality of this discrimination and upheld Congress's plenary power to set virtually any immigration restrictions it chose in the case of *Chae Chan Ping v. United States,* decided in 1889.[58]

The contradiction between the Statue's promise of liberty and Congress's exclusion of Chinese persons because of their race could not have been clearer. Notwithstanding popular hostility against them, appeals were made to the Chinese to contribute to the pedestal fund for the Statue of Liberty.

Responding to these appeals, Saum Song Bo wrote "A Chinese View of the Statue of Liberty" in 1885:

[T]he word liberty makes me think of the fact that this country is the land of liberty for men of all nations except the Chinese. I consider it as an insult to us Chinese to call on us to contribute toward building in this land a pedestal for a statue of Liberty. That statue represents Liberty holding a torch which lights the passage of those of all nations who come into this country. But are the Chinese allowed to come? As for the Chinese who are here, are they allowed to enjoy liberty as men of all other nationalities enjoy it? Are they allowed to go about everywhere free from the insults, abuse, assaults, wrongs and injuries from which men of other nationalities are free?

If there be a Chinaman who . . . desires to make his home in this land, and who, seeing that his countrymen demand one of their own number to be their legal adviser, representative, advocate and protector, desires to study law, can he be a lawyer? By the law of this nation, he, being a Chinaman, cannot become a citizen, and consequently cannot be a lawyer.

And this statue of Liberty is a gift to a people from another people who do not love or value liberty for the Chinese. Are not the Annamese and Tonquinese Chinese, to whom liberty is as dear as to the French? What right have the French to deprive them of their liberty?

Whether this statute against the Chinese [the Chinese exclusion law of 1882] or the statue to Liberty will be the more lasting monument to tell future ages of the liberty and greatness of this country, will be known only to future generations.

Liberty, we Chinese do love and adore thee; but let not those who deny thee to us, make of thee a graven image and invite us to bow down to it.[59]

While the Chinese were excluded altogether from the United States, women were excluded from the nation's political and economic life. Ironically, while Bartholdi used the female form to symbolize liberty, American women were not free. At the time of the Statue's arrival, women were unable to vote both in the United States and France. "Why were the socially unfree used to symbolize freedom?" ask two perceptive present-day commentators.[60] Of the six hundred guests officially invited to the dedication ceremony, only two were women, Mme. Bartholdi, wife of the sculptor, and Mme. Tototte de Lesseps, wife of a prominent Frenchman who spoke during the ceremony.[61] Women suffragists decried this inequality. During the dedication ceremony, a boat hired by the New York State Woman Suffrage Association cruised near and around the Statue.[62] Circling the Statue repeatedly, the suffragists complained loudly to the invited male officials and guests about their lack of access to the ballot and demanded equal treatment.[63]

Poet and suffragist Alice Duer Miller (1874–1942) wrote pointedly on the illusory promise of equality embodied in the Statue of Liberty, an equality available only to men during the struggle for women's suffrage.[64] These themes are prominent in Miller's "An Unauthorised Interview between the Suffragists and the Statue of Liberty," published in 1917:

> THE SUFFRAGISTS
> Lady robed in light,
> At our harbour standing,
> Equal law and right
> Promising, demanding,
> Can you tell us, do you know,
> Why you treat your daughters so?
>
> Do not think us pert,
> Insolent or teasing,
> But you seem a flirt,
> Only bent on pleasing
> That one-half of Human kind
> Who made Sister Justice blind.
>
> THE STATUE
> Be not deceived, my daughters, I'm not she—
> The winged Goddess, who sets nations free.
> I am that Liberty, which when men win
> They think that others' seeking is a sin;
> I am that Liberty which men attain
> And clip her wings lest she should fly again:
> I am that Liberty which all your brothers
> Think good for them and very bad for others.
> Therefore they made me out of bronze, and hollow.
> Immovable, for fear that I might follow
> Some fresh rebellion, some new victim's plea;
> And so they set me on a rock at sea,
> Welded my torch securely in my hand
> Lest I should pass it on, without command.
> I am a milestone, not an inspiration;
> And if my spirit lingers in this nation,
> If it still flickers faintly o'er these waters,
> It is your spirit, my rebellious daughters.[65]

The narrator's bitterness towards men is palpable. In the words of her Statue, men value only their own liberty, and curtail the liberty of women. Miller, however, lived to see the ultimate success of the women's suffrage movement. Women finally received a constitutional guarantee of their right to vote when the Nineteenth Amendment to the Constitution was ratified in 1920, over thirty years after the dedication of the Statue.

The contradiction between the liberty mythology and lived inequality remains unabated for many Americans. Of course, some progress has been made, some inequality alleviated. Women and blacks can vote. State-sponsored segregation has been declared unconstitutional. Discrimination because of national origin is said to violate our laws and our Constitution. So progress has been made. But progress toward equality without the achievement of equality is not enough. Continuing inequality is a continuing rebuke to the Statue of Liberty and its liberty mythology.

Laboulaye and Bartholdi succeeded in creating a lasting and international symbol of liberty, a source of freedom aspirations that remains powerful. The students whose freedom rebellion in Tienanmen Square was crushed by Chinese military authorities chose a modified version of the Statue of Liberty as their symbol of freedom and absence of repression.[66] Perhaps, as a repository of human desire for freedom, equality and dignity, the Statue has grown more powerful over time.

While its significance as a symbol of liberty has grown and endured, we have seen that the Statue has been a site of varied, developing and contested meanings. Its beginnings reveal no connection to the pro-immigration welcome that Emma Lazarus sought to inscribe upon it. And although the immigrant-welcoming interpretation grew over time, the Statue easily symbolized also the countercurrent of immigration restriction and nativism. Contrary to the perceptions of many, Thomas Bailey Aldrich's image of the Statue as a "white Goddess" and guardian of the gates seems to symbolize better the character of a country most of whose immigration history in law has been characterized by race-based restriction, rather than open welcome.

At the same time, the contradiction between the liberty myth and the inequality faced by many Americans also endures. As James Baldwin commented, "For a black American, a black inhabitant in this country, the Statue is simply a very bitter joke.... Meaning nothing, to us."[67] Or as Gordon Parks stated, "To be an American is one thing. To be an African American, which happens to be my lot, is another."[68]

One cannot, in the face of past and present contradictions, take the Statue of Liberty as a representation of the reality lived by many Americans. There are simply too many unresolved contradictions between the liberty ideal and the unfree state of many of our people. One must still ponder, after over one hundred years, the thoughts of Saum Song Bo: "Whether [exclusion] or the statue to Liberty will be the more lasting monument to tell future ages of the liberty and greatness of this country will be known only to future generations."

We are of those future generations. In this historical moment, we seem no closer to answering Saum Song Bo's paradox.

NOTES

I would like to thank Professors Linda S. Bosniak and Robert S. Chang for their insightful and helpful comments on an earlier draft of this chapter.

1. Bertrand Dard, "Liberty as Image and Icon," in Wilton S. Dillon and Neil G. Kotler, eds., *The Statue of Liberty Revisited*, 71 (Washington, D.C.: Smithsonian Institution Press, 1994).

2. I borrow the phrase "the way of a symbol" from the subtitle of the excellent book by Hertha Pauli and E. B. Ashton, *I Lift My Lamp: The Way of a Symbol* (Port Washington, N.Y.: Ira J. Friedman, 1969).

3. Christian Blanchet, *Statue of Liberty: The First Hundred Years*, 51 (New York: American Heritage, 1985) (English trans. Bernard A. Weisberger).

4. Id. at 62

5. Id. at 71–73.

6. Neil G. Kotler, "The Statue of Liberty as Idea, Symbol, and Historical Presence," in Dillon and Kotler, eds., *The Statue of Liberty Revisited*, 2.

7. Marvin Trachtenberg, *The Statue of Liberty*, 183–84 (New York: Penguin, 1977).

8. See Pauli and Ashton at 255–78, 279.

9. Even as the French donors of the Statue were creating it, the ideals for which it stood were vulnerable. As written by Seymour Drescher, "Even more directly threatening to the republic, sympathy for authoritarian and radical solutions was revealed in a series of challenges to the new regime. As late as 1885, on the eve of the presentation of the Statue of Liberty, monarchists and Bonapartists captured more than two hundred seats in the French Chamber of Deputies. Many monarchists and clerical opponents of the regime referred to their republic not as the maiden of liberty but as *la geuse*—'the slut.' " Seymour Drescher, "Liberty and Liberalism in Nineteenth-Century France and America," in Dillon and Kotler, eds., *The Statue of Liberty Revisited*, 17, 23.

10. Leslie Allen, *Liberty: The Statue and the American Dream*, 19 (New York: Statue of Liberty-Ellis Island Foundation, 1985).

11. Pauli and Ashton at 13.

12. Id. at 33–48. When Lincoln died, the people of France sent a medal, which said "honest Lincoln who abolished slavery, reestablished the Union, and saved the Republic, without veiling the *statue of liberty*" (emphasis added). The latter words appeared on the medal before there was any conception of the actual statue of liberty, illustrating the tie between French liberty and American antislavery.

13. Pauli and Ashton at 13.

14. Drescher at 22.

15. Pauli and Ashton at 13–14.

16. Drescher at 22.

17. Id.

18. Laboulaye's speech at the opera of Paris, April 25, 1876, quoted in Christian Blanchet, "The Universal Appeal of the Statue of Liberty," in Dillon and Kotler, eds., *The Statue of Liberty Revisited*, 27, 35.

19. Allen at 21.

20. Michael Kammen, *Spheres of Liberty*, 162 (Madison: University of Wisconsin Press, 1986).

21. Id.

22. Id. at 161.

23. Wilton S. Dillon, "The Ultimate Gift," in Dillon and Kotler, eds., *The Statue of Liberty Revisited*, 149; see also *The Statue of Liberty*, a film by Ken Burns, produced by Buddy Squires and Ken Burns, narrated by David McCullough, a Florentine Films Production in association with American Heritage (1986).

24. Pauli and Ashton at 221.

25. This was the name originally given to the statue by sculptor Auguste Bartholdi: "Liberty Enlightening the World."

26. Speech of President Grover Cleveland, reported in the *New York Times*, October 29, 1886.

27. John Higham, *Send These to Me: Jews and Other Immigrants in Urban America*, rev. ed., 74–75 (Baltimore: Johns Hopkins University Press, 1984).

28. Id. at 72.

29. Id.

30. Emma Lazarus, "The New Colossus," reprinted in Marvin Trachtenberg, *The Statue of Liberty* 214 n. 11.

31. Pauli and Ashton at 227.

32. Pauli and Ashton at 320–21; Higham at 72–74.

33. Higham at 73–74.

34. Id. at 77–78.

35. Id. at 74.

36. George Washington, "To the Members of the Volunteer Association and Other Inhabitants of the Kingdom of Ireland Who Have Lately Arrived in the City of New York," in *The Writings of George Washington*, vol. 27, ed. John C. Fitzpatrick (Washington, D.C.: Government Printing Office, September 1938) 253–54, quoted in Thomas Muller, *Immigrants in the American City*, 19 (New York: New York University Press, 1993).

37. Higham at 75. In the words of Rudolph J. Vecoli, "It was the immigrants themselves who imposed their own meaning on the Lady with the Torch." Rudolph J. Vecoli, "The Lady and the Huddled Masses," in Dillard and Kotler, eds., *The Statue of Liberty Revisited*, 40; Allen at 38.

38. See Jose Marti, *Marti on the U.S.A.*, 107 (Carbondale: Souther Illinois University Press, 1966) (trans. Luis A. Baralt).

39. Id. at 113. See also Pauli and Ashton at 286.

40. Marti at 113.

41. *New York Times*, October 29, 1886.

42. *New York Times*, October 29, 1886.

43. "The Statue of Liberty," a documentary film on the statue, begins with beautiful footage of the statue and a recitation of this part of the Declaration of Independence. During this film, when author James Baldwin is asked "What is liberty?" he responds by quoting this same text from the Declaration. Burns, *The Statue of Liberty*.

44. This paradox was aptly recognized by Gunnar Myrdal in his classic work *An American Dilemma: The Negro Problem and Modern Democracy*, 3–5, 23–25 (New York: Harper, 1944).

45. Rudolph J. Vecoli, "The Lady and the Huddled Masses," in Dillon and Kotler, eds., *The Statue of Liberty Revisited*, 49.

46. See Juan F. Perea, "Demography and Distrust: An Essay on American Lan-

guages, Cultural Pluralism and Official English," 77 *Minnesota Law Review* 269, 332–36 (1992).

47. Thomas Bailey Aldrich, *The Poems of Thomas Bailey Aldrich,* 275–76 (Boston: Houghton, Mifflin, 1907) (see also the Biographical Sketch at pp. xi–xvii.).

48. Id. (emphasis added).

49. Vecoli at 55.

50. Jose Marti's reporting on the unveiling ceremonies noted a group of black veterans marching in the parade. According to two commentators, "the sight of the Negro veterans obscured what then was happening to freedmen in the South." Pauli and Ashton at 284.

51. Frederick Douglass, "Life and Times of Frederick Douglass" (speech of August 1, 1880, in Elmira, New York), reprinted in Richard N. Current, ed., *Reconstruction* [1865–77], 173–74 (Englewood Cliffs, N.J.: Prentice-Hall, 1965).

52. Id.

53. 109 U.S. 3 (1883).

54. 163 U.S. 537 (1896).

55. Ellis Cose, *A Nation of Strangers: Prejudice, Politics and the Populating of America,* 48–52 (New York: Morrow, 1992).

56. Speech of President Grover Cleveland, reported in the *New York Times,* October 29, 1886.

57. See Cose at 51–57.

58. 130 U.S. 581 (1889).

59. Saum Song Bo, "A Chinese View of the Statue of Liberty," *American Missionary,* Vol. 39, No. 10 (October 1885).

60. Barbara A. Babcock and John J. Macaloon, "Everybody's Gal: Women, Boundaries, and Monuments," in Dillon and Kotler, eds., *The Statue of Liberty Revisited,* 84.

61. One reason offered for excluding women from the ceremony was paternalistic concern for their safety during the crowded ceremony. Trachtenberg at 216n. 20.

62. Id.

63. Kotler at 2.

64. For a brief biographical sketch of Alice Duer Miller, see *Alice Duer Miller, Selected Poems* v-viii (foreword by Denning Duer Miller) (New York: Coward-McCann, 1949).

65. Alice Duer Miller, *Women Are People!* 87 (New York: George H. Doran, 1917).

66. For a first-hand account of the creation of the "Goddess of Democracy," the symbol of democracy crafted by a group of Chinese students and inspired by the Statue of Liberty, see Tsao Hsingyuan and Fang Li Zhi, "Chinese Perspectives: A Beijing Chronicle and Chinese Views of Liberty, Democracy, and the Pursuit of Scientific Knowledge," in Dillon and Kotler, eds., *The Statue of Liberty Revisited,* 101–14.

67. Burns, *Statue of Liberty.*

68. Gordon Parks, quoted in *Newsweek,* July 10, 1995, 37.

IDENTIFYING THE
NEW NATIVISM
Its Ways and Means

The chapters in this part discuss the most prominent actual and proposed legislation to result from today's nativist impulse. Leo R. Chavez's chapter discusses California's Proposition 187 and fast-mushrooming restrictive federal immigration and citizenship legislation. Gleaning insight from the war metaphors used by proponents of these laws, Chavez also identifies the very specific attack on reproduction by immigrants and the attempted manipulation of the labor force wrought by recent legislation. Raymond Tatalovich's chapter on Official English provides insightful analysis on the causes of Official English laws in different states and explains their direct connection to conservative politicians and the politics of nativism.

4. IMMIGRATION REFORM AND NATIVISM

The Nationalist Response to the Transnationalist Challenge

Leo R. Chavez

On November 8, 1994, the voters of California overwhelmingly passed Proposition 187, which was, in the words of its supporters, to "Save Our State" by preventing "illegal aliens in the United States from receiving benefits or public services in the State of California."[1] As with many trends that begin in California, the anti-immigrant sentiment expressed in Proposition 187 rolled across the nation, as other states, some congressional representatives, and presidential candidates expressed the need to deny health care, education, and other publicly funded benefits to immigrants.

This chapter focuses on the "rhetoric of exclusion" embedded in the contemporary discourse on immigration reform.[2] The focus on anti-immigrant discourse reflects the notion that "the occasions, spaces, and modes of representation are themselves forms of power rather than mere reflections of power residing in the real, material 'facts of life,' and the 'big structures' through which the power of class, capital, or the state are expressed."[3] At the same time, the discourse of immigration reform is situated in a space that crosses over the borders of micropolitics and macropolitics. Local immigration reform discourse can become the national discourse, but in becoming national the local can become transformed.

As California's anti-immigrant discourse flowed across the nation, the anti-"illegal alien" focus of Proposition 187 broadened considerably. Discourse about immigration reform became a way of expressing anger about demographic changes brought on by immigration, targeting anyone who might be suspected of being "immigrant," "foreign looking," "un-American," or different. By eliminating or reducing these stigmatized groups, immigration reform would, in theory, "do something" about the source of the "problems" facing U.S. citizens, problems in the economy, education system, health care, and even the relations of local governments with the federal government. To the proponents of immigration reform, illegal immigrants are not the only problem; immigration in general is a threat to the "nation" that is conceived of as a singular, predominantly Euro-American, English-speaking culture. The "new" immigrants are *trans*nationalists, or people who maintain social linkages back in the home country; they are not bound by national borders and their multiple identities are situated in communities in different nations and in communities that cross nations.[4] Transnational migrants threaten a singular vision of the "nation" because they allegedly bring "multiculturalism" and not assimilation.[5] This was clearly part of U.S. Representative Newt Gingrich's intended message when, shortly after passage of Proposition 187, he promised that as Speaker of the House he would preside over a freewheeling congressional debate about the "cultural meanings of being American."[6]

Proponents of immigration reform, therefore, often cast their net on issues much wider than just illegal immigration. For example, flush with victory after passage of Proposition 187, the proposition's backers announced that their agenda was actually much broader and included affirmative action, bilingual education, and the promotion of English as the official language.[7] Their concerns led U.S. Representative Toby Roth (a Republican from Wisconsin) to introduce a bill that would effectively halt funding for bilingual education, abolish bilingual electoral ballots, and allow individuals to bring civil suits against institutions that violate English-only federal statutes.[8] The reason such a law is necessary, according to the bill itself, is because "It has been the long-standing national belief that full citizenship in the United States requires fluency in English."[9]

The question of who is an "American" and anti-immigrant discourse become entangled in revealing ways. For instance, on October 18, 1994, California State Senator Craven, a Republican from Oceanside, was quoted as saying "that the [California] state legislature should explore requiring all people of Hispanic descent to carry an identification card that would be used to verify legal residence."[10] By targeting "all Hispanics," citizens, legal residents, and undocumented immigrants, California Senator Craven defines all Hispanics as belonging to a suspect class. Why Senator Craven focuses only on Hispanics is not clear. After all, California's ethnic diversity includes many other ethnic groups, including undocumented Canadians and Europeans who overstay their visas. Perhaps the answer has to do with the assumptions about social evolution and progress implicit in immigration discourse.

Discredited nineteenth-century scientific notions about social evolution continue to underlie present-day discourse on national encounters. This discourse positions Euro-Americans and Europeans at the top of a hierarchical ordering of civilized ("developed" and "technologically advanced" being common metaphors for this hierarchy) societies in contrast to less civilized ("less developed" and "technologically backward") societies. Senator Craven expressed these assumptions when addressing a senate hearing on migrant workers held in San Diego in February 1993; he said that "migrant workers were on a lower scale of humanity."[11]

Gifts to charitable organizations provide another example of how anti-immigrant sentiments extend beyond a concern with "illegal aliens." In Orange County, California, donors to charities are increasingly stipulating that those who receive their gifts not be illegal aliens. In some cases, the donors specifically state that the recipients should be English speaking, or even non-Latinos to ensure their citizenship status. As one director of a charitable agency said, "I had to find someone white and English-speaking" to receive the donations.[12]

Perhaps one of the clearest statements about the threat of immigration to the "complexion" of American society comes from Pat Buchanan, a presidential candidate during the 1992 and 1996 elections. Buchanan said: "A nonwhite majority is envisioned if today's immigration continues." Given this prognosis, he argues that America needs a "time out" from immigration.[13] Buchanan would like a moratorium on all immigration to the United States, not merely closing the borders to undocumented immigrants.

The extent to which the anti-immigrant debate is racially polarized is suggested by voting patterns in California. Proposition 187 passed with 59 percent of the votes cast. But white Californians, in particular, appeared to be expressing sentiments of unease over immigration. Two out of three voting whites in California (about 67 percent) voted for the proposition, a significantly larger proportion than the vote among African Americans and Asian Americans (about half of each group voted for it) and Latinos (only 23 percent voted for it).[14] The voting block provided by white voters ensured passage of Proposition 187. Importantly, even though whites account for about 57 percent of California's population, they account for about 80 percent of the voters, thus their views take on tremendous power. In contrast, while Latinos account for 25 percent of the state's population, they accounted for only 8 percent of those voting.[15] White voters in California appear to be sending a symbolic statement about their concern over immigration and the "new" immigrants.

Since passage of Proposition 187 by the voters of California, a number of U.S. Representatives and Senators have submitted bills dealing with the "immigration problem." Following the assumption put forward by proponents of Proposition 187, that social services, not jobs, are the magnet drawing undocumented immigrants to the United States, national immigration reform proposals target aid to immigrants.[16] For example, Representative Ron Packard (Republican from Oceanside) proposed denying illegal immigrants federal benefits offered to victims of flooding in California.[17] In June 1995, a House task force chaired by Representative Elton Gallegly (Republican from Simi Valley) submitted its report urging an approach similar to Proposition 187 at the national level. The task force recommended denying all public services, except emergency health care, to undocumented immigrants. In order for hospitals to receive reimbursement for treating undocumented immigrants, however, they would have to notify the Immigration and Naturalization Service of the patients before they are discharged.[18] The task force also recommended allowing states to cut off public education to undocumented students. One of the task force's most contentious recommendations is to amend the U.S. Constitution to end automatic citizenship for U.S.-born children whose parents are undocumented immigrants.[19]

Representative Gallegly was an early proponent of this policy. In October 1991, he introduced legislation into Congress to amend the U.S. Constitution to deny citizenship to a child born in the United States if neither of the parents are citizens and if the child's mother is not at least a legal resident.[20] His argument is that even though this is a nation of immigrants, we must reduce immigration—both legal and undocumented:

We must recognize, however, that the United States is also a nation of finite resources and opportunities which must be available to and shared by all its citizens. Today, in many parts of this country our cities and towns are being overrun with immigrants, both legal and undocumented, who pose major economic and law enforcement problems for local governments and place an added burden on their already strained budgets.[21]

Although Gallegly's legislation focuses on the children of undocumented immigrants, his statement clearly makes little differentiation between legal and illegal immigrants. He views immigrants generally as a "problem," as outsiders, regardless of immigration status. Thus, his attempts to stop conferring citizenship on the children of undocumented immigrants appears as but one part of a broader agenda to rid the country of all "outsiders," that is, immigrants and their U.S.-born children.

Perhaps the shift in focus from undocumented immigrants to legal immigrants became complete in June of 1995 when the U.S. Commission on Immigration Reform, headed by Barbara Jordan of Texas, recommended that legal immigration into the United States be sharply reduced.[22] President Clinton has also suggested that "You can make a good case for modest reduction of the quota on legal immigration."[23]

These emerging views on legal immigration set the context for national immigration reform proposals that target all immigrants, including those legally in the country. For example, Representative E. Clay Shaw, Jr. (a Republican from Florida), proposed that only citizens be provided benefits such as Aid to Families with Dependent Children, food stamps, and Medicaid. Denying these benefits to legal residents, would, according to Representative Shaw, take away the attraction of people to come to this country, that is, welfare and the social safety net.[24] In all, the Republican legislative program for immigration reform that was brought to the U.S. House of Representatives in Proposition 187's wake would deny sixty kinds of federal assistance to millions of legal immigrants, including health programs, Social Security, Supplementary Security Income, disability payments, housing assistance, childhood immunizations, subsidized school lunches, job training, and aid to the homeless.[25] On March 24, 1995, the House of Representatives passed the Personal Responsibility Act, which included many of these proposals to limit social services to legal immigrants.[26]

The U.S. Senate followed the House's example when it passed its own bill on welfare policy on September 19, 1995. The Senate's bill cuts fewer benefits for legal immigrants than the House's but also restricts benefits for naturalized citizens who immigrate after the bill's enactment.[27] If enacted, this would be the first time in U.S. history that government benefits were denied naturalized citizens because they were not born in the United States, thus establishing a two-tiered or segmented structure for citizenship. But even if these parts of the bill are ultimately dropped, they indicate the willingness of policy-makers to treat naturalized citizens differently from U.S.-born citizens. This is a sign of a major reconceptualization of the relationship of immigrants to the nation.

Finally, the U.S. Congress is considering legislation that would reduce the number of legal immigrants from 800,000 to about 535,000 per year. This reduction would be accomplished by eliminating several preference categories for family reunification, including the preferences for foreign adult children and parents of U.S. citizens and legal residents, and for adult brothers and sisters of U.S. citizens. The aim of eliminating these preferences is to stop the network migration of extended family members, while allowing nuclear families to continue to reunite in the United States. Eliminating these preferences would shut the door on an estimated 2.4 million foreigners—mostly Mexicans and Filipinos—waiting in queues to enter the United States on the basis of family ties.[28]

In sum, the nativist revolt against undocumented immigrants that began in California quickly reached national proportions, targeting all immigrants. The policy recommendations emanating from state and federal legislators and the discourse spewing forth from presidential candidates are of the sort not heard with such force since the nativist movements of the late 1800s and the early twentieth century. Should some of these proposals come to pass—especially such dramatic changes as a constitutional amendment to deny citizenship to children born in the United States, and distinctions between citizens by birth and those naturalized—then this round of nativism will have ushered in some of the most profound changes in how America—the United States—perceives itself as a community, as a people, and as a nation. Traditional definitions of who deserves to be an American and receive the benefits of the social contract are being challenged and redefined in unprecedented ways.

As the nation rushes along the anti-immigrant current, it is important to contemplate how we arrived at this juncture in our history and to analyze the underlying nature the attack on immigrants is taking and its implications for the future. Why this level of nativism now? Why do immigration reform proposals target mainly women and children? Or, to put it another way, why target reproduction of the immigrant labor force? And, what does this tell us about the production of immigrant labor that specific sectors of our economy have grown to depend upon?

THE NEW NATIVISM IN HISTORICAL PERSPECTIVE

Why is anti-immigrant rhetoric so prominent in the contemporary discourse on the state of the nation? To answer this question, we must remember that Americans have always had a love-hate relationship with immigration, despite a congratulatory self-image as a "nation of immigrants." [For further treatment of the history of American nativism, see chapters 1 and 9–11 of this volume—*Ed.*] Because of America's history, "immigration" has become what anthropologists call a key symbol in American culture.[29] Immigration is such a central and powerful concept that it is endowed with a multiplicity of referents and meanings; it raises highly charged emotions, which can often be contradictory.[30] In short, nativism and xenophobia have been constant themes in American history, although they become prominent during specific historical moments. Contemporary anti-immigrant posturing can be traced to changes in immigration law, continued undocumented immigration, an economy undergoing repeated cycles of recession, and the end of the Cold War.[31]

In many ways, the "new" nativism sounds strikingly similar to the "old" nativism. In their book *The Immigration Time Bomb*, Richard Lamm, the ex-Governor of Colorado, and Gary Imhoff, an ex-official of the Immigration and Naturalization Service, warn about the perils of immigration in a way that is reminiscent of older laments:

At today's massive levels, immigration has major negative consequences—economic, social, and demographic—that overwhelm its advantages. . . . To solve the immigration crisis, we Americans have to face our limitations. We have to face the necessity of passing laws to restrict immigration and the necessity of enforcing those laws. If we fail to do so, we shall leave a legacy of strife, violence, and joblessness to our children.[32]

More recently, Peter Brimelow, himself an immigrant from the Great Britain, has vociferously echoed Lamm and Imhoff's dark scenario for a future of continued immigration.[33] America's problems, according to Brimelow, are due to immigrants who lack the cultural background of earlier European, especially British, immigrants. He argues that America needs to "rethink" immigration and calls for a "time out" from immigration.[34] Failure to restrict immigration, Brimelow warns, will lead America on the road to becoming an "alien nation."

Discourse surrounding Proposition 187 and subsequent immigration reform resonate with Lamm and Imhoff's and Brimelow's views, with their heavy emphasis on the conflict and threat to the nation posed by transnational migrants who do not respect traditional borders and the sovereignty of nation states. In arguing for the urgency of their cause, the proponents of immigration reform often characterize the immigrant as the "enemy" in metaphors of war. Immigrants become the new threat to national security and identity, filling the void left by the loss of the old enemies after the collapse of the Soviet Union and the end of the Cold War. In this respect, the anti-immigrant discourse of the 1990s corresponds to the new vision of "America First" put forward by Pat Buchanan and increasingly touted by Republican presidential candidates. The anti-internationalist stance of "America First" enthusiasts carries with it "a kind of nativistic foreigner-bashing," according to Jeremy Rosner of the Carnegie Endowment for International Peace.[35]

Immigrants as foreigners who threatened the American way of life was a central part of the Proposition 187 campaign in California. Proponents of Proposition 187 banked on the widely held perception that an "invasion" of undocumented immigrants was the cause of California's economic problems and eroding the lifestyles of U.S. citizens to the point of reducing the nation to a "Third World" country.[36] The reference to "Third World" is a strategic marker that metaphorically alludes to social evolution and the threat of immigration leading to a de-evolution of "American civilization."

U.S. Representative Dana Rohrabacher (a Republican from Huntington Beach, California), in arguing for passage of Proposition 187 shortly before the election, carried the war metaphor even further when he said, "Unlawful immigrants represent the liberal/left foot soldiers in the next decade."[37]

Another proponent of Proposition 187, Ruth Coffey, the director of Stop Immigration Now, frequently raised the specter of "multiculturalism," commenting that "I have no intention of being the object of 'conquest,' peaceful or otherwise, by Latinos, Asians, blacks, Arabs or any other groups of individuals who have claimed my country."[38] Of course, the irony of Ms. Coffey's statement appears to go unnoticed; as a result of the Mexican American War in the mid 1800s, the United States "conquered" California. An appeal to historical memory, however, can be subtle yet telling. Ronald Prince, one of the cofounders of the Save Our State (SOS) initiative, speaking to a gathering in Orange County, explaining how Proposition 187 would stop undocumented immigration, used a metaphor that harkened back to images of frontier justice, when Mexicans were routinely hanged by vigilante mobs: "You are the posse and SOS is the rope."[39]

Glenn Spencer, founder of the Voice of Citizens Together, a San Fernando Valley-based group that was a principal grassroots backer of Proposition 187, also put his views into a war metaphor framework. Before the November elections in California, he argued for passage of Proposition 187 because illegal immigration is "part of a reconquest of the American Southwest by foreign Hispanics. Someone is going to be leaving the state. It will either be them or us."[40] After the passage of Proposition 187, at a rally to deny public education to illegal immigrants and to denounce the Clinton Administration's proposed $40-billion aid package to Mexico, Spencer said, "It boils down to this: Do we want to retain control of the Southwest more than the Mexicans want to take it from us?" He went on to compare "the conflict" to the Vietnam war: "It's a struggle between two groups of people for territory."[41] Even when confronted with academic research that suggests immigrants generally assimilate and improve their economic well-being, Spencer's comment was that "What we have in Southern California is not assimilation— It's annexation by Mexico."[42]

Immigrants as a threat to national security, sovereignty, and control of territory is central to the war metaphors as used in debates about immigration. As Bette Hammond, the head of S.T.O.P.I.T. (Stop the Out-of-Control Problems of Immigration Today), a Marin County-based group that was an early and key organizer on behalf of Proposition 187, put it: "We've got to take back our country."[43] Newt Gingrich, speaking about immigration reform, also raised the sovereignty issue: "If they're illegal, why aren't they gone? Whatever law we have to pass to be able to protect American sovereignty and to be able to say we're not going to have illegal people in the United States, we should pass."[44]

According to Linda B. Hayes, the Proposition 187 media director for southern California, the loss of U.S. territory can occur as a result of the rapid demographic shifts caused by Mexican immigration. As she wrote in a letter to the *New York Times,*

By flooding the state with 2 million illegal aliens to date, and increasing that figure each of the following 10 years, Mexicans in California would number 15 million to 20 million by 2004. During those 10 years about 5 million to 8 million Californians would have emigrated to other states. If these trends continued, a Mexico-controlled California could vote to establish Spanish as the sole language of California, 10 million more English-speaking Californians could flee, and there could be a statewide vote to leave the Union and annex California to Mexico.[45]

Why people who left a country in search of economic opportunity and a better life would vote to return the state to that country is not explained. Nor is it clear why, in the year 2004, the children and grandchildren of immigrants—all U.S. citizens who did not grow up in Mexico and who will not have the same nostalgia for Mexico as their parents or grandparents— would vote to annex California to Mexico. Of course, such questions may be beside the point since nativist arguments rely more on emotional resonance than the marshaling of empirical evidence and support found in academic treatises.[46]

Proposition 187 and the proposals for immigration reform that followed, then, can be traced to xenophobia related to the changing complexion of immigrants, frustration with the ineffectiveness of the 1986 immigration law to control undocumented immigration, economic recessions, and a new nationalism. As anti-immigrant as the discourse appears, immigration reform targets predominantly women and children, that is, the reproduction of the immigrant labor force. Why is this and what does it mean?

TARGETING REPRODUCTION WHILE IGNORING PRODUCTION

Anthropologist Claude Meillassoux long ago reminded us of the importance of focusing on both production and reproduction when examining immigration.[47] Proposition 187 and most of the immigration reform proposals that followed it target social services, especially health care and education, as the principal attraction to immigrants, both legal and undocumented. The logic is that denial of social services to immigrants reduces the incentives for immigration and thus fewer immigrants will decide to come to the United States. This logic, however, targets reproduction—women and children— and does very little to stop the production-work of immigrant labor.

This is not to suggest that some proposals do not advocate increased funding for the Border Patrol and that the Justice Department does not occasionally "get tough" on employers, because both of these are true.[48] Rather, the point here is that most of the proposals for immigration reform focus on social services, targeting reproduction of the immigrant family and thereby reducing the costs associated with immigrant labor while maintaining, or even increasing, the profits of that labor. It is certainly true that immigrant families have reproductive costs, some of which are subsidized by society, such as education. Immigrant workers, on the other hand, have many benefits for production, since they cost society little to produce (the costs of raising and educating them were borne by their families and home societies), are often willing to perform low-wage work, are typically young and relatively healthy, and are often afraid to pursue, or are unaware of, their rights as workers. By targeting reproduction, immigration reform does very little to undermine the lucrative and highly profitable relationship between employers and workers.

Proposition 187 and most of the immigration reform proposals discussed above do not target production. They leave immigrant workers and their employers curiously out of the picture. For example, Proposition 187 did not advocate more funds for ensuring fair labor standards and practices, thus reducing the incentive for hiring immigrant, especially undocumented, labor. As Labor Secretary Robert B. Reich noted: "One reason that employers in the United States are willing to risk employer sanctions right now and hire illegal immigrants is because they can get those illegal immigrants at less than the minimum wage, put them in squalid working conditions, and they know that those illegal immigrants are unlikely to complain."[49] Nor did the proposition propose increased enforcement of employer sanctions. The implicit message is that we are going after the reproduction of the undocumented labor force not the laborer nor the employer.

The debate surrounding Proposition 187 provides further insight into this point. The proposition's proponents targeted those who are "breaking the law" and don't deserve social service benefits. Governor Wilson argued that "Californians are justifiably fed up with those who break the law and ignore the rules that govern a civilized society. Californians want people held accountable for their actions again—whether it's a career criminal, a deadbeat dad, or someone who violates immigration laws."[50] Proposition 187, however, targeted only undocumented immigrants' use of social services, not employers who might be breaking the law by hiring undocumented workers. Indeed, in correspondence between Pete Wilson and immigration authorities, Wilson often encouraged the immigration commissioner to stop raids on California companies, arguing that sweeping up undocumented workers caused unnecessary disruptions to business.[51] Such actions stand in marked contrast to anti-immigrant discourse, suggesting that production must be safeguarded but reproduction of the worker's family must be stopped.

Getting rid (the euphemism is "voluntary return migration") of spouses and children would reduce the costs associated with immigrant labor by removing those most likely to use social services. Parenthetically, a more cynical argument is that the objective in denying education and health care to undocumented immigrants is not to pressure them to return to their country of origin but to create a permanent underclass of low-educated, available low-wage workers. While I believe this is the practical outcome of the immigration reform proposals, I am assuming here that the goal of immigration reform is as stated: to remove the alleged incentives (social services) attracting undocumented immigrants to the United States. Research has shown, however, that undocumented immigrants come to the United States to work and rarely come to get an education.[52] It is the children of undocumented immigrants that are in the public school system. Research has also shown that immigrant women and children are more likely than immigrant men, especially among the undocumented, to use health services.[53] But even though they are more likely than adult males to use health services, immigrant women, particularly the undocumented, continue to face major health risks because they significantly underuse critical preventive medicine.[54] Despite the medical and financial implications, the first action Governor Wilson took after passage of Proposition 187 was to move to cut off prenatal care to undocumented women.[55] However, there is absolutely no evidence that if you deny health care for women and children, or deny education or school lunches for children for that matter, that it will do anything to reduce the economic magnet—jobs—that draws immigrant labor to the United States. This is true for both undocumented and legal immigration.

This relationship between production (positive) and reproduction (negative) is revealed most clearly in the proposals for a guest-worker program. At the same time that proponents of immigration reform appear to be clamoring for an end or reduction in immigration, there are serious proposals to bring foreign workers to the United States on a temporary basis to work in agriculture and highly competitive high-technology companies. Shortly after the November 1994 elections were over in California, Governor Wilson was in Washington promoting just such a new *bracero* or guest-worker program.[56] An advocate of providing California agribusiness low-cost seasonal labor (guest-workers) when he was a U.S. senator, Wilson again made his plea for a guest-worker program in an address to the Heritage Foundation. Wilson justified a guest-worker program as a way "to alleviate the pressure for illegal immigration created by Mexico's inability to produce enough jobs for its people." Wilson clearly stated his vision of a return to a use of primarily Mexican male labor that would exclude the workers' families: "It makes sense—it has in the past, it may well continue to do so in the future—to have some sort of guest-worker program. But not the kind of thing we have been seeing where there has been massive illegal immigration, where whole families have come and where they are . . . requiring services that are paid for by state taxpayers." [57] Harold Ezzell, a coauthor of Proposition 187 and a past official of the INS, has also suggested a guest-worker program as a means of meeting labor shortages that cannot be filled by U.S. workers. [58] Even Representative Gallegly, who is so adamant about denying citizenship to children born in the United States if their parents are not legal residents, acknowledged that there may be a need for immigrants to work in temporary jobs in the United States. [59]

This is the logical next step since a guest-worker program institutionalizes the perfect cost-benefit ratio for immigrant labor: bringing foreign workers produced with no costs and who are not allowed to bring their families, thus not incurring reproductive costs (health care, education) here. In essence, production without reproduction, workers without families, sojourners not settlers.

To a certain extent we have come full circle in the debate over immigration, especially immigration from Mexico. In 1911, the Dillingham Commission, which was established to study the immigration issue, argued that Mexican migration should be promoted as the best solution to the Southwest's labor problem. [60] Unlike Japanese, Chinese, and Southern and Eastern European immigrants, the Commission argued that Mexicans were "homing pigeons" who would work for a short time in the United States and then return to their families in Mexico. It even went so far as to exempt Mexicans from the head tax for immigrants that was established under the immigration laws of 1903 and 1907. The Commission's advocacy of single male workers allowed to work on a temporary basis—without their families accompanying them— was institutionalized in contract labor programs during the 1910s and later during the Bracero Program, which lasted from 1942 to 1964. Ultimately, however, even some temporary workers manage to bring their families to join them and become settlers. As Doris Meissner, Commissioner of the INS has observed, "History shows that every contract-worker program falls victim to the inexorable goal of workers who wish to reunite with their families or to become members of the community in which they work." [61]

Even undocumented workers, our unofficial guest-workers, and their families have a remarkable capacity to develop a sense of community in the United States. [62] Although they may have come originally as temporary migrants, over time they marry or bring their spouse and children to join them in the United States, have children born here who therefore become citizens (what I have termed "binational families"), have other relatives and friends living nearby, and have important networks in the labor market. [63] These social and familial developments increase the likelihood of settlement in the United States. [64]

FINAL THOUGHTS

What is new in the "new" nativism, perhaps, is the extent to which immigrants, even those who are legal residents and citizens, are being reimagined as less deserving members of the community.[65] What began as a prairie fire against undocumented immigrants quickly ignited into a major round of immigration reform, with immigrants facing denial of many social services. The benefits immigrants have historically brought to this "nation of immigrants" have become overshadowed by the cost of immigration. To be "immigrant" today is tantamount to being a "cost" to society, a cost that must be reduced if the nation is to get its house in order and balance its budget. In the discourse of contemporary social sciences, immigrants have become the less moral, undeserving, and threatening Other in society.

In the current discourse on immigration, race matters but in a less than obvious way. As Balibar has noted, the category of immigration has replaced the notion of race. In other words, rather than speaking in terms of biological differentiation, genetic inferiority, or social evolution, proponents of immigration reform cloak a "neo-racism" in a language that talks about "scales of humanity," "us and them," "conquest and sovereignty" and "a nonwhite majority."[66] Such phrasing alerts us to the fact that the "new" immigration from Latin America, particularly Mexico, and Asia is qualitatively different from the "old" immigration from Europe.

The new immigrants pose a transnationalist challenge to a narrow nationalist construction of the nation. In this sense, the current wave of immigration reform proposals reflect a nationalist response to this transnational challenge. Immigrants, it is said, are harbingers of a "nonwhite majority," multiculturalism, and an end of English dominance. As a consequence, they are depicted as posing a threat to the fiction of the "national culture" and the nationalist order of society. They undermine the notion of a singular American identity. Immigrants, as the transnational movements of people across borders—both political and cultural—underscore the disorder inherent in the order implied by the fiction of a singular cultural heritage.[67]

Thus enters the recurrent contradiction in America's immigration history. On the one hand, there are those who have desired immigrant labor because it provides a valuable asset to the economy. On the other hand are those Americans who believe immigrants threaten that which is "American." The specific nature of that threat may find different emphasis during any particular historical moment. In the current epoch, the threat is both cultural and fiscal. The families of immigrant workers have costs to society. Reducing society's obligations and responsibilities to immigrant families is way of balancing the budget but not necessarily a way to produce healthy and educated members of society. Nor are such policies sure to reduce the flow of immigrants, legal or otherwise. What do we get, then, from this new round of nativism? Rather than giving us an accurate portrayal of immigrant motives and behavior, the discourse of immigration reform tells us more about the fears and character of a nation under stress. In this sense, the new nativism is a lot like the old nativism.

NOTES

1. California Ballot Pamphlet 1994. On November 20, 1995, a federal district judge in Los Angeles ruled that the state of California is preempted from barring illegal immigrants from elementary and secondary education, and from federally funded health care and social welfare services. These issues are far from resolved, however, since the advocates for Proposition 187 intend to take their case to the U.S. Supreme Court. See Paul Feldman, "Parts of 187 Thrown Out," *Los Angeles Times* 21 November 1995: A1.

2. For an excellent analysis of the immigration debate in Europe, see Verena Stolcke, "Talking Culture: New Boundaries, New Rhetorics of Exclusion in Europe," *Current Anthropology* 36: 1–24, 1995.

3. Michael Peter Smith, "Postmodernism, Urban Ethnography, and the New Social Space of Ethnic Identity," *Theory and Society* 21: 493–531, 1992.

4. This view of transnational migrants converges with contemporary social theory. For example, see Linda Basch, Nina Glick Schiller, and Cristina Szanton Blanc, *Nations Unbound: Transnational Projects, Postcolonial Predicaments, and Deterritorialized Nation-States* (Amsterdam: Gordon and Breach, 1994). Also, postmodern definitions of identity critique the notion that a person must belong to only one community, geographically defined; rather, people have multiple and often contradictory identities, inhabiting a diversity of communities. See Michael Peter Smith, "Postmodernism, Urban Ethnography, and the New Social Space of Ethnic Identity," *Theory and Society* 21: 493–531, 1992. For a discussion of undocumented immigrants positioned in multiple communities, see Leo R. Chavez, "The Power of the Imagined Community: The Settlement of Undocumented Mexicans and Central Americans in the United States," *American Anthropologist* 96: 52–73, 1994; Roger Rouse, "Mexican Migration and the Social Space of Postmodernism," *Diaspora* 1: 8–23, 1991; and Michael Kearney, "Borders and Boundaries of State and Self at the End of Empire," *Journal of Historical Sociology* 4(1): 52–74, 1991.

5. Gebe Martinez and Patrick J. McDonnell, "Prop. 187 Forces Rely on Message—Not Strategy," *Los Angeles Times* 30 October 1991: A1.

6. Melissa Healy, "Gingrich Lays out Rigid GOP Agenda," *Los Angeles Times* 12 November 1994: A1.

7. Patrick J. McDonnell, "Prop. 187 Win Spotlights Voting Disparity," *Los Angeles Times* 10 November 1994: A3. See also Patrick J. McDonnell, "Is Prop. 187 Just the Beginning?" *Los Angeles Times* 28 January 1995: A1.

8. Charles King, "Too Narrow a View of Who's American," *Los Angeles Times* 21 September 1995: B11 (Orange County edition).

9. Charles King, "Too Narrow a View of Who's American," *Los Angeles Times* 21 September 1995: B11 (Orange County edition).

10. Maria C. Hunt, "Craven Says All Hispanics Should Carry I.D. Cards," *San Diego Union-Tribune* 18 October 1994: A1.

11. Maria C. Hunt, "Craven Says All Hispanics Should Carry I.D. Cards." *San Diego Union-Tribune* 18 October 1994: A1.

12. Leslie Berkman, "Some Attach Strings to the Spirit of Giving," *Los Angeles Times* 24 November 1994: B1 (Orange County edition).

13. Patrick J. Buchanan, "What Will America Be in 2050?" *Los Angeles Times* 28 October 1994: B11. See also John L. Graham, "Xenophobic Fears about a 'Nonwhite Majority' Are Nonsense," *Los Angeles Times* 27 November 1994: B17 (Orange County edition).

14. Patrick J. McDonnell, "Prop. 187 Win Spotlights Voting Disparity," *Los Angeles Times* 10 November 1994: A3. See also Philip Martin, "Proposition 187 in California," *International Migration Review* 24: 255–63, 1995.

15. Patrick J. McDonnell, "Prop. 187 Win Spotlights Voting Disparity," *Los Angeles Times* 10 November 1994: A3.

16. Kevin R. Johnson, "Public Benefits and Immigration: The Intersection of Immigration Status, Ethnicity, Gender, and Class," *UCLA Law Review* 42(6): 1509–75, 1995.

17. Lisa Richwine, "Packard Vows to Bar Illegal Immigrants from Flood Aid," *Los Angeles Times* 14 January 1995: B1 (Orange County edition).

18. Marc Lacey, "New Task Force Targets Illegal Immigration." *Los Angeles Times* 16 March 1995: A3.

19. Marc Lacey, "Immigration Report Gains Key Support," *Los Angeles Times* 30 June 1995: A34.

20. Elton Gallegly, "Gallegly Seeks to End Automatic Citizenship for Illegal Alien Children," press release of October 22, 1991, from the Office of Congressman Elton Gallegly, Washington, D.C., 1991.

21. Elton Gallegly, "Time to Amend Our Birthright Citizenship Laws," speech presented by Rep. Gallegly in the House of Representatives, October 22, 1991. Copy in author's files.

22. Janet Hook, "Immigration Cutback Urged by U.S. Panel," *Los Angeles Times* 8 June 1995: A1.

23. Alison Mitchell, "President Rebuts Some GOP Themes on Economic Woes," *New York Times* 5 September 1995: A1.

24. Elizabeth Shogren, "Plans to Cut Safety Net Leave Legal Immigrants Dangling," *Los Angeles Times* 21 November 1994: A1.

25. Aaron Epstein, "GOP Targets Legal Noncitizens," *Orange County Register* 27 December 1994: A1.

26. Elizabeth Shogren, "House OK's Welfare Overhaul that Cuts off Aid Guarantees," *Los Angeles Times* 25 March 1995: A1.

27. Elizabeth Shogren, "Senate Approves Shifting Control of Welfare to States," *Los Angeles Times* 20 September 1995: A1.

28. "Congress Moves on Immigration Reform," *Migration News* 2(10) October 1995: 1. Philip Martin, editor, *Migration News*, 1004 Eagle Place, Davis, CA 95616.

29. Clifford Geertz, *The Interpretation of Cultures* (New York: Basic Books, 1973).

30. See, generally, Stephen Steinberg, *The Ethnic Myth: Race, Ethnicity, and Class in America* (Boston: Beacon Press, 1981); John Higham, *Strangers in the Land: Patterns of American Nativism 1860–1925* (New York: Atheneum, 1985 [1955]); Stephen Jay Gould, *The Mismeasure of Man* (New York: W.W. Norton, 1981); Rita J. Simon, *Public Opinion and the Immigrant* (Lexington, MA: Lexington Books, 1985).

31. On these issues, see David M. Reimers, *Still the Golden Door: The Third World Comes to America* (New York: Columbia University Press, 1985); Frank D. Bean, Barry Edmonston, and Jeffrey S. Passel, *Undocumented Migration to the United States* (Washington, DC: Urban Institute Press, 1990); Rita J. Simon, *Public Opinion and the Immigrant* (Lexington, MA: Lexington Books, 1985); and Wayne A. Cornelius, "America in the Era of Limits," *Working Paper No. 3* (La Jolla, CA: Center for U.S.-Mexican Studies, University of California, San Diego, 1980).

32. Richard D. Lamm and Gary Imhoff, *The Immigration Time Bomb* (New York: Truman Talley Books, 1985).

33. Peter Brimelow, *Alien Nation: Common Sense About America's Immigration Disaster* (New York: Random House, 1995).

34. Peter Brimelow, "Time to Rethink Immigration?" *National Review* 22 June: 30–46, 1992.

35. Jim Mann, "GOP Candidates Warm to Anti-Foreign Policy," *Los Angeles Times* 24 September 1995: A3.

36. Gebe Martinez and Patrick J. McDonnell, "Prop. 187 Forces Rely on Message—Not Strategy," *Los Angeles Times* 30 October 1994: A1.

37. Gebe Martinez and Patrick J. McDonnell, "Prop. 187 Forces Rely on Message—Not Strategy," *Los Angeles Times* 30 October 1994: A1.

38. Gebe Martinez and Patrick J. McDonnell, "Prop. 187 Forces Rely on Message—Not Strategy," *Los Angeles Times* 30 October 1994: A1.

39. Patrick J. McDonnell, "Prop. 187 Heats up Debate over Immigration," *Los Angeles Times* 10 August 1994: A1.

40. Gebe Martinez and Patrick J. McDonnell, "Prop. 187 Forces Rely on Message—Not Strategy," *Los Angeles Times* 30 October 1994: A1.

41. Patrick J. McDonnell, "Is Prop. 187 Just the Beginning?" *Los Angeles Times* 28 January 1995: A1.

42. Spencer was quoted in Patrick J. McDonnell, "Study Disputes Immigrant Stereotypes, Cites Gains," *Los Angeles Times* 3 November 1995: A1. He was responding to the study "The Changing Immigrants of Southern California" by Dowell Myers, the first report from the research project California Immigration and the American Dream: Integration and Advancement of the New Arrivals (Los Angeles: School of Urban and Regional Planning, University of Southern California, November 1995).

43. Patrick J. McDonnell, "Prop. 187 Heats up Debate over Immigration," *Los Angeles Times* 10 August 1994: A1.

44. Melissa Healy, "House GOP Charts California Agenda," *Los Angeles Times* 13 November 1994: A1.

45. Linda B. Hayes, "Letter to the Editor: California's Prop. 187," *New York Times* 15 October 1994: 18.

46. For a discussion of the issues related to return migration among undocumented immigrants from Mexico and Central America, see Leo R. Chavez, *Shadowed Lives: Undocumented Immigrants in American Society* (Ft. Worth: Harcourt, Brace and Jovanovich College Publishers, 1992).

47. Claude Meillassoux, *Maidens, Meal and Money: Capitalism and the Domestic Community* (Cambridge: Cambridge University Press, 1975).

48. James Bornemeier, "Clinton Moves to Curb Illegal Immigration," *Los Angeles Times* 8 February 1995: A3. See also Janet Hook, "Clinton Moves to Speed Deportations," *Los Angeles Times* 7 May 1995: A1.

49. James Bornemeier, "Clinton Moves to Curb Illegal Immigration," *Los Angeles Times* 8 February 1995: A3.

50. Pete Wilson, "Sowing the Ground for a Better California," *Los Angeles Times* 24 October 1994: B11 (Orange County edition).

51. Paul Jacobs, "Wilson Often Battled INS, Letters Show," *Los Angeles Times* 25 September 1995: A3.

52. Leo R. Chavez, "Settlers and Sojourners: The Case of Mexicans in the United States," *Human Organization* 47: 95–108, 1988.

53. Leo R. Chavez, Wayne A. Cornelius, and O. W. Jones, "Mexican Immigrants and the Utilization of Health Services," *Social Science and Medicine* 21: 93–102, 1985; and Leo R. Chavez, Estevan T. Flores, and Marta Lopez-Garza, "Undocumented Latin American Immigrants and U.S. Health Services: An Approach to a Political Economy of Utilization," *Medical Anthropology Quarterly* 6: 6–26, 1992. Ruben Rumbaut, Leo R. Chavez, Robert Moser, Sheila Pickwell, and Sam Wishik, "The Politics of Migrant Health Care: A Comparative Study of Mexican Immigrants and Indochinese Refugees in San Diego," *Research in the Sociology of Medicine* 7 (Greenwich, CT: JAI Press, 1988), pp. 143–202.

54. Leo R. Chavez, Wayne A. Cornelius, and O. W. Jones, "Utilization of Health Services by Mexican Women in San Diego," *Women and Health* 11: 3–20, 1986.

55. Paul Feldman and Rich Connell, "Wilson Acts to Enforce Parts of Prop. 187; 8 Lawsuits Filed," *Los Angeles Times* 10 November 1994: A1.

56. Ronald Brownstein, "Wilson Proposes U.S. Version of Prop. 187," *Los Angeles Times* 19 November 1994: A1.

57. Ronald Brownstein, "Wilson Proposes U.S. Version of Prop. 187," *Los Angeles Times* 19 November 1994: A1.

58. Frank del Olmo, "Open the Door to Mexican Workers," *Los Angeles Times* 31 January 1995: B9 (Orange County edition).

59. Marc Lacey, "New Task Force Targets Illegal Immigration," *Los Angeles Times* 16 March 1995: A3.

60. Alejandro Portes and Robert L. Bach, *Latin Journey: Cuban and Mexican Immigrants in the United States* (Berkeley: University of California Press, 1985).

61. Doris Meissner, "Contract Workers: Human Exploitation," *Los Angeles Times* 30 January 1995: B9 (Orange County edition).

62. Leo R. Chavez, "The Power of the Imagined Community: The Settlement of Undocumented Mexicans and Central Americans in the United States," *American Anthropologist* 96: 52–73, 1994.

63. Leo R. Chavez, "Settlers and Sojourners: The Case of Mexicans in the United States," *Human Organization* 47: 95–108, 1988.

64. Leo R. Chavez, Estevan T. Flores, and Marta Lopez-Garza, "Here Today, Gone Tomorrow? Undocumented Settlers and Immigration Reform," *Human Organization* 49: 193–205, 1990.

65. Benedict Anderson, *Imagined Communities* (London: Verso, 1983).

66. Etienne Balibar, "Is There a 'Neo-Racism'?" In *Race, Nation, Class: Ambiguous Identities,* Etienne Balibar and Immanuel Wallerstein, eds. (New York: Verso, 1991), 17–28.

67. I credit Javier Inda with the notion of (dis)order, as he discussed it in "The Anthropology of Transnationalism," 1994 mimeo.

5. OFFICIAL ENGLISH AS NATIVIST BACKLASH
Raymond Tatalovich

In July 1992, Senator Robert C. Byrd (D-WV) made the point during floor debate that the United States should stop accepting immigrants who do not speak English. "I pick up the telephone and call the local garage," he said. "I can't understand the person on the other side of the line. I'm not sure he can understand me. They're all over the place, and they don't speak English. We want more of this?" Later Byrd apologized for the remark, saying, "I regret that in the heat of the moment I spoke unwisely." [1] Whether or not Byrd saw the error of his ways, others were not apologetic for insisting that Americans speak English and that English be the "official" language of the nation. By mid-1995, more than one-third of the House of Representatives had signed on as cosponsors of H.R. 123, introduced by Congressman Bill Emerson (R-MO). This legislation was introduced first on January 5, 1993, when the Democratic Party controlled Congress and the White House, but with the Republican majority in the 104th House of Representatives walking in lock-step with Speaker Newt Gingrich, it would not be unexpected to learn that Emerson's bill was adopted.

OFFICIAL ENGLISH LAWS

Before 1980, only three states had adopted legislation to establish English as their official language, and all three were historical curiosities although like-minded attitudes prompted those enactments. In 1920, Nebraska passed a constitutional amendment to affirm English against the desires of Germans and others to speak their native tongues. Three years later, Illinois passed a law making "American" its official language (amended in 1969, whereby English was substituted for American), but here the motivation was anti-

English sentiment. The Nebraska and Illinois enactments were a backlash from World War I.[2] In 1978, Hawaii codified English and Hawaiian as official languages, though section 4 of the Hawaii constitution specifies that "except that Hawaiian shall be required for public acts and transactions only as provided by law." Thus, both languages are official but the amendment gives primacy to English.

During 1981–1990, ten Southern and Midwestern states established Official English by statute, but politically a more important development was the 1986 referendum vote in California, where a sizeable Spanish-speaking population resides, which amended its state constitution for that purpose. Three more referenda in 1988 in Florida, Arizona, and Colorado along with another in Alabama, in 1990 when voters ratified a constitutional amendment proposed by the state legislature, meant that fifteen states had joined the contemporary Official English movement. Since then, Louisiana, Montana, South Dakota, and New Hampshire have followed suit, meaning that, at this writing, twenty-two states have official language laws on the books. Every state in the South has adopted these laws and the others are Midwestern, Mountain, or Southwestern states. Only New Hampshire in the Northeast corridor has such an enactment. On the other hand, "English-Plus" laws or resolutions establishing official multilingualism were adopted in 1989 by heavily Hispanic New Mexico and in the Northwest by Washington and Oregon.

If opponents can find anything to salvage from this ominous trend, it is the fact that all but a few of these laws are purely symbolic and have no policy implications.[3] For example, Section 3–3–31 of the Mississippi code reads: "The English language is the official language of the State of Mississippi." And Chapter 145–12 of the general statutes of North Carolina states:

English is the common language of the people of the United States of America and the State of North Carolina. This section is intended to preserve, protect and strengthen the English language, and not to supersede any of the rights guaranteed to the people by the Constitution of the United States or the Constitution of North Carolina. . . . English is the official language of the State of North Carolina.

Moreover, the purpose was not to discourage foreign language instruction nor, for that matter, bilingual education although the presumption was that such programs be "transitional" and designed to move non-English speakers into classes taught in English as soon as possible. Opposition to federal bilingual education mandates led to Virginia's 1981 law, which was not amended until 1986 to allow for bilingual educational assistance. However, "in the states that followed, the pattern was for amendments to exempt foreign language and bilingual instruction from the general prohibition against non-English languages. And the declarations of official English were never strengthened by amendment; where amendments were added, they had the effect of softening the enforcement language of the laws."[4]

So why bother enacting such symbolic laws which seem to have no effect other than causing linguistic minorities to feel that they are being discriminated against? The purpose of my research on Official English has been to determine what motivations were behind this policy agenda and to assess whether the agitation was elite-driven or a mass movement. I argue that the Official English controversy will have developed in three stages by the time it fully becomes a national political issue.

STAGE I: NATIVISM REVISITED

The enactments of North Carolina, South Carolina, Georgia, Alabama, Mississippi, Arkansas, Kentucky, Tennessee, Indiana, North Dakota, and (to a lesser degree) Virginia were non-issues. In this group of "statutory" states, Official English laws were passed by state legislatures, whereas the referendum process was used in four other states during the 1980s. Mainly (Southern) Democrats and some Republicans were cosponsors of the Official English bills, and governors of both parties signed the bills into law, including then Governor Bill Clinton of Arkansas. The statutes were enacted by overwhelming majorities in both houses of the state legislature, with 92 percent of state senators and 88 percent of state representatives who voted doing so in the affirmative.[5] A detailed analysis of legislative voting behavior indicates, however, that a racial cleavage surfaced in Alabama, Mississippi, North Carolina, and Tennessee, meaning that white Democrats joined forces with white Republicans but that African American legislators (virtually all of whom were Democrats) tended to vote against this legislation or abstain from voting.

The multivariate analysis, used to predict the pattern of voting behavior and legislative sponsorship of Official English bills, included demographic variables as proxies for grassroots opinion and attributes of the legislators to assess whether the agitation was a bottom-up or top-down phenomenon. The results led me to conclude that, among the statutory states, "the movement for official English is elite driven; it does not represent a groundswell from mass opinion. Attributes of the legislators (party, race, gender) were far more important in explaining sponsorship and voting behavior than the characteristics of their home counties. This implies that political dynamics within the legislatures, rather than a commonality of constituency pressures from outside, were the driving force behind action on official language laws."[6] While the patterns varied among states and across groups of states, the state legislators who were more supportive of Official English were Republicans, whites irrespective of their party affiliation, and men.

My review of newspaper coverage shows that the local press gave scant, if any, attention to the legislative efforts to establish Official English, probably because the laws were not intended to correct any real problems in those states. These states have very small percentages of Spanish speakers, according to the Census, so clearly whatever motivated these legislators was not related to any tangible fear that non-English speakers posed a threat to the power structure. Indeed, interviews with the key sponsors, legislative histories, and news reports suggest that the legislators were acting as "trustees" during the agenda-setting stage. They were following their own policy agenda rather than constituency opinion. This caveat should not mask the political result, however, that polls conclusively show that the public supports Official English laws, at least in the abstract.

Spearheading the cause of Official English is U.S. English, which in mid-1995 boasted membership of 620,000.[7] It was organized in 1983, but the origins of discontent with bilingualism and multiculturalism predate its founding. Local controversies fueled a backlash over official biculturalism in Dade County, Florida in 1980, over federally mandated bilingual education in Virginia in 1981, and over bilingual ballots in San Francisco in 1983 (where newly organized U.S. English gave assistance to the local opposition). U.S. English was founded one year prior to the enactments of Indiana, Kentucky, and Tennessee, and interviews with the key Indiana and Tennessee legislative sponsors indicated that they were motivated by personal experiences to oppose bilingualism in the United States.[8]

Today, however, there seems little doubt that the current activism at the state and federal levels is being orchestrated by this single-issue group. Its newsletter, which gives a state-by-state summary of its efforts to achieve Official English legislation in the remaining twenty-eight states, took credit that "in just three months, South Dakota, Montana and New Hampshire all enacted U.S. English-sponsored legislation" to codify an official language.[9]

The best evidence for the assertion that the actions of most states which adopted Official English laws during the 1980s and 1990s was the result of a nativist impulse—a general animosity towards foreigners—is the fact that so few non-English speakers live in those states. Even though Asians are the target of anti-foreign sentiments in certain localities, still the main focus are Spanish speakers generally and Hispanics in particular. In no case was any state compelled to adopt Official English because of the fear that the Anglos would be overrun by Spanish speakers. In 1985, Spanish speakers represented 7.3 percent of the U.S. population, and the eleven states that adopted Official English statutes during the 1980s are conspicuous for *not* having

many Spanish-speaking peoples or any other linguistic minorities. Less than
1 percent of the population in Alabama, Arkansas, Kentucky, Mississippi,
Tennessee, Georgia, North Carolina, South Carolina, and Virginia is Hispanic. In Indiana, the figure was below 2 percent, and North Dakota in the
mid-1980s had 3,400 Hispanic inhabitants. The statistics are equally low in
the four states which acted during the early 1990s. For South Dakota, the
number of Hispanics was 3,700 and 5,700 in New Hampshire; the 10,800
figure in Montana represented 1.2 percent of its population while Louisiana
topped this listing with 1.9 percent Hispanic in 1985.[10]

There is a scholarly literature that links white fear of some minority group
to reactionary politics, notably the case of African Americans in the South,[11]
but the fear threshold is related to a sizeable presence or a growing concentration of minorities in a locale. This explicitly "racist" dynamic is not the
motivating factor behind the diffusion of Official English laws to this subgroup of states. On the other hand, because virtually the entire South is
included among these states, there is evidence to suggest that Official English
is a modern residue of nativist sentiment dating back to the post-World War
I era.

LINKING PAST NATIVISM TO PRESENT NATIVISM

The classic work on nativism in American history argues that it embodies
anti-Catholicism, xenophobia, and a sense that Anglo-Americans were superior.[12] The last period of nativism followed World War I and culminated in
passage of the 1924 National Origins Act which established a "quota"
system that grossly disadvantaged Southern European, Asian, and African
immigrants to the benefit of Northern European immigrants. That law governed our immigration policies until the 1960s, and more than one observer
has noted the racist overtones of that legislation. The law was enacted by
overwhelming margins in the Senate (62–6) and the House of Representatives
(323–71), but there was a regional division in the vote. On the final roll call,
83 percent of Republicans and 81 percent of Northern Democrats but 100
percent of Southern Democrats voted yea. What seemed paradoxical was
my finding that "states (mostly Southern) with populations of foreign-born
residents and Catholics *below* the national average cast 98 percent of their
votes for enactment."[13]

To determine who represented the leading edge of nativist sentiment in
Congress, a close reading of the debates revealed an amendment by James
Begg (R-Ohio), narrowly passed on a 198–193 roll call, which highlighted
extreme anti-foreign sentiments. Without belaboring the details,[14] the Begg
Amendment was targeted at aliens *entering* the United States, not those
already residing in the country, and thus, Begg argued, to impose on residents

the "burden of proof" that they immigrated to the United States legally "is contrary to the practice and the basic principles of the United States in guaranteeing everybody, when accused of any crime, the right of a supposition of innocence until they are proven guilty."[15] In other words, "liberals" of that day included this proviso to assist aliens living in the United States in their fight against deportation, which explains why 122 more representatives voted "yea" on the Begg Amendment even though they also voted "yea" on final enactment of the 1924 Act. The votes against the Begg Amendment, therefore, can be taken as the hard-core opposition to foreigners.

The empirical question, then, is whether there is any relationship between how state congressional delegations voted on the Begg Amendment in 1924 and how state legislatures acted on Official English laws during the 1980s. Multivariate analysis confirms that the linkage between these two episodes is not explained by random chance even though they span nearly six decades.[16] The adoption by Louisiana of an Official English law in the 1990s gives more support to the interpretation that nativism is (though not exclusively) a Southern phenomenon. The seventeen state congressional delegations that cast 90 percent to 100 percent of their votes *against* the Begg Amendment included ten Southern States, all of whom enacted Official English laws: Alabama, Arkansas, Florida, Kentucky, Georgia, Louisiana, Mississippi, North Carolina, South Carolina, and Virginia. Then, as now, this group of states was not distinguished by having large numbers of foreign-born according to the 1920 Census; 1.5 percent was the average percentage for these ten states.[17] In Tennessee, all eight Democrats voted against the Begg Amendment; two Republican Congressmen voted in the affirmative.

Of the other statutory states, today most would be counted among the most socially homogeneous states of the union. With the exception of solidly Midwestern Indiana (whose population was only 5.2 percent foreign-born in 1920), at that time there were sizeable numbers of immigrants in North Dakota (with 20.4 percent foreign-born in 1920), New Hampshire (20.6 percent), Montana (17.4 percent), and South Dakota (13.0 percent),[18] which explains why seven of the eight Congressmen from those states voted *for* the Begg Amendment. If nativism in the South can be attributed to the demographic makeup of its population—home to more "native" Americans than any other region—the experience of those Mountain states indicates that the cycle of nativism means that old immigrant groups, once established, will turn against new immigrant groups.

The outlier among Southern states is Florida, because its Official English law was the result of a referendum campaign. Florida is a mixed case because it is Southern but also home to a substantial number of Cubans who are Spanish speakers. In Florida, and elsewhere where large minorities of Spanish speakers reside, the state legislature refused to enact an Official English law.

As a result, the agitation took on characteristics of a mass movement, with all the adverse implications associated with direct democracy. This scenario affected not only Florida but also California, Arizona, and Colorado. Only in Texas, which lacks a popular initiative to force such issues on the ballot, was a referendum on Official English avoided. So different were the political dynamics in these states that I have characterized them as reflecting Stage II in the development of the controversy over Official English.

STAGE II: REFERENDA POLITICS

A generalized anti-foreign backlash likely fueled this movement in the statutory states simply because there are so few Spanish speakers in the South, where most enactments occurred. However, the dynamics of conflict in the "referendum" states—Arizona, California, Colorado, and Florida—which codified English by popular initiative could lead one to racist interpretations: perceived grievances by the dominant Anglo population against a sizeable, and growing, minority of non-English speakers gave rise to the Official English agitation. This view gains credibility because an outpouring of public support for Official English occurred in those states. Taking the experiences of these four states (with appropriate caveats added for Florida), there are commonalities which are distinctive and unlike the situation in the "statutory" states that enacted Official English.

The numbers of Spanish speakers in these referendum states are substantial, so the potential for racial or linguistic conflict is magnified. By 1985, these states ranked among the top seven in percentage of Hispanics in the population: New Mexico 37.8 percent, Texas 22.8 percent, California 22.1 percent, Arizona 16.8 percent, Colorado 11.9 percent, New York 10.6 percent, and Florida 9.8 percent.[19]

Though some localities in New York have considered Official English legislation (notably Suffolk County where the largest Hispanic community outside of New York City resides),[20] there has been little sustained effort at the state level. In Texas, where a backlash could be expected, legislative efforts during the late 1980s were derailed by the Democratic controlled state legislature and specifically by the ability of the Mexican American Legislative Caucus to secure commitments from enough representatives to kill any attempt to place the issue on the ballot. Texas does not have a popular initiative and a two-thirds vote is required in the 150–member House and the 31–member Senate to use referendum to approval proposed constitutional amendments.[21]

The Texas experience was repeated elsewhere, which explains why the advocates of Official English resorted to a popular initiative. Attempts to persuade the Democratic controlled Florida and California legislatures to enact Official English laws failed, and in Colorado a bill that seemed destined to be approved was withdrawn after Governor Roy Romer, a Democrat, threatened a veto. The Arizona legislature was controlled by Republicans but when faced with a sustained outcry from Hispanic and Native American leaders, the chief legislative sponsor backed down. Not deterred, the activists turned to mobilizing a grassroots movement to gather enough signatures to force the issue on the ballot. These episodes offer early warning signs of how the Official English controversy will evolve in Stage III, the stage of partisan conflict at the national level, and thus they deserve more scrutiny.

In each state, the referendum campaign received direct and indirect support (though not necessarily to launch the petition drive, as shown by Colorado) from U.S. English. Such groups as Arizonans for Official English, the California English Committee, the Colorado Official English Committee, Florida English, and the American Ethnic Coalition (in Texas) spearheaded those campaigns. The debate over "English Only" or "English Plus" (the phrase coined by those favoring multiculturalism and bilingualism) is a moral conflict over language as an emotional symbol of a group's status in American society. I have argued that moral conflicts are characterized by conflict between single-issue groups, especially by the defenders of the normative status quo.[22] For their part, the opposition rallied its forces through such ad hoc coalitions as Arizona English, Californians United Committee against Proposition 63, Colorado Unity, and Speak Up Now for Florida.

Established interests, certainly trade associations or labor unions, are reluctant to become involved in moral conflicts that do not touch their economic self-interest. But invariably some established organizations do take sides, typically against Official English. These included bilingual educators, religious groups (especially the Roman Catholic Church since Hispanics are predominantly Catholic), spokespersons of mainstream Protestant and Jewish churches, and reliably the ACLU or its local affiliates. Since these laws are patently anti-Spanish, Hispanic community leaders and political elites were drawn into the battle in Texas and Arizona, though Asians and other ethnic minorities also joined the alliance in California. In contrast, leaders of the Cuban community in Dade County were reluctant players, to the chagrin of bilingual activists. However, once they increased their numbers on the Dade County Commission (to six of thirteen members), they quickly acted to repeal the 1980 Official English ordinance which had divided Anglos and Cubans in south Florida long before the 1988 referendum adopting an Official English amendment to the state constitution.[23]

The ranks of the opposition included the political establishment—or more accurately the Democratic establishment; the GOP was divided between its rank-and-file and its elected leadership in some instances. High profile Democrats in Arizona, Colorado and California were generally unified against the referenda, whereas state GOP organizations endorsed Official English in Arizona and Texas. The leading promoters in the Arizona and Colorado legislatures were Republicans as were the vast majority of legislative sponsors in California and Texas. It was calculated that 93 percent of state senators and 96 percent of state representatives who cosponsored Official English bills in California, Colorado, and Arizona were Republicans.[24] However, some Republicans who held statewide offices were reluctant to offend Hispanic voters and thus publicly opposed those initiatives: Governors George Deukmejian (R-CA)and Evan Mecham (R-AZ) and U.S. Senators Bill Armstrong (R-CO) and John McCain (R-AZ). In light of his 1994 gubernatorial campaign which demonized illegal aliens as a burden to California taxpayers, it is noteworthy that Pete Wilson (R-CA), formerly a U.S. Senator, had endorsed the California Official English referendum in 1988.

Here, Florida offers an important qualification which will have bearing on the bilingualism debate as it moves onto the national political arena. Most legislative sponsors of the ill-fated Official English bills in its legislature were Democrats, a pattern which was more typical of Southern states than of the Western states which held referenda. Whereas Hispanics in the Southwest tend to vote Democratic, the large Cuban population of South Florida is doggedly loyal to the Republican Party.[25] For that reason, Florida Republicans would have fewer political incentives to push the Official English agenda than would Democrats who could appeal to non-Hispanic whites and black voters. Moreover, tensions between the African American and Cuban American communities of South Florida already have surfaced over political spoils. A deadlock over redistricting following the 1990 Census pitted Republicans and Cubans against Democrats and blacks in the state legislature.[26] The reverse political logic would encourage Republicans to promote Official English in Western and Southwestern states in order to drive a wedge between Hispanics and the majority of white voters.

THE RHETORIC OF REFERENDUM CAMPAIGNS FOR OFFICIAL ENGLISH

Where the political debate over Official English was subdued in the statutory states, where legislatures enacted these laws, the public rhetoric was explosive during the referenda campaigns. Invariably the charge of racism was hurled against the advocates of "English Only" and nowhere did it reach such a fever pitch as in Arizona. The degree of controversy surrounding its Proposition 106 was due to the punitive nature of the referendum proposal and, more importantly, by the revelations unearthed in the now-famous Tanton Memo. As a result, Arizonans barely approved the proposition by a

50.5 percent vote margin, much lower than the landslides recorded in Florida, California, and Colorado.

John Tanton, M.D., was chairman and founder of U.S. English. His roots go back to Petroskey, Michigan where he began an ophthalmology practice in the early 1960s. Tanton worked with Planned Parenthood Federation and later with Zero Population Growth (ZPG), having served as its president during 1975–77. When he failed to convince the ZPG board of directors to deal with immigration, he founded another group called Federation for American Immigration Reform (FAIR), which today advocates a moratorium on immigration to the United States. Later, he joined Senator S. I. Hayakawa (R-CA) to form U.S. English. An executive director of ZPG said that "there is a path" from organizations like ZPG and Planned Parenthood to concerns about immigration and language.[27]

The Tanton Memo, he said, was inspired to stimulate discussions at the WITAN IV conference on the consequences of immigration to California and the United States. Tanton covered a range of topics including the impact of unrestricted immigration on political conflict:

Is apartheid in southern California's future? The demographic picture in South Africa now is startlingly similar to what we'll see in California in 2030. In southern Africa, a white minority owns the property, has the best jobs and education and speaks one language. A non-white majority has poor education, jobs and income, owns little property, is on its way to political power and speaks a different language.

In the California of 2030, the non-Hispanic whites and Asians will own the property, have the good jobs and education, speak one language and be most Protestant and "other." The blacks and Hispanics will have the poor jobs, will lack education, own little property, speak another language and will be mainly Catholic. Will there be strength in this diversity? Or will this prove a social and political San Andreas Fault?[28]

On culture, he wrote: "Will Latin American migrants bring with them the tradition of the mordida (bribery), the lack of involvement in public affairs, etc.? . . . Will blacks be able to improve (or even maintain) their position in the face of the Latin onslaught?" And adding a perspective on race and class, Tanton asked: "What will be the fate of blacks as their numbers decline in relationship to Hispanics? As they lose political power, will they get along with the Hispanics? Relations are already heavily strained in many places."[29]

With the likelihood that immigrants would reproduce at higher rates, Tanton concluded: "Perhaps this is the first instance in which those with their pants up are going to get caught by those with their pants down!" Then he broached "the theory of a moratorium: the pause in immigration between

1930–1950, combined with the assimilating experience of fighting side by side in the trenches of World War II, gave us a needed pause so that we could assimilate the mass of people who came in the early years of the century. Do we again need such a pause?"[30]

Immediately leaders of the anti-106 campaign in Arizona labeled the Tanton Memo as "the Nazi memo" and said that its content resembled the discussions held by Adolf Hitler and his advisers as they plotted the rise of Nazism. According to William Meek, a political consultant with the opposition forces: "I think it's clear he's a racist. . . . He's a racist in the pure sense, because he's sitting there looking at demographic information and simply assuming that because there's going to be more of them (minorities) than there are of us, that there's going to be a conflict."[31]

This political bombshell led to the resignation of Walter Cronkite, once the anchorman for CBS-TV evening news, from the advisory board of U.S. English and caused Linda Chavez, its president, to resign as well. Chavez viewed the Tanton Memo as "anti-Catholic" and "anti-Hispanic" and her decision also was prompted by information she received from a journalist about financial contributions to U.S. English, FAIR, and Population Environment Balance. When told that those moneys came from people who advocated forced sterilization and who subsidized the reprinting of *Camp of the Saints*,[32] which Chavez labeled "a paranoid, racist fantasy" about "Third World people sort of taking over the world. In a certain point in political life, you realize that perceptions are reality. I just don't want to be in a position to defend those actions."[33] All this ultimately had an effect on Tanton, who stepped down from his official position with U.S. English.

The accusation that Official English advocates were mean-spirited if not racist was made in California, Florida, and Colorado but the level of accusations and countercharges in Arizona had an effect on the electorate; its referendum was almost defeated by the voters. But this was the exception that proves the rule: the decisive vote outcomes in California (73 percent), Colorado (64 percent), Florida (84 percent), and Alabama (89 percent) signaled that Official English has substantial public support. The analysis of election statistics and opinion polls in these referenda states allow us to evaluate alternative hypotheses about which population groups are most likely to favor this kind of legislation.

HYPOTHESES TO EXPLAIN POPULAR SUPPORT FOR OFFICIAL ENGLISH

The racial hypothesis, which may have more relevance to the referenda states than the statutory states, assumes that a majority-minority conflict exists; non-Hispanic whites would be most opposed to Spanish speakers. Journalists and academics[34] have observed that the potential exists for serious rivalries between African Americans and Hispanics, two minority groups who seek economic mobility and political influence and, if so, then presumably blacks have special reasons to be opposed to Spanish speakers. From historical accounts we learn that fear of job loss mobilized the working class and lower socioeconomic-status groups to oppose foreigners.[35] Political tolerance is also linked to class, notably to educational levels, since college educated people generally are more supportive of civil liberties and accepting of differing life styles. For both these reasons, one would anticipate that Official English would find more support from lower income, education, and occupational groups.

The political hypothesis is that Official English is promoted by Republicans and conservatives for electoral purposes. Bilingualism is another wedge issue—like abortion, school prayer, or gun control—that can be used to peel away Southerners, Catholics, and blue-collar workers from their traditional loyalties to the Democratic Party.

Finally, the nativist hypothesis suggests that an anti-foreign cultural trait among Americans (despite our being a nation of immigrants) is the motivating factor. James Crawford believes that a "cultural conservatism" provides an intellectual defense of the "Anglo-American" national culture and rationalizes attacks on bilingualism.[36] It is difficult to measure this cultural phenomenon directly; if support for Official English is cultural, then presumably it would extend across racial, class, and partisan lines.

County votes in the five Official English referenda (including Alabama) were subjected to statistical analysis to evaluate these hypotheses, and the results were consistent if not conclusive. In California, Colorado, and Florida, those counties with disproportionate numbers of Spanish speakers gave *less* support to those referenda, and the percentage of residents with a college education also depressed the vote for Official English in California and Colorado. But the strongest predictor in Alabama, Arizona, and California was a political variable; counties that gave disproportionate votes for President Reagan's reelection in 1984 also gave higher levels of support to codifying the English language. This "Reagan" variable was second-ranked in importance in Colorado and also Florida, which gives support to Jack Citrin's view that "the political right is the core of the 'official language' movement, but the movement attracts support from all along the ideological spectrum."[37]

Most likely there are multiple forces interacting today: race, politics, and culture. Opinion polls find that whites are more supportive of Official English than blacks (who sometimes express disapproval) and obviously Hispanics are more opposed. But the level of approval rises when you control for party and/or ideology: conservatives and Republicans are even more supportive than Anglos because at least one subgroup—self-proclaimed liberals—often register their disapproval of Official English.

Most intense scrutiny has been given to polling results in California since Proposition 63 was a harbinger of future developments. Dyste examined a California Poll three months before the November 1986 referendum and determined that "the strongest supporters of Proposition 63 were Whites, conservatives, and less educated . . . [while the] strongest opponents were Hispanics and Asians, the highly educated . . . and liberals."[38] A multivariate analysis of 1986 California exit polls indicated to Citrin and his associates "widespread support for the English Language Amendment in almost every segment of the electorate. To be sure, Hispanic and Asian voters were less likely to approve Proposition 63 than the other two ethnic groups, but blacks and whites did not differ significantly in their support." Any "cracks in the general consensus about the desirability of 'official English' also were strongly related to party and ideology. Registered Republicans were more likely than registered Democrats to vote for Proposition 63. . . . And this divergence in outlook grows even larger when we compare voters grouped by their evaluation of President Reagan's job performance . . . or other indicators of 'social' liberalism-conservatism."[39]

A bivariate examination of 1988 exit polling on "English as the only official language of the U.S." led Schmid to conclude that "the most striking finding is the marked difference in support for this legislation between Hispanics and Anglos at all educational and income categories in both California and Texas." Moreover, in both states more than three-fourths of Republicans and conservatives favored Official English whereas the "only Anglo group [in California] where the majority consistently opposed Official English was among self-reported liberals."[40]

Whereas Proposition 63 had obtained majority approval from whites (72 percent), blacks (67 percent) and Asians (58 percent) but opposition from most Hispanics,[41] a re-analysis of public attitudes based on a 1989 California Poll led Sonntag to conclude that "the official English issue is not dividing the population along language lines; indeed, there is broad consensus *for* official English legislation."[42] In other words, by 1989 Sonntag found that two-thirds of blacks (66.7 percent) and Asians (67.3 percent) but *also* nearly as many Hispanics (63.9 percent) favored the passage of Proposition 63. We can only speculate about what caused the shift in Hispanic attitudes; certainly it is conceivable that, in the aftermath, when cooler heads prevailed, Spanish speakers understood the law to be purely symbolic and with no effect on their lives. It was this realization—that Official English was nothing more than a symbolic slap-in-the-face—which caused the Cuban leadership in Dade County not to squander their political resources on a lost cause of trying to defeat Amendment 11.[43] Looking ahead to the future of Official

English, there may be solace in Sonntag's observation that "language issues are not particularly salient in the United States, as they are in such countries as Belgium where they do indeed function as a powder keg."[44] What is ominous are trends in Stage III to move beyond symbolism and enact legislative barriers to immigration.

STAGE III: PARTISAN CONFLICT

All indications are that my prognosis that Official English will become a partisan issue appear to be true. The 104th Congress is now considering H.R. 123, known as the "Language of Government Act of 1995," but so far its cosponsors include 148 Republicans and only 16 Democrats. A more detailed examination of those backers of H.R. 123 also indicates a linkage between the efforts by states to codify the English language and this latest effort to establish an official language for the United States Government.

TABLE 3.1 1995 Congressional Co-Sponsors of H.R. 123

	Republicans	Democrats
Referenda States	34 (100 percent)	0
Statutory States	54 (82 percent)	12 (18 percent)
Other States	*60 (94 percent)*	*4 (6 percent)*
TOTALS	148 (90 percent)	16 (10 percent)

U.S. English Update, Vol. XII, No. 2 (Summer 1995), p. 5.

In 1993, during the 103rd Congress, similar legislation attracted 77 Republicans and 16 Democrats as sponsors so virtually the entire increase is due to the GOP. Indeed, the partisan makeup at that time was 83 percent R-17 percent D[45] so the appeal of this legislation has grown only because the Republicans took control of the 104th Congress. The other constant in the political calculus is the heavy representation of sponsors—three-fifths—from states with existing Official English laws. As was the case with state legislative sponsors, a degree of bipartisanship exists in the statutory states but *all* congressional sponsors from the four referenda states are Republicans, which also is consistent with the findings on state legislative sponsorship.

In the crowded Republican field of presidential contenders, only Senator Robert Dole (R-KS) was viewed as a moderate when compared to such conservatives as Senator Phil Gramm (R-TX) and Patrick Buchanan, the columnist and former Nixon speechwriter. Since the GOP primary attracts highly motivated conservatives and given the growing importance of the Christian Right to Republican electoral successes in 1994, Dole became outspoken on various "social" issues to solidify his conservative credentials.

One such issue was Official English, and in September 1995 Senator Dole traveled to Indianapolis to address the 77th national convention of the American Legion. He told the Legionnaires that multilingual education should be ended. "Insisting that all our citizens are fluent in English is a welcoming act of inclusion, and insist we must," he declared. "We need the glue of language to help hold us together. We must stop the practice of multilingual education as a means of instilling ethnic pride or as a therapy for low self-esteem or out of elitist guilt over a culture built on the traditions of the West." In his litany of attacks on affirmative action, the advertising and television industries, political correctness, and efforts by the federal government to "glorify other cultures" and wage "war on traditional American values," Dole warned the nation to "return as a people to the original concept of what it means to be American" and debate subjects "the arbiters of political correctness" would prefer to avoid. "Our diversity," he added, "requires us to bind ourselves to the American idea in every way we can— by speaking one language, taking pride in our true history and embracing the traditional American values that have guided us from the beginning."[46]

If Dole's words are taken at face value, then a host of related issues have become conceptualized in the latest wave of nativism. Multiculturalism, bilingualism, political correctness, and intellectual elitism are components of a current unease which Dole, and the GOP, seem prepared to exploit for every political advantage. What he did not mention was *the* issue that catapulted these other issues onto the national political stage: immigration.

It takes somebody to dramatize the political power of an issue, and that person was fellow Republican Pete Wilson, Governor of California. In his uphill battle for reelection in 1994, Wilson exploited the issue of illegal immigration at a time when a referendum campaign was underway in California to deny them government benefits. In praising a seven-month U.S. Border Patrol "blockade" in El Paso, and asking that it be implemented in San Diego as well, Wilson declared that "if you have the resources, you can in fact control the border" and if congressional leaders had "one-tenth the guts of the illegal immigrants" who crossed our borders each day, they would provide those resources.[47] Also heading toward the November 1994 ballot was a petition drive by Save Our State, which had gathered 600,000 signatures for a Proposition 187 to deny public education and nonemergency medical aid to illegal aliens and to require teachers, health care workers, and the police to report any "apparent illegal immigrants" to federal authorities. Wilson endorsed Proposition 187 and his ploy worked; he soundly defeated his Democratic opponent, who was against the referendum, and forced incumbent Democratic Senator Dianne Feinstein, who expressed concerns about unrestricted immigration but avoided endorsing Proposition 187, to take a stand. In the end, Feinstein narrowly edged out her Republican rival, multimillionaire Michael Huffington (who strongly embraced Proposition 187), even though she chose to oppose Proposition 187 as too draconian a measure.

But the lesson was not lost on politicians that immigration reform was a hot political issue. One author of Proposition 187--which 86 percent of respondents approved in an early *Los Angeles Times* poll—was Harold Ezell, a former regional chief with the Immigration and Naturalization Service, who argued that without social services the illegals would "go back to where they came from."[48] Because of adverse commentary by the media and some political leaders coupled with raucous street demonstrations, backing for Proposition 187 eroded to the point where it won enactment by a 59 percent-41 percent vote margin. Exit polls determined that immigration was even more important than crime or taxes, and people who cited the immigration issue gave nearly two-thirds of their votes to Governor Wilson. Those voting for the referendum did so to send a protest message and force the federal government to deal with illegal immigration, while 41 percent of those who voted against Proposition 187 called it racist. Only the majority of whites (54 percent) backed Proposition 187; Latinos were solidly opposed (78 percent) while African Americans (44 percent to 56 percent) and Asian Americans (46 percent to 54 percent) voted against Proposition 187 though a sizeable minority of both groups showed their support.[49]

Events seem to be moving the country toward Stage III at an alarming pace, and the referenda states are leading the way. Florida had filed a lawsuit against the federal government in April 1994, seeking $1.5 billion in reimbursement for social services provided to illegal immigrants. "The people of Florida are saying, 'Enough,' to paying an unfair share of providing services to illegal immigrants," stated Democratic governor Lawton Chiles (one of the few Democratic incumbents to survive the 1994 GOP landslide): "We refuse to pick up Washington's tab any longer."[50] Similar legal actions were announced by Arizona and California, both with Republican governors, and Texas joined the parade of lawsuits although its governor, Ann Richards (a Democrat who was defeated in 1994) avoided attacking immigrants but rather couched the issue in budgetary terms.[51] A study by the Urban Institute, which the federal government commissioned, found that illegal immigrants in the seven states with the largest numbers (CA, NY, FL, TX, NJ, IL, AZ) contributed $1.9 billion in state and local taxes but the costs to these states was greater. Educating the children of illegal immigrants alone cost $3.1 billion.[52] While it would be convenient to explain the anti-foreign backlash as a rational response to fiscal crisis, many fewer states than the twenty-two with Official English laws have such burdens.

Undoubtedly linguistic politics is intertwined with the immigration issue, and there are many indications that Americans now think that the country needs to halt the flow of illegals and legals. The 1990 Census reported that 14 percent of the 230 million in the United States over age five speak a language other than English at home, a jump of 38.1 percent since 1980. This increase was mainly caused by Hispanic immigration,[53] and it was reported that Hispanic children are less likely than other newcomers to state a preference for knowing English rather than their native tongue.[54]

Negative attitudes toward the "new" immigrants have been recorded in surveys during the 1990s. In June 1993, a *New York Times*/CBS News poll found that 61 percent felt that immigration should be decreased and, moreover, the number of respondents saying that "most of the people who have moved to the United States in the last few years are here illegally" rose from 49 percent in 1986 to 68 percent in 1993.[55] A Gallup Poll of July 1993 found that 65 percent favored a reduction in immigration, a view expressed by 49 percent in 1986, by 42 percent in 1977 and only 33 percent in 1965. Majorities also believed that immigrants "mostly threaten American culture" or "cost the taxpayers too much by using government services like public education and medical services." Such resentment was targeted at recent immigrants, not older immigrant groups: 62 percent said there are "too many" immigrants from Latin American and Asian countries whereas 52 percent indicated that the number from Europe was "about right." Those most hostile towards Latin American immigration tended also to disapprove of President Clinton and were conservatives, Republicans, Southerners, and whites.[56]

While the leading edge of the nativist backlash has strong partisan and ideological overtones, there are enough "liberal" voices supporting Official English to argue that the phenomenon is more universal than particularistic. The national sample in the 1992 National Election Study showed overall that 65 percent favored Official English, and no partisan, ideological, socioeconomic, or racial subgrouping gave less than majority approval for "a law making English the official language of the United States, meaning government business would be conducted in English only" (including 56 percent of liberals). My attempt to use multivariate analysis to pinpoint the key variables was not successful because the model predicted no better than by chance. However "non-Hispanic whites, people with lower educational achievement, and Republicans were more likely to be supporters of official English laws."[57]

One leading proponent of both immigration restrictions and a renewed "Americanization" campaign was Barbara Jordan, the late Congresswoman (D-TX), who served as chair of the U.S. Commission on Immigration Reform. Created by the Immigration Act of 1990 (P.L. 101–649), the Commission's two volume report on legal and illegal immigration expressed a decidedly conservative viewpoint. In 1994, the Commission recommended "that illegal aliens should not be eligible for any publicly-funded services or assistance except those made available on an emergency basis or for similar compelling reasons to protect public health and safety . . . or to conform to constitutional requirements."[58] Prospective employers would be required to verify a job applicant's immigration status through a computer registry based on Social Security and Immigration and Naturalization Service files. And the other recommendations included short-term federal aid to "offset at least a portion of certain identifiable costs to states and localities" from illegal immigration.

Its second report, in 1995, called for slowly cutting legal immigration by one-third from a yearly average of 830,000 to 550,000, and favored allowing the immediate relatives of U.S. citizens (parents, spouses and children under 21) the right to immigrate without a waiting period but eliminated any such preferences for relatives beyond the nuclear family. Although nobody from U.S. English was represented on the Commission, its endorsement of an Americanization effort must have been especially satisfying to them: "The Commission supports effective Americanization of new immigrants, that is the cultivation of a shared commitment to the American values of liberty, democracy, and equal opportunity." In explaining its rationale, the Commission declared that the United States, "one of the most successful multiethnic nations in history" has united "immigrants and their descendants from all over the world around a commitment to democratic ideals and constitutional principles" which "permit and protect religious and cultural diversity within a framework of national political unity." However:

Religious and cultural diversity does not pose a threat to the national interest as long as public policies ensure civic unity. Such policies should help newcomers learn to speak, read, and write English effectively. They should strengthen civic understanding in the teaching of American history for all Americans. They should lead to the vigorous enforcement of laws against hate crimes and of laws to deter and to punish discrimination. Of course, such policies should encourage the naturalization of immigrants as the path to full civic participation.

At the same time, immigration to the United States should be understood as a privilege, not a right. Immigration carries with it obligations to embrace the common core of the American civic culture, to become able to communicate— to the extent possible—in English with other citizens and residents, and to adapt to fundamental constitutional principles and democratic institutions.

The Commission did not endorse Official English, but its future research agenda would include considering "other public policies that are believed by some to encourage ethnocentrism in the name of multiculturalism or to promote political separatism in the name of civil rights. For example: Do bilingual education and affirmative action as applied to immigrants and their children promote or diminish civic unity? Now that immigrants come from more than 160 nations and many more ethnic groups, it is extremely important that public policies facilitate, not inhibit, the Americanization of newcomers."[59]

Official English is an issue that is not particularly salient for most Americans though it carries the potential, given the politics of the moment, to become a highly charged and emotional cause. If anti-immigrant grievances are based on economics, then the contagion of conflict might not have extended beyond a few states with sizeable numbers of Spanish speakers. But this issue is surrealistic to the degree that popular passions can be inflamed by the accumulation of symbolic indignities to the nation.

In 1993, the news stories told us that upwards of 100,000 people chanted "Ingles No!" to express opposition to a law making both Spanish and English the official languages of Puerto Rico.[60] Also that year the media reported that federal district judge Alfredo Marquez, a Hispanic, for the first time in the nation's history permitted the oath for naturalized citizenship to be given in Spanish.[61]

In 1995 it was the highly publicized account of a child-custody dispute in Texas before State District Judge Samuel C. Kiser. The child's Mexican father mainly spoke English but her mother used only Spanish at home, and Kiser declared that the mother was "abusing that child and you're relegating her to the position of housemaid." As he continued: "Now, get this straight. You start speaking English to this child because if she doesn't do good in school, then I can remove her because it's not in her best interest to be ignorant. The child will only hear English."[62] Liberal columnist Bob Green rose in Kiser's defense, saying:

The household maid comment was a dumb thing for the judge to say. But lost in the criticism he received for saying it was the wisdom of the other part of his comment. Because, despite our nation's new devotion to the concept of multiculturalism, people who do not have a proper command of English are, indeed, at a disadvantage—and children who are not taught English early are at a special disadvantage. So much attention is being given to ethnic pride—so many people seem to be more interested in what country they came from than what country they're living in now—that the basic connective value of a common language has been devalued.[63]

Greene then cited efforts by U.S. English to enact Official English because, in its words, " '[a]s the U.S. increases its commitment to cultural diversity, a commitment to the common bond of English becomes more and more essential to maintaining clear, precise communication.' " He concluded with the oblique comment, "In some quarters this notion is somehow regarded as highly controversial."[64] How fast things change. It was seven years ago when the prestige of U.S. English was at a low ebb, reeling from charges of racism during the Arizona referenda campaign and suffering organizational turmoil. Now U.S. English is quoted in the liberal press and never before has its political agenda seemed more appealing.

The Republicans in the House of Representatives did not need much encouragement to curb immigration but the Jordan Committee report gave them added ammunition. The House Judiciary Committee on Immigration and Claims was formulating a bill to cut legal immigration by one-third, requiring that job seekers be eligible to work in this country, and with other restrictions like speeding the deportation of illegal aliens.[65] Whether congressional Democrats will ally themselves with the Republicans as the 1996 election season unfolds or become defenders of linguistic minorities is an open question at this point. On other social issues Democratic presidents have been "constrained not to abandon liberalism" by taking an ambiguous or neutral position against GOP attacks.[66] But President Clinton may not act according to that script.

Bill Clinton campaigned in 1992 as a "new" Democrat but promptly changed to an old-time liberal to promote such controversial issues as gays in the military and restructuring the health care system. His repudiation on Election Day, when Republicans captured both houses of Congress for the first time since 1954, caused Clinton to resurrect a centrist image as he began preparations for the 1996 presidential election campaign. While he generally praised the work of the Jordan Commission and endorsed immigration reductions, Clinton has been mum on specifics other than his earlier position in favor of federal aid to help states pay the costs of imprisoning illegal immigrants.[67] Since immigration reforms and Official English legislation have not been approved by Congress, as yet, Clinton has not had to take a public position on those matters.

As Quebec voters went to the polls to decide a 1995 referendum to separate from Canada (which was barely defeated), House of Representatives Speaker Newt Gingrich (R-GA) made known his views on the subject. "If we don't insist on renewing our civilization, starting with insisting on English as a common language, we are just going to devour this country. Watch the Canadian results today," Gingrich told a business forum in Atlanta. The Quebec referendum was "a serious warning to all Americans that allowing bilingualism to continue to grow is very dangerous and that we should insist on English as a common language," he later told reporters.[68] Speaker Gingrich added that Congress would consider legislation in 1996, which Senate Majority Leader Robert Dole (R-KS) also endorsed, to make English the nation's official language.

Taking issue with that position, Secretary of Education Richard W. Riley charged that "these efforts to make English the 'official' language and to eliminate programs that teach English are more about politics than improving education."[69] But can we expect a courageous defense of bilingualism by President Clinton? Will he employ a veto threat to stop that legislation, and, if faced with the prospect of a veto-proof majority favoring Official English, what are the odds that Bill Clinton will veto the legislation anyway and "go public" to champion the "English-Plus" position? Not great, if his previous actions as governor of Arkansas are any indication.

Bill Clinton was governor when the Arkansas Official English law was passed, but he disavowed that legislation during the presidential campaign. In April 1992, he gave this response to a question via satellite from a reporter attending the annual meeting of the National Association of Hispanic Journalists: "I probably shouldn't have signed the one that passed, but it was passed by a veto-proof majority," Clinton said. "I agreed to sign it only after we changed the law to make it clearer that it would not affect bilingual education, something that I have always strongly supported."[70] Of course, Clinton could have taken a principled stand against the legislation, lobbied to defeat the measure, and, if unsuccessful, forced its enactment over his veto, which is how Governor Romer (D-CO) successfully derailed the 1987 legislative effort in his state.

It seems abundantly clear that the push for Official English at the national level is a Republican agenda, one which has influenced the GOP presidential contenders for the 1996 nomination. These political dynamics confirm that Republicanism and conservatism represent the leading edge of this social movement. As Professor Kenneth Meier succinctly put it, "nativism and its contemporary guise, conservatism, are the driving forces behind this policy movement."[71] The Official English movement, one might add, was a leading indicator that this latest manifestation of nativism would eventuate as a broader anti-foreign backlash. Thus the parallels between the 1920s and the 1980s are quite remarkable.

That we are heading towards a retightening of the nation's immigration laws—a throwback to the National Origins Act of 1924—seems certain. And Official English was a precursor to this policy shift, just as immigration curbs in the 1920s were preceded by efforts to impose literacy tests on newcomers to America. Those who then favored a "restrictionist policy did so not merely, perhaps not primarily, because they wished to reduce the total volume of immigration, but, more important, because they wished to eliminate the 'new' while perpetuating the 'old' immigration. This was the logic of the literacy test."[72] But the literacy test enacted into law over President Wilson's veto in 1917 did not satisfy the forces of nativism, who turned their energies to gaining immigration restrictions.

We do not know whether President Clinton will follow Wilson's example when he is confronted with Official English legislation but, looking ahead, do not expect a Bill Clinton to veto immigration "reforms" during 1996, in the midst of a presidential election campaign. In Congress, the political dynamics today are not much different than they were in the 1920s. Then (as now) immigration controls were promoted by congressional Republicans; the 1924 law was known as the Johnson-Reed Act after its two Senate and House GOP sponsors. But on the final roll, the 1924 Act passed the lower house of Congress by a lopsided 323–71 margin that showed 83 percent of Republicans *and* 81 percent of Democrats voting in the affirmative. Today the congressional Republicans are tightly cohesive, and indications are that very few Republicans in either house of Congress will stand opposed to immigration reform. Democrats may well follow suit, which would mean that the widespread legislative support fueled by anti-foreign hysteria during the 1920s is about to be repeated during the 1990s.

NOTES

1. "Remark on Immigrants Brings Byrd's Apology," *New York Times,* July 27, 1992, p. 8.

2. Both enactments are discussed in Raymond Tatalovich, *Nativism Reborn? The Official English Language Movement and the American States* (Lexington, KY: University Press of Kentucky, 1995), pp. 33–62 and 65–69.

3. Those laws which did threaten the rights of Spanish-speakers in California and especially in Arizona have been nullified by federal courts though ultimately the United States Supreme Court is likely to accept an appeal from one of these states.

4. Tatalovich, *Nativism Reborn?* p. 223.

5. Ibid., p. 237, Table 8.5.

6. Ibid., p. 242.

7. *U.S. English Update,* Vol. XII, No. 2 (Summer 1995): 8.

8. See Tatalovich, *Nativism Reborn?* pp. 200–204.

9. *U.S. English Update,* Vol. XII, No. 2 (Summer 1995): 1.

10. U.S. Department of Commerce, Bureau of the Census, *Population Estimates by Race and Hispanic Origin for States, Metropolitan Areas, and Selected Counties, 1980–1985,* Current Population Reports Series P-25, no. 1040–RD-1 (Washington, DC: U.S. Government Printing Office, 1989), p. 69.

11. Earl Black and Merle Black, "The Wallace Vote in Alabama: A Multiple Regression Analysis," *Journal of Politics* 35 (August 1973): 730–36; Robert A. Schoenberger and David R. Segal, "The Ecology of Dissent: The Southern Wallace Vote in 1968," *Midwest Journal of Political Science* 15 (August 1971): 583–86; Michael W. Giles and Melanie Buckner, "David Duke and Black Threat: An Old Hypothesis Revisited," *Journal of Politics* 55 (August 1993): 702–13.

12. John Higham, *Strangers in the Land: Patterns of American Nativism, 1860–1925* (New York: Atheneum, 1965).

13. Tatalovich, *Nativism Reborn?* p. 72.

14. Tatalovich, *Nativism Reborn?* pp. 71–80.

15. Congressional Record, 68th Cong., 1st Sess., April 12, 1924, vol. 65, part 6, p. 6252.

16. Tatalovich, *Nativism Reborn?* p. 80–83.

17. U.S. Department of Commerce, Bureau of the Census, *Abstract of the Fourteenth Census of the United States, 1920* (Washington, DC: U.S. Government Printing Office, 1923), p. 103.

18. Ibid.

19. U.S. Department of Commerce, Population Estimates by Race and Hispanic Origin for States, Metropolitan Areas, and Selected Counties, 1980–1985, ibid., p. 69.

20. Eric Schmitt, "As the Suburbs Speak More Spanish, English Becomes a Cause," *New York Times,* February 26, 1989, p. E6.

21. Tatalovich, *Nativism Reborn?* pp. 160–68.

22. See Raymond Tatalovich and Byron W. Daynes, eds., *Social Regulatory Policy: Moral Controversies in American Politics* (Boulder, CO: Westview Press, 1988), pp. 210–14.

23. "Dade County Commission Repeals English-Only Law," *New York Times,* May 19, 1993, p. A8.

24. Tatalovich, *Nativism Reborn?* p. 227, Table 8.1.

25. Dario Moreno and Christopher L. Warren, "The Conservative Enclave: Cubans in Florida," in Rodolfo O. de la Garza and Louis DeSipio, eds., *From Rhetoric to Reality: Latino Politics in the 1988 Election* (Boulder, CO: Westview Press, 1992), pp. 127–45.

26. Larry Rohter, "A Black-Hispanic Struggle over Florida Redistricting," *New York Times,* May 30, 1992, p. 6.

27. William Trombley, "California Elections: Prop. 63 Roots Traced to Small Michigan City; Measure to Make English Official Language of State Sprang from Concern over Immigration, Population," *Los Angeles Times,* October 20, 1986, part 1, p. 3.

28. Andy Hall, " 'English' Advocate Assailed," *Arizona Republic,* October 9, 1988.

29. Ibid.

30. Ibid.

31. Ibid.

32. Originally published in France in 1973, there were two printings in the United States in 1975, one in London in 1977, and again in the United States in 1982 and 1984. The title of the 1984 volume, which predated the revelations to Chavez, was Jean Raspail, *The Camp of the Saints: The End of the White Race,* translated by Norman Shapiro (Brooklyn, NY: Revisionist Press, 1984).

33. Andy Hall, "Two in U.S. English Quit over Charges of Racism," *Arizona Republic,* October 18, 1988.

34. Paula D. McClain, "The Changing Dynamics of Urban Politics: Black and Hispanic Municipal Employment—Is There Competition?" *Journal of Politics* 55 (May 1993): 399–414; Paula D. McClain and Albert K. Karnig, "Black and Hispanic Socioeconomic and Political Competition," *American Political Science Review* 84 (June 1990): 535–45.

35. John Higham, *Strangers in the Land: Patterns of American Nativism, 1860–1925* (New York: Atheneum, 1965), pp. 45, 266–67.

36. James Crawford, *Bilingual Education: History, Politics, Theory, and Practice.* (Trenton, NJ: Crane, 1989), pp. 63–65.

37. Jack Citrin, "Language Politics and American Identity," *Public Interest,* no. 99 (Spring 1990): 104–5.

38. Connie Dyste, "The Popularity of California's Proposition 63: An Analysis," in Karen L. Adams and Daniel T. Brink, eds., *Perspectives on Official English* (New York: Mouton de Gruyter, 1990), p. 144.

39. Jack Citrin, Beth Reingold, Evelyn Walters, and Donald P. Green, "The 'Official English' Movement and the Symbolic Politics of Language in the United States," *Western Political Quarterly* 43 (September 1990): 544.

40. Carol Schmid, "The English Only Movement: Social Bases of Support and Opposition among Anglos and Latinos," in James Crawford, ed., *Language Loyalties: A Source Book on the Official English Controversy* (Chicago: University of Chicago Press, 1992), p. 204–6.

41. Citrin, Reingold, Walters, and Green, "The 'Official English' Movement and the Symbolic Politics of Language in the United States," p. 544.

42. Selma K. Sonntag, "Political Saliency of English as Official Language." Paper delivered to the Annual Meeting, Western Political Science Association, Newport Beach, CA, March 22–24, 1990, p. 2.

43. Tatalovich, *Nativism Reborn?* pp. 96–97.

44. Sonntag, "Political Saliency of English as Official Language," p. 2.

45. Tatalovich, *Nativism Reborn?* p. 253.

46. B. Drummond Ayres, Jr., "Dole Sounds a Bold Alarm on Education," *New York Times,* September 5, 1995, p. A8.

47. "Wilson: Border Blockade Works," *USA Today,* April 22, 1994, p. 3A.

48. Seth Mydans, "Californians Trying to Bar Service to Aliens," *New York Times,* May 22, 1994, p. 10.

49. Daniel M. Weintraub, "Crime, Immigration Issues Helped Wilson, Poll Finds; Election: Proposition 187 Wins Among Whites, but Loses among All Other Ethnic Groups, Exit Survey Shows," *Los Angeles Times,* November 9, 1994, part A, page 1.

50. "Florida Sues U.S. over Aid to Aliens," *New York Times,* April 12, 1994, p. A10.

51. Sam Howe Verhovek, "Texas Plans to Sue U.S. over Illegal Alien Costs," *New York Times,* May 27, 1994, p. A7.

52. Deborah Sontag, "Illegal Aliens Put Uneven Load on States, Study Says," *New York Times,* September 15, 1994, p. A8.

53. Felicity Barringer, "Immigration in 80's Made English a Foreign Language for Millions," *New York Times,* April 28, 1993, pp. A1, A10.

54. Deborah Sontag, "A Fervent 'No' to Assimilation in New America," *New York Times,* June 29, 1993, p. A6.

55. Seth Mydans, "A New Tide of Immigration Brings Hostility to the Surface, Poll Finds," *New York Times,* June 27, 1993, pp. 1, 14.

56. David W. Moore, "Americans Feel Threatened by New Immigrants," *Gallup Poll Monthly,* no. 334 (July 1993): 3–5, 13.

57. Tatalovich, *Nativism Reborn?* p. 181. Also see Table 6.1 on pages 178–79.

58. U.S. Commission on Immigration Reform, *U.S. Immigration Policy: Restoring Credibility* (Washington, DC: U.S. Government Printing Office, 1994), p. 115.

59. U.S. Commission on Immigration Reform, *Legal Immigration: Setting Priori-*

ties, Executive Summary (Washington, DC: U.S. Government Printing Office, 1995), pp. 30–31.

60. " 'Ingles, No!' Puerto Ricans Shout," *New York Times,* January 25, 1993, p. A9.

61. "New Citizens Take the Oath in Spanish," *New York Times,* July 3, 1993, p. 7 (photo).

62. Sam Howe Verhovek, "Mother Scolded by Judge for Speaking in Spanish," *New York Times,* August 30, 1995, p. A9.

63. Bob Greene, "In Plain English, Not a Bad Idea," *Chicago Tribune,* September 3, 1995, section 5, page 1.

64. Ibid.

65. Robert Pear, "House GOP Moves to Cut Immigration," *New York Times,* June 22, 1995, p. A10.

66. Tatalovich and Daynes, eds., *Social Regulatory Policy: Moral Controversies in American Politics,* pp. 216–17.

67. Tim Weiner, "Aid Proposed in Jail Costs for Aliens," *New York Times,* April 23, 1994, p. 10.

68. "Gingrich Finds Bilingual Moral in Canada's Secession Ballot," *Washington Post,* October 31, 1995, p. A10.

69. Elizabeth Shogren, "Gingrich Assails American Bilingualism as 'Dangerous,' " *Los Angeles Times,* October 31, 1995, part A, p. 13.

70. Gwen Ifill, "The 1992 Campaign: Reporter's Notebook; Bush and Clinton Spar, but out of Arm's Reach," *New York Times,* April 25, 1992, section 1, p. 10.

71. Tatalovich, *Nativism Reborn?* quote on back cover.

72. Oscar Handlin, *Race and Nationality in American Life* (Garden City, NY: Doubleday, 1957), pp. 75–76.

CAUSATION OF THE NEW NATIVISM
Why Is It Happening Now?

One of the most challenging aspects of the new nativism is to explain why it is happening now. The chapters in this part seek to explain and to provide understanding of today's nativism from several vantage points. Thomas Muller explains it as a function of economic uncertainty, ethnic and cultural differences between new arrivals and the existing population, and a large, sustained inflow of immigrants. Jean Stefancic then describes the crucial role of conservative think tanks and foundations in financing and providing institutional legitimacy for the nativist agenda. Stefancic's work demonstrates the personal and organizational links between the Official English movement and proponents of current immigration reforms. Patricia Zavella focuses on California, describing it as a "paradise lost" for whites as a result of major economic changes. She then documents the lived experiences of two families, one Mexican American and one white, in their own words as they struggle to exist and find meaning in this devastating paradise lost.

6. NATIVISM IN THE MID-1990s

Why Now?
Thomas Muller

Few readers would disagree with the proposition that anti-immigrant sentiment, as expressed in public opinion polls, legislative initiatives and media reports, reached a post World War II peak in the mid-1990s. This discontent was evident in Congress, where a majority is about to revamp the legislation that forms the basis for the nation's immigration policy. Among other measures, the proposed 1995 Immigration Act would limit the number of immigrants admitted annually by about a third.[1]

It is difficult to identify the causes for this apparently sudden political reaction. How can one explain the eruption, when only a few years ago Congress passed, by a comfortable margin, the most liberal Immigration Act since we restricted the inflow of aliens during the 1920s?[2] One approach to understanding the rise of the negative response to recent immigration is to view the current sentiment from a historical perspective.

Comprehending the cyclical character of anti-immigrant fervor provides a framework to explain the combination of forces that shape public opinion on this issue. [For detailed treatment of the historical precursors of today's nativism, see chapters 2 and 9–11 of this volume—*Ed.*] An examination of prior periods when anti-immigrant sentiment peaked—the 1840s, the 1880s, and the 1920s—reveals several common conditions. These include: (1) economic uncertainty and job insecurity among the nation's population, (2) social, ethnic and cultural disparities between new arrivals and the native majority, and (3) a large and sustained immigrant inflow.

Since 1980, about 15 million aliens, mostly Mexicans, Central Americans, and Asians entered in the United States.[3] These immigrants and their children now comprise about 10 percent of the nation's population. However, in some of the larger metropolitan centers, as much as a third of the population are post-1965 immigrants and their descendants. Nationally, three of each ten new workers is an immigrant.[4] This concentration of mostly non-white immigrants has accelerated the outflow of native-born residents from Los Angeles, New York and other cities with large immigrant populations to the outer perimeters of these areas or to sparsely populated states.

ECONOMIC CAUSES OF NATIVISM

The economic mood of the nation in the mid-1990s can best be described as uncertain. Although the sharp economic downturn that marred the first years of the decade has been reversed, several longer term, noncyclical trends have emerged. First, average earnings continue to lag, although unemployment rates have fallen below 6 percent. Second, income has become more concentrated, with the most affluent segment of the population absorbing a larger share of total income. Although immigration has been identified as one potential cause for both phenomena, its role is uncertain. In terms of earnings, recent studies consistently find that the impact of immigrants has been small.[5] Wages of those without a high school education continue to fall relative to those with college degrees. Concurrently, immigrants, particularly Hispanics, comprise a considerable share of the young labor force with limited education. Their presence has contributed, but only modestly, to the widening wage gap. More important factors are technological change, international trade, and deunionization.

To the extent that immigrants contribute to the downward pressure on unskilled worker wages, this effect is concentrated in areas with a large immigrant presence. Hispanics, who typically form the bulk of these workers, absorb a substantial share of reduced earnings. Non-Hispanic immigrants, especially Asians and Europeans, have education and skill levels commensurate with the native population. As such, they are less likely to be part of the low skill labor pool than Hispanics.

Most upper- and middle-class Americans understand that they benefit from low wages paid to immigrants. In their absence, these households would have to pay more for child care, meals in restaurants, clothing, and fresh vegetables from California or Florida. Senior citizens also gain from young immigrants because our elderly population depends on a large labor pool to finance the Medicare and Social Security trust funds. For the elderly, wage disparities attributable to immigration are not an issue.

Because income redistribution is not a widely understood concept, the public does not associate immigration with rising disparities. Changes in income distribution since the 1960s have benefited the most affluent portion of the population, and few noncitizens are among its ranks. For example, the downsizing of large corporations, which is totally independent of immigration, hurts both middle income and lower income employees. Such downsizing, however, is greeted with cheers on Wall Street, and corporate stockholders garner sizable profits from this action.

Rapid technological change, one factor forcing corporate restructuring, is also causing job obsolescence at rates not observed in earlier decades. Transnational capital mobility and the lowering of transit barriers allows American corporations to purchase inexperienced labor overseas, with the products exported to the United States. Compared to global economic and technological changes, immigration does not have a significant role in explaining rising income disparities leading to wealth concentration.

Competition for jobs was a rallying cry of anti-immigrant groups during earlier periods, but is a less emotional issue for most Americans today. Although some continue to believe that foreign-born workers as a group are replacing the native-born work force, there is no empirical data to demonstrate such an effect. Yet the fear of job loss or displacement continues to haunt many, perhaps a majority of American workers. Although most Americans are willing to accept the premise that immigrants not only take jobs but also create employment, job uncertainty and wage stagnation is causing the public to seek a simplistic explanation for these conditions.

Anxiety about low wage jobs is partially muted because in periods of relatively low employment there is little competition for such jobs. Nonetheless some blacks, such as Representative Major Owens (D-NY), have concerns. In 1990, Representative Owens warned that increasing the level of legal immigration was another step in the creation of a permanent underclass. Owens did not persuade others that blacks would be hurt, and the bill he argued against passed Congress by a comfortable majority. In addition to blacks, a few other groups, including associations representing engineers, complained at the time that the presence of foreign-born professionals reduced their employment opportunities. This concern remained unheeded until the 1990s, when lay-offs in defense industries and cutbacks in federally sponsored research curtailed job opportunities for these professionals. Until recently, few skilled, white-collar workers grasped that a new threat to job security emerged: some of their own jobs are being exported to countries with lower wages. Many native-born engineers and programmers are not competing for jobs primarily with foreign-born engineers in the United States (whose earnings are comparable to their own) but increasingly with professionals in other nations functioning as subcontractors to American corporations.

A comparatively new immigration-linked fear is the use of public services by immigrants, particularly illegal aliens. This issue was not in the forefront

when nativism peaked in previous eras because the government sector was
small. Publicly funded social services were not widely available until the
1930s. Although complaints about "paupers" arriving as immigrants
emerged two centuries ago, the current outcry can be traced to California's
fiscal crisis of the early 1990s. The cost of education and welfare was rising
in the state at a time when the economy was stagnating. Proposition 187
passed in part because of public anxiety about the size of the alien population
but also because rising social service costs were attributed to these aliens.

Although lower courts have declared key provisions of Proposition 187
unconstitutional, the political significance of its passage should not be under-
estimated. Since the 1920s, California has set the pace for the nation in
popular culture as well as political movements. It should therefore not be
a surprise that two years after the passage of Proposition 187 Congress
incorporated various limitations on federal assistance for legal aliens.

The service demand issue has been the focus of considerable media attention. Not yet fully resolved are arguments within the academic community as
to whether or not immigrants as a group place a disproportionate demand
on government services. Most of the available evidence confirms the perception that certain groups of immigrants (Hispanics and refugees in particular)
receive a higher proportion of some public services than their share of the
population.[6] This is attributable to both demographic differences (these immigrant groups tend to have large families) and their low income. An often-
quoted study by The Urban Institute concludes that immigrants as a group
create fiscal surplus. A full accounting of all costs and revenues of both the
local and federal level would not, however, reach the same conclusion. On
the other hand, the net public sector "deficit" resulting from the immigrant
presence is relatively small at the national level and concentrated in a few
populous areas of the nation.

To what extent have these economic issues fueled the recent surge of anti-
immigrant sentiment? Whether or not immigrants contribute to rising wage
and wealth disparities is fodder for debate among economists but the general
public has only limited appreciation of these issues. However, the demand
for public services, as demonstrated by the ease with which Proposition 187
passed, is unquestionably on the mind of the voter.

The vast majority of American workers are not impacted directly, or even
indirectly by new immigrants. Therefore, fear that their jobs are threatened
by aliens is not frequently expressed by native-born workers. A more reasonable explanation why economic concerns fan anti-immigrant sentiment is the
frustration of many workers who feel that their earnings are stagnant and
their job insecurity is rising. Unable to identify a specific cause, immigrants
can be seen as a convenient target for some to vent their anger. Although the
sponsor of the 1995 Immigration Act, Congressman Lamar Smith of Texas,

asserts that minority workers may be hurt by alien jobholders, minority job issues are not the underpinning for the anti-immigrant upsurge. Economic conditions were more severe and unemployment rates among blacks and whites substantially higher in both the early 1980s and early 1990s than in the mid-1990s, yet the level of nativism observed now failed to materialize. Although economic concerns can strengthen anti-immigrant sentiment, we need to search elsewhere for the root causes of the nativist resurgence.

SOCIAL DISCONTENT

Segments of the American public, particularly more affluent groups, continue to benefit economically from immigration. These benefits tend to offset politically real or perceived costs of immigration among lower income households. Given this balance, there is little doubt that in the absence of noneconomic concerns, the policy status quo would remain. The surge in nativist sentiment can only be explained by a rise in what can be broadly described as social discontent.

In this and other respects, conditions in the mid 1990s parallel the mid 1920s. The 1924 Immigration Act passed at a time when the national economy had already recovered from the brief but deep postwar recession. The fear that millions of war refugees would swamp the nation never materialized, and industry was again seeking new workers. Organized labor, fearing low wages, continued to press for restriction. But unions held little sway in Congress, where business interests exerted considerable, if not dominant, leverage.

In the more "politically correct" environment of the 1990s, few would admit that the ethnicity or appearance of new immigrants is the basis of their negative views regarding much of the foreign-born population. Until very recently, anti-alien sentiment based on race or ethnicity would not be exposed in public.[7] In contrast to the 1920s, when "racial inferiority" was a belief widely acknowledged by the media, today's environment is not conducive to traditional nativism. Nonetheless, I would argue that the increased visibility of new immigrants, the sight of veiled women in suburban supermarkets, the proliferation of mosques in large cities, the prevalent sound of Spanish in the streets, and the proliferation of small businesses with Korean, Indian, Arabic, and other ethnic advertising have aroused middle-class resentment in the 1990s similar to that observed nearly a century earlier. As the number of the post 1965 immigrants rises and their economic status improves, immigrants move from the urban core outward. This exposes more middle-class suburban Americans to distant languages and alien cultures. Rising discomfort frequently accompanies this exposure.

Language is one of the irritants. The growth of Spanish has now reached a level that the nation is close to being a two-language society, causing added uneasiness among those who believe the English language should have exclusive domain. The role of language in the current environment cannot be ignored. Although new immigrants converse in dozens of distinct languages, only Spanish is perceived as a potential threat to the dominance of English. But because the most populous areas of the nation are de facto two-language societies, legislation to legally establish English as the national language will not slow this trend. The proliferation of Spanish in the media, popular culture and advertising are an indication that the business community, if not government, has recognized the emerging bilingual society. The trend may raise fears among some of a Quebec on the Hudson next century. But most of the counties directly north of the Rio Grande have been predominantly Hispanic for decades, demonstrating cultural fusion rather than fragmentation.

The language and related bilingual education debate, which has been brewing for many years, is not fundamentally nativist. Few can reasonably doubt that a common language has contributed to the ability of the United States to mold earlier waves of immigrants into a coherent society. The fact that a solid majority of ethnic French Canadians voted to separate from the English-speaking provinces shows the hold of culture and language, although both groups have lived in close proximity on two continents for centuries.[8] But neither can one demonstrate that the United States is in danger of being splintered along a fault line of language. The fact that English is now the dominant language of business, science, and politics across all continents only confirms the urgency for new immigrants to learn the language. Nonetheless, some have seized this issue as another reason for restricting immigration.

The mid-1990s case against immigration from the right has been articulated by the *National Review*. The editor of this conservative journal argues that the arrival of aliens has sharpened the sense of ethnic differences and has promoted multiculturalism among native Americans. He further argues that black/white tensions have been exacerbated by other ethnic groups with their focus on multiculturalism.

A glance at the social history of the 1960s suggests that the rise of several black movements during that volatile decade sparked assertions of ethnic identity among other groups, and in particular, among Hispanics. But whatever the sequence of events leading to the focus on group identity, some conservatives believe that large scale immigration will inevitably lead to fragmentation.

Broad, essentially sociopolitical and cultural concerns about immigrants have always been present. These concerns tend to remain dormant until events thrust this discontent above the surface. Several shocks in the early

1990s that depicted the vulnerability of the national fabric strengthened the fear of ethnic division and brought the issue to the forefront. The Los Angeles riots were the first of these events. While parts of the city were smoldering, several commentators identified the root cause of the disturbances as the conflict between Afro-Americans and newly arrived Hispanics.[9] All expressed the fear that more immigrants could exacerbate interethnic strife in Southern California.

The bombing of the New York City Trade Center by Islamic aliens was the first demonstration in decades of how immigration from volatile nations could result in domestic terrorism. The unrelated Cuban and Haitian crises which followed that event precipitated a mass outflow across the sea to the Florida shore. The fear that liberal entry policies could create additional waves of refugees prompted the White House to modify its long standing Haitian refugee policy. Even the Oklahoma City bombing, a product of indigenous violence, fanned fears of international terrorism.

The fragmentation issue has gained considerable support among the many middle-class, politically moderate Americans concerned about racial polarization. Although racial conflict has been a characteristic of the nation since its inception, events in late 1995—the O. J. Simpson verdict, the black male march in Washington, D.C., and the response to these events dramatized the racial divide between blacks and whites. The inability to heal this conflict 130 years after the Civil War raises the serious question of how the nation will deal with more racial diversity. The volatile issue of race relations has become intertwined with immigration policy. Since immigration is the pivotal cause for rising racial and ethnic diversity, the black-white divide is fodder for those anxious to sharply limit immigration.

Interethnic violence raging across the globe from Africa to the former Soviet Union and Bosnia has contributed to the understandable fear that multiethnic societies molded into nations must either fully assimilate or break apart. The United States, we should recall, is atypical of most other countries in this respect. No serious attempt at separation has taken place with the one exception of the North-South struggle culminating in the Civil War. The situation in Bosnia is seen by the media both in terms of religion and nationalism. Given that a considerable number of new immigrants to the United States are Moslem, some can envision the nightmare scenario of a domestic Bosnia in the next century, with the nation fragmented into ethnic enclaves.[10]

THE POLITICAL ARENA

Every cause or movement that garners strong public support quickly finds expression in the political arena. When legislators perceive public discontent on issues such as immigration, there is a rush to sponsor bills aimed at responding to the concerns of their constituents.

When the 1990 Immigration Act was being considered by Congress, groups which opposed the measure such as FAIR (The Federation for American Immigration Reform) could not find influential opponents. Because most of the public was indifferent or unaware of the proposed legislation, the bill was passed with little fanfare and limited debate. As immigration was not on the national agenda, few among the general public were aware that the bill considerably increased the number of annual admissions. Had the measure been delayed for a year or two, the downturn in the economy would have galvanized substantial opposition, and made its passage very unlikely.

The 1992 presidential campaign focused on economic issues, particularly the deep recession, and essentially ignored immigration. In the early stages of the political campaign, Pat Buchanan made an anti-immigration stance a focal point of his platform. However, his "America First" position was not a serious challenge to the Republican political establishment. The party saw no political advantage from what was acknowledged to be a divisive issue. Other established conservatives, including columnist George Will, opposed Buchanan's view. With the Republican nomination of George Bush assured, and the Democratic candidate openly seeking the Hispanic vote in California and Texas, immigration was off the agenda of both parties.

The 1996 presidential race promises to be different. Pat Buchanan again sought the Republican nomination. In the early months of the 1996 campaign, he assured his audience that if elected, all immigration would be halted for five years. As public sentiment has become more nativist, Buchanan's view is likely to find a more receptive audience than in the earlier campaign. An ex-candidate for the Republican nomination, Governor Pete Wilson of California, also staked a claim to the nomination on the basis of his immigration record. Although not opposed to legal immigration, his focus on Proposition 187 indicated that Wilson was seeking support among those in his party concerned about aliens. His withdrawal from the race suggested that one issue candidates have little support.

Senator Dole, the leading candidate of his party, stated that "ethnic separatism" is a threat to American unity. This belief was the basis for his call to have English declared our national language. His comments were a signal that immigration among the mainstream politicians is not as much an economic concern as a social issue.

The beliefs held by these candidates is not to suggest that the Republican Party is dominated by anti-immigrant elements. Newt Gingrich is not anxious to tackle the legal immigration issues, nor is the House Majority Leader, Dick Armey. Governor George Bush of Texas, like his father earlier, takes a dim view of immigration as a political issue. Finally, two well-respected conservatives not running for office, Bill Bennett and Jack Kemp, questioned the wisdom of Proposition 187. In contrast to California, illegal immigrants and their use of public services is of little concern among Texas business interests who are more anxious about promoting trade with Mexico than controlling aliens crossing their border to find work. Bush and other Texans also recognize the political risk of antagonizing the Hispanic population.

The current immigration debate has caused a deep schism among conservatives. This division is by no means new. Conservative business leaders such as Andrew Carnegie spoke on behalf of immigrants a century ago while other wealthy conservatives were anxious to stop all immigration. Some of the most conservative groups continue to support liberal entry, as do several leading business publications including the *Wall Street Journal*. The position of these proponents is that economic benefits associated with open trade and migration outweigh potentially adverse social consequences.

But other conservatives including the editor of the *National Review* argue the opposite, that social costs are high, and the economic benefits minimal.[11] Their position is that the economic benefits are primarily redistributional, with immigration helping the rich while hurting the poor. This neo-Marxian approach is very surprising, given the strident anti-left tone of the *National Review*. Notably, the same publication favors tax and social service policies that would be expected to increase the gap between the poor and the affluent.

Liberals are likewise divided on the issue. For example, Michael Link, the senior editor of the *New Republic,* takes liberals to task for avoiding the immigration debate. His thesis is that both legal and illegal immigrants hurt low wage black and white Americans. Link cites the same sources and arguments as the editor of the *National Review*. Immigration may well be the only subject on which the views of the two editors converge. Hispanic groups are blamed by Link for their political influence on liberals seeking their vote. Asian-owned businesses in minority neighborhoods are criticized for their nepotism, thus hurting job opportunities for blacks seeking work in the ghetto enterprises.

Although many liberals do not share these views, there has been some shift toward an anti-immigrant position. In fact, Link explicitly calls on pro-labor liberals and nonracist populists on the right to unite and jointly back legislation to sharply curtail the flow of immigrants. A well-respected traditional liberal, Arthur Schlesinger, Jr., has also expressed the fear that multiculturalism, likely to increase as a result of immigration, could lead to a "tower of Babel."

The current convergence of the political left and right in their views on immigration is reminiscent of the early 1920s. During this era, business strongly backed open immigration to obtain unskilled labor. Today, business also supports the admission of labor. The one difference is that in today's global economy, it is highly skilled professionals that industry seeks overseas.

The attitude of the President has always been crucial in setting the course of the immigration debate.[12] Therefore, President Clinton's initial positive response to the report of the nonpartisan U.S. Commission on Immigration Reform provides an indication of the national direction. The report issued in the summer of 1995 recommended that the number of legal admissions should be curtailed by about a third. Another recommendation was that employers seeking the admission of workers based on their needed skills pay a substantial fee for the privilege. Both proposals strike one as surprisingly political for a nonpartisan group. The Commission findings and recommendations, as those of the numerous earlier commissions on immigration formed to advise Congress, appear to follow public sentiment. The Commission had the opportunity to gauge public sentiment at a series of public hearings across the nation and their findings may have been influenced by these hearings. The fact that the White House was favorably disposed to the Commission's findings suggests that this position carries some political advantage.[13]

To what extent is the political backlash on immigration attributable to the continuing presence of illegal aliens? Many observers including this writer, expressed the view in 1986 that measures passed by Congress in that year would do little to stem the tide. But Proposition 187 was perhaps less of a protest against illegal aliens than a response to the California economic and fiscal crisis. There is little doubt, however, that the continuing illegal flow has hardened public sentiment on all immigration. Yet the Immigration Reform Commission in its 1994 report to Congress was unwilling to recommend harsh steps necessary to curtail illegal entry.

Any person who spends a week or so at our Southern border recognizes that the current approach of building more barriers and other measures proposed by the Commission to strengthen border enforcement are doomed to failure. To seriously stem the flow could require a reduced pace of economic activity between the United States and Mexico. Slower movement of goods would result from a more intensive border crossing point processing of trucks. Sharp increases in border patrols and surveillance, including the use of military personnel and equipment and severe measures against those who cross illegally and against employers who hire these workers would be essential steps. I am not necessarily advocating these measures, but stating that if the Commission is serious about the problem, it should be willing to publicly admit that such measures, and not their proposed agenda, are essential to seriously reduce the inflow. One has the impression that the Commission and others wish to allay public concerns not by effective, if troublesome, measures to reduce the illegal flow, but by the easier path of reducing legal entry levels.

NATIVISM: THE LONGER VIEW

Given the ebbs and tides in nativist sentiment, predicting the effects of the current wave is a risky proposition. One could well argue that the wave has already crested and will slowly recede following the Congressional debate on immigration and the 1996 election. In the early 1990s, as we have already observed, unexpected events quickly aroused passions. Nonetheless, public attitudes may soften were a sense of job security and economic well-being restored. Were, however, influential conservatives and liberals to join forces to constrain immigration and to link some of the nation's woes to immigrants, the surge would reach a new high before receding.

We know that public attention shifts quickly, and immigration may not be a media subject as other issues take the national spotlight. A hot item of debate today could be quickly discarded and dismissed as of only academic interest within a year. The American public, continually bombarded by various real or fabricated crises, cannot remain focused on any one issue for long.

Some may argue that current nativism is motivated primarily by illegal immigration. Were illegal entry constrained, the concern would presumably be resolved. One has to agree that there is a fundamental non-economic difference between legal and illegal entry. One group enters the nation at the invitation of society, the other violates its sovereignty.

Yet, I could argue that there would be a backlash even in the absence of any illegal entry. It is not as much the legal status of aliens but rather their ethnic, cultural and religious diversity that is the origin of most anti-immigrant sentiment. Senator Alan Simpson who heads the Committee on Immigration expressed this belief, stating that "curbing, even stopping, illegal immigration is not enough."[14]

There is a strong consensus in Congress that illegal immigration should be curtailed. No doubt additional legislation will emerge to discourage illegal entry, although the chances are dim of substantially slowing this flow with legislative action. In part, this is because we are unwilling to recognize that promoting such trade-generating measures as NAFTA encourages illegal immigration. It is, for example, extremely difficult, if not impossible, to inspect the thousands of trucks crossing our borders daily. Business owners and shippers balk at the cost of lengthy crossing delays that careful inspections would require. Similarly, more commercial air and sea traffic increases the difficulty of controlling entry from nations outside the Western Hemisphere. Steps necessary to seriously impair illegal entry and the hiring of illegal aliens would likely be too Draconian for public acceptance. Only in case of a national emergency or an economic depression could such measures be accepted by both conservatives and liberals.

In the short run, the real question is whether or not Congress will pass legislation to reduce legal immigration by a third or more prior to the 1996 election. If this issue is debated by the full House and Senate before the summer of 1996, it is very likely that a version of the Smith bill approved by the House Subcommittee on Immigration would pass and be signed into law. If so, this would represent the first significant success for nativists in many decades.

The legislative outcome will ultimately depend on the ability of conservatives and liberals to forge a temporary alliance on this issue. The immigration debate, as noted earlier, has caused a deep schism among conservatives and liberals. Some of the nation's most conservative press promote liberal immigration, as do the nation's leading business journals. These publications hail free trade policies and favor relatively free movement of labor across the border. Their view is that economic benefits associated with open trade outweigh any potentially adverse social consequences. Other conservatives, led by the *National Review* editors argue that the economic benefits of immigrant workers are limited and offset by their high demand for services. But one suspects that what concerns these opponents of liberal entry is not primarily the well-being of the unskilled ghetto workers but social issues. Multicultural and ethnic divergence is seen as weakening the moral fiber of the nation. Prior to the mid 1990s, these views were muted; more recently, the sentiment has reached center stage.

Notwithstanding various pressures, it is doubtful that strong legislation aimed at illegal entry will materialize. Several forces work against it, including fears that our Constitutional rights may be infringed, resistance from some business interests who utilize undocumented workers, and the difficulty as well as high cost of implementing such legislation. Therefore, illegal entry could rise as legal entry is curtailed because more unskilled workers than now enter legally may be needed, particularly in services.

Groups that comprise today's sanitized nativists are likely to achieve their objective of curtailing legal immigration, but it may be a pyrrhic victory. The size of the current immigrant population assures that the ethnic and racial composition of the population will continue to change significantly even if additional legal immigration is reduced to a trickle. Reducing the flow of these immigrants would slow the process, but given high birth rates among many immigrant groups, the rate of change would remain substantial.

The passage of the 1995 Immigration Act would mark the end of an era—the three decades between 1965 and the mid 1990s—that will leave a deep and permanent imprint on this nation. These decades will be recalled as the time during which the United States permanently shifted from a single language, biracial society to a multiracial, multicultural, and bilingual nation. Only future generations can evaluate the costs and benefits of this profound change. But I would argue that the demographic change will be viewed by future historians as the most important domestic event during the second half of the twentieth century. Nativism in whatever form cannot change this reality.

NOTES

1. H.R. 2202, to be cited as the "Immigration in the National Interest Act of 1995" sets reduced worldwide numerical limits on family sponsored and other categories of immigrants. It also changes the preference system for family members, limits refugee admissions, restricts benefits for aliens, and includes numerous provisions for border enforcement.

2. The 1990 Immigration Act (P.L. 101–649) established a flexible worldwide level of 700,000 visas, a higher number than established in 1965. Changes in the 1990 Act resulted in a 27 percent increase in family-based immigrants between the FY 1987–1991 annual average and the FY 1993 total (U.S. Commission on Immigration Reform 1994 Report to Congress, p. 191).

3. The 15 million count derived as follows:

LEGAL ENTRANTS

FY 1980–FY 1993	11.6 million (INS Yearbooks)
FY 1993–FY 1995 (Est.)	1.7 million
Total Legal 1980–95	13.3 million
Undocumented 1980–95	2.5 million* (Bureau of the Census)
Total	15.8 million

*Assumes two-thirds of all undocumented came between 1980–95.

4. Between 1980 and 1994, 24.2 million new jobs were added to the economy. On the basis of about 15 million new immigrants, approximately 7.3 million immigrant workers were employed.

5. See, for example, Robert H. Topel, *The Impact of Immigration on the Labor Market* (University of Chicago and National Bureau of Economic Research, Cambridge, Mass., January 1988), and Francisco L. Rivera-Batiz, "Substitution and Complementarily between Immigrant and Native-Born Labor in the United States" in *U.S. Immigration Policy Reform in the 1980s*, ed. Francisco L. Rivera-Batiz et. al. (New York: Praeger Publishers, 1991).

6. The proportion of Hispanics attending public schools in California and Texas, as a percentage of the Hispanic population, is considerably higher than among the balance of the population due to larger families among Mexican immigrants and native born Mexicans. The proportion of Hispanics eligible for federal programs aimed at low income households is also larger because a higher percentage than in the general population are below the poverty level. For a detailed analysis of service costs associated with immigrants, see George J. Borjas and Stephen I. Trejo, "Immigrant Participation in the Welfare System," *Industrial and Labor Relations Review* 44 (January 1991).

7. The widely publicized, if controversial *The Bell Curve* by Richard J. Herrnstein

and Charles Murray (New York: Free Press, 1994) brought into the spotlight again the issue of race and intelligence. On the basis of IQ and SAT tests results, the authors show that certain races and ethnic groups score higher than others on these tests. For recent immigrants as a group they calculated the mean IQ to be 95 (somewhat below average), essentially unchanged since the 1960s (p. 359).

8. Quebec nationalists blamed the immigrant vote for the 50.4 percent vote against separation in late 1995. Surveys indicated a preference among immigrant groups for the English language and a united Canada. Had immigrants not voted, Quebec would have approved the referendum to become independent.

9. Edward N. Luttwak, "The Riots: Underclass vs. Immigrants," *New York Times,* May 15, 1992, p. A29 and Joe Kotkin "America on Hold, Can We Learn to Rebuild the Nation?" *Washington Post,* May 31, 1992, p. C1.

10. The December 1995 agreement brokered by the United States and enforced by American troops called for maintaining Bosnia as a multiethnic nation. In fact, the mass transfer of ethnic groups is in full force. As a result, there will be a de facto division based on religion and ethnicity.

11. See, for example, John O'Sullivan, "America's Identity Crisis," *National Review,* November 21, 1994, p. 36.

12. For a discussion of this issue, see Thomas Muller, *Immigrants and the American City* (New York: New York University Press, 1993).

13. The White House has not taken a formal position on the immigration bills being considered by the House and Senate.

14. William Branigan, "Sen. Simpson Offers Overhaul of Legal, Illegal Immigration; Bill Would Limit Employment, Family Sponsorship," *Washington Post,* November 4, 1995, p. A8.

7. FUNDING THE NATIVIST AGENDA
Jean Stefancic

As the essays in this volume show, there are a number of ways one can look at the new nativism. One can see it as a resurgence of the 1920s nativist movement, or as a response to changing demographics in the United States, or as an obsession with eugenics and the need to control reproduction. One can see it in terms of socioeconomic stresses and competition over shrinking resources and jobs. One can see it, even, as America's need to define a new enemy within, now that the Cold War has ended.

This chapter seeks to explore causation in terms of material conditions. I examine the role conservative funding has played in advancing certain aspects of the nativist agenda—in particular the Official English movement, Proposition 187 and related immigration reforms. Conservative money and talent have backed each of these efforts through a linked group of action committees, think tanks, voluntary associations, and foundations, all of which have been manipulating national consciousness in a highly effective manner.

Just as happened during earlier periods of nativist sentiment, today we are seeing a resurgence in calls for maintaining one official language, for denying public benefits to aliens, illegal or not, for regaining control over our borders, and for redefining citizenship more narrowly. Conservative money and action groups have backed all these causes. Where does that money come from? How are the groups related? Who are the key players? How have they been so effective in mobilizing public and political opinion in recent years?

By the end of the century, the number of non-English speakers in the United States is expected to reach forty million. Many believe that the lack of a common language will lead to the fragmentation of society and balkanization. As a result, public interest groups, such as U.S. English, and lobbying groups, such as English First, organized to promote an English Only agenda.

BEGINNINGS

The beginning of the Official English movement, which holds that multilingualism erodes the English language and fragments society to the detriment of our national heritage, is marked by a 1982 proposal by the late Sen. S. I. Hayakawa (R-Calif.) to make English the official language of the United States. Although Congress held hearings over a three year period, Hayakawa's proposals for English language legislation did not pass.

In 1987, the effort was renewed. Six bills were introduced into the U.S. Senate and House to amend the Constitution and make English the official language. Supporters of the English Only movement lobbied and petitioned conservative Republicans, namely Senator Steven Symms of Idaho and then Representative Norm Shumway of California, to endorse several of the six bills. Although none of the bills passed, the issue remained a live one. As of March 1995, a number of bills had been introduced in the 104th Congress to make English the official national language.

The most popular bill, proposed by Rep. Bill Emerson (R-Mo.) with 160 Republican cosponsors, carries an exception to English Only strictly for emergency services. Other bills required that citizenship ceremonies be performed in English, ballots be printed only in English, and bilingual education be ended. Supporters of the bills, such as Daphne Magnuson of U.S. English, believe that an amendment is needed to preserve a common language bond in the United States.[1]

Opponents counter that the Founding Fathers did not place any such provision in the Constitution and that these measures are punitive and divisive. Others, such as James Crawford, author of *Hold Your Tongue,* add that the English Only movement is just another of a long line of coercive measures used to target linguistic minorities which have included Native Americans, Chinese, Yiddish, and now mainly Spanish-speaking persons. Crawford argues that immigrants are learning English faster than ever and that Hispanics have no goal to make Spanish a common language.[2]

BREAKTHROUGHS: CALIFORNIA AND BEYOND

Although an amendment to the U.S. Constitution declaring English the official language of the United States has not been passed, at the state level efforts have been more successful. In November 1986, California passed Proposition 63 by a 3–1 margin, making English the state's official language and requiring that steps be taken to meet that end. Consequently, the California Constitution now requires the legislature to "preserve and enhance the use of English." The initiative was critical to the English Only movement because, of the six states that had passed official English legislation, California was the first to encode this requirement into its constitution. The initiative indicated a sharp departure in that state's stance, since previously California had passed broad legislation protecting those who do not speak English. Over $1,000,000 was spent in support of the California proposition, including $500,000 from U.S. English, the nation's largest and most powerful activist group in the English Only movement.[3] The momentum of the California campaign in 1986 led to the introduction of the six bills at the federal level in 1987.

A BROAD COALITION FORMS

California's momentum also inspired broad action around the country at the state level. New groups formed while established groups redoubled their efforts. U.S. English was founded in 1983 by Dr. John Tanton, a semi-retired Michigan ophthalmologist, and the late Sen. S. I. Hayakawa. Canadian-born and of Japanese ancestry, Hayakawa, a well-known semanticist, became president of San Francisco State University, where he opposed student protests in the 1960s by ripping wires out of a sound truck. Not one to back away from controversy, he further alienated liberals by proclaiming that the U.S. internment of Japanese Americans during World War II was justified. Tanton, on the other hand, for many years was regarded as a moderate liberal activist interested in ecology and population issues. He belonged to groups with overlapping agendas, such as the Sierra Club, the National Audubon Society, Planned Parenthood, and Zero Population Growth. When a group resisted serving one of his interests, Tanton often created a new one. For example, as president of Zero Population Growth, Tanton began to assert that immigration was the main cause of overpopulation. Many members complained; eventually his position became unacceptable to the group. In 1979, he left to found the Federation for American Immigration Reform (FAIR). Then, after FAIR declined to participate in the English Only movement, Tanton—never discouraged—founded U.S. English.[4]

Though FAIR and U.S. English focus on two separate targets (FAIR on the economic consequences of immigration, U.S. English on the cultural divisiveness of official multilingualism), the two issues, states James Crawford, were "inextricably intertwined" in Tanton's mind. And indeed, according to Crawford, not only did the two organizations share the same director—Tanton—but also the same office space, general counsel, PAC treasurer, direct-mail consultant, and funding benefactor.[5]

U.S. English soon grew to a membership of 620,000 nationwide. It strives to make English the official language of the U.S. government through a constitutional amendment, as well as to aid state level campaigns to that same end. Its other goals include "action to end policies which require government agencies to conduct their official business in multiple languages; enforcement of English language and civics requirements for naturalization; English proficiency as a national priority; expanded opportunities to learn English quickly in our schools and in the workplace."[6] U.S. English does not support English-only workplaces, perhaps because the organization realizes that many small and medium-sized businesses would oppose such a rule.

In 1986, Tanton wrote an inflammatory memo for a study group called WITAN, made up of members of U.S. English, FAIR, and like-minded organizations. He derived the name WITAN from the Old English word *witenagemot,* meaning council of wise men to advise the king.[7] The memo asks a series of questions addressing the consequences of immigration in California, including the following:

Will the present majority peaceably hand over its political power to a group that is simply more fertile?

Will Latin American migrants bring with them the tradition of the mordida (bribe), the lack of involvement in public affairs, etc.? What in fact are the characteristics of Latin American culture, versus that of the United States?

[E]thnicity is a more acceptable term than race. It should also be noted that 50% of all Hispanic surname people on the census forms designate themselves as White. So perhaps we should speak of Hispanic Whites and non-Hispanic Whites, to further diffuse the issue. Is Anglo a better term than White? LANGUAGE IS *VERY* important here.

What are the differences in educability between Hispanics (with their 50% dropout rate) and Asiatics (with their excellent school records and long tradition of scholarship)?

Since the majority of the retirees will be NHW [Non-Hispanic Whites], but the workers will be minorities, will the latter be willing to pay for the care of the former? They will also have to provide the direct care: How will they get along, especially through a language barrier?[8]

Although the document was not intended to become public, it was found and published by the *Arizona Republic,* a Phoenix newspaper, a month before Arizonans were to vote on an English Only initiative.

Opponents of U.S. English claimed the memo revealed the true motives of the English Only movement. Arthur J. Kropp, then president of People for the American Way, called for the immediate resignation of U.S. English board members, declaring, "The scandal has laid bare the ugly core of the English-only movement. The real motivation for too many of the movement's leaders is racism, plain and simple. The leaders of U.S. English have grossly misrepresented their real purpose."[9] As a result of the controversy, Tanton, as well as a number of advisory board members who wished to distance themselves, including Linda Chavez and Walter Cronkite, quickly resigned.

U.S. English responded that a majority of its leaders, as well as many of its members were minority group immigrants. How could its policies be racist? In addition, the organization maintained that its support of English only is anti-racist in that it would be discriminatory to print government and official documents in Spanish and English, and not in any of the other 150 languages spoken in the United States.[10] Despite the controversy, scandal, and resignations, U.S. English successfully mounted winning campaigns in the 1988 elections in Florida, Colorado, and Arizona where voters, by small margins, made English the official language in their respective states.

U.S. English underwent significant reorganization during the following two years. Power struggles broke out between Tanton's allies and enemies. An internal audit revealed a misuse of funds; at the time of writing, the IRS was examining U.S. English for discrepancies in tax year 1990.[11] Nevertheless, the organization seems to have weathered the crisis. In January 1991, it commissioned a survey which purported to find 78 percent of registered voters in favor of designating English the official language of government.[12] Following that, it initiated a "Campaign for Our Common Language" to promote such legislation and attracted hundreds of supporters to a rally in Washington, D.C. to lobby for the effort.[13]

Funding for U.S. English comes from membership dues and grants. In 1993, U.S. English reported more than $6,000,000 in contributions, with almost $4,000,000 of that spent on program services.[14] Aside from the $20 membership dues, U.S. English receives funding from the Laurel Foundation and reportedly from the Pioneer Fund.[15] Both groups have supported a number of scholars and projects that focus on race, intelligence, and eugenics, and are intensely controversial.

The Laurel Foundation, established by Mellon heiress Cordelia Scaife May, has supported the Tanton network of organizations over a period of years. Between 1983 and 1989, according to James Crawford's examination of IRS forms 990 and 990-F, Cordelia Scaife May donated at least $5,800,000 to FAIR, U.S. English Foundation (formerly U.S. English), Population-Environment Balance (formerly Environmental Fund), and U.S. Inc. (Tanton's umbrella corporation).[16]

The Laurel Foundation contributed $5,000 toward the distribution of the first U.S. reprint of Jean Raspail's controversial 1973 novel, *Camp of the Saints,* which depicts starving refugees from the Third World swarming over Europe and causing chaotic change and disruption.[17] In addition, Laurel helped fund Garrett Hardin's *Living within Limits: Ecology, Economics, and*

Population Taboos. Hardin is a cofounder of Zero Population Growth and a board member of FAIR, as well as a WITAN participant. An academic with impressive credentials, Hardin supports incentives for sterilization and argues that multiculturalism leads to social chaos,[18] adding a gloss of respectability for positions that, until very recently, could not be uttered.

How else does U.S. English make use of its funds? In addition to agitating for legislative reform, U.S. English sponsors and directs a number of subsidiary groups working for its cause, including Mothers of Multicultural English (MOME), Learning English Advocates Drive (LEAD), and the Institute for Research in English Acquisition and Development (READ). MOME is a New York city group of about six hundred members of different ethnicities, many of whom are immigrant mothers who insist that their children be taught in English only. Director Anita Cloutier de la Garza, not herself Hispanic, is married to a Mexican American surgeon. She argues that to work and function in today's United States, immigrant children must have a thorough command of English which bilingual education impedes.[19]

LEAD, a grassroots California-based advocacy group, was founded in 1987 by Sally Peterson, a Los Angeles Unified School District elementary school teacher. Like de la Garza, Peterson and her fellow teacher-members believe that bilingual education is ineffective and that immigrant children should be taught subjects such as math and history only in English. Why would teachers object so strenuously to a subject that other teachers teach? Part of the reason may be financial: In 1989, LEAD supported an initiative that would have denied special stipends awarded to certified bilingual teachers for their language abilities. Peterson caught the attention of Stanley Diamond, Tanton's successor as chairman of U.S. English, who praised her stand saying that she is "bucking the well-entrenched, institutionalized, bilingual administration." In 1989, LEAD claimed 20,000 members and a budget of less than $25,000, with financial support coming from U.S. English and English First, in addition to its $10 dues.[20]

The READ Institute was founded in 1989 to carry out research into the failings of bilingual education. READ studies purport to show that native-language teaching injures older students by slowing their acquisition of English, resulting in a high dropout rate. The organization urges requirements for bilingual or native-language instruction be rescinded by federal and state government. In 1991, READ received a boost when Rosalie Porter, author of *Forked Tongue: The Politics of Bilingual Education* and director of E.S.L. (English as a Second Language) and bilingual education programs in Newton, Mass., took over as director. Started with a grant of $62,000 from U.S. English, READ also receives support from the Laurel Foundation and English Language Advocates, another Tanton organization. Though Porter concedes that "less than half" of READ's budget comes from U.S. English, she insists that it has not endorsed any political agenda. Board and advisory panel members include Christine Rossell, Boston University political science professor and occasional expert witness on the defects of bilingual education; Abigail Thernstrom, former academic and currently a senior fellow at the Manhattan Institute, who rarely seems to find anything good to say about Hispanic causes; and Richard Estrada, columnist and former research director of FAIR.[21]

English First, a spin-off group of U.S. English, declares itself a lobbying organization and actively engages in working for legislative reform. It was founded in 1986 and currently claims about 100,000 members. The organization, whose logo is the Statue of Liberty, has three basic goals: "make English America's official language; give every child the chance to learn English; and eliminate costly and ineffective multilingual programs."[22]

Members of English First trace the fall from grace to the early 1960s when the federal government passed extensive legislation containing multilingual requirements. In an early fundraising letter, English First described non-English-speaking groups as "remain[ing] stuck in a linguistic and economic ghetto, many living off welfare and costing working Americans millions of dollars every year."[23] The organization justifies its harsh views by quoting immigrants who embrace English and believe that their own language should be used only at home. Funding for English First comes largely from its $28 per year membership dues.[24]

The organization's president, Lawrence Pratt, is a most versatile conservative. In addition to directing English First, he serves as the head of two other lobbying groups, Gun Owners of America and Committee to Protect the Family. Pratt also served as secretary of the Council for Inter-American Security, which believes that the increase in Hispanic immigration is a threat to America. A document issued by the Council in 1986 declared, "Hispanics in America today represent a very dangerous, subversive force that is bent on taking over our nation's political institutions for the purpose of imposing Spanish as the official language of the United States." Pratt attempts to soften his image by pointing out that he is fluent in other languages.[25] (How could one who speaks Spanish, Haitian, or Mandarin be prejudiced against people whose skins are brown, black, or yellow?)

English First has taken a leadership role in English Only efforts in Georgia and Pennsylvania. In April 1995, Jim Boulet, legislative director of English First, wrote to the editor of the *Atlanta Journal and Constitution*, criticizing the English Only bill being considered in the state because it authorized the printing of official documents in other languages other than English and allowed language rights to be enforced in court. Although the bill passed in the Georgia House and Senate, it was vetoed by the governor. In Allentown, Pennsylvania, English First sent 4,000 letters to voters asking for support of city council candidates who backed the city's new English Only law. English First became engaged in what seemed to be a minor local election because HUD was taking an interest in the new law as a possible violation of federal rights.[26]

Recently a third group called English Language Advocates (ELA), has entered the English Only foray, where it has assumed the role of and become a hard-line rival of U.S. English. Standing by his WITAN memo, John Tanton (something of an all-purpose immigrant basher) founded ELA, which campaigned for California's Official English Proposition 63. Chaired by equally versatile Robert Park, who also serves as chair for Arizonans for Official English, ELA is currently appealing a 1994 9th Circuit ruling declaring Arizona's official English initiative unconstitutional. ELA argues that the initiative process strengthens community, and without a common language society is destined to become a Tower of Babel.[27]

KEEP THEM OUT AND BE MEAN TO THEM WHILE THEY'RE HERE

Once English Only measures were in place, many of the same actors turned their attention to other fields. On October 5, 1993, ten people, called together by Ron Prince and California Republican Assemblyman Richard L. Mountjoy, met to talk about illegal immigration.[28] After a day of discussion they agreed to launch a statewide petition for an initiative to deny public benefits to illegal immigrants. Two former top INS officials, Alan Nelson and Harold Ezell, were credited with creating the initiative that came to be known as Proposition 187, but they had quite a bit of assistance. In addition to Nelson and Ezell, others who helped were Prince and Mountjoy, political consultants Robert and Barbara Kiley (the mayor of Yorba Linda), and civilian police employee Barbara Coe.[29]

Prince, Coe, and Bill King, a former INS border agent, then formed the California Coalition for Immigration Reform and chose the name "SOS" (Save Our State) for the campaign, while reportedly eating at a Mexican restaurant.[30] Nelson and Ezell, previously active in immigration reform efforts, established Americans Against Illegal Immigration (AAII), to aid the many grassroots groups that sprang up to support the Proposition 187 campaign. Howard Jarvis Taxpayers Association and Butcher, Forde and Mollrich, the political consulting firm that successfully ran the Proposition 13 campaign in 1978 that limited California property taxes, both made significant contributions to AAII.[31]

Proposition 187, which passed comfortably on November 8, 1994, has several key provisions. The proposition does the following: prohibits illegal immigrants from public schools and universities; bars them from medical care at facilities receiving public funds (preventive and prenatal care are not available, although emergency and maternity care are); requires schools, hospitals and social service agencies to report suspected illegal immigrants (including those who are parents of native born children) to state and federal authorities; and excludes them from social service programs such as disability insurance, family planning, and foster care.

Proponents of the proposition argued that those who violate immigration laws (even children) should not benefit from taxpayer-funded education. California law enforcement organizations opposed to the proposition replied that children who would be excluded from schools would still remain in the state, becoming an unskilled and uneducated class drawn to crime.

Initiative proponents also argued that because health care funding for citizens was already in jeopardy, illegal immigrants should not receive a free ride. However, opponents such as Dr. Brian D. Johnston, secretary of the Los Angeles County Medical Association, argued, "If we do not immunize undocumented children, we will increase the incidence of measles, whooping cough, mumps, rubella, diphtheria, and hepatitis B in all children, not just the undocumented."[32]

TAKING SIDES

Proposition 187 was roundly endorsed by California Governor Pete Wilson, former GOP presidential candidate Patrick Buchanan, the California Republican Party, the California Coalition for Immigration Reform, Stop the Out-of-Control Problems of Immigration Today (S.T.O.P. I.T.), and a grassroots network of groups advocating immigration reform.[33]

Opponents of Proposition 187 included President Bill Clinton, U.S. Senator Dianne Feinstein, Los Angeles County Sheriff Sherman Block, Los Angeles County Board of Supervisors, Los Angeles City Council, the Peace Officers Research Association of California, the California Organization of Police and Sheriffs, California Parent-Teacher Association, California School Boards Association, California State Employees Association, Mexican American Legal Defense and Education Foundation, League of Women Voters, American Jewish Congress, Sierra Club, and the *Wall Street Journal, Los Angeles Times, USA Today, Orange County Register,* and *San Francisco Chronicle.*[34]

In addition, some of California's most powerful institutions opposed the proposition. Taxpayers against 187 was a coalition of four groups that would suffer losses if the initiative passed: California Medical Association, California State Council of the Service Employees International Union, California Teachers Association, and California Labor Federation, AFL-CIO.[35]

Other influential opponents of the initiative included Republican California gubernatorial candidate Ron Unz, who opposed affirmative action, bilingual education, multiculturalism and welfare, but did not support Proposition 187. National conservatives Jack Kemp and Bill Bennett, while stoutly declaring their undying opposition to illegal immigration, nevertheless went on to say "concerns about illegal immigration should not give rise to a series of fundamentally flawed, constitutionally questionable 'solutions' which are not consonant with our history; which would prove ineffectual; and which would help contribute to the nativist, anti-immigration climate." [36] Conservative think tanks such as Empower America also opposed the initiative, as did leaders from the Alexis de Tocqueville Institution and the Reason Foundation who signed a statement in opposition to the initiative. Milton Friedman, Cato Institute's Steve Moore, and representatives of the Heritage Foundation, the American Enterprise Institute, and the Christian Coalition participated in a letter-writing campaign against the initiative.[37]

THE DOLLARS ROLL IN

Funding to oppose Proposition 187 came from a variety of sources: $321,896 from the California Teachers Association, $139,837 from the California State Council of Service Employees, $100,000 from Univision Television Group, Inc., a New Jersey-based Spanish television network with stations in Los Angeles and San Francisco, and $5,000 from Monica Lozano, associate publisher of the Spanish language newspaper *La Opinion.* As of September 30, 1994 opponents of the Proposition had raised $836,937.[38]

Supporters of Proposition 187 raised slightly more than half that amount but apparently used it to better effect. The largest portion of funding in support of Proposition 187 came from institutions and political groups. Of the $486,044 that the campaign raised from January 1, 1993, to September 30, 1994,[39] $136,482 consisted of "in-kind" contributions such as stationary, postage, and signs, of which Assemblyman Richard Mountjoy donated $43,500. Among the largest cash contributions were $86,678 from the Republican party, $27,850 from Mountjoy, $25,000 from California state Senator Don Rogers, and $15,740 from Americans Against Illegal Immigration.[40]

The remainder of the contributions came from a significant number of volunteers, with 58 percent of the individual contributions coming from retirees, totaling $26,904. Consultants attributed retirees' support to their belief that illegal immigrants receive services that come at the cost of reduced benefits for the elderly, their resentment over bilingualism, and their acceptance of reports that illegal immigrants place a heavy burden on taxpayers.[41] The campaign also received $2,000 from Prince to get the campaign started and a loan of $20,000 in May 1994. Coe contributed in excess of $15,000, and the ubiquitous John Tanton donated $100.[42]

HAND IN GLOVE: A FAIR INFERENCE

FAIR caused a great deal of controversy over its endorsement and possible connection with Proposition 187. When the campaign got underway, the coauthor of Proposition 187, Alan Nelson, served as a part-time consultant and lobbyist for FAIR, for which he was paid $70,000. However, Nelson and the executive director of FAIR insist that FAIR had no part in Proposition 187's drafting or the campaign that placed it on the ballot.[43]

The real controversy behind FAIR's backing of Proposition 187 lay in its connection to the Pioneer Fund, which has promoted the eugenics movement and funded research aimed at proving the biological inferiority of minorities. Though FAIR denies it used Pioneer Fund money to support Proposition 187, it received $1,100,000 from the Pioneer Fund between 1982 and 1992, more than $600,000 of it since 1988, making FAIR the second largest of the Pioneer Fund's twenty-two grant recipients.[44]

A VERY SPECIAL ORGANIZATION

Long the world's leading backer of race-IQ research, the Pioneer Fund (which the reader met briefly earlier) has recently resumed its interest in the fate of immigrants. Established in 1937 by Wickliffe Draper, a New England textile industrialist, the Fund's first president, eugenicist Harry Laughlin, was influential in lobbying for anti-immigration legislation in 1924. Laughlin also wrote the Model Eugenical Sterilization Law, subsequently adopted by thirty states, and soon afterward used by the Nazis as a model for their own sterilization program. Soon after receiving an honorary degree from the University of Heidelberg in 1936 for his work in eugenics, Laughlin advocated that Hitler be made an honorary member of the American Eugenics Society. He later supported Senator Joseph McCarthy, fought against the *Brown v. Board of Education* decision, and advocated shipping blacks back to Africa.[45]

More recently, the Fund provided support to Garrett Hardin to write *Living within Limits,* in addition to providing research grants to Phillipe Rushton, Richard Lynn, Arthur Jensen, and Michael Levin, all latter-day eugenicists and architects of race-IQ theories. Many of these authors were cited by Charles Murray and Richard Herrnstein in their recent book *The Bell Curve.* Current president Harry Weyher insists that the Pioneer Fund does not engage itself in, or take any position on, the political issues brought up by such research. It merely gives money to what it considers worthy projects.[46]

The Fund also gives money to the American Immigration Control Foundation (AICF) because, as Weyher admits, both organizations work toward ending Third World immigration. Pioneer has contributed over $200,000 through the years to AICF, and other Pioneer grant recipients serve on the AICF board. AICF recently published John Tanton and Wayne Lutton's *The Immigration Invasion,*[47] a book which may have been inspired by Jean Raspail's *The Camp of the Saints.* FAIR's executive director Dan Stein defends FAIR's financial backing from the Pioneer Fund by saying, "I don't give a s—— what they do with their money. . . . My job is to get every dime of Pioneer's money. . . . And if they [FAIR's critics] don't like what Pioneer is doing . . . why don't they take it up with Pioneer?" He notes that FAIR receives contributions from forty other foundations, including Leland Fikes, Weedan, Carthage, S. H. Cowell, Henry Luce, as well as the Pasadena Area Residential Aid-a-Corporation.[48]

Although FAIR may not have been a major player from the beginning, it quickly became one. As one staffer put it, "These guys at FAIR have come out of nowhere to damn near shape the whole immigration debate." FAIR took credit for the success of four bills in California in 1993: new driver's licenses will not be issued without proof of legal status, increased deportation of undocumented prisoners will be stepped up, local sanctuary decrees will no longer be valid, and government jobs will be denied to illegal immigrants.[49]

As the campaign progressed, more think tanks issued studies. When an Urban Institute report concluded that benefits for the business sector offset the costs of services to illegal immigrants, FAIR changed its approach. Ira Mehlman, FAIR-California media director, stated, "The U.S. is more than an economy. Do we really want a society with a half-billion people in it?" Emphasizing population control, Mehlman continued, "American birth rates are more or less stabilized. Burgeoning growth comes primarily from immigration—two new San Franciscos every year."[50] FAIR has also publicized reports, such as those conducted by Rice University professor Donald Huddle and the Center for Immigration Studies in Washington, D.C., finding that high levels of legal as well as illegal immigration are placing a burden on the environment. Huddle's report was underwritten by Carrying Capacity Network, a nonprofit Washington-based group that calls attention to the connection between environmentalism and population control.[51]

OTHER STATES FALL INTO LINE

After Proposition 187 passed in California, conservative think tanks in other states began to focus on the effects of illegal immigration. Tom Tancredo, president of the Independence Institute, a conservative think tank in Golden, Colorado, declared that the initiative reflected broad-based economic concerns, not racial ones. According to Tancredo, "What we see in this proposition passing in California is part of a bigger phenomenon. There's a strong anti-federal government feeling. The government has been unable to control the border in California. The people voted to take care of the problem."[52] At a conference in Denver, the Independence Institute called for a petition drive to place a measure similar to Proposition 187 before Colorado voters in 1996. Institute representatives reason that Proposition 187, even if declared unconstitutional, is a useful measure around which to unite a conservative constituency, which in turn would support the Institute's program of eliminating bilingual education and multicultural curricula in schools.[53]

Around this time, the Institute issued a study entitled "Compassion or Compulsion: The Immigration Debate and Proposition 187," which found that of the 3.5 million population in Colorado, 142,000 are non-U.S. citizens and about 50,000 are illegal immigrants. It declares that taxpayers in Colorado pay $8 million per year to incarcerate illegal immigrants, between $5 and $13 million per year to educate their children, and as much as $22 million per year for welfare and health care. The study also highlighted the sociopolitical expense of immigration, quoting John O'Sullivan, editor of the National Review: "Immigration and the multiculturalism it feeds are threatening to dissolve the bonds of common nationhood and the underlying sense of a common national destiny, bringing forward the danger of a Balkanized America." Sounding a familiar refrain, Tancredo emphasized that the Independence Institute believes "a common language is an extremely important element of nationhood." (Tancredo and the Independence Institute also call for elimination of bilingual education which they believe is "both educationally unsound and politically divisive.")[54]

DISSENSION WITHIN THE RANKS

Immigration reform at the federal level after the passage of Proposition 187 exposed a sharp division within the Republican Party. Many Republicans, as the reader knows, favor entrepreneurial values and as little government regulation as possible. This faction sees little wrong with immigration, particularly in areas and industries that are heavily reliant on immigrant labor. Another group of Republicans, however, resist spending above all. Immigrants simply cost too much money—money which should be reserved for the needs of those who are already here. Republican leader Jack Kemp predicts, "If Proposition 187 goes national that would be something on which the soul of our party would be decided."[55] William F. Buckley, Jr., founder of the *National Review*, writes that while "the dispute on immigration policy within the right had up until just now exercised itself in the theoretical playing grounds," after the success of Proposition 187, "the two camps are now out in the open, moving towards one another with sabers drawn." [56]

Republicans confronted this conflict almost immediately upon taking control of Congress in January 1995. Invoking their "Contract with America," which they had pledged to bring to a floor vote within one hundred days, Republican leaders opted to eliminate many federal services to legal immigrants, including housing assistance, Medicaid, free childhood immunizations, and subsidized school lunches—sixty federal programs in all. Cato's Steve Moore applauded these developments: "Our belief is that nobody should get these programs, but if welfare is not going to be eliminated outright, then we argue that it should be for citizens only." [57] Shortly thereafter, Senator Richard Shelby (R-Ala.) introduced sweeping reform legislation, the "Immigration Moratorium Act," placing a five-year moratorium on legal immigration, and reducing it by at least two-thirds, down to 325,000 a year instead of the current one million. FAIR executive director, Dan Stein, praised Shelby and insisted that "[w]e will not have real immigration reform unless Congress reduces legal immigration numerically, structurally, and radically." FAIR also predicted that immigration reform will become a key issue in the 1996 presidential election if Congress fails to pass major legislation in 1995. [58]

As we have seen, conservative money and brains have been central to the success of the English Only and immigration reform movements. A collection of think tanks, ad hoc community groups, and lobbyists have shrewdly and effectively manipulated the way America thinks on these issues, producing change in a remarkably short period of time. They solicit money intelligently, targeting different sectors—corporate elites at one end, fearful retirees on tight budgets at the other—with different messages. Just as important, they spend their money wisely, commissioning papers, holding conferences, mailing reports to key legislators, and taking out ads in newspapers, so as to achieve the greatest possible effect.

Most Americans are swayed, not so much by emotional appeals, as by facts. In order to change once cherished beliefs, they need to be convinced that immigrants hurt their job chances, that American culture is under attack, that immigrants consume huge quantities of social services, and that new immigrants do not wish to learn English, whether these are true or not. Most university researchers will not make such bald statements; they know reality is more complex than that. The conservative think tank leaps nimbly into the breach. Unlike a university, the think tank need not compete for funds. Its research is not subject to peer review. Its work may be unabashedly ideological. The conservative think tank, then, supplies the veneer of respectability for the new nativism, making anti-immigrant measures seem sensible, humane, and ethically and economically sound. In the face of the right-wing juggernaut, liberals have marshaled nothing comparable. Liberal philanthropy, with few exceptions, cannot match the dedicated and effective fundraising we have seen on the part of the right. No liberal think tank operating today exhibits the dynamism of Cato or Independence, nor the dogged, half-deluded perseverance of Pioneer. Nor has the left been able to capture the nation's attention through glib phrases and media catchwords, such as reverse discrimination, political correctness, swarthy hordes, carrying capacity, breeding factories, and Tower of Babel.

Unless progressive people mobilize to counteract the slick operators of the right, America's complexion will continue to change as radically as it has done over the past thirty years. We will become a nation whose official policy disdains foreignness, other languages, and other cultures and people.

NOTES

1. Maria Puente, " 'English Only' Movement Picks up Steam," *USA Today,* Mar. 14, 1995, at 4A.

2. James Crawford, *Hold Your Tongue* (Reading, Mass.: Addison-Wesley, 1992), 43–44, 121–29.

3. Gail Diane Cox, " 'English only': A Legal Polyglot," *Nat'l L.J.,* Oct. 26, 1987, at 1; Letta Tayler, States News Service, Dec. 9, 1987, available in LEXIS, Nexis Library, arcnws File.

4. Crawford, *Tongue,* at 150, 151–53.

5. Ibid., at 153.

6. U.S. English Foundation, Inc. and Affiliate, *Financial Statements,* 5 (1993).

7. Crawford, *Tongue,* at 154.

8. John Tanton, WITAN IV Memo, Oct. 10, 1986. Copies of the memo can be obtained from People for the American Way (202) 467-4999.

9. "People For/U.S. English; People for Calls for Resignations from U.S. English Board; Members Include Walter Annenberg, Arnold Schwarzenegger, Saul Bellow," *Business Wire,* Oct. 19, 1988, available in LEXIS, Nexis Library, arcnws File.

10. "U.S. English Slams Bustamante Proposal for Government Operations in Spanish," *U.S. Newswire,* Oct. 17, 1991, available in LEXIS, Nexis Library, arcnws File.

11. U.S. English, *Financial,* at 7.

12. "Poll Shows Americans Overwhelmingly Support Official English," *Business Wire,* Feb. 5, 1991, available in LEXIS, Nexis Library, arcnws File.

13. Katherine Ely, "Common Language Supporters Rally at U.S. Capitol," *U.S. Newswire,* Sept. 17, 1991, available in LEXIS, Nexis Library, arcnws File.

14. U.S. English, *Financial,* at 3. The annual report does not disclose the sources of U.S. English's funding.

15. Michael Pye, *The Scotsman,* Oct. 17, 1994; Salim Muwakkil, "The Ugly Revival of Genetic Determinism," *San Francisco Examiner,* Dec. 6, 1994, at A14; Michael Lind, "Brave New Right," *The New Republic,* Oct. 31, 1994, at 24; Ruth Conniff, "The War on Aliens: The Right Calls the Shots," *The Progressive,* Oct. 1993, at 22.

16. Crawford, *Tongue.*, at 157–58, 267n. 2.

17. Ibid. at 158; Conniff, *War on Aliens.*

18. Crawford, *Tongue,* at 159, 166; Alexander Cockburn, "Follow the Money; Environmental Politics; Beat the Devil," *The Nation,* Sept. 5, 1994, at 225.; and Patrick J. McDonnell and Paul Jacobs, "FAIR at Forefront of Push to Reduce Immigration; Population: Group's Roots are in the Environmental Movement. It is now an Influential Player in Border Issues," *Los Angeles Times,* Nov. 24, 1993, at A1.

19. Wendy Lin, "Choosing the Right Language of Learning," *Newsday,* Oct. 16, 1991, News at 26.

20. Richard Lee Colvin, "A Lead Role in Bilingual Controversy; Teacher's Emphasis on English Puts Her in the Center of Storm," *Los Angeles Times,* June 18, 1989, Metro, part 2 at 1.

21. Crawford, *Tongue,* at 225–28, 275n. 16; Carol Innerst, "Studies Hit Native-Language Education; Bilingual Program Reported Failing," *Washington Times,* Mar. 9, 1995, at A6.

22. *English First,* "Does America Need Official English?" (pamphlet on file with author).

23. Cox, " 'English only.' "

24. *English First,* "Does America Need Official English?"

25. Tayler, *States News Service.*

26. Dan Fricker, "English First Asks Voters to Pick Tropiano, Frey," *Morning Call,* May 14, 1995, at B5.

27. "English Language Advocates Move Swiftly to Define Arizona 'Official English' Amendment," *PR Newswire,* Dec. 12, 1994, available in LEXIS, Nexis Library, curnws File.

28. Gebe Martinez and Doreen Carvajal, "Prop. 187 Creators Come under Closer Scrutiny; Initiative; From Secret Location, Political Veterans and Novices Lead the Campaign against Illegal Immigration," *Los Angeles Times,* Sept. 4, 1994, at A1.

29. Paul Feldman, "Figures behind Prop. 187 Look at Its Creation," *Los Angeles Times,* Dec. 14, 1994, at A3.

30. Martinez and Carvajal, "Prop. 187 Creators."

31. Ed Mendel, "Immigration Control Could Zoom into Law—If Its Time Has Come," *San Diego Union-Tribune,* Aug. 1, 1994, at A1.

32. Paul Feldman, "Proposition 187, Measure's Foes 'Try to Shift Focus From Walkouts to Issues,' " *Los Angeles Times,* Nov. 4, 1994, at A3.

33. Pamela Burdman, "Closing the Door on Illegal Immigrants," *San Francisco Chronicle,* Oct. 23, 1994, at 11/Z1; "Decision '94," *Los Angeles Times,* Oct. 30, 1994, at W9.

34. Ibid.

35. Mendel, "Immigration Control."

36. *Press Conference,* Federal News Service, Nov. 21, 1994, available in LEXIS, Nexis Library, curnws File; James E. Garcia, "Kemp, Bennett Unlikely Allies with Proposition 187," *Austin American-Statesman,* Nov. 20, 1994, at E1.

37. Morton M. Kondracke, "Prop. 187 Is Sinking: Immigration-Bashing to Collapse with It?" *Roll Call,* Nov. 3, 1994; Feldman, "Figures Behind."

38. Susan Ferriss, "Elderly Ante up Most Donations for Prop. 187; But Anti-Immigrant Initiative's Opponents Raise More Funds Overall," *San Francisco Exam-*

iner, Oct. 16, 1994, at A1; Pamela J. Podger, "Ballot Measures Attract Big Money," *Fresno Bee,* Oct. 17, 1994, at B3.

39. Podger, "Ballot Measures."

40. Ferriss, "Elderly Ante Up."

41. Ibid.

42. Martinez and Carvajal, "Prop. 187 Creators"; Pamela Burdman, "Campaign Watch," *San Francisco Chronicle,* Sept. 10, 1994, at A4.

43. Ed Mendel, "Prop. 187 Opponents Question FAIR Funding," *San Diego Tribune,* Sept. 8, 1994, at A4.

44. Paul Feldman, "Group's Funding of Immigration Measure Assailed," *Los Angeles Times,* Sept. 10, 1994, at B3; Alexander Cockburn, "In Honor of Charlatans and Racists; 'The Bell Curve' Pays Tribute to Some of History's Most Notorious Pseudoscientific Hatemongers," *Los Angeles Times,* Nov. 3, 1994, at B7.

45. For an excellent history of the eugenics movement in the United States and its relationship with that in Germany prior to World War II, describing the role of members of the Pioneer Fund, see Stefan Kuhl, *The Nazi Connection* (New York: Oxford University Press, 1994); for articles on the recent activities of the Pioneer Fund, see Adam Miller, "Professors of Hate," *Rolling Stone,* Oct. 20, 1994, at 114; "About the 'Bell Curve,' Footnotes From Hell," *Newsday,* Nov. 9, 1994, at A42; John Sedgwick, "The Mentality Bunker," *GQ,* Nov. 1994, at 228.

46. Harry F. Weyher, "Fund Stays Totally Hands Off," *Toronto Star,* April 23, 1995, at A22.

47. Adam Miller, "About the 'Bell Curve' "; Samuel Francis, "The Usual Suspects against Immigration Reform," *Washington Times,* Aug. 8, 1994, at A19.

48. Conniff, "War on Aliens"; Mendel, "Prop. 187 Opponents."

49. Marc Cooper, "The War against Illegal Immigrants Heats Up," *Village Voice,* Oct. 4, 1994, at 28.

50. Ibid.

51. "Immigration Drains California," *Arizona Republic,* Oct. 1, 1994, at B7.

52. Maureen Harrington, "Coalition Protests 'Racist' Measure; Coloradans Outraged by Calif. Proposition," *Denver Post,* Nov. 11, 1994, at B1.

53. Reuben S. Villegas, "Recapping Busy Week in Latino Community," *Rocky Mountain News,* Nov. 28, 1994, at 3N.

54. Tom Tancredo, "Make a Candidate Sweat—Ask about Illegal Immigrants," *Denver Post,* Apr. 30, 1995, at E1.

55. Michael Doyle, "Wilson Lashed on Immigration," *Sacramento Bee,* Nov. 22, 1994, at A1; Marc Sandalow, "Republicans Battle Over Immigration for 'Soul of Party,' " *San Francisco Chronicle,* Nov. 22, 1994, at A3; Robert Suro, "Kemp Camp vs. Proposition 187; Immigration Issue Splitting the GOP," *The Record,* Nov. 22, 1994, at A18.

56. Robert Suro, "Kemp Camp."

57. Robert Suro, "GOP Would Deny Legal Immigrants Many U.S. Benefits," *Washington Post,* Dec. 24, 1994, at A1.

58. "Senator Shelby Introduces an Immigration Moratorium Bill; Growing Public Sentiment Demands Real Reform," *PR Newswire,* Jan. 6, 1995, available in LEXIS, Nexis Library, curnws File.

8. THE TABLES ARE TURNED
Immigration, Poverty, and Social Conflict
in California Communities
Patricia Zavella

In popular culture, California is the "golden state." Premised on its founding as a state soon after the gold rush, and with the convergence of plentiful sunshine, fertile land, and the importation of water, California has abundant natural resources upon which to build agribusiness, tourism, and eventually manufacturing which attracted those seeking the good life. From the point of view of booster historians, the golden state is replete with stories of early white migrants of European origins, who quickly became the majority, as having found paradise. And in myth and reality, California became the place that invents the future, then markets it to the rest of the world.[1] Sunny California is where new products, new life styles, and new communities were formed, a place where everyone—from dust bowl Oakies to Cambodian peasants to Mixtecos from Oaxaca—could come and find work and a home of their own. California once epitomized the American dream. Currently, however, we hear more about how California living is harsh, no longer the state of golden opportunities, a place where the "rush" is out of the state.

In *Racial Fault Lines*, Tomás Almaguer shows how California history can been seen as a series of racial divides where white supremacy was constructed through racializing discourses and practices, a "fundamental pattern [that] took shape during the last half of the nineteenth century."[2] The new nativism we see in California—expressed through the attempt to pass the English-Only proposition, and more recently in the passage of Proposition 187 and the introduction of the California Civil Rights Initiative—reflects a sense of loss of white control over the affairs of the state. Indeed, Proposition 187 was an explicit attempt to "save our state" from inundation by immigrants, who—in this wave—are predominantly of color. This sense of California as "paradise lost" by white citizens is one of the cultural undertones of the current racial tensions we are experiencing in the state today, especially regarding Latinos. The sense of "loss" is ironic, for from the point of view of people of color, California history has been filled with repression and struggle with the displacement of Native Americans and then Spanish Mexican *Californians* from their land and culture, and the importation of a series of different racial groups—Chinese, Japanese, Filipinos, and more recently, Asians and Latinos from a variety of countries—who were recruited to labor in the fields, factories, and shops.

Once settling in California, Mexican immigrants are stigmatized on the basis of race and gender.[3] Racialization is a process by which social, economic, and political forces determine the content and importance of racial categories, and by which they are in turn shaped by racial meanings.[4] What is new about the fin de siècle nativism is that white supremacy has been undermined by global economic restructuring, which has created tremendous wealth while increasing the vulnerability of white citizens and has spurred the Latinization of California—the massive migration and settlement of Latino workers, increasingly with families who utilize schools and social services. Fueled by populist-inspired political measures that do not address the root causes of these transformations, California has become a site of racial tension and social conflict.

The contemporary sense of loss that originated in the California economy, which beginning in the 1980s, began a process of restructuring that had profound implications for the state and local communities. In particular, the changing Santa Cruz County economy has relied heavily on immigrant labor, and may serve as a case study of the reactions and tensions felt by different demographic and social groups. Two low-income families—Mexican farm workers and a white female single parent—are profiled here, illustrating how these tensions are experienced by human actors.

RECENT CHANGES IN THE CALIFORNIA ECONOMY

One set of changes in the economy is the result of restructuring of particular industries, such as electronics, food processing, and garments, seeking ways to remain competitive in an increasingly global market place where labor costs in the third world, or in the U.S. sunbelt, make California too expensive by comparison. The more dramatic phenomenon is the movement of firms out of the state, especially the labor and/or pollution-intensive activities. A recent study of business migration from California over the past decade estimates job loss at between 168,000 to 224,000, with Mexico receiving over one fourth of those cases.[5] The reasons are fairly well known—high overhead costs in California, especially dealing with industrial waste, water shortages, workers compensation, inflated rents, increasing insurance rates, or rising litigation costs. But the overwhelming factor is the cheaper labor, especially in nearby Mexico. These plant closures brought devastating economic and social dislocations for California communities.

When you couple these job losses with the thousands of jobs lost through military base closures in the 1980s, the picture becomes truly grim.[6] Between 1988 and 1993, twenty-two major bases in fourteen counties have been designated for closure or realignment in California, which affected over 29,000 civilian staff and almost 81,400 military staff.[7]

Another form of job migration has been the loss of expansion in jobs. In electronics especially, the frenzy of introducing new products that will organize our lives and provide instantaneous access to global telecommunications masks uneven internal industrial development. What is less readily apparent are the firms with large market shares and research and development budgets that are expanding employment in areas such as the Silicon Valley or southern California as well as establishing new factories in less expensive areas of the United States. The "Silicon Gulches" or "Silicon Deserts" of the sunbelt offer tax incentives, city sponsored industrial parks, lower housing costs, and especially cheaper labor make for a more attractive site for new factories.[8] The other source of expansion has been to the Third World, especially to the U.S.-Mexico border region.[9] Like electronics, garments and food processing have experienced their own "out sourcing" to the Third World and the sunbelt, and to the extent that they remain in California, increasingly rely on immigrant labor forces.[10]

Less visible are the changes occurring in California agriculture, the "backbone" of the state economy. It is well known that California farms have become efficient producers of capital on the strength of immigrant Mexican labor.[11] California agriculture is a fifteen billion dollar industry that provides the "salad bowl and fruit plate of America." In the late 1980s, the state produced 98 percent of the nation's broccoli, 63 percent of celery, 75 percent of cauliflower, 98 percent of processed tomatoes, and 74 percent of lettuce.[12] The overwhelming majority of California's one million farm workers are migrants from Mexico. Unknown to many Californians, Mexican rural communities have become specialized reproducers of agricultural migrant workers who, with small land holdings, must rely on U.S.-earned wage remittances to ensure basic survival at home. Palerm and Urquiola argue that these two phenomena constitute a "binational system of agricultural production and reproduction," and this relationship is so intertwined that neither link can be correctly understood without reference to the other.[13]

The Bracero Program of 1941–64—an Executive Agreement between Mexico and the United States—initially was designed to make up for World War II-led labor shortages (including the internment of the Japanese), but eventually became Public Law 78 on the basis of growers' pressure for contract workers. In the peak year of 1956, 445,000 Mexican workers were recruited through this program and Braceros (contract workers) averaged 11 percent of all farm labor and 30.2 percent of all hired labor in the state.[14] In important agricultural counties, Braceros formed much larger percentages of the seasonal farm worker population.[15]

During this period in Mexico, hundreds of Mexican men flocked to Bracero recruitment centers. Eventually, peasant small land holders became the core group of Braceros because landless peasants often relocated permanently either to the U.S.-Mexico border region, or settled permanently in the United States. In the central Mexican state of Guanajuato, up to 85 percent of the adult male population in one community had participated in the program. With high local unemployment and favorable wage differentials because of a devalued peso, Braceros received up to ten times the prevailing local wage.

Of more long term consequence, the Bracero program provided migrants with a knowledge base and with personal relationships with employers: these individuals then began to migrate to California on their own, without documentation. With the aid of employers who provided housing or employment letters, many of these early migrants established immigrant communities which would provide the infrastructure of support for other migrants to find jobs, housing, and adjust to life in the United States.

Beginning in the early 1980s, U.S. agriculture experienced a crisis as export markets dissolved, farm prices dropped, and land values eroded, creating severe economic strains on farmers. California farmers survived by shifting to specialized high-value fruit and vegetables and marketing to high income markets such as in Japan. These were labor intensive crops, however, and required the expansion of farm worker jobs. This in turn spurred increased migration from Mexico. Fruit crops have distinct peak harvest periods and tend to create seasonal employment, while vegetable crops tend to create permanent or semi-permanent jobs because production occurs almost the whole year. (With subsidized water and cheap labor, one of the largest farm worker jobs is irrigators, workers who move the irrigation pipes around the fields.)

During the 1980s, Mexico experienced its own economic crisis, precipitated by the decline in oil prices, which resulted in difficulties repaying foreign loans, the devaluation of the peso and increased value of the dollar, defunding of state rural agricultural programs, as well as the stock market crash of 1987. Mexican citizens experienced this crisis in terms of the erosion of real wages, high unemployment in many industrial and service jobs, increased underemployment, and spiraling inflation.[16] Meanwhile, the wage differential between Mexico and the United States had skyrocketed. The only alternative for many was to migrate to the United States, risking apprehension by the Border Patrol. The remittances sent back to home communities in Mexico not only amounted to a significant cash inflow, but enabled remaining household members to survive and to lessen the number of migrating workers. The human capital characteristics of migrants began to change, with more workers with higher education and skill levels and/or urban labor market experience. Beginning in the 1980s, more women began migrating as well, accompanied by male kin or utilizing their own social networks. They too sought work in California fields, or found jobs in food processing, in the service sector, or in urban low-waged jobs.

The availability of long-term jobs has enabled many migrants to establish a second home in California, in which they remain for longer periods of time, and they are increasingly settling permanently. These processes have fueled the *latinization* of rural California, where immigrant farm workers have become the majority population and have changed the character of rural life in these communities.[17] Moreover, increasingly Mexican migrants are originating in indigenous communities in Mexico, with Mixtecs and Zapotecs forming the newest wave of migrants who often experience increased discrimination and exploitation not only by whites but by Chicanos and mestizo Mexicanos.[18] Rural Latino communities have become places of concentrated and persistent poverty, dual societies in which a few Anglos are the landowners, professionals, and white-collar workers. In these communities, social relations—including networks, church affiliations, political differences, and ethnic expressions—often resemble those in Mexico from which the migrants came.

The presence of Latinos in urban areas is somewhat different, in part because they do not form a majority of the population in large cities, but certainly with their barrios and vibrant social and cultural life, migrants are a strong presence as well. Latinos in urban and suburban areas also experience disproportionately high poverty rates, visible even in the third generation after settling in the United States.[19]

Integral to the system of binational production and reproduction is the construction of binational kin relations among Mexicanos. While Mexicans have a long history of utilizing kinship and social networks for support in coping with migration, recently there have emerged "binational households" that maintain homes on both sides of the border and practice income sharing, resource pooling, and mutual assistance.[20] According to one study, 90 percent of Mexican migrants in California sent money to family members, maintained businesses, constructed homes in Mexico, or attracted relatives and friends to California as permanent settlers or seasonal migrants.[21] Household members can move easily between the two countries, not only to find employment but to attend weddings or other social gatherings, a process facilitated by members becoming U.S. citizens or permanent residents. Given the transnational nature of Mexicans' work and family lives, scholars increasingly are abandoning the term "immigrants" for "transnational migrants."[22]

The system of binational agricultural production and reproduction has become further integrated recently through the post-NAFTA economic crisis in Mexico, which sparked another migrant flow[23] and increased American corporate investment in agriculture in Mexico, which has led to some California job loss.[24]

One of the consequences of the economic changes of the 1980s and 1990s was that the U.S. wealthy got richer while the middle and working classes saw real wages decline and became vulnerable, unable to survive health catastrophes or struggling to pay rising college fees for their children or the purchase of new homes in rising housing markets. This widening class divide is exacerbated by a transference of wealth along racial lines, as family incomes and net worth increased for whites overall, while they fell among blacks and Latinos.[25]

The poor, meanwhile, fell further behind. One study found that 12.5 percent, or 3.6 million, Californians lived in poverty in 1989: "By 1992, California was experiencing the worst economic downturn since the Great Depression: 4.9 million Californians (15.9 percent) lived in poverty, including one out of every four children."[26] It has been estimated that 2.7 million Californians use emergency food services, and nearly half of low-income California families spend at least 70 percent of their income on housing.[27] Using 1993 population and income date, Linda Neuhauser and her colleagues conservatively estimate that "8,400,000 Californians are 'food-insecure'—that is, they may have uncertain access to adequate food through normal channels and are at risk of some degree of hunger."[28] People of color have disproportionately high poverty rates. In one study where the poverty rate was 12.2 percent for whites, it was 33.1 percent for African Americans, 30.6 percent for Hispanics, and 15.3 percent for Asians.[29] And the statistic that too often gets overlooked: most poor people are white.

Some scholars are arguing that these changes are not the product of cycles of expansion and recession but reflect more serious structural changes in the California economy. Regional Planner Stephen Cohen and his colleagues predicted in 1993 that "a moderate national recovery will not translate into a comparable California recovery,"[30] and indeed their predictions have been realized. Despite the recent announcement that the number of Americans living in poverty dropped by 1.2 million in 1995, the first decline since 1989, California remained the exception. California's 1994 poverty rate of 17.9 percent was essentially unchanged from the previous year, and California was one of the few states where median household incomes actually fell—by 2.1 percent—between 1992 and 1994.[31] With some of the highest housing markets and costs of living in the country, the dream of home ownership is becoming increasingly remote for Californians. The social expectation that hard work would pay off in tangible benefits or economic mobility is not longer applicable to thousands of people.

The California economy might be the basis of social cleavages, but immigration and politics played a role as well. Nationally, Latinos experienced unprecedented demographic growth at nearly ten times the rate of non-Hispanic whites and more than five times that of blacks between 1980 and 1990.[32] In California, we experienced a great deal of that growth in population, with the majority of in-migrants coming from Mexico and Latin America. Data on immigration are notoriously unreliable because of census under counts, especially of the undocumented who make it their business to go unnoticed. Despite this, the census bureau estimates that about half of the national total of undocumented immigrants came to California.[33]

Despite the structural reasons for their immiseration and migration, the media and conservative political pundits worry whether the "brown hordes" of Mexican and Central American immigrants, with their high fertility rates, will soon deplete American jobs and social services and bemoan the "culture of poverty" among the poor.[34]

The most sensitive issue regarding this new wave of immigrants is their possible use of social services. The only public services that undocumented immigrants can receive, however, are emergency medical care, prenatal care and K-12 education.[35] "Except for refugees, immigrants who arrived in the past decade [1980s] receive public assistance at significantly *lower* rates than native-born Americans."[36] Compared to blacks and whites, Latinos receive the lowest amount of cash derived from income-transfer programs such as Social Security, welfare, and unemployment and other social programs.[37] Moreover, when refugees are excluded, immigrant use of public benefits actually *decreased* during the 1980s."[38] The major cost of immigrants settling in California is in the education of their children. These costs, however, are offset by the taxes paid by settled migrant workers, which rise with length of time in the United States. "The average household incomes of both legal immigrants and refugees who entered before 1980 are higher than natives. Overall, annual taxes paid by immigrants to all levels of governments more than offset the costs of services received, generating a net annual surplus of $25 billion to $30 billion."[39]

Despite evidence to the contrary, the concern with abuse of social services was evident in the passage of the 1986 Immigration Reform and Control Act (IRCA). Ostensibly designed to impede illegal immigration, legislators (with grower pressure) allowed for a period of transition, recognizing the importance of migrants to California agriculture. Thus, the Special Agricultural Worker Program provided a window of opportunity for farm workers who qualified to apply for legal permanent residence and eventually U.S. citizenship. The Replenishment Agricultural Worker Program (RAW) allows new immigrant workers to enter the United States between 1990 and 1993, and after working three consecutive seasons, they too would qualify for permanent resident status. The H-2A program allows seasonal workers to be brought in to work temporarily when farmers cannot meet their labor needs. It has been estimated that about one million California Special Agricultural Workers applied for "amnesty" so they could receive permanent residence.[40] Ironically, based upon the hopes of qualifying for the RAW program or possible family reunification legislation passed by Congress, it appears that even more Mexican migrants have moved to California.

The 1994 vote on Proposition 187, where almost 5 million Californians voted in favor, demonstrates a statewide attempt to control the border. Latinos who work, pay taxes and contribute to society certainly felt as they had been disfranchised in this election. It has been estimated that there are 4.5 million non-U.S. citizen Latinos—legal and undocumented—who if they had voted might have significantly altered the outcome of a ballot measure directly affecting them.[41]

Racial and class divides are clearly evident in California today. Middle and working class whites find themselves becoming a minority population, surrounded by immigrants who seem to thrive with their growing numbers, and unable to make the American dream a reality for themselves. In Santa Cruz County, we see these fault lines in microcosm.

SANTA CRUZ COUNTY

With spectacular coastline, accessible beaches with strong surf, and abutting pine-forested mountains, Santa Cruz County has long been an important vacation and retirement area. Tourist infrastructure—beginning with the construction of private rail roads (built with Chinese labor), grand hotels, the now over one hundred-year-old Boardwalk, and a plethora of beach side cottages—was designed for bourgeois pleasures, and luring tourists continues to be a major source of revenue for the county today.[42] Agriculture was the other half of the foundation of the Santa Cruz County economy beginning in the nineteenth century, concentrated in south county. Like their counterparts elsewhere in the state, recruiters sought out Chinese, Japanese, and Filipino workers, who then settled in the area.[43] By the mid-twentieth century, the area experienced a gradual settlement of whites of European heritage who became the majority population. As in other parts of the state, local developers continue to advertise Santa Cruz County as a paradise, a place to shop, have fun, retire, or raise a family.[44]

Mexicans were relatively late arrivals to the area. Donato's study of Mexicans in the Pajaro Valley's schools in south county indicates that in 1930 there were only seven Mexican-descent students enrolled at Watsonville High, followed by eighteen in 1940, fourteen in 1945, and ninety-four in 1950.[45] Unlike large metropolitan areas like Oakland or Los Angeles, without World War II-led industrial development, Santa Cruz County never attracted large numbers of blacks. Donato shows that it wasn't until the late 1950s that Mexican American students became a noticeable group in the Pajaro Valley in south county. When the University arrived in the mid-1960s, Santa Cruz County was a sleepy retirement and agricultural community, with conservatives at the helm, whites in the majority.[46] The pressing political issues centered around zoning and congestion in neighborhoods near the beaches, and there was a decidedly pro-growth sentiment in the political arena.

Beginning in the late 1960s, Santa Cruz County began experiencing a number of dramatic changes. Chicanos and Mexican and Central American immigrants began settling in the area—the latter displaced by immiseration and political turmoil in their home countries; all attracted to jobs in agribusiness and the service sector, and facilitated by social networks and small immigrant communities, such as the Beach Flats, that enabled people to find housing and jobs. In 1973, Spanish-surname students constituted 34 percent of the total enrollment of the local high school, although Mexican American teachers were only 7 percent of the staff. By 1984, Latinos made up 57 percent of total enrollment.[47] Meanwhile there was noticeable "white flight" as Anglos moved to the suburbs, escaping the Latinization occurring in south county.[48] In some south county classrooms today, its hard to find any Anglo students, and the Latino children are predominantly Spanish speakers—that is, children of immigrants. Like other California counties, Santa Cruz found itself suddenly "Latinized"—containing enclaves, where about 30 percent of their residents are Latino. Watsonville in south county is easily a "majority enclave," a city where two thirds of the residents are Latinos—especially during peak harvest season.[49]

The presence of Latinos can be seen in a number of ways. Local outdoor markets, for example, resemble those in the Latin America, with products sold bilingually and varied costumes or accents indicating migrants from far to the south. Even Safeway was spurred into a multicultural response, offering tortillas and other foods for the burgeoning Latino population in a large section of local stores. Unique to Santa Cruz, official census tallies find that 75 percent of the total county population is white, and Hispanics are officially 20 percent. This figure significantly undercounts Latinos, however, especially undocumented immigrants. Local activists argue that south county is 60 percent Latino. In contrast to other counties, the census finds that in Santa Cruz County, blacks are only 1 percent of the population, Asian or

Pacific Islanders are over 3.4 percent, and American Indians are less than 1 percent.[50] Besides the visibility of many Latino residents, there are numerous Latino-run business, a bilingual newspaper, Latino cultural and arts organizations, and increased political clout by Latino activists.[51]

The transformations in populations can be seen in the local labor market. The county economy diversified over time so that agriculture now provides only about a fifth of total employment. The service sector—fueled by Silicon Valley spillover in software development (primarily in small firms) and retail trade, are highly dependent on tourism and provide another fifth each. The public sector and schools (including the University of California) provide 16 percent of all employment, while manufacturing—some generated by electronics production—provides 13 percent of total employment.[52] The better paying jobs—software engineers, professors—are overwhelmingly male and white; while retail clerks, clerical workers, electronics production, or fast food workers are usually female and often of color.[53]

In this diversified economy, unemployment consistently remains high—especially in Watsonville where it has hovered around 22 percent—even as the state is moving out of the recession.[54] As would be expected with low-paying jobs and seasonal industries, official poverty rates are high. Among adults in 1990, 20 percent of Hispanics, 19 percent of blacks and American Indians, and 9 percent of whites and 9 percent of Asians were living in poverty. Seventy-three percent of those who live in poverty in this county are white (these rates are actually lower for Asians and higher for whites in the state as a whole).[55]

As in the robust informal economy, each sector of the economy has race and gender segregation. "Surf City" (the City of Santa Cruz, the county seat) still attracts major sports tournaments and regional day-trippers.[56] Tourist spots are likely to employ Mexican immigrants at the bottom of the job ladder as busboys and gardeners for men, and maids and domestics for women, while waiters and managers in the fancy hotels or restaurants are usually white men or women. There is anecdotal evidence that in some night spots, stereotypically looking "beach bunnies" or "surfers" (those who are blond and blue-eyed) are hired first.

In south county, agribusiness continues to be a major employer, despite contraction in food processing that provoked a strike by Watsonville cannery workers in 1985.[57] Farm workers are over 90 percent Latino, more often male than female;[58] while food processing's race and gender matrix replicates what I found in the late 1970s in the Santa Clara Valley—predominantly Mexican women.[59] Those who found jobs in agriculture became ensconced in the increasingly longer work season, so that Latinos now include long-term settlers and temporary migrants.[60] With the decline of the United Farm Workers union, agricultural wages for some jobs have fallen to below minimum wages, based on piece rates. In 1993 a strawberry picker earned $3.70 an hour plus 60–65 cents per box.

Housing has been a problem in this county. Political initiatives, including the 1978 statewide Proposition 13 and local ordinances that created a countywide green belt and restricted apartment construction (Measure O, passed in 1979), and repeated rejection of rent control—created a situation where rental housing is very limited and expensive. This was exacerbated after the 1989 Loma Prieta earthquake, which destroyed a significant number of housing units, especially in south county. (One-room, unfurnished studio apartments start at $500 and go up; the cost of buying a home is one of the highest in the country, and is beyond the reach of most low-income residents.) Coupled with lax enforcement of building codes, especially in south county, there has been a proliferation of illegal housing units. It is not uncommon to find multiple family households, or very large households of men living in cramped conditions, especially during the harvest season. Farm worker housing is in such demand that attempts to tear down the old, partially renovated Murphy's worker camp was delayed because it would displace two hundred people with nowhere to go.[61] In addition to the lack of housing is the persistence of residential segregation, with several Latino barrios located throughout the county. The Beach Flats, located next to the Boardwalk, is the most visible and is considered a political embarrassment since incoming tourists can see the lack of recreational facilities, overcrowded conditions, and Latino men hanging out on the streets.[62]

Besides the local ordinances and Proposition 13, other political events were important. Grassroots neighborhood organizing, a coalition of liberal-left organizations, and help from the student vote culminated in the "take over" of City Council beginning in the 1981 election. The liberals elected a male socialist, feminist mayor. Since then, local politics has become highly polarized and rancorous.[63] The "progressives" have successfully pushed for increased funding for social services at the expense of business interests, and according to a current city council member, has better social service funding than almost any county or city in the United States. In the mid-1980s when the homeless became a visible national problem, a study conducted on the local homeless made the following observation: That about one third were "the new poor"—that is, white males with relatively high educational levels, another third were displaced mental health patients, and another third were "voluntary street people." The voluntary homeless apparently preferred living on the streets, and found Santa Cruz a congenial place because of the temperate weather (it doesn't snow), forests to camp in, liberal climate offering shelters and soup kitchens, and "quality of street life"—that is, friendly fellow travelers.[64] By 1993, it was estimated that there were over 3,000 homeless people living in Santa Cruz County, with 450 of them being children and youth.[65] The increase in homeless white men can be seen today in a local highly visible labor shape up that used to include mainly Latinos but on some days includes predominantly white men.

Beginning in the 1970s, Santa Cruz County also became a site of gay and lesbian visibility, as local gay and lesbian activists joined the city council electoral campaigns, and pushed for queer-sensitive social services. There is a gay-lesbian-bisexual community center oriented towards youth, a magazine *(Lavender Reader)* which profiles gay and lesbian couples, local businesses and political events, a pride parade (carefully organized so as not to conflict with the one in San Francisco), bars, large entertainment venue (the annual fund raiser, a Gay Evening in May, in local parlance, GEM is held in the Civic Auditorium), and there was an openly gay City Council member. There is talk of a local lesbian baby boom, with births through artificial insemination, and lesbian mothers can find support through local workshops aimed at their special problems. Gay and lesbian leaders have raised community consciousness about "alternative families," and when Queer Nation organized a "kiss-in" demonstration at the mall, they made the point, "were here, we're queer, and we're not going shopping." Santa Cruz has been dubbed a lesbian utopia. Santa Cruz County, then, has become a center of diversity, where race, gender, sexuality and class refract to create various visible "communities"; this particular mix is somewhat unusual for suburban California.

The political discourse about the poor is highly charged and polarized. Along with predictable hand wringing over these demographic, social and political changes, conservatives allege that Santa Cruz is becoming a liberal bastion. They reacted by contesting several liberal-led symbolic fights—whether Santa Cruz should be declared a sanctuary for Central Americans in the mid-1980s, the 1994 infamous "lookism" ordinance that was implicitly about gay and lesbian rights. And the discourse often includes stereotypes about the poor and uses underclass terminology—such as allegations that drug dealers are taking over Beach Flats or that immigrants come here to use social services. Epithets—such as "voluntary homeless," "street bums," or "grunge factor"—are used to blame the homeless for their plight.[66] Coded terms like "the new poor" or "alternative poor"—that is, white people—contain the implicit notion that these people are different from "traditional poor"—that is, people of color.

Besieged by immigrants and the homeless, struggling to fund social services because of recessionary pressures and Proposition 13, increasingly looking to federal support for social agencies, Santa Cruz County's dilemmas are classic Californian. And like in other counties, political pressure recently pushed the City Council to the right. After numerous skirmishes where local business people protested the deleterious effects of street people and local activists protested that the camping ban (in effect since the late 1960s) and inadequate shelters force people onto the streets, the City Council took action. With the Council's blessing, health officials started enforcing ordinances that restrict local organization, "Food not Bombs," from feeding of the poor on the streets. The City Council passed constitutionally questionable ordinances regulating panhandling and forbidding sitting on side walks. (One suggestion was that panhandlers should apply for permits, although that did not pass.) Like San Francisco and Los Angeles, the City of Santa Cruz is now at the vanguard of the regulating the behavior of the homeless, with other communities rushing to copy these local ordinances.

In this complex and shifting local political economy, where the political discourse about poverty has become contested terrain, I have been conducting life histories among the multiracial poor—mainly during 1992–1993 prior to the passage of Proposition 187. I am trying to find the "hidden poor," that is, those who are not homeless and therefore highly visible (there are good national and local studies) or not necessarily fitting criteria for being officially poor, that is the "working poor." I have explicitly sought out "low-income people." Informants, then, self-selected based on their own perceptions that they are "low income." Replicating the major racial groups settling in the area, I am seeking out whites and Latinos—mainly Chicanos and Mexican immigrants.[67] I am trying to get a sense of the practice of daily life—that is, how people manage with low incomes—and whether this varies from cultural constructions of what "family" should be.

These subjects reveal the complex ways they try to support themselves, the contingencies of constructing households where social support and sharing of resources ease their difficulties, and what "family" means in the context of troubled circumstances and underclass ideology in popular culture. The overwhelming pattern is the flexibility of their lives, especially in work, intimate relationships and support networks.

Being poor in this county means that one's relation to the means of production is tenuous at best. Women as well as men struggle and strategize—often unsuccessfully—to find stable jobs with good pay and benefits in the area, or hang on to them in the face of contracting employment. Among the poor, then, there are strata, ranging from those who struggle to make ends meet, at the bottom of the working class, to those provided material aid from the state (such as AFDC, workers' compensation, or social security), to those with informal economy incomes so low that one wonders how they survive. Some fit traditional expectations of the poor with their low educational levels. The poor in this county also include those with very high educational levels—all sixteen of the white people I've interviewed have some college (usually community college courses taken when they were virtually free); a few have college degrees either from Mexico or the United States.

In this county, a college education will not necessarily translate into a good job. A significant percentage of those who are officially poor in this county have a college education. The highly educated Mexican immigrants find themselves especially vulnerable, putting in stints as day laborers before moving up to bilingual semi-professional jobs that are underpaid for their educational requirements or prior experience, and which are often temporary because of soft money funding.

Race is embedded in this social construction of class, including racial difference in experiences (completing an education, finding work in the labor market, or moving to Santa Cruz to begin with). At one extreme are the Mexicanos (particularly the undocumented), with stories of numbing poverty and no job options in Mexico, differential proletarianization and internal migration there, and perhaps domestic violence or male abandonment for women. Immigrants provide classic stories of extraordinary borrowing of resources to make the journey *al norte* harrowing tales of crossing the border, and the final long journey to northern California, avoiding Border Patrol check points and thieves, coping with vehicles breaking down or lying in trunks the whole time. People spend huge amounts on repaying loans back home or becoming documented through unscrupulous lawyers, providing economic and social support to others in similar situations, and living in cramped conditions, often for years at a time. More so than others, Mexicanos are living in the margins, leading, as Leo Chávez says, "shadowed lives." [68] Many travel back and forth between the United States and Mexico, saving the huge sums for bus, air fare or the use of their own cars from their meager incomes. My informants behave like others in this transnational labor pool, supporting businesses or kin in Mexico, and occasionally are able to unite disrupted "binational" families, often a difficult project economically and socially.

The stigmatization of transnational migrants can be seen in their treatment once arriving to the United States. Despite internal variation—regarding educational levels, for example—most immigrants have completed elementary schooling, while a few have college degrees—and different regions of origin in Mexico (most are mestizos from classic sending areas like western Mexico, while others are indigenous people from Oaxaca in southern Mexico), once settling in Santa Cruz County, Mexicanos are treated alike, like "Mexicans." Many informants expressed their anger or fear of verbal or occasionally physical assaults; they have experienced what they characterize as discrimination in hiring, or finding housing, or are forced to work extra hours or tasks without extra pay.

Among the Chicanos, the social construction of race and ethnicity is varied and complex, often in reaction to stereotypes about Mexican immigrants. Second and third generation Chicanos sometimes find little in common with Mexican immigrants (evidenced in statements supporting the regulation of immigrants). These informants often have integrated social networks with whites, and, if their parents are immigrants, may contest aspects of "traditional" Mexican culture while experiencing little economic mobility themselves. Dominique Ponce, for example, found a "good" job with the county as a clerical worker with her high school education, youth, and bilingual skills—a job her mother could never have taken. Yet when Dominique became pregnant, had to return home, and started receiving AFDC, she submitted to her family's strict norms regarding parenting and dating. She characterized moving in with her parents as, "It is really hard." And, while Chicanos will occasionally find discrimination in the labor market or in finding housing, they do not have the same experiences of "super exploitation" described by Mexican immigrants.

The whites also had varied ethnic origins and expressions of ethnic identity, from those who claim none or who only serve ethnic dishes at holidays, to those immersed in or contesting ethnic families.[69] White women often expressed a sense that being single parents was difficult and a concern for their ethnic kin. Sullivan Green, for example, saw her Italian American parents (who wanted her to "settle down") as too "old country." Others, like single parent Esther Strange, contested her parents' Swiss-Lutheran-military strictures that she should marry. (In speaking about ethnicity, white informants often referred to family.)

There are also gender differences, ranging from getting social capital to enter the job market, contending with sex segregated work, and gendered families. Often discouraged from pursuing education, women struggled to move up the job ladder, coping with sexism and poor working conditions. Some women—Mexican, Chicana and white—contested traditional expectations that marriage would provide them with economic stability, for their own experiences showed the fragility of men's employment and of marriages. Others, like Shirley Bywater and Minifred Cadena attempted to fulfill the American dream of intact nuclear family despite the temporary job forays into other parts of the country by their spouses. These women are single-parents in circumstances, but not by self-perceptions. The quotidian struggles of low income families reveal how families are trying to survive in this local political economy.

THE CABAÑAS FAMILY

Lucio Cabañas was born in Jalisco, Mexico, and finished the sixth grade in school. He is thirty-eight years old, lives in Watsonville, and identified himself as "Hispano." Lucio has lived in Santa Cruz County since 1970. When he was fifteen years old, he migrated to Tijuana, then with the help of some relatives, he migrated illegally to the United States (he has since become a permanent resident). He moved to Watsonville and worked in the field for several months. [The quotations that follow throughout this chapter are excerpts from interviews with the referenced person—*Ed.*]

Well, the work ended. In that time we didn't have the right to unemployment benefits, well we worked in the fields. After the season the people would travel back to Mexico, no? Because the work had finished and the little work there was during the winter, well they gave it to the supervisors or persons with more influence. So the majority returned back to Mexico. And being illegal, well we had to suffer on one side [of the border] and then the other, because, well, also we suffered the crossing, not the *coyote* (smuggler), no?

Lucio returned to Mexico and lived in Tijuana with a group of families of fellow workers. He returned to Watsonville and worked in the fields again. He lived in a number of different apartments before meeting his wife, María, and settling down. The Cabañas returned to Mexico to celebrate their church wedding in María's home community.

In 1977, Lucio got a job at the Green Giant food processing factory, where he worked for thirteen years. María worked there as well, and was laid off when he was. During this time Lucio and María had five children, all of whom were born in Watsonville. Lucio was laid off when the factory closed to move operations to Mexico in 1990. He was unemployed for one and a half years, and during this time Lucio took English as a Second Language classes, learned to read and write in English, and received job training in construction. He appreciated learning English and the ability to figure out strategies for how to proceed in finding a job. He found the training in construction, however, of little value (he did not get a job in construction) and he believed that the training was too costly for U.S. taxpayers (of which he was one).

After a long job search, Lucio returned to farm work, picking strawberries. He earns $3.70 an hour plus 60–65 cents per box. He picks between 25 and 26 boxes a day for a total wage of $41.75 a day or about $200 a week. María also attended ESL classes and received some clerical training. She has worked in various jobs, then experienced carpel's tunnel syndrome in her wrist and can no longer work. She has a workmen's compensation case pending and worked part time at a school cafeteria. Meanwhile her mother, who had lived with them for years, became ill and María helped her mother travel to Mexico so she could live in her own home.

Through a process of "down skidding," Lucio and María have become part of the working poor. They did not qualify for AFDC for their U.S.-born children since they were homeowners and were making payments on a car. Yet they were in danger of losing their home and had a hard time making ends meet.

Lucio and other members of his village in Mexico decided that they wanted to form an organization to deal with migrant workers' problems at work and with human rights abuses. Their initial goals were oriented towards their home communities:

We saw the necessity of taking up again the consciousness of those people, especially with those from my village, and we formed a mutual aid committee. Among ourselves we rediscovered the necessities that were lacking in our little village. And what we could do. Then we got together many of the necessities that there were and between—well it was a group of about twenty participants, sixteen or twenty in the committee—that we met periodically and well we did a few projects that lasted a long time.

Eventually, Lucio and María belonged to four other organizations. María was also active in the predominantly Mexicano parent-led demonstrations against the School Board's spending cuts and threats to dismiss teachers. (These demonstrations resulted in the reinstatement of busing of children to school, facilitated when one of the parents discovered some missing funds on a computer print out of the budget.) María explained her participation in these different organizations by saying, "I'm marginalized, but I want there to be justice." Lucio is now working in the United Farm Workers' new organizing campaign. Their oldest daughter is attending a California university, majoring in math, and is doing well in school.

While their political participation may be somewhat unusual, the Cabañas family is very similar to other farm workers in the area regarding their household structure. The recent local survey found that farm worker households are large (6.8 members on average), with 2.6 workers per household. Forty-eight percent are nuclear families, while 41 percent are households formed by extended family groups. Thirty-five percent had full time, year-round employment, while 65 percent had seasonal/temporary farm jobs. The vast majority earned income below the official poverty level (gross averages of $15,203). California farm workers like Lucio and María Cabañas live in overcrowded rural communities characterized by concentrated and persistent poverty, despite their best efforts to improve their lot. While life seems hard to them, it is an improvement over their situations in Mexico, and they came to the United States with expectations that they would struggle to better themselves.

SULLIVAN GREEN

Of Italian American heritage and a strict Catholic family with eight children, forty-two-year-old Sullivan Green was a single parent with one child. Her former spouse was an immigrant from Latin America and Sullivan left the marriage because of domestic violence. Sullivan's early labor market experience included working in fast food, as a retail sales clerk, telephone soliciting, and then in several nurseries, propagating plants, planning landscaping, working as a sales representative, driving a large truck around the northern part of the state, then managing a nursery. Despite her high level of on-the-job training and increased skills, most of these jobs paid close to minimum wage. Meanwhile she took classes part time, working towards a degree in horticulture. Eventually she became certified by the State of California Nurserymen, passing tests in etymology and landscaping. Her best job was working for the City of Santa Cruz, which provided higher hourly wages and medical benefits. She recalled this job with pride. The downtown mall was beautiful with the flowers she planted, and local newspaper articles about her work turned her into a minor celebrity: "We were always in the papers, were admired, and we were respected. And I had full control as an adult, to handling situations and plants and ordering and it was really fabulous. I got to use my education and my learning to its maximum."

The passage of Proposition 13 put her job into jeopardy, and with her "attitude" for asking people not to smash the flower beds, she was told she would be cut back to part-time work. She resigned instead. Her marriage to a man with no English skills, and therefore limited labor market options himself, and birth of her son meant that her part-time jobs in the service sector as waitress or as sales clerk, were even more important. Feeling threatened, her spouse took charge of her wages, then changed the bank account to his name so she did not have access to it. She went back to school, commuting by bus to San Jose State University, thirty miles away: "I decided to go back to school because of that drive, where you're losing your life." As her marriage deteriorated, she quit school three courses shy of her B.A. She has held her current job as a food sales clerk for many years, and her hourly wage is a respectable $9.80 an hour. But her job provides no medical benefits. Because her asthmatic son is often sick, she frequently misses work, and her annual gross income in 1992 was $10,800. Sullivan believed that she would have been more aggressive about pursuing her education if she had been encouraged: "Education was not expected for women. Matter of fact, it was better to do typing, possibly if you needed to work, go to secretarial school or get married and they would take care of you. This was how I was raised. We were not expected to be bright, we were expected just to be women."

After asking her for a residence and job history, I asked the general question, "have you ever experienced any discrimination or prejudice?" Sullivan responded, "sure, living here, because I'm white. It's very interesting. The tables are turned." Sullivan qualified for subsidized housing and lives in an apartment complex in which the overwhelming majority of residents are Latinos. Sullivan considers herself to be racially tolerant, "my parents didn't raise me to believe that all white is right. So therefore the best thing that I thought I could pass to my son would be the same thing. But it doesn't work." Particularly galling is that, in contrast to her own hard work, her neighbors do not seem to follow her example: "Of the sixteen places that are here, there's only three women who work and we're all white. All of us are single moms. Everyone else that lives here are not single parents; they have families and they don't work. Sometimes neither of them [the couple] work."

Moreover, Sullivan and her son experienced a series of rebuffs from their neighbors. Her son was teased by the Latino children, with occasional fights or exclusions from parties, and she characterized this as prejudice. She found that her efforts to work with the parents of the offending children produced few results: "I went over that and said, 'well, we need to work this out. You need to apologize to him; you need to shake hands like this.' But you always have one parent—me—going out there." She felt hurt that her neighbors would not afford her customary courtesies, like informing her when the laundry was free: "All of a sudden, no one seems to understand English, right? Sometimes I get in such a tizzy." Sullivan does not speak Spanish so her attempts to communicate with her neighbors are difficult. And her attempts to get her neighbors to turn down their music received a "patronizing" response: "They say, 'well, you could write a letter and get signatures; we're not too sure it's going to work.' " She characterized these experiences as "subtle things" that heightened her awareness of racial prejudice: "And I understand now. I'm among it. I get to see now how they have felt in their past, or how they feel now. It makes me think, 'now I know what it's like, but no one should ever feel like that.' " These social conflicts, despite her best efforts not to be prejudiced herself, and to teach her son not to name call, is evidence that prejudice is "a social thing," something that "I'm going to rise above."

Sullivan feels extreme pressure by her parents to "just find a nice guy and settle down," yet finds the possibilities for meeting men difficult. She is well aware that as a single parent, the expectations of achieving "normal" social rewards are minimal. "I have no idea what my life has in store for me. My goal is, I want to be a homeowner; I would love to own a house. I would love to have a job where I'm respected and appreciated, and I really want medical benefits. That was on my Christmas list. For me, health insurance would be fantastic. To get a mammogram maybe would be a delight." With over $4,400 in debts, including a student loan, her health takes low priority.

Sullivan could qualify for Medi-cal or food stamps but refuses to apply for several reasons: "I'm trying not to be part of the system. I will take other things that come my way [such as subsidized housing and her son's free lunches at school], but I'm trying to pay my way." Furthermore, "I hate them [eligibility workers] interrogating me, asking all these questions. I dislike that they know everything about me anyway. They make you feel bad, like you're cheating them. Make you feel like a victim. I'm not a victim. I'm a very happy woman and I try to take advantage of being positive on all the things that are given to me. I feel more in control. I feel I'm proud of myself. You don't have to feel as though you're down and out." Her independence and control come at quite a price. Recently her son had a critical asthma attack, in which she had to rush him to the emergency room. "They asked me, 'how are you going to pay for this' and my son's in the back room yelling, 'I'm getting a headache,' then I say 'cash.' 'Are you sure?' I just got paid, and I take out my wallet and lay it down—$480. They'll take my son now." Her sense of fury was mitigated by her belief "that was the hardest thing I ever did, but I never weakened for him. It was a very sad thing."

Sullivan scrupulously manages her money, purchasing clothing and household items at the local flea market, and once a year selling items with her son to generate cash. "We go out to dinner afterwards and we usually break even. It's a fun thing to do, and then we give the rest to the Women's Shelter. That's how I raised him. There's always less fortunate than what we are. And sometimes I tell him, I don't have the money right now. We might be broke, but we're not poor." Despite her difficult economic situation and social tensions in her apartment complex, Sullivan does not want to see herself as a "desperate single mother," someone who says "poor me, I do it all myself." She is proud of her self-sufficiency and distances herself from "the poor." Poor people are people like her neighbors, Latinos with large families, sometimes out of work, receiving food stamps or Medi-cal. To identify with the poor would threaten her self-esteem and force her to confront that her situation of being "broke" is not temporary and continues despite her best efforts. Sullivan attempts to establish some modicum of control over her life and a sense of self-respect despite being in circumstances in which "the tables are turned," she as a white person does not have access to the good life. Despite her good intentions, she resents that others appear to have a free ride.

CONCLUSION

Low-income people in Santa Cruz County experience poverty as multilayered and complex, certainly grounded in the regional political economy which in the early nineties (like the rest of the state) revealed the underside of the California dream. In contrast to underclass theory and popular images about their dysfunctional culture, however, these informants are both active historical agents and vary enormously in lives they construct under extraordinary constraints.

The sense that paradise is lost is a cultural undertone we experience in

California today. Of course this is a one-sided metaphor, for some of "us" believe that the paradise was never accessible. And those of us who feel that they no longer have control over their lives do not realize that this paradise was never under their control to begin with. The myth of the California dream, seemingly played out in real lives, seemed possible as long as the engine of economic growth and unlimited resources drove development. As we now see the mobility of capital, the downsizing of federal resources in base closures and lost military contracts, the inability of cities to house, feed, police, or transport their multiracial populations under scarce resources, the illusionary nature of the California dream is laid bare. Meanwhile, Mexican and white families in California work and struggle toward fulfillment of their own dreams.

NOTES

For their helpful comments on different versions of this chapter, I would like to thank John Borrego, Micaela di Leonardo, Ramón Gutiérrez, Mike Rotkin, and Paule Cruz Takash. Thanks to the UC MEXUS program and the Chicano/Latino Research Center at the University of California, Santa Cruz, both of which provided financial support for this project.

1. Stephen S. Cohen, Clara Eugenia García, and Oscar Loureiro, "From Boom to Bust in the Golden State: The Structural Dimension of California's Prolonged Recession," Working paper 64, The Berkeley Roundtable on the International Economy, University of California, Berkeley, September 1993.

2. Tomás Almaguer, *Racial Fault Lines: The Historical Origins of White Supremacy in California* (Berkeley: University of California Press, 1994), p. 1.

3. This view contrasts with that of immigration theorists who focus on settlement as a process, or who focus on internal variation in the transnational immigrant pool such as gender and legal status. For studies of settlement processes of immigrants, see Douglas Massey, "The Settlement Process among Mexican Migrants to the United States," *American Sociological Review* 51 (1986): 670–85; Leo R. Chávez, *Shadowed Lives: Undocumented Immigrants in American Society* (New York: Harcourt Brace Jovanovich College Publishers, 1991). For a discussion of the importance of gender and legal status, see Pierrette Hondagneu-Sotelo, *Gendered Transitions: Mexican Experiences of Immigration* (Berkeley: University of California Press, 1994).

4. Michael Omi and Howard Winant, *Racial Formation in the United States: From the 1960s to the 1980s* (New York: Routledge and Kegan Paul, 1987), chap. 2.

5. Stephen S. Cohen, Clara Eugenia García, and Oscar Loureiro, "From Boom to Bust in the Golden State: The Structural Dimension of California's Prolonged Recession," Working paper 64, The Berkeley Roundtable on the International Economy, University of California, Berkeley, September 1993.

6. Base closures have been mitigated by federal assistance, most often before job loss actually began. For a discussion of plant closures during the 1980s in California, see Philip Shapira, "The Crumbling of Smokestack California: A Case Study in Industrial Restructuring and the Reorganization of Work," Working paper no. 437,

Institute of Urban and Regional Development, University of California, Berkeley. For a discussion of plant closures in the food processing industry, see Patricia Zavella, *Women's Work and Chicano Families: Cannery Workers of the Santa Clara Valley* (Ithaca: Cornell University Press, 1987), esp. Chapter 6.

7. Cynthia A. Kroll, Josh Kirschenbaum, Mary Corley, Lyn Harlan, et al., "Defense Industry Conversion, Base Closure, and the California Economy: A Review of Research and Planning Activities for Recovery," Institute of Urban and Regional Development, Working Paper 632, February 1995, p. 7. The conversion of Fort Ord in Monterey to educational usage, including the opening of California State University, was the result of over fifteen million in federal funds.

8. For a discussion of Silicon Valley spillover to the sunbelt, see Louise Lamphere, Patricia Zavella, and Felipe Gonzáles, with Peter B. Evans, *Sunbelt Working Mothers: Reconciling Family and Factory* (Ithaca: Cornell University Press, 1993).

9. Patricia Fernández-Kelly, *For We Are Sold, I and My People: Women and Industry in Mexico's Frontier* (Albany: State University of New York Press, 1983); Devon G. Peña, *The Terror of the Machine: Technology, Work, Gender and Ecology in the U.S.-Mexico Border* (Austin: University of Texas Press, 1996).

10. Karen Hossfeld, "Hiring Immigrant Women: Silicon Valley's 'Simple Formula,' " in Maxine Baca Zinn and Bonnie Thornton Dill, *Women of Color in U.S. Society* (Philadelphia: Temple University Press, 1994), pp. 65–94; Louise Lamphere, Alex Stepick, and Guillermo Grenier, eds., *Newcomers in the Workplace: Immigrants and the Restructuring of the U.S. Economy* (Philadelphia: Temple University Press, 1994); Maria Patricia Fernández Kelly and Anna M. García, "Economic Restructuring in the United States: Hispanic Women in the Garment and Electronics Industries," *Women and Work: An Annual Review* 3 (1988): 49–65.

11. Carey McWilliams, *Factories in the Field* (Boston: Little, Brown, 1939); Walter Goldschmidt, *As You Sow* (Glencoe, IL: Free Press, 1947); Ernesto Galarza, *Farm Workers and Agri-business in California, 1847–1960* (Notre Dame: University of Notre Dame Press, 1977); Ernesto Galarza, *Merchants of Labor: An Account of the Managed Migration of Mexican Farm Workers in California, 1942–1960* (Santa Barbara: McNally and Loftin, West, 1978).

12. Ann Foley Scheuring, *A Guidebook to California Agriculture* (Berkeley: University of California Press, 1983), cited in Juan Vicente Palerm and José Ignacio Urquiola, "A Binational System of Agricultural Production: The Case of the Mexican Bajio and California," in Daniel G. Aldrich, Jr., and Lorenzo Meyer, eds., *Mexico and the United States: Neighbors in Crisis* (Berkeley: Borgo Press), pp. 311–66, at 314.

13. Palerm and Urquiola, "A Binational System of Agricultural Production," p. 311.

14. Ernesto Galarza, *Merchants of Labor,* p. 79, cited in Palerm and Urquiola, "A Binational System of Agricultural Production," p. 323–24.

15. There is regional variation in Mexico regarding the length of time that migrants have been coming to work in the United States. In a heavy sending area of Guanajuato, 1930–40 is the time when the Cárdenas administration enforced land reform, which spurred the migration of small peasant farmers to work in the United States, so the period of migration is about sixty years. The migration history of western Mexico (the states of Jalisco, Michoacán, Zacatecas, Colima, Aguascalientes, Nayarit, and Guanajuato) is over one hundred years, initiated by U.S. recruiters who journeyed to Mexico. For a discussion of the history of migration from Guanajuato,

see Palerm and Urquiola, "A Binational System of Agricultural Production," p. 313; for a discussion of migration from western Mexico, see Douglas S. Massey, Rafael Alarcón, Jorge Durand and Humberto González, *Return to Aztlan: The Social Process of International Migration from Western Mexico* (Berkeley: University of California Press, 1987).

16. Alejandro Álvarez Béjar and Gabriel Mendoza Pichardo (translated by John F. Uggen), "Mexico 1988–1991: A Successful Economic Adjust Program?" *Latin American Perspectives* 78:20 (Summer 1993): 32–45.

17. Juan Vicente Palerm, "Farm Labor Needs and Farm Workers in California, 1970–1989," unpublished report for the State Employment Development Department, 1991.

18. Carol Zabin, Michael Kearney, Anna García, David Runsten, and Carole Nagengast, *Mixtec Migrants in California Agriculture: A New Cycle of Poverty* (Davis: California Institute for Rural Studies, 1993).

19. David E. Hayes-Bautista et al., *No Longer a Minority: Latinos and Social Policy in California* (UCLA: Chicano Studies Research Center, 1992); Aída Hurtado et al., *Redefining California: Latino Social Engagement in a Multicultural Society* (UCLA: Chicano Studies Research Center, 1992).

20. Carlos G. Vélez-Ibañez and James B. Greenberg, "Formation and Transformation of Funds of Knowledge Among U.S.-Mexican Households," *Anthropology and Education Quarterly* 23, no. 4 (1992), 313–34; Carlos Vélez-Ibañez, "U.S. Mexicans in the Borderlands: Being Poor without the Underclass," in Joan Moore and Raquel Pinderhughes, eds., *In the Barrios: Latinos and the Underclass Debate* (New York: Russell Sage Foundation, 1993), pp. 195–210; and Juan Vicente Palerm, "Farm Labor Needs and Farm Workers in California." Also see Aída Hurtado, "Variations, Combinations, and Evolutions: Latino Families in the United States," in Ruth E. Zambrana and Maxine Baca Zinn, eds., *Latino Families: Developing a Paradigm for Research, Practice, and Policy* (Thousand Oaks, CA: Sage Publications, 1994).

21. Juan Vicente Palerm, "Farm Labor Needs."

22. These scholars stress the construction of "transnational" lives by Latinos, where economic relations, political power, cultural forms, and identities are situated in and contextualized by Latin American and U.S. social formations. See Roger Rouse, "Making Sense of Settlement: Class Transformation, Cultural Struggle, and Transnationalism among Mexican Migrants in the United States," *Annals of the New York Academy of Sciences* 645 (July 1992): 25–52; Carol Zabin et al., *Mixtec Migrants in California Agriculture.*

23. Esther Schrader, "Peso Plunges Mexico into Uncertainty," *San Jose Mercury News,* November 10, 1995, p. 1C.

24. Kirby Moulton and David Runsten, "The Frozen Vegetable Industry of Mexico," Cooperative Extension Working Paper, University of California, Berkeley, 1986.

25. Rebecca Morales and Frank Bonilla, eds., *Latinos in a Changing U.S. Economy* (Newbury Park, CA: Sage Publications, 1993), p. 1.

26. Linda Neuhauser, Doris Disbrow, and Sheldon Margen, "Hunger and Food Insecurity in California," *California Policy Seminar Brief* 7:4 (April 1995): 3.

27. Linda Neuhauser et al., "Hunger and Food Insecurity in California," pp. 3 and 4.

28. Linda Neuhauser et al., "Hunger and Food Insecurity in California," p. 5.

29. R. A. Zaldivar, "Poverty Rate Hits '90's High," *San Jose Mercury News,* September 7, 1994. In a 1992 survey, approximately 22 percent of Latino families

were living in poverty, compared to 22 percent of blacks, 18 percent of Asians, and 7 percent of Anglos. See David Hayes Bautista et al., *No Longer a Minority*, p. 13.

30. Stephen S. Cohen et al., "From Boom to Bust in the Golden State," p. 3.

31. "Number of Poor in U.S. Declines," *The San Jose Mercury News*, October 6, 1995, p. 4A.

32. Rebecca Morales and Frank Bonilla, eds., *Latinos in a Changing U.S. Economy*, p. 1.

33. *San Francisco Chronicle*, August 7, 1993, p. 1, cited in Stephen S. Cohen et al., "From Boom to Bust in the Golden State," p. 33.

34. For one example of this hysteria, see Michael Meyer, "Los Angeles 2010: A Latino Subcontinent," *Newsweek*, November 9, 1992, pp. 32–33. For a critique of cultural models which blame the poor for their own immiseration, see Maxine Baca Zinn, "Family, Race, and Poverty in the Eighties," in Barrie Thorne and Marilyn Yalom, eds., *Rethinking the Family: Some Feminist Questions* (Boston: Northeastern University Press, 1992), pp. 71–89; Patricia Zavella, "Living on the Edge: Everyday Lives of Poor Chicano/*Mexicano* Families," in Avery Gordon and Christopher Newfield, eds., *Mapping Multiculturalism?* (Minneapolis: University of Minnesota Press, 1996).

35. Estevan Flores, "Research on Undocumented Immigrants and Public Policy: A Study of the Texas School Case," *International Migration Review* 18, no. 3 (1984): 505–23.

36. Michael Fix and Jeffrey S. Passel, with María E. Enchautegui and Wendy Zimmermann, *Immigration and Immigrants: Setting the Record Straight* (Washington, DC: Urban Institute, 1994), p. 6, emphasis in the original.

37. Hayes-Bautista et al., *No Longer a Minority*, p. 166; also see Mark Testa and Marilyn Krogh, "Nonmarital Parenthood, Male Joblessness, and AFDC Participation in Inner-City Chicago" (final report prepared for the Assistant Secretary for Planning and Evaluation, November 1990), p. 83.

38. Michael Fix, Jeffrey S. Passel, et al., *Immigration and Immigrants*, p. 6, emphasis in the original.

39. Michael Fix, Jeffrey S. Passel, et al., *Immigration and Immigrants*, p. 6.

40. Palerm and Urquiola, "A Binational System of Agricultural Production," p. 350.

41. Approximately 4.8 million people voted *yes*, while 3.3 million voted *no* on Prop. 187. See Alexander Cockburn, "Beat the Devil," *The Nation*, December 5, 1994.

42. Sandy Lydon, *Chinese Gold: The Chinese in the Monterey Bay Region*. (Capitola: Capitola Book Company, 1985); Betty Lewis, *Watsonville: Memories that Linger* (Santa Cruz: Otter B Books, 1986, vols. 1 and 2).

43. There is evidence of a few blacks who settled in the area beginning in the nineteenth century. Betty Lewis discusses "Jim Broadis—Runaway Slave," who arrived in Watsonville about 1850, and she mentions a south county place known as "Nigger Hill." During the nineteenth century, there was a local "colored school" for south county black children. See Betty Lewis, *Watsonville* (vol. 2), chapter 12 and (vol. 1), p. 101.

44. One commentator dubbed the Central Coast California's "middle kingdom." See Dan Walters, *California: Facing the 21st Century*, 2d ed. (Sacramento: California Journal Press, 1992).

45. Ruben Donato, "In Struggle: Mexican Americans in the Pajaro Valley Schools,

1900–1979," Ph.D. Dissertation, Stanford University, 1987. Also see in Maria Eugenia Matute-Bianchi, "Ethnic Identities and Patterns of School Success and Failure among Mexican-Descent and Japanese-American Students in a California High School: An Ethnographic Analysis," *American Journal of Education* 95 (1986): 233–55.

46. Michael E. Rotkin, "Class, Populism, and Progressive Politics: Santa Cruz, California, 1970–1982," Dissertation, University of California, Santa Cruz, History of Consciousness Board, 1991.

47. See Ruben Donato, "In Struggle," pp. 82 and 128. Also see Maria Eugenia Matute-Bianchi, "Ethnic Identities and Patterns of School Success and Failure among Mexican-Descent and Japanese-American Students in a California High School: An Ethnographic Analysis," *American Journal of Education* 95 (1986): 233–55.

48. Ruben Donato, "In Struggle," p. 83.

49. See Juan Vicente Palerm, "Farm Labor Needs and Farm Workers in California"; and Paule Cruz Takash, "A Crisis of Democracy: Community Responses to the Latinization of a California Town Dependent on Immigrant Labor," Dissertation, Anthropology Department, University of California, Berkeley, 1990.

50. U.S. Bureau of Census, *1990 Census of Population and Housing: Population and Housing Characteristics for Census Tracts and Block Numbering Areas, Santa Cruz, CA PMSA.* (Washington, DC: U.S. Government Printing Office, 1993), p. 38, Table 8.

51. League of United Latin American Citizens, for example, was one of the plaintiffs in the redistricting suit against the City of Watsonville; activist Celia Organista has a column in the notoriously conservative newspaper, *The Santa Cruz Sentinel.* For a discussion of the lawsuit, see Paule Cruz Takash, "A Crisis of Democracy."

52. Employment Development Department, Annual Planning Information, Santa Cruz Metropolitan Statistical Area, Report, 1990, pp. 8, 11.

53. University of California, Santa Cruz, "Executive Order 11246 Affirmative Action Program for Minorities and Women, September 1, 1994–August 31, 1995," unpublished report.

54. For nonagricultural employment, see Employment Development Department, *Annual Planning Information, Santa Cruz Metropolitan Statistical Area,* 1990, pp. 8, 11; for agricultural employment, see Santa Cruz County Farmworker Housing Committee, County Farm Worker Housing Needs.

55. Children's Network, "The Santa Cruz County Report Card: The State of Our Children, 1992–93," unpublished report, 1993.

56. Community Chautaugua, "Focus Group Report: Tourism," report by the Beach Area Outlook Conference, 1994.

57. See Frank Bardacke, "Watsonville: How the Strikers Won," *Against the Current* (May/June 1987): 15–20. This strike was immortalized in the award winning documentary, "Watsonville on Strike," directed by Jon Silver. Also see Brian Frith Smith, "Stereotypes about Mexicanos in the Mass Media: News Coverage from the Watsonville Cannery Workers Strike, 1985–1987," Honors Senior Thesis in Latin American Studies, 1993.

58. Based on a survey of 688 farm workers and 81 farm worker employees, this study aimed to provide information for the development of farm workers housing in Santa Cruz County by public and private entities, and to help alleviate substandard conditions of existing farm worker housing. Santa Cruz County is eligible for Community Development Block Grants, and housing has been identified as a pressing

need. The Santa Cruz Housing Market Area includes the unincorporated Pajaro, just over the Monterey county line, and other small neighborhoods where many farm workers reside. See Santa Cruz County Farmworker Housing Committee, "Santa Cruz County Farm Worker Housing Needs," unpublished report, 1993.

59. See Frank Bardacke, "Watsonville: How the Strikers Won"; and Frank Bardacke, *Good Liberals and Great Blue Herons* (Santa Cruz: Center for Political Ecology, 1994).

60. Santa Cruz County Farmworker Housing Committee, "Santa Cruz County Farm Worker Housing Needs," p. 10.

61. Marianne Biasotti, "Farmworkers Seek to Keep Camp Open," *Santa Cruz Sentinel,* January 26, 1994, p. 1.

62. See Community Chautaugua, "Focus Group Report: Property Owners," report by the Beach Area Outlook Conference, 1994. Once the focus group reports were compiled, the Beach Area Outlook Conference (sponsored by the Seaside Company which owns the Boardwalk) convened various community forums, whose purpose was to discuss how to redevelop the Beach Area. Several wild schemes were suggested, ranging from constructing a Children's museum (competing with one in San Jose, half an hour away) to building a conference center. Also see Nicole Dubis, "I Am Not Heard Here," Community Studies senior thesis on women in the Beach Flats.

63. See Rotkin, cited *supra* n. 46.

64. These observations were based on a survey of 103 homeless people, as well as in-depth interviews with 31 participants, and interviews with shelter workers and participant observation. See William Friedland and Robert Marotto, "Streetpeople and Straightpeople in Santa Cruz, California: A Report of the Downtown Study," University of California, Santa Cruz, 1985 (unpublished report).

65. *The Santa Cruz Sentinel,* January 14, 1993, cited in Children's Network, "The Santa Cruz County Report Card: The State of Our Children, 1992–93" (unpublished report, 1993), p. 28. Also see Toni Nelson Herrera, "CASAS HOY!" Community Studies senior thesis on women in a Watsonville homeless shelter.

66. Lee Quarnstrom, "It's Time to Get the Bums Off Our Streets," *San Jose Mercury News,* November 20, 1995, p. 1B.

67. I have interviewed 35 individuals thus far: 11 Mexicanos, 10 Chicanos, and 14 whites; all were found through "snowball sampling."

68. Leo R. Chávez, *Shadowed Lives.*

69. For discussions of white ethnicity, see Micaela di Leonardo, *The Varieties of Ethnic Experience: Kinship, Class, and Gender among California Italian-Americans* (Ithaca: Cornell University Press, 1984); and Ruth Frankenberg, *White Women, Race Matters: The Social Construction of Whiteness* (Minneapolis: University of Minnesota Press, 1992).

NATIVISM PAST

Historical Context and the New Nativism

The chapters in this part provide essential links between past and current nativism by presenting selected aspects of American nativism in history. Kevin R. Johnson's chapter chronicles images of the alien in legal history and demonstrates the profound influence of racial differences in the construction and implementation of immigration law. Gilbert Paul Carrasco then focuses on the historical relationships among Mexican labor, the U.S. government, and business interests. The alternating currents of invitation followed by deportation shed much light on the anti-Mexican character of much of today's nativism. Dorothy E. Roberts places the new nativism into the context of the eugenics movement. She describes how formerly discredited race-based conceptions of American citizenship form an integral part of the new nativism.

9. THE NEW NATIVISM
Something Old, Something New, Something Borrowed, Something Blue
Kevin R. Johnson

The new nativism in the United States represents a fascinating combination of diverse influences. Modern nativism is "something old," part and parcel of a legacy of xenophobia in this nation that may be traced to long before Benjamin Franklin derided German immigration to colonial Pennsylvania. There is, however, "something new" about the emerging nativism as well.[1] Since 1965, an increasing proportion of the immigrants to the United States have been people of color.[2] As painfully learned by the descendants of Chinese and Japanese immigrants of a century ago, the assimilation of immigrants of color into the American mainstream generally is not as easy as it is for European immigrants.[3] This perceived failure historically has resulted in no small part from the refusal of dominant society to accept racial minorities, regardless of immigration status, as full-fledged members of the national community. The changing demographics of immigration mean that an increasing number of immigrants will face barriers to assimilation. It also has helped create a strain of nativism that may prove longer lasting, perhaps more volatile and divisive (though hopefully not as violent and probably less overtly racist), than previous ones.

An aspect of the new nativism is "something borrowed" as well. Xenophobia, of course, is not unique to the United States but is endemic to many societies. For example, nativist turmoil in Europe, remarkably similar in many ways to that in the United States, thrives as the century comes to a close.[4] This is not altogether surprising. The European settlers of the New World brought with them many traditions from their mother countries. The fear of the other is one of them.[5]

There is also "something blue" about the new nativism. The future is nothing less than ominous for the new immigrants and their descendants in the United States. Due to the changing demographics of immigration, the new nativism in all likelihood will not disappear quietly into obscurity as immigrants assimilate into U.S. society. If the 1990s are any indication, the coming years are likely to bring great volatility and rancor in the public debate about immigration. Indeed, race, ethnicity, and immigration status, and the intersection of these increasingly overlapping characteristics, may prove to be the social dividing lines in the United States for the foreseeable future.

The analysis of the new nativism in this chapter will be through the lens of the law. From that vantage point, we shall see how the virulent strain of race-based nativism of the 1990s influenced immigration and immigrant law and policy and how this has been the case in past anti-immigrant epochs. In examining nativism's historical roots in the United States, we also will see that the dominant images of the immigrant in society at any time in history greatly affect the formation of the law and policy toward immigrants.[6] Moreover, we shall see that immigrants of color have been singled out for particular antipathy, the most negative imagery, and the harshest of laws and policies.

Illustrating the importance of the racial composition of the immigrant stream, the immigration debate historically has been especially volatile whenever significant numbers of people of color immigrated to this country from non-Western nations. Consideration of this fact is crucial to a full understanding of nativism in the modern era. The heightened hostility toward immigrants of color, and the overlap between race and immigration status, was evident in the campaign over Proposition 187, a punitive measure passed by California voters in November 1994 that would eliminate most public benefits and services for undocumented persons. In the initiative's wake, Congress acrimoniously debated legislation that would greatly restrict immigration. Though allegedly directed at "illegal aliens" regardless of race, the initiative in fact was aimed at undocumented persons from Mexico.

In the end, my contention is that the race and color of immigrants, and the perception of racial difference, exacerbates nativist responses to immigrants in the United States. This stands in stark contrast to the conventional wisdom about immigrant assimilation—that all immigrant groups, white ethnic groups included, have faced nativist responses initially but eventually assimilated into the American mainstream. That conception suggests that the current nativism, like all others, will pass as the assimilation process unfolds. The truth of the matter, however, is that immigrants of color never have, and perhaps never will, be fully assimilated into U.S. society. They instead join a racially stratified society with deep inequalities. This stratification will forever deny them the opportunity available to their white counterparts to be fully integrated into the national community.

I. THE HISTORICAL INFLUENCE OF RACE ON IMMIGRATION LAW AND POLICYMAKING

As a result of the immigration backlash of recent years, "nativism" has entered common parlance. It is traditionally defined as the "intense opposition to an internal minority on the grounds of its foreign (i.e., 'un-American') connections. . . . [N]ativism translates into a zeal to destroy the enemies of a distinctively American way of life." [7] This definition of nativism, which is not based on the race of the immigrants, focuses on the "foreign," "un-American" characteristics of the "internal minority." Nativist sentiment historically has been directed at the most different group of immigrants of an era, including the Irish with their Catholicism and Germans who spoke a language other than English. [8]

At various times in U.S. history, however, the difference of race has inflamed nativist sentiment. [9] This makes perfect sense if one considers the central importance of race in this country. People of color who are citizens often are viewed as the other, foreign, un-American, and an internal minority. [10] Dominant society views immigrants of color, especially those of a non-Western cultural heritage who speak a language other than English, as more foreign and more un-American than other immigrants. Put differently, an immigrant of color suffers the disadvantaging impact of race that white ethnic immigrants do not. [11] Although nativism most definitely has touched the lives of European immigrants, these immigrant groups have found it easier to ultimately become integrated into the American community. [12]

The idea that the racial composition of the immigrants of the day affects the strength and volatility of the nativist reaction finds strong support in the historical record. The most virulent nativist episodes in the United States coincided with times of immigration of people of color to this country.

A. Images of the Chinese in the 1880s

The need for low wage labor to construct the transcontinental railroad spurred Chinese immigration to the United States in the 1800s. Anti-Chinese sentiment flourished in response, a fact reflected in the judicial opinions of the era. For example, in broadly interpreting a statute prohibiting a Chinese person from testifying "in favor of, or against a white man," the California Supreme Court observed in 1854 that Chinese immigrants were

a distinct people, living in our community, recognizing no laws of this State except through necessity, bringing with them their prejudices and national feuds, in which they indulge in open violation of law; whose mendacity is proverbial; a race of people who nature has marked as inferior, and who are incapable of progress or intellectual development beyond a certain point, as their history has shown; differing in language, opinions, color, and physical conformation; between whom and ourselves nature has placed an impassable difference.[13]

The hostility toward the Chinese grew to even greater heights when the economy turned sour. Anti-Chinese sentiment was at its worst in California where many demanded legislation to force the Chinese out of the state. At the 1878 California constitutional convention, for example, proponents of Chinese exclusion expressed alarm about the "Oriental invasion."[14] In response to pressures from Californians, the United States Congress passed a series of laws known as the "Chinese exclusion acts" designed to halt further immigration from China and to encourage the deportation of Chinese persons already here.[15] Each law was increasingly severe. One went so far as to subject a Chinese immigrant unlawfully in the country to imprisonment at hard labor without a trial by jury.[16] Another required that a Chinese person establish lawful presence in this nation through "at least one credible white witness."[17]

As one might expect, the Chinese exclusion laws and related legislation were challenged as violating the Constitution. In rejecting such a challenge to one of the laws, the U.S. Supreme Court said the following about Chinese immigrants:

They were generally industrious and frugal. Not being accompanied by families, except in rare instances, their expenses were small; and they were content with the simplest fare, such as would not suffice for our laborers or artisans. The competition between them and our people was for this reason altogether in their favor, and the consequent irritation, proportionately deep and bitter, was followed, in many cases, by open conflicts, to the great disturbance of the public peace.

The differences of race added greatly to the difficulties of the situation. . . . They remained strangers in the land, residing apart by themselves, and adhering to the customs and usages of their own country. It seemed impossible for them to assimilate with our people or to make any change in their habits or modes of living. As they grew in numbers each year the people of the coast saw . . . great danger that . . . our country would be overrun by them unless prompt action was taken to restrict their immigration.[18]

This and other judicial opinions of the era emphasized that Chinese immigrants were racially different, foreign, and, in effect, un-American. Deeply negative images of the Chinese, exacerbated by the difference of race, obviously influenced the legislatures that enacted the exclusion laws as well as the courts that upheld them. Chinese immigrants found it impossible to assimilate. This resulted in no small part from resistance to their assimilation by dominant American society. Neither the courts nor the body politic accepted the Chinese as members of the national community. As noncitizen outsiders, the Chinese had little chance to influence the political process.

B. More of the Same: The Alien Land Law Cases and Japanese Internment

The Chinese exclusion acts were not the last of the efforts to exclude unwanted immigrants from Asia. Amendments to immigration laws in place near the turn of the last century sought to limit migration from nations in Asia in addition to China (as well as to exclude anyone with Asian blood).[19] In that spirit, a number of Western states passed laws, which came to be known as the "alien land" laws, that limited the rights of aliens ineligible to naturalize to own agricultural lands. Although these laws did not specifically target Japanese noncitizens, the laws unquestionably were directed at them, since they were ineligible for naturalization under federal law at the time.

A heavy dose of racism and nativism influenced the enactment of the alien land laws. The campaign culminating in the passage of a law in 1920 by California voters "depicted [the Japanese] as degenerate mongrels and the voters were urged to save 'California—the White Man's Paradise' from the 'yellow peril.' . . . Opponents of the initiative measure were labeled 'Jap-lovers.' "[20] Despite this racist backdrop, the Supreme Court rejected constitutional challenges to the laws.[21]

Even those who attacked the alien land laws appealed to nativist and racist themes that dominated the times, illustrating how deeply entrenched these views were. For example, an attorney challenging the Washington law argued to the Supreme Court that

it cannot be said that the subjects of Russia and Turkey are attached to or respect the American Government or its institutions; *or that the admission to citizenship of the Zulu, the Kaffir, the cannibals of the Congo and the tribes of Ashantee and Dahomey, contribute to the success and preservation of our government and civilization.* . . . Japan stands among the foremost nations today, not only in civilization, accomplishment, civic pride, but in all those national attributes which make her one of the great recognized powers. Her nationals, resident in America, are notably law-abiding and industrious, and actuated by civic pride which well might be emulated by American citizens. Many of them have been residents of the State for years, have made it their permanent homes.[22]

Note the emphasis on difference in terms of the race, in addition to the political views, of foreign citizens other than the Japanese. Note also the attempt to establish how the Japanese embraced "American" values and thus could not be classified as "un-American."

Like the Chinese exclusion acts, the alien land laws were influenced by many factors, including a desire to eliminate "competition by alien Japanese in farming."[23] Still, racism pure and simple worsened the nativist reaction. Disenfranchised and demonized, the Japanese, similar to the Chinese, were in no position to defend themselves in the hostile political climate.

There is one difference in the anti-Japanese outburst during this time from previous ones that is worth noting—a difference that served as a bell-weather for the future. Political leaders at the time who advocated restriction of Japanese immigration claimed that the tenor of the debate had improved and that the laws were not motivated by race. For example, California Governor William D. Stephens proudly emphasized that, although the Japanese caused economic and social problems for the state,

it is with great pride that I am able to state that the people of California have borne this situation and seen its developing menace with a patience and self-restraint beyond all praise. California is proud to proclaim to the Nation that despite this social situation her people have been guilty of no excesses and no indignities upon the Japanese within our borders. No outrage, no violence, no insult, and no ignominy have been offered to the Japanese people within California.[24]

Though this sort of denial may seem incredible today, it is not atypical. To the contrary, such denial may be the norm in any period of nativism. Nativists often deny that they are nativists and point to past nativist epochs as "true" or "real" examples of nativism. Similar themes, including the claim that Proposition 187 is not nativist, racist, or anti-immigrant, can be seen in the immigration debate in the 1990s.

The anti-Japanese sentiment of this era, fanned by the hostility toward Japan during World War II, facilitated one of the most notorious examples of racism in U.S. history. In the infamous case of *Korematsu v. United States*,[25] the Supreme Court upheld the decision to place Japanese persons, citizens and aliens alike, in internment camps. Societal views of the Japanese undoubtedly influenced both the policy judgment and the Supreme Court's refusal to disturb it. Consider the Court's statements about the Japanese in one internment case:

There is support for the view that social, economic, and political conditions which have prevailed since the close of the last century, when the Japanese began to come to this country in substantial numbers, have intensified their solidarity and have in large measure prevented their assimilation as an integral part of the white population. In addition, large numbers of children of Japanese parentage are sent to Japanese language schools outside the regular hours of public schools in the locality. Some of these schools are generally believed to be sources of nationalistic propaganda, cultivating allegiance to Japan. Considerable numbers . . . of American-born children of Japanese parentage have been sent to Japan for all or a part of their education.[26]

As was the case for the Chinese in the 1800s, we see concern expressed with the inability of people of color who immigrated to the United States (or whose forbears did) to assimilate and become less un-American and less foreign. This is true even though many of the Japanese interned were not immigrants at all but citizens born in the U.S. What the Court failed to acknowledge was that the "failure" of Japanese Americans, including citizens such as Fred Korematsu, to fully assimilate resulted from racially discriminatory laws that made this impossible, such as the law denying Japanese immigrants the ability to naturalize and become members of the U.S. political community.[27]

Social tensions, most notably the war with Japan, inevitably influenced the internment decision. Similarly, World War I contributed to antipathy toward German immigrants.[28] However, the impact of race is reflected in the decision to intern the Japanese but not the Germans. This disparate treatment highlights the difference that race makes in nativist responses to the immigrants of the day.

C. Mexican Immigrants, "Illegal Aliens," and Law Enforcement

As the century comes to a close, concern with "illegal aliens" in the United States dominates debate about immigration reform. Though the term "illegal aliens" fails to identify immigrants of a particular nationality, study of its use in context reveals clearly that, at least in the Southwest, the term refers to undocumented Mexicans and plays off of stereotypes about Mexicans as criminals.[29] The terminology better masks nativist sympathies than the popular vernacular that it replaced—"wetbacks"[30]—which is even more closely linked to Mexican immigrants.[31]

Reminiscent of the Chinese immigrants of the nineteenth century, undocumented workers from Mexico long have served as a disposable labor force in the United States, especially in Southwestern agriculture.[32] As one might expect, the United States has been schizophrenic in its views about undocumented Mexican labor. On the one hand, Mexicans often are characterized as hardworking and performing labor that many "Americans" will not.[33] On the other hand, they serve as convenient scapegoats when the U.S. economy turns for the worse. Woody Guthrie captured the essence of this ambivalence:

> Some of us are illegal and some are not wanted,
> Our work contract's out and we have to move on;
> Six hundred miles to that Mexican border,
> They chase us like outlaws, like rustlers, like thieves.[34]

The contrasting views are reflected in the changing government attitudes toward enforcing the immigration laws with respect to undocumented Mexicans in the twentieth century. For example, major governmental efforts were made to force large numbers of Mexicans, including U.S. citizens, to move to Mexico during the Great Depression.[35] Following World War II, a perceived labor shortage in agriculture provoked Congress to establish the Bracero Program, which allowed the temporary importation of Mexican labor.[36] Even after the program's dismantling, the U.S. Border Patrol informally collaborated with growers to ensure ready availability of cheap undocumented labor in the Southwest.[37] Coming full circle, the Border Patrol implemented a mass deportation program in 1954 officially known as "Operation Wetback."[38]

The U.S. Supreme Court has focused considerable attention on cases touching upon illegal Mexican immigration. Such immigration, in the Court's view, is a "colossal problem"[39] posing "enormous difficulties"[40] and "formidable law enforcement problems."[41] Individual justices have observed that immigration from Mexico is "virtually uncontrollable"[42] and that the nation "is powerless to stop the tide of illegal aliens—and dangerous drugs—that daily and freely crosses our 2,000-mile southern boundary."[43] Even renowned liberal Justice Brennan stated, "No one doubts that the presence of large numbers of undocumented aliens in the country creates law enforcement problems of *titanic proportions*."[44] Ignoring the heated debate among social scientists about the contribution of undocumented immigrants to the economy, the Court has stated unequivocally that undocumented Mexicans "create significant economic and social problems, competing with citizens and legal resident aliens for jobs, and generating extra demand for social services."[45] Such perceptions inspired Chief Justice Burger to include an extraordinary appendix to an opinion describing in remarkable detail "the illegal alien problem,"[46] which focused exclusively on unauthorized migration from Mexico.

The Court's decisions, however, cannot be explained by raw nativism or anti-immigrant, perhaps anti-Mexican, sentiment. Alex Aleinikoff thoughtfully identified the "good alien/bad alien" pattern to the Court's decisions in the 1980s. The Court tends to treat lawful permanent residents ("good aliens") and others who entered through lawful channels more favorably than illegal entrants ("bad aliens") who are "uninvited guests, intruders, trespassers, law breakers."[47]

By focusing exclusively on the noncitizen's immigration status, the "good alien/bad alien" distinction fails to consider the other salient characteristics of immigrant populations, such as race, culture (including language), and class, which often are considered to be linked to a certain immigration status. Undocumented immigrants include a relatively large percentage of Mexicans, though perhaps not as great as popularly thought. The dominant image of a bad alien often is an undocumented Mexican or some other person of color, perhaps a Haitian or a Chinese person travelling by sea, from a developing nation. Analyzing the impact of these variables on the Court's reasoning is hazardous because, unlike the decisions of the late 1800s, or even those earlier in the twentieth century, blatant xenophobic statements generally are absent from the decisions, a qualitative departure from past nativist eras.[48] The same is true for the law and policymaking process. Nevertheless, it is difficult to contend that the ethnicity of the Mexican undocumented population has had no impact on the antipathies for this immigrant group.

Historical analysis of the responses to Chinese, Japanese, and Mexican immigrants to the United States shows how race has exacerbated the nativist response. Other social forces obviously come into play as well. Economic fears, for example, contributed to antipathy for Chinese, Japanese, and Mexican noncitizens. National security concerns contributed to the U.S. government's decision to intern the Japanese. Nonetheless, the color of the immigrants influenced their harsh treatment under the law.

II. THE INFLUENCE OF RACE ON NATIVISM AT THE CLOSE OF THE TWENTIETH CENTURY

We have seen that the color of the immigrants historically has inflamed public opinion. Race and immigration status combine to enhance their unpopularity. Events in the United States and Europe at the close of the century offer further support for this thesis.

A. The U.S. Experience

Until 1965, national origin quotas in the U.S. immigration laws favored immigration from northern and western Europe and discriminated against those from most other nations.[49] In the egalitarian spirit of the civil rights movement, Congress eliminated the quotas in 1965, a move that greatly changed the demographics of U.S. immigration over the last third of the twentieth century. An increasing proportion of the immigrants to this nation have been groups constituting racial minorities in this country. For example, while less than 154,000 persons lawfully immigrated to the United States from Asia from 1951–60, over 2.7 million came from 1981–90.[50] Similarly, while less than 300,000 Mexican immigrants lawfully came to the United States from 1951–60, over 1.6 million came from 1981–90 and almost one million in 1991 alone.[51]

This change has had a distinct impact on some high-immigration states, with California being a prominent example. In response to the demographic changes wrought by immigration, nativist sentiment slowly built momentum before reaching a fever pitch in the 1990s. Although many factors were at work, including job displacement and a simple fear about the number of persons immigrating to the United States, the race of the immigrants unquestionably influenced nativism's resurgence. Opinion polls, for example, suggest that the general public prefers European over Latin American, Asian, and African immigration and that whites are more likely than nonwhites to express concern with excessive immigration.[52]

Consistent with history, the changing demographics of immigration have influenced the operation of the laws. Even with the elimination of the national origin quotas system, annual quotas on the number of immigrants who may be admitted from a country disparately affect immigrants from certain nations. The nations affected generally are developing ones populated by people of color who must wait in longer lines for admission to the United States than persons from developed nations populated predominantly by white persons.[53] In addition, Congress, through a series of acts culminating in the ironically named "diversity" visa program created in 1990, sought to subtly encourage European migration and thus reverse the trend in the racial composition of the immigrant population.[54]

Nevertheless, because the immigration laws do not discriminate on the basis of race, they can be defended as "color blind." Similarly, modern restrictionists regularly deny that race is the reason for their dismay with immigration. They instead employ other non-race-based arguments—that too many people are immigrating to the United States, that immigrants (particularly "illegal aliens") take jobs from U.S. citizens, especially the poor and minorities, that "they" contribute to overpopulation that damages the environment, that "they" overconsume public benefits and adversely affect already-strapped state and local government budgets, that "they" contribute to the crime problem, and that "they" cause interethnic conflict and refuse to assimilate.[55] Some restrictionist arguments approach the boundaries of racism, such as claims that today's immigrants speak languages other than English, which is "un-American,"[56] and that the new immigrants come from different, "un-American" cultures.[57]

Consider briefly the U.S. response to immigrants from Asia. Though the overtly racist views expressed about Asians seen in the past are rarely found in modern mainstream discourse about immigration, anti-Asian sentiment remains alive and well in the United States. Increased Asian immigration since 1965 has reinvigorated such sentiment.[58] The antipathy even applies to refugees, perhaps the most revered immigrants in the American consciousness. Indeed, the Refugee Act of 1980, often praised as humanitarian, was motivated in part by the desire to end the Executive Branch's ad hoc admission of sizeable numbers of refugees from Southeast Asia.[59]

In light of the sea change in modern sensibilities about race in the United States, the fact that the race of immigrants ordinarily is not expressed as a reason for restricting immigration should not be surprising. As sociologist

David Riesman observed in discussing the negative public reaction to Vietnamese refugees in the 1970s, racist " 'attitudes have been generally repressed since World War II by the almost uniformly antiracist attitude of the enlightened stratum of our society.' "[60] Unlike past anti-immigrant eras, most consider it impermissible to expressly rely on race as a reason for restricting immigration.[61]

The issue of race most frequently enters the debate when immigrant activists claim that restrictionist measures, or those who advocate them, are racist. Restrictionists counter by claiming that such accusations are aimed at silencing debate over much-needed immigration reform.[62] [For an in-depth analysis of the contested meaning of "nativism," see chapter 15 in this volume—*Ed.*] Besides this sort of back-and-forth, race normally is submerged in the public discourse about immigration. It nevertheless would be foolish in light of this nation's history to conclude that the race of the immigrants coming to the United States is irrelevant to the debate. The fact that racist statements persistently reappear in, even if they do not dominate, public discourse suggests that at least some restrictionists object to the racial composition of the immigrant population.[63] Moreover, because much racism is of an unconscious nature,[64] it is difficult to gauge its influence on the views of restrictionists.

Though modern restrictionists rarely invoke the race and ethnicity of immigrants as a reason to restrict immigration, it often is a subtext to the debate. An immigration article in the September 1993 issue of the *American Bar Association Journal,* a mainstream periodical of the legal profession, nicely captures this phenomenon. The headline on the cover read "Alienation" with a picture of Haitians on a rickety boat. With the aid of photographs of Chinese and Haitian immigrants, the story focused on these immigrants along with Central Americans and Mexicans.[65] The "Alienation" article thus almost exclusively addressed immigration of people of color.

When considering the concrete impact of race on this nation's immigration policies in the modern era, one need look no further than those noncitizens who were subject to the U.S. government's harshest treatment in the waning years of the twentieth century. Mass detention of Central American asylum-seekers, combined with heavy-handed tactics designed to encourage them to "voluntarily" return home rather than pursue their legal claims, became the norm in the 1980s.[66] Haitians fleeing violent political turmoil were subject to increasingly harsh detention and interdiction policies culminating in one in which U.S. coast guard cutters intercepted boats on the high seas and returned desperate Haitians to a land where they feared persecution, without any attempt to determine whether their fear was valid.[67] The 1990s have seen increasing efforts to seal the southern border with Mexico to halt illegal immigration, although it has been estimated that over 60 percent of the undocumented persons in this country come from nations other than Mexico.[68] The unprecedented harsh treatment accorded some Mariel Cubans, many of whom are black and ostracized by the established white Cuban American community in the United States,[69] included indefinite detention in high security federal penitentiaries because Cuba will not accept their return.[70]

Some may object to the suggestion that these policies are "racist." That, however, misunderstands the argument. Rather, the claim is that the race and ethnicity of the noncitizens subjected to these harsh policies *influenced*, not *dictated*, the formulation and retention of the harsh measures. The race of the affected persons permitted the U.S. government to ratchet up the intensity of the policies without significant public opposition. Public reaction to the policies described above might have been negative if the noncitizens were more "American," less foreign, and more like "us."[71] Other factors, including economics, foreign policy, public opinion, and fears of mass migration, inevitably entered into the decisionmaking calculus as well. It is not plausible to contend, however, that the race of the immigrants in no way influenced the decisions.

B. Europe Compared

The United States is not the only nation in the world that grappled with xenophobia in the twentieth century. Europe experienced a resurgence of nativism in the early 1990s, often of a much more violent nature than the U.S. variety. Europeans also generally appear less inhibited than Americans about expressing a distaste for foreigners. In stark contrast to the United States,[72] no European nation proclaims with pride that it is a "nation of immigrants." To the contrary, most view themselves—and happily so—as nations of emigration rather than immigration.

Such sentiment finds expression in the generally restrictive nature of the immigration and naturalization laws of most European nations. Characteristic of this, the European Union, which in theory plans to allow relatively free migration between member nations, is much stricter on immigration from outside the Union.[73] This has been referred to as the "Fortress Europe" mentality, which has alarmed persons concerned with the humanitarian treatment of refugees.[74]

The most pressing immigration issue of the 1990s in Europe has been the great increase in political asylum applications. The increase prompted immigration reform efforts, particularly in Germany, and, not coincidentally, a fount of anti-immigrant sentiment.[75] To reduce the number of asylum-seekers, as well as the number granted asylum, Germany went so far as to amend its constitution.[76] Vicious attacks on Turks in Germany, many of whom had lived in that country for years, became all-too-common-place. Similar attacks on "foreigners" also took place in other European nations.[77]

As in the United States, the race and ethnicity of the immigrants to European nations directly correlated with the resurgence of nativism. Attacks on "asylum abuse" in Germany, for example, masked deeper-seated public hostility toward immigrants of color.[78] Immigration control measures in England are in no small part aimed at limiting immigration of blacks.[79] A popular European stereotype of " 'foreigners' " is of "a large, undifferentiated mass of garlic-reeking Muslim fanatics."[80] A French stereotype is that, because of racial and cultural differences, immigrants would never be " 'integrated' " into French society: "migrants are presented as noisy and dirty; their children are accused of being unbearable, disrespectful to people and the law, and when grown up, of being delinquents and drug addicts and dealers."[81] This, of course, resembles the contentions made in the United States about immigrants' alleged failure to assimilate.

III. THE IMPORTANCE OF RACE: PROPOSITION 187 AS AN EXAMPLE OF THE NEW NATIVISM

As previously mentioned, immigration restrictionists in the United States have increasingly focused on the economic and related impacts of immigration and downplayed the role of race as motivating their demands. Economic concerns, including ever-tightening governmental budgets, undoubtedly contributed to perhaps the most fiery debate about immigration in the latter half of the twentieth century. Nonetheless, careful study reveals that the racial demographics of immigration heightened societal anxiety and helped fuel the calls for restriction. Proposition 187 is perhaps the most prominent example.

In 1994, the California electorate rebelled in a manner that brought immigration to the forefront of national attention. The voters passed Proposition 187, an initiative known by proponents as "Save Our State" or "SOS," thus conveying a crisis mentality. The measure is reminiscent of past nativist outbursts in the United States. Proposition 187 supporters repeatedly proclaimed that "we" must be *saved* from "illegal aliens." Like the legal responses to the immigrants of yesteryear, the measure attempted to halt the alleged harms caused by unwanted noncitizens in our midst.

If implemented,[82] Proposition 187 would bar undocumented persons from receipt of most public benefits, social services, and a public education.[83] The measure also attempts through a variety of means, including requiring local law enforcement authorities to notify the Immigration and Naturalization Service of suspected undocumented persons, to facilitate the deportation of criminal aliens. Proposition 187 thus attempts to deal with two very unpopular sorts of undocumented immigrants: those who consume public benefits (in fact, undocumented immigrants are ineligible for most public benefits) and criminals. As the Mexican ambassador to the United States observed, " 'There is an equation now in California that goes: Illegal immigrants equal to Mexicans, equal to criminals, equal to someone who wants social services.' "[84] This fits in nicely with the long history of governmental attempts to discourage the migration of criminals and benefit recipients into the jurisdiction.[85]

Typical of modern nativism, proponents of Proposition 187 offered reasons in support of the measure that on their face were not invidious, such as concern with the fiscal consequences of undocumented immigration. The fact that Proposition 187 threatened to cost much more money than it promised to save places in serious doubt whether fiscal considerations were the primary motivation for the measure's strong support.[86] For example, the initiative would cut off prenatal care provided by the state to undocumented women. However, "studies have shown that every dollar spent on prenatal care *saves* between two and ten dollars in future medical care costs."[87]

The Proposition 187 campaign demonstrated that economic considerations were not the sole motivation for the initiative. Drafters of the initiative often expressed plainly nativist sentiments. For example, one drafter of Proposition 187 stated that " 'illegal aliens are killing us in California. . . . Those who support illegal immigration are, in effect, *anti-American*,' "[88] a statement that falls within the textbook definition of nativism. Similar to the imagery employed by nativists of past generations, proponents of the initiative, in the pamphlet distributed to voters, claimed that the initiative would be the first step in ending the "ILLEGAL ALIEN invasion."[89] This invasion imagery carries with it connotations of a loss of control over society that contributes to restrictionist sentiment.[90]

Concern with the race of the immigrant "invaders" was reflected in the deeply negative portrayal of the undocumented in the Proposition 187 campaign.[91] California Governor Pete Wilson used television advertisements expressing support for the measure that showed shadowy figures attempting to run across the Mexican border with the narrator stating that " '*They* keep coming.' "[92] As this advertisement illustrates, undocumented Mexicans were the "illegal aliens" targeted by Proposition 187.

The importance of the race of the "illegal aliens" at issue is evident from the statements of other prominent supporters of the initiative. One 187 drafter, Harold Ezell, who as a high level Immigration and Naturalization Service official in the 1980s provoked controversy by suggesting that " 'illegal aliens' " should be " 'caught, skinned and fried,' "[93] emphasized that the initiative enjoyed great support because " 'the people are tired of watching their *state run wild and become a third world country*.' "[94] Another sponsor employed deeply troubling racial imagery from another sad era of American history: " 'you are the posse . . . and SOS [Proposition 187] is the rope.' "[95]

Some leading proponents expressed the fear that the undocumented "invasion" would culminate in "a Mexico-controlled California [that] could vote to establish Spanish as the sole language of California, 10 million more English-speaking Californians could flee, and there could be a statewide vote to leave the Union and annex California to Mexico."[96] In a similar vein, Barbara Coe, another 187 drafter, expressed fear of the " 'militant arm of the pro-illegal activists, who have vowed to take over first California, then the Western states and then the rest of the nation.' "[97] In Coe's mind, so-called Third World immigrants and crime are inextricably linked:

"You get illegal alien children, Third World children, out of the schools and you will reduce the violence. That is a fact. . . . *You're not dealing with a lot of shiny face, little kiddies. . . . You're dealing with Third World cultures who come in, they shoot, they beat, they stab and they spread their drugs around in our school system.* And we're paying them to do it."[98]

In the face of such comments, Proposition 187 supporters, consistent with the trend in modern debates about immigration, strongly denied that the measure was anti-immigrant or racist. Perhaps an extreme example of this type of denial is the statement of the founder of a group in Arizona seeking to place a Proposition 187-style measure on the ballot who emphasized that it was " 'not a racial issue. My friends have never heard a racist word out of me. *I just don't like wetbacks.*' "[99]

Elaborating on the defense of the measure's intentions, proponents claimed that it was not anti-immigrant, but simply anti-*illegal* immigrant. However, as has been the case in Europe, an attack on one group of noncitizens may mask anti-foreign sentiment generally. Certainly those persons sympathetic to a blanket anti-foreigner, anti-Mexican stance readily supported Proposition 187. The Ku Klux Klan, for example, apparently endorsed the measure.[100] Nor was the eventual response provoked by Proposition 187 limited to undocumented persons. Not surprisingly, soon after the initiative's passage, Congress considered legislation—going well beyond concern with *illegal* immigration—to bar the receipt of a variety of public benefits to immigrants *lawfully* in the United States and to greatly limit *legal* immigration to this country.[101]

Once the xenophobic genie is let out of the proverbial bottle, it is difficult to make distinctions between various sorts of immigrants or even to limit the impacts of nativism exclusively to immigrants. This phenomenon offers clues about the concern of some minority groups about the rise of nativism in the United States. As the Chinese, Japanese, and Mexican experiences suggest, nativism generally is not limited to aliens of a particular immigration status but ordinarily is directed at all persons of a group, whatever their immigration status, perceived to be different and "un-American." Latinos and Asian Americans often are treated by society as foreigners, even if they are long-term lawful permanent residents or citizens. It would not be extraordinary for an Asian American citizen to be asked which country she is from[102] or for a Latino citizen in the Southwest to be approached by Border Patrol officers.[103] The same is not true for many other groups of lawful permanent residents and citizens whose roots can be traced to Europe. Consequently, even when restrictionists advocate a desire to limit only illegal or legal immigration, such policies have ripple effects on certain minority communities traditionally viewed as foreign by the dominant culture.

Still, the general lack of blatant racist appeals in the debate over Proposition 187 arguably represents progress. Unlike the days of old, restrictionists cannot expressly rely on racism and maintain public credibility. However, as is true with respect to racial discrimination generally, racism in the immigration debate is more subtle and difficult to detect than has been the case historically. Arguments for immigration restrictions, even if based in part on racial concerns, may be clothed in what at first glance appears to be neutral window-dressing. Though concern with Mexican migration undoubtedly influenced the passage of Proposition 187, the primary focus was on more neutral, noninvidious considerations, such as the immigration status of the noncitizens at issue and the fiscal consequences on state and local government. The public emphasis on such factors obfuscates the influence of race on the initiative's passage and demonstrates the general difficulties in attempting to evaluate the impact of race on the immigration debate.

In sum, as historically has been true, social forces, such as economic uncertainty and national security concerns, influence nativist sentiment.[104] Proposition 187 and the related efforts of the federal government to limit immigration were influenced by economic and fiscal concerns that dominate the times. Nonetheless, the debate over the initiative demonstrates how the color of the immigrants inflamed the public debate and contributed to their harsh treatment.

In this brief walk through one facet of U.S. immigration history, we have seen how the difference of race has increased the nativist hostility toward the immigrants of the day. From this history, we can speculate about the future. As the Japanese learned during World War II, the disadvantages facing racial minorities in the United States do not magically disappear once someone becomes a citizen. Regardless of citizenship status, members of minority groups not infrequently are treated as foreign and un-American. Today's immigrants of color and their descendants are likely to suffer hostility because of their race for the indefinite future and forever be subject to the charge that they refuse to assimilate.[105]

The difference that race makes compels recognition of the fact that not all immigrants are created equal. Though the treatment of immigrants of European stock to this country has not always been praiseworthy, the worst and longest lasting chapters of nativism have coincided with the immigration of people of color to the United States. This frequently is either understated or ignored. The race of the immigrants helps explain the vehemence of the nativist outbursts of the 1990s. Because the current immigrant stream is composed predominantly of people of color, we can expect similarly strong nativist reactions in the future, especially during times of economic uncertainty or other types of social stress.

In considering ways of changing the tenor of the public debate of immigration, we must recognize the common interests of immigrants and people of color generally. "[I]mmigration has added new complexity to inequality, exposing sharp class differences within established racial and ethnic groups. Immigration by itself does not create these divisions. But it can add to and sometimes exacerbate them." [106] The racial dynamics are complicated by the fact that some minority citizens, particularly African Americans, have long complained that immigrants displace them in the job market.[107] A modern, deeply complex incantation of this claim is the powerfully made objection to immigrant eligibility for affirmative action programs.[108]

As we enter the twenty-first century, those interested in social change must begin to address the racial dynamics of immigration. We should learn the lessons of history. We should see that the debate about immigration is part of a larger social debate about race in the United States.

NOTES

Thanks to Nipa Rahim, Aleem Ullah Khan Raja, and E. Dion Costa for their excellent research assistance and to Minty Siu Chung for commenting on a draft of this chapter. The thoughtful comments of the editor of this book, Juan Perea, greatly improved this chapter. The U.C. Davis School of Law and the U.C. Berkeley Center for German and European Studies provided much-appreciated financial support for this research.

1. See Nathan Glazer, "Debate on Aliens Flares beyond the Melting Pot," *New York Times*, April 23, 1995, at sec. 4, p. 3 ("every time anti-immigration sentiment rises, there is something new as well as much in the way of prejudice, ethnocentrism and racism that is old").

2. For analysis of the changing racial and ethnic demographics of immigration in the post-1965 period, see *Immigration and Ethnicity: The Integration of America's Newest Arrivals* (Barry Edmonston and Jeffrey S. Passel, eds., 1994).

This chapter's analysis considers the impact of "race" with the understanding that it to a large extent is a social as opposed to a biological construct. See Ian F. Haney López, "The Social Construction of Race: Some Observations on Illusion,

Fabrication, and Choice," 29 *Harvard Civil Rights-Civil Liberties Law Review* 1 (1994).

3. See Pat K. Chew, "Asian Americans: The "Reticent" Minority and Their Paradoxes," 36 *William and Mary Law Review* 1, 33–38 (1994) (discussing outsider treatment afforded to Asian American citizens by dominant society); Sharon M. Lee, "Asian Immigration and American Race-Relations: From Exclusion to Acceptance," 12 *Ethnic and Racial Studies* 368 (1989) (concluding that, although blatant discrimination against Asian Americans is a thing of the past, Asians are not completely accepted as "Americans"); see also Robert S. Chang, "Toward an Asian American Legal Scholarship: Critical Race Theory, Post-Structuralism, and Narrative Space," 81 *California Law Review* 1241, 1286–1314 (1993) (detailing exclusion and marginalization of Asian Americans in United States).

4. See Jost Delbrück, "Global Migration-Immigration-Multiethnicity: Challenges to the Concept of the Nation-State," 2 *Indiana Journal of Global Legal Studies* 45, 56–57 (1994) ("The notion of 'Überfremdung' [translated as the " 'fear of over-foreignization' "]—common coin in Europe—seems to have become a marketable notion in the United States as well") (footnote omitted).

5. See Ronald Takaki, *The Tempest in the Wilderness: The Racialization of Savagery, in Discovering America: Essays on the Search for an Identity* 58 (David Thelen and Frederick E. Hoxie, eds., 1994) (analyzing similarities in the views of the English in the 1700s and 1800s of the Irish and the Indians in New World, including that both were "uncivilized" and "savages"). See, generally, Merryl Wyn Davies, Ashis Nandy, and Ziauddin Sardar, *Barbaric Others: A Manifesto on Western Racism* (1993) (analyzing centuries of history of European construction of the feared "other"); Bernard McGrane, *Beyond Anthropology: Society and the Other* (1989) (to same effect).

6. This relationship is explored in Kevin R. Johnson, "Los Olvidados: Images of the Immigrant, Political Power of Noncitizens, and Immigration Law and Enforcement," 1993 *Brigham Young University Law Review* 1139.

7. John Higham, *Strangers in the Land* 4 (2d ed. 1988) [hereinafter Higham, *Strangers*].

8. See *id.* at 29–30; Kenneth L. Karst, *Belonging to America* 81–104 (1989). Hostility toward white ethnic immigrants in the United States contributed to the return of a significant number to their country of origin. See David A. Hollinger, *Postethnic America: Beyond Multiculturalism* 152–53 (1995).

9. See Higham, *supra*, at 131–57. As Higham observed, "*no* variety of anti-European sentiment has ever approached the violent extremes to which anti-Chinese agitation went in the 1870s and 1880s." *Id.* at 25 (emphasis added). He theorized that, unlike the nationalistic nature of the reaction against European immigrants, both anti-Chinese and anti-Mexican sentiment was ethnocentric and racial. See *id.* at 344.

10. See Kimberlé Crenshaw, "Race, Reform and Retrenchment: Transformation and Legitimation in Antidiscrimination Law," 101 *Harvard Law Review* 1331, 1360 (1988) ("[T]he creation of a clearly visible 'other' whose interests are seen as being opposed in every way to the interest of those who identify—by virtue of color and culture—with the dominant class is a hegemonic tool used to maintain legitimacy").

11. The disadvantaging impact of ethnicity, along with immigration status, on the provision of public benefits is analyzed in Kevin R. Johnson, "Public Benefits and

Immigration: The Intersection of Immigration Status, Ethnicity, Gender, and Class," 42 *UCLA Law Review* 1509 (1995) [hereinafter Johnson, *Public Benefits*].

12. See Nathan Glazer and Daniel Patrick Moynihan, *Beyond the Melting Pot* 313 (1963) (stating that a "good general rule" is "that except where color is involved . . . the specifically national aspect of most ethnic groups rarely survives the third generation") (emphasis in original deleted). See, generally, Mary C. Waters, *Ethnic Options: Choosing Identities in America* (1990) (analyzing voluntary assumption of ethnicity by middle-class white descendants of immigrants). Jewish immigrants may represent an exception to this rule. See John Higham, *Send These to Me: Immigrants in Urban America* 153–74 (rev. ed. 1984) (discussing anti-Semitism in United States).

13. *People v. Hall*, 4 Cal. 399, 404 (1854).

14. *The Chinese Exclusion Case (Chae Chan Ping v. United States)*, 130 U.S. 581, 595 (1889); see *Chew Heong v. United States,* 112 U.S. 536, 569 (1884) (Field, J., dissenting) (justifying laws restricting Chinese immigration because, absent such restrictions, "from the unnumbered millions on the opposite shores of the Pacific, vast hordes would pour in upon us, overrunning our coast and controlling its institutions").

15. See, generally, Bill Ong Hing, *Making and Remaking Asian America through Immigration Policy 1850–1990*, at 1–36 (1993); Ronald Takaki, *Strangers from a Different Shore: A History of Asian Americans* 79–131 (1989). For a fascinating discussion of the various legal challenges organized by the Chinese community to various state and federal laws aimed at the Chinese in the nineteenth century, see Charles J. McClain, *In Search of Equality: The Chinese Struggle against Discrimination in Nineteenth Century America* (1994).

16. See *Wong Wing v. United States*, 163 U.S. 228 (1896) (invalidating law).

17. See *Fong Yue Ting v. United States*, 149 U.S. 698 (1893). In upholding this law, the Supreme Court emphasized that "Chinese laborers [are] of a distinct race and religion, remaining strangers in the land, residing apart by themselves, tenaciously adhering to the customs and usages of their own country, unfamiliar with our institutions, and apparently incapable of assimilating with our people." *Id.* at 717; see *id.* at 743 (Brewer, J., dissenting) (claiming that the law violated the Constitution even though it "is directed only against the obnoxious Chinese").

18. *The Chinese Exclusion Case (Chae Chan Ping v. United States)*, 130 U.S. 581, 595 (1889) (emphasis added); see *id.* at 625 (stating that restriction of immigration from China "was essential to the peace of the community on the Pacific Coast, and possibly to the preservation of our civilization there"); see also *Chew Heong v. United States,* 112 U.S. 536, 566–69 (1884) (Field, J., dissenting) (stating similar views).

19. See Hing, *supra*, at 27–36.

20. *Oyama v. California*, 332 U.S. 633, 658–59 (1948) (Murphy, J., concurring) (footnote omitted); see also *Takahashi v. Fish & Game Comm'n*, 334 U.S. 410, 422–27 (1948) (Murphy, J., concurring) (detailing how a California statute barring issuance of commercial fishing licenses to persons ineligible for citizenship was "but one more manifestation of the anti-Japanese fever which has been evident in California since the turn of the century").

21. See *Cockrill v. California*, 268 U.S. 258 (1925) (upholding California law); *Frick v. Webb*, 263 U.S. 326 (1923) (same); *Webb v. O'Brien*, 263 U.S. 313 (1923) (same); *Porterfield v. Webb*, 263 U.S. 225 (1923) (same); *Terrace v. Thompson*, 263 U.S. 197 (1923) (upholding Washington law).

22. *Terrace v. Thompson,* 263 U.S. 197, 203 (1923) (statement of counsel for appellants) (emphasis added).

23. *Sei Fujii v. State,* 38 Cal. 2d 718, 735, 242 P.2d 617, 628 (Cal. 1952).

24. *Gov. William D. Stephens, of California, Presents the Original Question to Secretary of State Bainbridge Colby, Washington, D.C., in United States House of Representatives, Hearings before the Committee on Immigration and Naturalization on Japanese Immigration,* 66th Cong. 71 (1921).

25. 323 U.S. 214 (1944).

26. *Hirabayashi v. United States,* 320 U.S. 81, 96–97 (1943) (emphasis added) (footnotes omitted). In the better known internment case of *Korematsu,* the Court relied heavily on *Hirabayashi*'s reasoning. See *Korematsu,* 323 U.S., at 216–19.

27. See Juan F. Perea, "Ethnicity and the Constitution: Beyond the Black and White Binary Constitution," 36 *William and Mary Law Review* 571, 582–87 (1995).

28. See, e.g., *Meyer v. Nebraska,* 262 U.S. 390 (1923) (reviewing application of state law aimed at German immigrants that prohibited teaching of foreign language).

29. See Richard Delgado and Jean Stefancic, "Images of the Outsider in American Law and Culture: Can Free Expression Remedy Systemic Social Ills?" 77 *Cornell Law Review* 1258, 1273–75 (1992) (detailing stereotypes about Mexican Americans, including that of the "bandido," in popular U.S. culture).

30. See, e.g., *Diaz v. Kay-Dix Ranch,* 9 Cal. App. 3d 588, 590 n. 1, 88 Cal. Rptr. 443, 444 n. 1 (1970); Richard K. Park, "Illegal Entrants: The Wetback Problem in American Farm Labor," 2 *University of California at Davis Law Review* 55 (1970).

31. Justices Douglas and Brennan have recognized the subtle impact that terminology has in the legal treatment afforded noncitizens. See *Hurtado v. United States,* 410 U.S. 578, 604 (1973) (Douglas, J., dissenting) ("We cannot allow the Government's insistent reference to these Mexican citizens as 'deportable aliens' to obscure the fact that they come before us as innocent persons who have not been charged with a crime"); *id.* at 599 (Brennan, J., concurring in part, dissenting in part) (agreeing with Justice Douglas on this point); see also Gerald L. Neuman, "Aliens as Outlaws: Government Services, Proposition 187, and the Structure of Equal Protection," 42 *UCLA Law Review* 1425, 1429 (1995) ("[T]he discourse of legal [immigration] status permits coded discussion in which listeners will understand that reference is being made, not to aliens in the abstract, but to the particular foreign group that is the principal focus of current hostility") (footnote omitted).

32. See, generally, Mario Barrera, *Race and Class in the Southwest: A Theory of Racial Inequality* (1979); Kitty Calavita, *U.S. Immigration Law and the Control of Labor: 1820–1924* (1984).

33. See David G. Gutiérrez, *Walls and Mirrors: Mexican Americans, Mexican Immigrants, and the Politics of Ethnicity* 47–48 (1995) (collecting statements of political leaders in early 1900s to effect that migration of Mexican labor to the United States was necessary because Mexicans were willing to perform work that native born persons were not).

34. Woody Guthrie, *Deportee,* in *The Woody Guthrie Songbook* 72 (Harold Leventhal and Marjorie Guthrie, eds., 1976). Thanks to Michael Scaperlanda for bringing this song to my attention.

35. See, generally, Camille Guerin Gonzales, *Mexican Workers and American Dreams: Immigration, Repatriation, and California Labor 1900–1939,* at 77–94 (1994); Abraham Hoffman, *Unwanted Mexican Americans in the Great Depression* (1974).

36. See, generally, Kitty Calavita, *Inside the State, the Bracero Program, Immigration, and the I.N.S.* (1992).

37. See Julian Samora, *Los Mojados: The Wetback Story* 48–51 (1971).

38. See Juan Ramón García, *Operation Wetback: The Mass Deportation of Mexican Undocumented Workers in 1954*, at 139 (1980).

39. *United States v. Valenzuela-Bernal*, 458 U.S. 858, 864 n.5 (1982).

40. *United States v. Cortez*, 449 U.S. 411, 418 (1981).

41. *United States v. Martinez-Fuerte*, 428 U.S. 543, 552 (1976).

42. *Plyler v. Doe*, 457 U.S. 202, 237 (1982) (Powell, J., concurring).

43. *United States v. Ortiz*, 422 U.S. 891, 899 (1975) (Burger, C. J., concurring in judgment). Similar concerns have influenced policymakers. For example, in arguing for an overhaul of immigration enforcement in 1981, then-Attorney General William French Smith proclaimed, "We have lost control of our borders." *Immigration Reform and Control Act of 1983: Hearings on H.R. 1510 before the Subcommittee on Immigration, Refugees, and International Law of the House Committee of the Judiciary 6*, 98th Cong., 1st Sess. 1 (1983) (testimony of Attorney General William French Smith).

44. *Immigration and Naturalization Service v. Delgado*, 466 U.S. 210, 239 (1984) (Brennan, J., dissenting in part) (emphasis added).

45. *United States v. Brignoni-Ponce*, 422 U.S. 873, 878–79 (1975).

46. *United States v. Ortiz*, 422 U.S. 891, 900 (1975) (Burger, C. J., concurring in judgment) (excerpting *United States v. Baca*, 368 F. Supp. 398, 402–8 [S.D. Cal. 1973]).

47. T. Alexander Aleinikoff, *Good Aliens, Bad Aliens and the Supreme Court*, in 9 *In Defense of the Alien* 46, 47 (1986).

48. Indeed, some claim that concern with unauthorized migration does not "represent a new form of nativism" at all. David A. Martin, *Disentangling the Strands of U.S. Immigration Policy Reform*, in *Controlling Immigration: A Global Perspective* 101 (Wayne A. Cornelius, Philip L. Martin, and James F. Hollifield, eds., 1994).

49. See Stephen H. Legomsky, "Immigration, Equality, and Diversity," 31 *Columbia Journal of Transnational Law* 319, 328 (1993).

50. See *U.S. Department of Justice, 1993 Statistical Yearbook of the Immigration and Naturalization Service* 27–28 (1994) (Table 2); see also Hing, *supra*, at 79–120 (analyzing the impact of the quota system's elimination on the Asian American community in the United States).

51. See *U.S. Department of Justice, supra*, at 27–28 (Table 2).

52. See Jack Citrin et al., "Is American Nationalism Changing? Implications for Foreign Policy," 38 *International Studies Quarterly* 1, 16 (1994) (reviewing poll data). Matters are complicated by the fact that public opinion polls also suggest that the most recent immigrants of the day, regardless of race, are the most disfavored. See Rita J. Simon and Susan H. Alexander, *The Ambivalent Welcome: Print Media, Public Opinion and Immigration* 45–46 (1993).

53. See Legomsky, *supra*, at 328.

54. See *id.* at 329–30.

55. See, e.g., Richard D. Lamm and Gary Imhoff, *The Immigration Time Bomb: The Fragmenting of America* (1985).

56. See, generally, Juan F. Perea, "Demography and Distrust: An Essay on American Languages, Cultural Pluralism, and Official English," 77 *Minnesota Law Review* 269 (1992).

57. See Bill Ong Hing, "Beyond the Rhetoric of Assimilation and Cultural Plural-ism: Addressing the Tension of Separatism and Conflict in an Immigration-Driven Multiracial Society," 81 *California Law Review* 863, 874–75 (1993).

58. See, generally, U.S. Commission on Civil Rights, *Civil Rights Issues Facing Asian Americans in the 1990s,* at 22–48 (1992) (documenting hate crimes directed against Asian American immigrants and citizens).

59. See Deborah Anker and Michael Posner, "The Forty Year Crisis: A Legislative History of the Refugee Act of 1980," 19 *San Diego Law Review* 9, 30–42 (1981).

60. Roger Daniels, "Majority Images—Minority Realities: A Perspective on Anti-Orientalism in the United States," 2 *Prospects* 209, 210 (1976) (quoting Riesman and citing from his letter to *Time,* June 2, 1975).

61. But see Peter Brimelow, *Alien Nation: Common Sense about America's Immi-gration Disaster* (1995) (arguing that immigration should be restricted in part be-cause it is changing the racial demographics of the United States).

62. See, e.g., *id.* at 116–17; Lamm and Imhoff, *supra,* at 19–22.

63. See, e.g., Douglas Jehl, "Buchanan Raises Specter of Intolerance, Critics Say," *Los Angeles Times,* March 17, 1992, at A1 (quoting Patrick Buchanan, Republican Presidential candidate: " '[I]f we had to take a million immigrants in say, Zulus, next year, or Englishmen, and put them up in Virginia, what group would be easier to assimilate and would cause less problems for the people of Virginia?' ").

64. See, generally, Charles R. Lawrence III, "The Id, the Ego, and Equal Protec-tion: Reckoning with Unconscious Racism," 39 *Stanford Law Review* 317 (1987).

65. See John Jefferson, "Alienation: Is There a Legal Solution to the Immigration Mess?" *ABA Journal,* Sept. 1993, at 54.

66. See *Orantes-Hernandez v. Thornburgh,* 919 F. 2d 549 (9th Cir. 1990).

67. See *Sale v. Haitian Centers Council, Inc.,* 113 S. Ct. 2549 (1993) (rejecting legal challenges to Haitian interdiction and repatriation). See, generally, Harold Hongju Koh, "The 'Haiti Paradigm' in United States Human Rights Policy," 103 *Yale Law Journal* 2391 (1994).

68. See *Immigration and Naturalization Service, Estimates of the Unauthorized Immigrant Population Residing in the United States, by Country of Origin and State of Residence: October 1992,* at 14 (1994).

69. See Mark S. Hamm, *The Abandoned Ones: The Imprisonment and Uprising of the Mariel Boat People* 74–75 (1995).

70. See, e.g., *Barrera-Echavarria v. Rison,* 44 F. 3d 1441 (9th Cir. 1995) (en banc) (upholding indefinite detention of Mariel Cuban in United States because Cuban government would not allow his return).

71. See, e.g., James Harney, "Critics of U.S. Policy See Racist Overtones," *USA Today,* Feb. 3, 1992, at 2A (quoting law professor Stephen Legomsky to effect that public " 'would never stand for [treatment of Haitians] if the boat people were Europeans' ").

72. See, e.g., *Foley v. Connelie,* 435 U.S. 291, 294 (1978) ("As a Nation we exhibit extraordinary hospitality to those who come to our country, which is not surprising for we have often been described as 'a nation of immigrants.' ").

73. I say "in theory" here because there have been difficulties in implementing the European Union's free migration provisions. See Sarah Helm, "Britain Will Block EU Moves to End Frontier Checks," *Independent,* July 13, 1995, at 11; see also Bernhard Santel, *Loss of Control: The Build-Up of a European Migration and Asylum Regime,*

in *Migration and European Integration: The Dynamics of Inclusion and Exclusion* 75, 83, 88 (Robert Miles and Dietrich Thränhardt eds., 1995) (noting anxiety about removal of border controls between European Union member nations).

74. See James C. Hathaway, "Harmonizing for Whom? The Devaluation of Refugee Protection in the Era of European Economic Integration," 26 *Cornell International Law Journal* 719 (1993); Gerald L. Neuman, "Buffer Zones against Refugees: Dublin, Schengen, and the German Asylum Amendment," 33 *Virginia Journal of International Law* 503 (1993) [hereinafter Neuman, "Buffer Zones"].

75. See Philip L. Martin, *Germany: Reluctant Land of Immigration, in Controlling Immigration, supra,* at 213 (stating that "[a]s the number of asylum applicants rose, so did German attacks on foreigners").

76. See Sam Blay and Andreas Zimmermann, "Recent Changes in German Refugee Law: A Critical Assessment," 88 *American Journal of International Law* 361 (1994).

77. See, e.g., Eric Geiger, "Deadly Campaign against Immigrants in Austria Evokes Nazi Past," *San Francisco Chronicle,* Aug. 19, 1995, at A10 (reporting "wave of letter bombs and booby traps" directed at immigrants in Austria); Frederic Niel, "France: French Skinhead Confesses in Moroccan's Drowning," *Reuter News Service*—Western Europe, May 11, 1995 (reporting drowning in River Seine of Moroccan immigrant by French skinheads during May Day march by National Front); Andrew Gumbel, "Italy: Racism Darkens Rome's Riviera," *Independent,* January 6, 1995 (reporting random shooting of Moroccan in Italy).

78. See Neuman, "Buffer Zones," *supra,* at 509–16.

79. See Abdul Paliwala, *Law and the Constitution of the 'Immigrant' in Europe: A UK Policy Perspective in Nationalism, Racism, and the Rule of Law* 77 (Peter Fitzpatrick, ed., 1995); Zig Layton-Henry, *Britain: The Would-Be Zero Immigration Country, in Controlling Immigration, supra,* at 293.

80. See Tore Bjorgo, *Role of the Media in Racist Violence, in Racist Violence in Europe* 96, 110 (Tore Bjorgo and Rob Witte, eds., 1993).

81. Michel Wieviorka, *Tendencies to Racism in Europe: Does France Represent a Unique Case, or Is It Representative of a Trend? in Racism and Migration in Western Europe* 57 (John Solomos and John Wrench, eds., 1993); see, e.g., Marlise Simons, "France Takes Tougher Line on Foreigners," *New York Times,* July 23, 1995, at sec. 1, p. 4 (reporting that France's new conservative government was taking a tough stance on illegal immigration and that public opinion polls showed that French citizens favored limiting legal as well as illegal immigration, particularly that from developing nations).

82. As of December 1995, Proposition 187 was the subject of litigation that appeared likely to ultimately make its way to the U.S. Supreme Court. During the pendency of the litigation, the courts enjoined implementation of the measure's most significant, and controversial, provisions.

83. The denial of an elementary and secondary school public education to undocumented children conflicts with *Plyler v. Doe,* 457 U.S. 202 (1982), which held that the denial of such education under a Texas law violated the equal protection clause of the Fourteenth Amendment of the Constitution.

84. Marc Sandalow, "Mexican Envoy Berates State on Immigration," *San Francisco Chronicle,* July 6, 1994, at A1 (quoting Mexican ambassador to United States).

85. See, generally, Gerald L. Neuman, "The Lost Century of American Immigra-

tion Law (1776–1875)," 93 *Columbia Law Review* 1833 (1993) (recounting history of state regulation of immigration of poor and criminals before the first comprehensive federal immigration laws).

86. This is explored in greater detail in Johnson, *Public Benefits, supra,* at 1568–70.

87. See *Lewis v. Grinker,* 965 F. 2d 1206, 1219 (2d Cir. 1992) (citation omitted) (emphasis added).

88. Patrick J. McDonnell, "Prop. 187 Turns up Heat in U.S. Immigration Debate," *Los Angeles Times,* Aug. 10, 1994, at A1 (quoting Ron Prince) (emphasis added).

89. Tony Miller, Acting California Secretary of State, *California Ballot Pamphlet: General Election November 8, 1994,* at 54 (Argument in Favor of Proposition 187) (capitals in original).

90. See Peter H. Schuck, "The Message of 187," *American Prospect,* Spring 1995, at 85 (stating that the passage of Proposition 187 apparently was "an expression of public frustration with a government and civil society that seem out of touch and out of control").

91. The salience of race in the initiative campaign is analyzed in detail in Kevin R. Johnson, "An Essay on Immigration Politics, Popular Democracy, and California's Proposition 187: The Political Relevance and Legal Irrelevance of Race," 70 *Washington Law Review* 629, 650–61 (1995).

92. See John Marelius, "Wilson Ad out to Ease Prop. 187 Drumbeat," *San Diego Union-Tribune,* Oct. 25, 1994, at A3 (describing advertisement) (emphasis added).

93. See Olga Briseno, "Mister Migra, Harold Ezell," *San Diego Union-Tribune,* Aug. 23, 1989, at F1 (quoting Ezell).

94. Daniel B. Wood, "Ballot Vote on Illegal Immigrants Set for Fall in California," *Christian Science Monitor,* June 1, 1994, at 1 (quoting Ezell) (emphasis added).

95. McDonnell, *supra.*

96. Pamela J. Podger and Michael Doyle, "War of Words," *Fresno Bee,* Jan. 9, 1994, at A1 (quoting Coe) (emphasis added). Coe later wrote in a similar vein that "[v]iolent crime is rampant. . . . Illegal-alien gangs roam our streets, dealing drugs and searching for innocent victims to rob, rape and . . . murder. . . ." Barbara Coe, "Keep Illegals out of State," *USA Today,* Oct. 12, 1994, at 12A.

97. *Id.*

98. *Id.*

99. Maria Puente, "States Setting Stage for Their Own Prop. 187's," *USA Today,* Nov. 18, 1993, at 60 (emphasis added).

100. See "To File a Motion for Request for Leave to File a Brief" submitted by Kleagle and Representative of the Ku Klux Klan San Joaquin Valley, filed in Court of Appeals for the Ninth Circuit Case No. 9555186 (May 19, 1995) (expressing support for Proposition 187 and requesting that court of appeals expedite ruling in a case involving a challenge to the measure and, more importantly, that the court uphold it in face of legal challenges).

101. See, e.g., H.R. 2202, 104th Cong., 1st Sess. (1995) (bill entitled "Immigration in the National Interest Act" designed to deter illegal immigration, reduce legal immigrant levels, and restrict benefits to aliens); see also Steven A. Holmes, "Congress Plans Stiff New Curb on Immigration," *New York Times,* Sept. 25, 1995, at A1 (summarizing congressional proposals to reduce legal immigration).

102. See Chew, *supra,* at 33; see also Mari J. Matsuda, "Public Response to Racist

Speech: Considering the Victim's Story," 87 *Michigan Law Review* 2320, 2329–31 (1989) (offering story helping to explain why Asian Americans fear racial slurs more than whites).

103. See Suzanne Espinosa, "Snafu Underscores Civil Rights Issues: Born in U.S.A.—But Deported," *San Francisco Chronicle,* Oct. 22, 1993, at A1 (reporting that a U.S. citizen was deported to Mexico after arrest by Border Patrol while fixing the roof of his parents' home).

104. See, generally, Higham, *Strangers, supra.*

105. Cf. Derrick Bell, *Faces at the Bottom of the Well: The Permanence of Racism* (1992) (contending that racism is a permanent fixture of U.S. society).

106. National Board of the Changing Relations Project, *Changing Relations: Newcomers and Established Residents in U.S. Communities* 5 (1993).

107. See Lawrence H. Fuchs, *The Reactions of Black Americans to Immigration, in Immigration Reconsidered: History, Sociology and Politics* 293 (Virginia Yans-McLaughlin, ed., 1990).

108. See Brimelow, *supra,* at 217–18, 263–64.

10. LATINOS IN THE UNITED STATES

Invitation and Exile

Gilbert Paul Carrasco

I. INTRODUCTION

Throughout the history of the United States, there have been periods of labor shortage and labor surplus. In times of labor shortage, the United States has enthusiastically welcomed immigrants to fill gaps in the labor pool. More often than not, however, available employment has been characterized by harsh working conditions, enormous amounts of physical labor, and minimal remuneration. In addition to abject working conditions, immigrants have also faced discrimination and resentment.[1]

During periods of labor surplus or economic stress, immigrants in the United States have been subjected to particular cruelty. Americans, led by various nativist organizations and movements such as the Know-Nothing Party in the 1850s or, more recently, U.S. English or California's "Save Our State" campaign, have blamed immigrants for the country's economic woes. Such xenophobic bigotry has resulted in calls for anti-immigrant legislation (including restrictions on immigration for whichever immigrant group was targeted at the time), attempts to deny public services (including elimination of bilingual education for school-aged immigrants and the American citizen children of undocumented immigrants), and, ultimately, deportation.

Mexican immigrants have usually been the subject of these seesaw trends. One reason for this is that Mexico and the United States share a common border. The border between the two countries stretches for two thousand miles and is evidenced in some places by a fence, but at most points merely by an imaginary line in the sand or by the Rio Grande River.[2] A border that has historically been easy to traverse, this proximity facilitates immigration, both legal and illegal, as well as expulsion.

Due to their great distance from the United States, Europeans historically could not make the journey to where their labor was needed (typically the Southwestern United States) before the need was met. The only immigrants left within reach of the American Southwest were Mexicans and Asians. The Chinese and the Japanese have their own regrettable history of discrimination in the United States.[3] [For a detailed discussion of this history, see chapters 2 and 9 in this volume—*Ed.*] The laws and policies that temporarily ended immigration from Japan and China left Mexico as the only source to fill the labor vacuum.[4] Mexican laborers have since become the United States' disposable labor force, brought in when needed, only to fulfill their use and be unceremoniously discarded, a trend that has been recurring for over 150 years.

Before we go any further, it may be helpful to define terms that will be used in this essay because they are often used interchangeably or with varying definitions. "Mexican" is a person from Mexico; "Mexican American" is an American of Mexican descent; "Latino" is a person of Latin American ancestry; and "Anglo" is an American of Anglo-Saxon, European, or other non-Latino extraction.[5]

II. CYCLES OF INVITATION AND EXILE

A. From the Gold Rush to World War I

Early migration into the United States was aided by negligible border restrictions and virtually no immigration laws.[6] The first wave of Mexican laborers was drawn to California by the Gold Rush shortly after Mexico ceded California to the United States under the terms of the Treaty of Guadalupe Hidalgo in 1848.[7] The Gold Rush drew people from all over the world, triggering rapid population growth. Because most people who flocked to California wanted to strike it rich in their own mines, unskilled manual labor was scarce and laborers were needed to work not only in Anglo-owned mines but also to construct the railroads and to farm in agricultural areas.[8] The work was backbreaking, low-paying, and often dangerous, so it was difficult to find Anglos who would do it.

In addition to fulfilling labor demands, Mexicans brought with them knowledge of mining. Anglos came to California with dreams of striking it rich but had little practical experience or knowledge of how to do it. Anglos, however, soon acquired the knowledge, tools, and techniques of Latino miners.[9]

Unfortunately for Latinos, a need for their labor and knowledge did not translate into good attitudes toward them. Popular accounts of Latinos during that period were influenced by manifest destiny, "scientific" theories of racial miscegenation, and the Mexican War. These accounts provided the Anglo miner with a negative stereotype of the Latino that led to discrimination and hostility.[10] These hostilities took the form of threats, violence, and restrictive legislation directed against Mexicans and Mexican Americans.[11] Examples of these hostilities include posters appearing in mining areas threatening violence to any "foreigners" who remained where "they had no right to be"; vigilante groups expelling Latinos from mines claiming that mineral rights and wealth in America were reserved for "Americans"; the imposition of a Foreign Miners' Tax Law; assaults; and lynchings.[12]

In addition to the negative stereotypes and misconceptions, anti-Latino attitudes were also fueled by greed for the much coveted gold. Latinos who labored in the fields, on the railroads, or in the mines of Anglos were not as persecuted and discriminated against as those who sought their own fortunes in the mines. Nevertheless, although nonminers were not as persecuted as miners, there are recorded incidents of whole towns being put to the torch, rioters shooting any Mexican in sight, random murders, and other vigilante actions throughout this period.[13]

Even while Latinos were being persecuted, their labor was needed, especially in jobs that were low-paying and labor-intensive. Such jobs included ranching, agriculture (especially for crops such as cotton and sugar beets), laying the rails that traverse the Southwest (a task made harder because most of the terrain is desert, semidesert, and/or mountainous), and mining (where, although their knowledge of mining techniques proved invaluable, they received lower wages for the same work that their unskilled Anglo counterparts did).[14]

There was such a demand for Mexican labor in some labor-intensive occupations that employers held Mexicans captive. One such industry was the Colorado sugar beet industry. Sugar beets require attention almost year-round and, therefore, need a semipermanent labor force. When farmers could not persuade Mexican laborers to stay year-round to perform the arduous labor, they resorted to coercion. Coercive tactics employed by farmers took different forms. One such tactic was to refuse to make final wage payments to their employees so that they were unable to leave; thus, they had to remain in the area until the following season to collect their pay. Essentially, farmers had a captive work force without rights of citizenship or the ability to leave.[15]

B. World War I through the Great Depression

Although there were periods of economic trouble in 1907 and 1921 when immigrants were blamed for many of the problems, Mexican immigrants were generally welcomed into the United States until the 1930s and the Great Depression.[16] Prior to the Depression, U.S. immigration policies were aimed mainly at keeping out Asians and southern and eastern Europeans, while allowing Mexican laborers to immigrate. For example, within a year of the enactment of the most restrictive immigration legislation in U.S. history — the Immigration Act of 1917—the first foreign labor program was initiated.

In response to pressure from agricultural employers in the Southwest, Congress included provisions in the law that allowed entry into the United States of "temporary" workers who would otherwise be inadmissible under the Act.[17] This temporary worker program, or the first *bracero* program as Kiser and Kiser called it, was enacted for the duration of World War I and was extended until 1922, four years after the war ended.[18] Although this program did not include the Mexican government's proposals to guarantee the contracts of immigrant workers as did later *bracero* agreements, it was the blueprint upon which the later programs were based.

After the Depression began, Latinos found themselves unemployed and unwanted. Jobs that Latinos had been doing for years were no longer available, either because the jobs were no longer there or because they were being performed by Anglos who were forced to resort to that type of labor.[19] Because Latinos were historically ill-paid, many had little or no financial reserves and had no choice but to go on welfare or other relief programs. Another result of the Depression was that Mexican workers and immigrants were no longer welcomed. In fact, they were so unpopular that many were driven from the country. For example, Latinos in Oklahoma were threatened with being burned out of their homes,[20] in Indiana a mob forced railworkers to "give up their jobs,"[21] and in Texas signs were displayed warning Mexicans to get out of town.[22]

As the Depression lingered and county, state, and federal budgets dwindled, governments sought ways to cut welfare costs. One method used was to deny welfare benefits to Mexican laborers. This action, labeled "fair and humane" by government agents, was a move to reduce the labor surplus and at the same time to reduce welfare rolls.[23] No longer welcome in the United States, and with no way to sustain themselves, many Mexicans began a mass exodus to Mexico.

The Mexican migration was heralded by governments of various jurisdictions. They decided to expedite this process by sending lawful resident Mexican workers back to Mexico rather than carry them on the public welfare rolls; however, this decision was problematic for a variety of reasons. Legally, to expel Mexicans from the United States was as costly as keeping them afloat when their funds were depleted. Consequently, instead of using costly legal maneuvers such as public hearings and formal deportation proceedings, social workers resorted to betraying Mexicans by telling officials that they wanted to return to Mexico. This duplicitous tactic, of course, lowered the cost of expulsion considerably.[24] It also, however, effectively deprived many of due process.

This treachery toward Latinos continued throughout the Depression. Tragically, some, if not most, of the repatriated Latinos were lawful permanent residents of the United States. They had lived in the United States for decades, establishing homes and roots. Another result of repatriation was that many families were separated. In some instances, either one or both parents was an "alien," but children, having been born and raised in the United States, were American citizens.[25] In some cases, the children were allowed to stay in the United States while their parents were repatriated, but in many other cases such U.S. citizens were themselves "repatriated." By the end of the Depression, over 400,000 Latinos were "repatriated" to Mexico without any formal deportation proceedings, including thousands of American citizens.[26]

These repatriation programs naturally sparked protest from the Mexican government. In response to the protests, the Los Angeles Chamber of Commerce issued a statement assuring Mexican authorities that the city was in no sense unfriendly to Mexican labor. The communique stated further that the repatriation policy was designed solely to help the destitute. This was supposedly the case when invalids were removed from County Hospital in Los Angeles and shipped across the border.[27]

C. World War II and the *Bracero* Program

When the Great Depression ended at the onset of World War II, so did the labor surplus that the Depression had created. Agricultural growers in the Southwest, however, began as early as 1940 to petition agencies of the United States for permission to use foreign labor to fill labor shortages, a precedent established during World War I.[28] Shortly after Mexico declared war on the Axis powers on June 1, 1942, the Department of State contacted it about the importation of labor. The Mexican government doubted that the labor shortage really existed and viewed the efforts of the State Department as a way of obtaining cheap labor.

Cognizant of the deportation and repatriation of Latinos during the Great Depression, the Mexican government, to protect its citizens from harsh treatment and discrimination, entered into a formal agreement with the United States. This protection was provided by a government-to-government accord signed on July 23, 1942. The Mexican Labor Program, or the *Bracero* Program as it is more commonly known, was first implemented on August 4, 1942 and was funded by the U.S. President's emergency fund. The *Bracero* Program was renewed on April 26, 1943.

Under the *bracero* agreement, Mexico would permit its citizens to work in the United States for temporary, renewable periods under agreed-upon conditions. The conditions stipulated methods of recruitment, transportation, standards of health care, wages, housing, food, and the number of hours the *braceros* were allowed to work. There was even a stipulation that there should be no discrimination against *braceros.* A violation of these conditions was supposed to have resulted in the suspension of *braceros'* availability for the violating area.[29] Unfortunately, the conditions were, for the most part, ignored by both the growers and the U.S. government; thus, migrant laborers were subjected to most oppressive working environments.

Braceros across the country were compelled to endure poor food, excessive charges for board, substandard housing, discrimination, physical mistreatment, inappropriate deductions from their wages, and exposure to pesticides and other dangerous chemicals.[30] Although Texas was not the only state that violated the conditions of the agreement, discrimination toward *braceros* there was so bad that Texas lost its privilege to utilize *bracero* labor until after the war.[31]

To illustrate how important *bracero* labor was, we need only look at the impact on Texas of losing *braceros.* To fill its labor needs, Texas was forced to recruit local Mexican Americans, college students, school children, and prisoners of war.[32] As a result, the cotton wages in Texas rose 236 percent during the war years, contrasted with California, where cotton wages increased 136 percent.[33]

The upshot of the *Bracero* Program was that the U.S. government provided growers with cheap labor. Agricultural growers preferred hiring *braceros* to American citizens for two reasons. First, growers were able to set the wages that would be paid *braceros* instead of basing their remuneration on the principle of supply and demand or on collective bargaining agreements. Second, *braceros* tended to be males who traveled alone, while Americans had their families with them, thus making it easier to provide transportation and housing for *braceros.*[34]

A secondary effect of the *Bracero* Program was that it provided the United States with soldiers to fight the war. Although *braceros* were initially brought in to replace Japanese Americans who were sent to internment camps and Americans who went into the armed services or the defense industry, *braceros* additionally freed up many Mexican Americans for the armed services. Deferments were given to those who held defense industry jobs, few of whom were Mexican American, while workers in the agricultural industry, heavily staffed by Mexican Americans, were eligible for the draft. In short, Mexican Americans in the agricultural industry were sent off to the war while *braceros* were imported to replace them.[35]

While in the armed forces, Latinos distinguished themselves as fierce and reliable soldiers. Throughout the course of World War II, no Latino soldier was ever charged with desertion, treason, or cowardice.[36] The bravery of

Latino troops was recognized in the many medals awarded to Mexican Americans, including the Congressional Medal of Honor (the United States' highest honor), the Silver Star, the Bronze Star, and the Distinguished Service Cross. Seventeen Mexican Americans received the Congressional Medal of Honor for action in World War II and Korea. These seventeen Latino soldiers represent the highest proportion of Medal of Honor winners of any identifiable ethnic group. Because Mexican Americans seem to have gravitated to the most dangerous sections of the armed forces, they were overrepresented on military casualty lists.[37]

Ironically, when the Mexican American soldiers returned home, they were treated no better than they had been before they left. In Texas, a funeral parlor in Three Rivers refused to bury Félix Longoria, an American soldier decorated for heroism, because he was of Mexican descent. This obviously racist action sparked a storm of controversy that ended with the intervention of then Texas Senator Lyndon B. Johnson, who secured burial for Longoria in Arlington National Cemetery.[38] Sergeants José Mendoza López and Macario García, each awarded the Congressional Medal of Honor, were refused service in restaurants and diners because of their Mexican heritage.

Sergeant García, however, decided to challenge such discrimination against Latinos. García, after being told that he would not be served because he was a "Mexie," admonished the proprietor to serve him, declaring, "[If I am] good enough to fight your war for you, I'm good enough for you to serve a cup of coffee to." The merchant in charge of the diner refused to serve García and went so far as to attempt physically to remove García from the diner. García defended himself. The altercation ended with the arrival of the police. The police sent everyone home and ordered the diner closed for the night to end the incident. Later, after the incident was recounted over the national news, Sergeant García was arrested and charged with aggravated assault in an attempt by the city to save face.[39]

After the war, American soldiers returned to work, ending the labor shortage. Growers in the agricultural industry were, nonetheless, reluctant to give up *bracero* labor. Under the influence of agribusiness, Congress kept the program alive. The pressure they brought to bear was not enough to keep the program going on indefinitely, however, and the *Bracero* Program came to an end in December of 1947. Nonetheless, despite the termination of the *Bracero* Program, the use of Mexican labor did not end.

For nine months after the end of the *Bracero* Program, while no agreement existed between the United States and Mexico, the number of undocumented workers in the United States increased dramatically. Both governments became concerned with the increase and pushed for renewed labor negotiations. These negotiations led to a new *bracero* agreement in August of 1949. In addition to providing labor to the United States, the new *bracero* agreement stressed a reduction in the flow of undocumented workers from Mexico and the legalization of undocumented workers already in the United States.[40]

The program resulted in 238,439 undocumented workers being recruited into the work force between 1947 and 1951, when mass legalization ended.[41] Mass legalization ended for two reasons. First, it was ineffective in stemming the tide of undocumented workers coming into the country. Most importantly, the enactment of Public Law 78 on July 12, 1951, in response to the outbreak of the Korean War, created a new *bracero* program.

Under the new program, the U.S. Department of Labor was given administrative control of migration and essentially became a labor contractor. Public Law 78 conferred on the Secretary of Labor the responsibility for the certification of the need for the *braceros;* for authorization of their recruitment in Mexico; for transportation of the *braceros* to the labor camps; for guaranteeing the terms of their labor contracts; and for setting the prevailing wage. The new *bracero* agreement also rectified some problems of the prior agreements. The *braceros* were to enter contracts for periods of time ranging from six weeks to six months instead of year-long contracts. The *braceros* were also guaranteed work for at least 75 percent of the time for which they had contracted, as well as being paid the wages set by the Secretary of Labor.[42]

D. From the Korean War to "Operation Wetback"

Public Law 78 did not stem the tide of undocumented workers. Further, immigration authorities started finding undocumented workers in industrial jobs, causing labor unions to proclaim undocumented traffic as destructive to their welfare. As a result of these complaints, on June 17, 1954, Herbert Brownell, Jr., the U.S. Attorney General, ordered a crackdown on illegal immigration and a massive deportation drive, "Operation Wetback."[43]

This crackdown on illegal immigration and the ensuing process of deportation were left to the Commissioner of Immigration, Joseph P. Swing. Swing, a retired army general and reputed "professional, long-time Mexican hater," developed "Operation Wetback" along the lines of a military campaign.[44] "Operation Wetback" was a two-fold plan that coordinated the border patrol to prevent undocumented aliens from getting into the United States while rounding up and deporting those who were already here.

"Operation Wetback" went beyond its scope, however, and Americans of Mexican descent were also deported, stirring up memories of the mass deportations of the 1930s.[45] Many of those deported were denied the opportunity to present evidence that would have prevented their deportation. Between 1954 and 1959, "Operation Wetback" was responsible for over 3.7 million Latinos being deported. Of that number, an unknown amount were American citizens. In their haste to deport "illegals," only 63,500 persons were removed through formal deportation proceedings.[46] The rest of the deportees left the United States "voluntarily."[47]

In addition to violating the civil liberties of American citizens via questionable expulsions, "Operation Wetback" violated the human rights of the people being deported. Deportations were characterized by disrespect, rudeness, and intimidation. There were even reports of immigration officers "collecting fares" from persons being deported.[48]

Ironically, the *bracero* program was in effect while "Operation Wetback" was being executed. Public Law 78 was extended until it finally was allowed to lapse in December of 1964.[49] Although the *bracero* program was originally intended to be an emergency remedy for labor shortages during World War II, it survived the war by almost twenty years. Further, more *braceros* were hired in single years after the war than were hired during all of the years of the war combined.[50]

E. Modern Labor Programs

Even after the *bracero* program ended, importation of Mexican labor continued under the McCarran-Walter Immigration Act of 1952. Under the Act, immigrants from Mexico were permanently admitted to the United States to ensure there would be enough laborers. To guarantee there would be a sufficient labor force available under the Act, the Department of Labor lowered the admission standards for Mexican workers just days before the expiration of Public Law 78 and the *Bracero* Program.[51]

Although many Mexican citizens were issued visas, or "green cards," that would allow them to live and work in the United States, most preferred to reside in Mexico. These people, known as commuters because they traversed the border regularly to get to work, maintained the *bracero* lifestyle by working in the United States for days, weeks, or even months at a time, only to return to Mexico. As well as emulating *bracero* work patterns, these migrant workers performed similar jobs to the *braceros'* (i.e., low-skilled or service oriented). In 1977, there were approximately one million Mexican resident aliens in the United States, according to the Immigration and Naturalization Service.[52] The actual number of commuters is unknown due to inaccurate records and varying numbers of commuters from day to day.[53]

The McCarran-Walter Act also established a fallback *Bracero* Program. The "H-2 program" revived all the worst parts of the *Bracero* Program.[54] Under the "H-2 program," the U.S. Department of Labor has power to admit foreign labor for temporary jobs if able, willing, and qualified domestic workers can not be found at the time and place where they are needed.[55] Similar to the mistreatment suffered by workers in the *Bracero* Program, these migrants are totally dependent on the growers for employment. If the worker proves himself to be hard-working and faithful, he might be asked to return again the following year; if not, he can be deported without an appeal.[56]

In 1986 the United States went through its most recent mass legalization program. The Immigration Reform and Control Act of 1986 ("IRCA") gave legal status to undocumented persons who had been in the United States from January 1, 1982 to the time of application (between May 5, 1987 and May 4, 1988).[57] Like the McCarran-Walter Act, the IRCA provided special status to migrant farmworkers.[58] The IRCA offered legal status to special agricultural workers who could prove that they spent at least ninety "man-days" during a qualifying period doing agricultural work on specified crops. The end result of the IRCA was to legalize millions of undocumented workers and fill a labor shortage caused by the most recent immigrant expulsion, "Operation Jobs."

Another method of obtaining Mexican labor has been accomplished through the exportation of jobs. This phenomenon is euphemistically called the Border Industrialization Program or, as it is more familiarly known, the *Maquiladora* Program. The program is a system of concessions vis-à-vis Mexico that allows manufacturing and assembly plants or *maquilas* to be located in border towns in Northern Mexico and exportation of their products directly to the United States.[59] Other concessions granted by Mexico have included exemptions from labor and environmental regulations.[60]

The exemptions granted by Mexico do more than help American companies enter Mexico; they help American companies exploit Mexican labor. The *maquilas* have proven to be a financial success, but only at the expense of Mexican laborers suffering under poor working conditions, inadequate wages, deteriorating environmental conditions, and the inability to take any legal actions against their employers.[61]

History shows that whenever labor is needed, it is sought out in Mexico and discarded when the need is over, with little regard for Mexican Americans who are often ensnared in the same net. This was true with the U.S. repatriation programs during the Depression in the 1930s and "Operation Wetback" in the 1950s.

Due to intense exploitation suffered by migrant workers, their productive capacities are used up early in their lives and they have to be replaced by new waves of younger immigrants.[62] For the United States, employment of migrant workers represents a significant savings in producing and reproducing "human capital" because they stay in the United States only temporarily.[63] Even though the United States needs Mexican labor, migrant laborers arrive to face more than exploitation and brutal working conditions. They face racism, xenophobia, and discrimination. Although Latinos both within and outside the United States have come to recognize the American perspective that they are dispensable and disposable when the need for their labor diminishes, their struggle for human dignity continues, notwithstanding the seemingly inexorable cycle of invitation and exile.

NOTES

The author would like to acknowledge his research assistant, Elliott M. Castaneda, Villanova University School of Law Class of 1997, for his invaluable assistance with this essay.

1. U.S. Commission on Civil Rights, *The Tarnished Golden Door: Civil Rights Issues in Immigration* (Sept. 1980), 1.

2. "One year ago, along the border running east from Imperial Beach, Calif., the authorities built a 14-mile steel fence, installing searchlights and motion detectors and fielding hundreds of new agents." Sam Dillon, "Suddenly, the Inflow of Mexicans Seems to Slow," *New York Times,* Nov. 24, 1995, at A3.

3. In 1882, the United States began the era of racial and ethnic selectivity by enacting outright restrictions on the arrival of people from China. The Chinese Exclusion Act of May 6, 1882, ch. 126, 22 Stat. 58-59, suspended the immigration of Chinese laborers for ten years. The Act was extended in 1892 by Ch. 60, 27 Stat. 25, in 1902 by Ch. 641, 32 Stat. 176, and in 1904 it was extended indefinitely by Ch. 1630, 33 Stat. 428. The Act was finally repealed in 1943 allowing for a quota of 105 Chinese immigrants a year and declaring the Chinese eligible for naturalization by Ch. 344, 57 Stat. 600 (1943).

The Gentleman's Agreement was a compact between the governments of Japan and the United States in which Japan was supposed to stop the emigration of its citizens and the United States was supposed to end discrimination against the Japanese. See, generally, Gilbert Paul Carrasco, "The Golden Moment of Legalization," in X *In Defense of the Alien* 32, 32–34 (Lydio F. Tomasi ed., Center for Migration Studies 1988) (discussing "America's historical treatment of immigrants").

See *Korematsu v. United States,* 323 U.S. 214 (1944) (upholding a conviction for violating a military order that excluded persons of Japanese ancestry from the west coast of the United States); Eugene V. Rostow, "The Japanese American Cases—A Disaster," 54 *Yale L.J.* 489 (1945) (criticizing the Korematsu decision).

4. Julian Samora and Patricia Vandel Simon, *A History of the Mexican American People* (University of Notre Dame Press, rev. ed. 1993), 136.

5. "Anglo" originally meant someone of Anglo-Saxon ancestry but has since evolved to include all Europeans.

6. Other than the Alien Act of 1798, Ch. 58, 1 Stat. 570 (giving the President authority to expel aliens who posed a threat to national security), the first U.S. immigration law was enacted in 1877 in an effort to stop the importation of Chinese labor. It barred the admission of convicts and prostitutes. The first immigration laws establishing quotas were enacted in 1921 and codified in 1924. John Crewdson, *The Tarnished Door: The New Immigrants and the Transformation of America* (Times Books 1983), 91–97.

7. The Treaty of Guadalupe Hidalgo ended the Mexican American war and approved the prior annexation of Texas by the United States. Further, the treaty ceded to the United States the area now encompassed by the States of Arizona,

California, Nevada, and Utah, and parts of Colorado, New Mexico, and Wyoming for the price of 15 million dollars (later reduced to ten million dollars). The Treaty of Guadalupe Hidalgo is reprinted in Wayne Moquín, *A Documentary History of the Mexican Americans* (Praeger 1971), 183.

8. Ruth S. Lamb, *Mexican Americans: Sons of the Southwest* (Ocelot Press 1970), 105.

9. Among the things that Anglos acquired from Latinos were the Spanish mining law, including the concept of "staking a claim," the *batea,* a flat-bottomed pan with sloping sides used to take gold from streams, and the *arrastra,* a machine used to extract gold from quartz. Id. at 99–100.

10. Richard H. Peterson, "Anti-Mexican Nativism in California, 1848–1853: A Study of Cultural Conflict," from *Southern California Quarterly* 62 (1980) reprinted in *Historical Themes and Identity: Mestizaje and Labels* (Antoinette Sedillo López ed., Garland Publishing 1995), 193.

11. Mexican citizens living in territory ceded to the United States under the Treaty of Guadalupe Hidalgo had the option of becoming American citizens.

12. Peterson, *supra* note 10, at 181–92.

13. Matt Meier and Feliciano Rivera, *The Chicanos: A History of Mexican Americans* (Hill and Wang 1972), 75–77.

14. The testimony of Representative Addison T. Smith of Idaho provides a description of the work conditions and his opinion on why Latinos are suited for the job: "[I]t is very tiresome work for anyone except persons who are small in stature, because they have to get down on their knees a great deal of the time and crawl along the rows and weed out the extra plants, and a large man such as you or myself, figuratively speaking, would have a good deal of difficulty in engaging in that sort of work with any degree of comfort for probably more hours per day. We might stand it two hours." Robert P. Lipshultz, "American Attitudes toward Mexican Immigration" (M.A. thesis, University of Chicago 1962), reprinted in *Readings on La Raza: The Twentieth Century* (Matt S. Meier and Feliciano Rivera eds., Hill and Wang 1974), 66–67.

There was ample cheap Latino labor available. Even after many of the major rail lines were completed, Latinos comprised more than 70 percent of the section crews and 90 percent of the extra maintenance crews. Carey McWilliams, "The Great Invasion" from *The Mexicans in America* (Teachers College Press 1968), reprinted in *Readings on La Raza: The Twentieth Century* (Matt S. Meier and Feliciano Rivera eds., Hill and Wang 1974), 13.

Manuel P. Servín, "The Role of Mexican-Americans in the Development of Early Arizona," in *An Awakened Minority: The Mexican-Americans* (Manuel P. Servín ed., 2d ed., Glencoe Press 1974), 28–30.

15. Lamb, *supra* note 8, at 108.

16. Jorge A. Bustamante and James D. Cockcroft, "Unequal Exchange in the Binational Relationship: The Case of Immigrant Labor," in *Mexican/U.S. Relations: Conflict and Convergence* (Carlos Vásquez and Manuel García y Griego eds., UCLA Chicano Studies Research Center Publications 1983), 316.

17. Vernon M. Briggs, Jr., "Foreign Labor Programs as an Alternative to Illegal Immigration: A Dissenting View," in *The Border that Joins: Mexican Migrants and U.S. Responsibility* (Peter G. Brown and Henry Shue eds., Rowman and Littlefield 1983), 225.

18. George C. Kiser and Martha Woody Kiser, *Mexican Workers in the United*

States: Historical and Political Perspectives (University of New Mexico Press 1979), 6.

19. As a result of the Midwest Dust Bowl, more than 350,000 Anglos found themselves unemployed and willing to work for the low wages usually earned by Latinos. Francisco E. Balderrama and Raymond Rodríguez, *Decade of Betrayal: Mexican Repatriation in the 1930s* (University of New Mexico Press 1995), 76.

20. Carlos H. Zazueta, "Mexican Political Actors in the United States and Mexico: Historical and Political Contexts of a Dialogue Renewed" in *Mexican/U.S. Relations: Conflict and Convergence* (Carlos Vásquez and Manuel García y Griego eds., UCLA Chicano Studies Research Center Publications 1983), 450.

21. Balderrama and Rodríguez, *supra* note 19, at 99.

22. Id. at 99.

23. Matt S. Meier and Feliciano Rivera, *Readings on La Raza: The Twentieth Century* (Matt S. Meier and Feliciano Rivera eds., Hill and Wang 1974), 79.

24. The Southern Pacific Railroad "discovered that, in wholesale lots, the Mexicans could be shipped to Mexico City for $14.70 per capita." The cost to Los Angeles County to repatriate one shipment of 6,024 Mexicans: $77,249.29. It would have cost $424,933.70 in aid if they had stayed in Los Angeles, a total savings of $347,684.41. Carey McWilliams, "Getting Rid of the Mexican" from *The American Mercury*, 28 (March 1933), reprinted in *Readings on La Raza: The Twentieth Century* (Matt S. Meier and Feliciano Rivera eds., Hill and Wang 1974), 86.

25. Under the Fourteenth Amendment of the U.S. Constitution, "[a]ll persons born or naturalized in the United States, and subject to the jurisdiction thereof, are citizens of the United States and of the State wherein they reside," U.S. Const., Amend. XIV, Cl. 1.

26. The exact numbers are unknown, but estimates range from 400,000 Mexicans and many thousand American citizens, Office of Research, Advocacy and Legislation, National Council of La Raza, *Beyond Ellis Island: Hispanics-Immigrants and Americans* (1986), 4, to approximately 500,000 people, with more than half being American citizens. U.S. Commission on Civil Rights, *supra* note 1, at 10.

27. McWilliams, *supra* note 24, at 89.

28. Richard B. Craig, *The Bracero Program* (University of Texas Press 1971), 37–38.

29. Samora and Simon, *supra* note 4, at 138–39.

30. Id. at 213–14.

31. Id. at 140.

32. Meier and Rivera, *supra* note 13, at 210.

33. Id. at 210–13.

34. Samora and Simon, *supra* note 4, at 139.

35. Robin Fitzgerald Scott, "Wartime Labor Problems and Mexican-Americans in the War," from "The Mexican-American in the Los Angeles Area, 1920–1950: From Acquiescence to Activity," reprinted in *An Awakened Minority: The Mexican-Americans* (Manuel P. Servín ed., 2d ed., Glencoe Press 1974), 134.

36. Office of Research, Advocacy and Legislation, National Council of La Raza, *Beyond Ellis Island: Hispanics—Immigrants and Americans* (1986), 26.

37. Meier and Rivera, *supra* note 13, at 186–87.

38. Id. at 190–91.

39. Harold J. Alford, "War" from *The Proud Peoples: The Heritage and Culture*

of Spanish-Speaking Peoples in the U.S., reprinted in *Readings on La Raza: The Twentieth Century* (Matt S. Meier and Feliciano Rivera eds., Hill and Wang 1974), 147–49.

40. Meier and Rivera, *supra* note 13, at 224.

41. Manuel Garcia y Griego, "The Importation of Mexican Contract Laborers to the United States, 1942–1964: Antecedents, Operation, and Legacy" in *The Border that Joins: Mexican Migrants and U.S. Responsibility* (Peter G. Brown and Henry Shue eds., Rowman and Littlefield 1983), 65.

42. Meier and Rivera, *supra* note 13, at 225–26.

43. Juan R. Garcia, *Operation Wetback: The Mass Deportation of Mexican Undocumented Workers in 1954* (Greenwood Press 1980), 183.

44. Id. at 172.

45. U.S. Commission on Civil Rights, *supra* note 1, at 11.

46. Office of Research, Advocacy and Legislation, National Council of La Raza, *supra* note 36, at 4.

47. Meier and Rivera, *supra* note 13, at 228.

48. Garcia, *supra* note 43, at 215–16.

49. Meier and Rivera, *supra* note 13, at 230.

50. TEMPORARY CONTRACT LABOR FROM MEXICO

Year	Total	Year	Total	Year	Total	Year	Total
1942	4,203	1948	33,288	1954	310,476	1960	427,240
1943	52,098	1949	143,455	1955	390,846	1961	294,149
1944	62,170	1950	76,519	1956	444,581	1962	282,556
1945	49,454	1951	211,098	1957	450,422	1963	195,450
1946	32,043	1952	187,894	1958	418,855	1964	181,738
1947	19,632	1953	198,424	1959	447,535		
						Total	4,914,156

Samora and Simon, *supra* note 4, at 140.

51. The "11th hour" admission standards made it easier for Mexican workers to enter the United States by lowering "greencard" requirements to allow workers that would not normally be admittable. Meier and Rivera, *supra* note 13, at 230.

52. Briggs, *supra* note 17, at 225.

53. Samora and Simon, *supra* note 4, at 140.

54. See, generally, Richard A. Boswell and Gilbert Paul Carrasco, *Immigration and Nationality Law: Cases and Materials* (2d ed., Carolina Academic Press 1992), 256–57.

55. See 8 U.S.C. §1101 (a)(15)(H).

56. Briggs, *supra* note 17, at 231–32.

57. See amendments to 8 U.S.C. §1255a, Sec. 245A.

58. See 8 U.S.C. §1324a.

59. Garcia y Griego, *supra* note 41, at 65.

60. Joan M. Smith, "North American Free Trade and the Exploitation of Working Children," 4 *Temp. Pol. and Civ. Rts. L. Rev.* 57, 74 (1994).

61. Id. at 74; see also Chris Kraul, "There's One Boom in Mexico's Bad Times," *Philadelphia Inquirer,* Nov. 23, 1995, at D2.

62. Bustamante and Cockcroft, *supra* note 16, at 313.

63. Id. at 313.

11. WHO MAY GIVE BIRTH TO CITIZENS?

Reproduction, Eugenics, and Immigration

Dorothy E. Roberts

The new campaign against immigrants operates from the interior, as well as on the perimeters. An important strand of political theory regarding immigration holds that exclusion at the border is necessary for political citizenship to flourish within.[1] But the regulation of membership in the national community does not only involve patrolling our borders to prevent disfavored groups from entering. The present nativism also includes efforts to restrict who may give birth to citizens within the nation's boundaries. Two types of legislation currently proposed accomplish this end: laws that prohibit certain immigrants from using reproductive health services and the elimination of automatic citizenship to U.S.-born children of undocumented aliens.

Laws restricting the birth of citizens attempt concretely to control the demographics of the country. They are designed to reduce the actual numbers of disfavored groups in the population, but their broader impact is mainly metaphysical. They send a powerful message about who is worthy to add their children to the future community of citizens. Denying dark-skinned immigrants the right to give birth to citizens perpetuates the racist ideal of a white American identity.

I. LAWS REGULATING THE BIRTH OF CITIZENS

Charges against illegal immigration are often directed not at foreign workers themselves but at the presence of their families.[2] Immigration opponents argue that dependents of undocumented aliens drain local social service resources, imposing an unacceptable burden on taxpayers. These accusations are often accompanied by claims that immigrants have higher fertility rates than the rest of the population. In this view, undocumented families pose an uncontrollable internal threat to the nation's economic, cultural, and political stability.[3]

As a result of these sentiments, key anti-immigration proposals target the *children* of undocumented immigrants. California, the state containing the largest number of documented and undocumented immigrants, has become the focus of national attention regarding immigration reform. In 1993 alone, the California state legislature introduced 21 bills directed at stemming illegal immigration.[4] Governor Pete Wilson's 1994 electoral campaign centered on proposed anti-immigrant measures including the denial of welfare benefits to undocumented aliens and elimination of automatic citizenship for their children born in the United States.[5]

A. Denying Reproductive Health Services to Immigrants

California's most successful effort against illegal immigrants is the referendum initiative Proposition 187, designed "to prevent illegal aliens in the United States from receiving benefits or public services in the State of California."[6] The battle over Proposition 187 became a pivotal issue in the 1994 governor's race, with advocates declaring that it would end the "illegal alien invasion" and ultimately "save our state."[7] Three weeks before the election, an estimated 70,000 demonstrators held a march in Los Angeles to condemn the initiative.[8] Proposition 187 nevertheless passed by a 3–2 margin.[9]

The initiative prohibits local and state agencies from providing publicly funded social services, education, welfare, and nonemergency health care to any person whom they do not verify as either a U.S. citizen or a lawfully admitted alien. Government agencies are also required to report any applicant whom they suspect is an illegal immigrant.

The debate about Proposition 187 focused on the economic consequences of illegal immigration. The initiative's preamble declares that "The People of California . . . have suffered and are suffering economic hardship caused by the presence of illegal aliens in this state." The common perception that immigrant families use a disproportionate share of public assistance programs is hotly contested. Several studies have discovered that state and national rates of welfare dependency among immigrants is about the same as that of the general population.[10] The Urban Institute, for example, recently reported that 93.4 percent of the foreign-born residents in the United States do not receive public assistance, concluding that they create a net benefit of $28.7 billion annually.[11] Moreover, immigrants at the turn of the century, often extolled for their self-reliance, were actually more likely than today's immigrants to receive welfare: more than half of public welfare recipients in

1909 were immigrant families, making them three times more likely than native families to depend on public assistance.[12]

Although Proposition 187 covers a number of public services, its proponents stressed its bar to public assistance for reproductive care. Illegal immigrants had been eligible only for emergency Medi-Cal services, but California had chosen to provide prenatal care to undocumented pregnant women. Proposition 187 eliminated these services. An official estimate that nearly two out of three babies delivered at Los Angeles county hospitals in 1991 were born to undocumented mothers became the initiative's rallying point.[13] (This figure was probably inflated due to county officials' unscientific survey methods and confusion of legal and illegal immigrants.) The first step newly reelected Governor Pete Wilson took to enforce Proposition 187 was to issue an executive order directing health care providers to discontinue prenatal services for illegal immigrants.[14] According to a Wilson spokeswoman, the governor believes that pregnant women need prenatal services, but "they should just go back to their country to get them."[15]

The requirement that health workers report their patients whom they suspect of being illegal aliens will further deter pregnant women from seeking the medical care they need.[16] Moreover, by directing public health care facilities to deny services to people suspected of being illegal aliens, Proposition 187 will reduce medical care for many people who look or sound "foreign," even though they are here legally. At best, Proposition 187 will deter undocumented immigrant women from having children in the United States. At worst, it will lead to a rise in maternal and infant deaths.

B. Denying Birthright Citizenship to Children

Another example of regulating the birth of citizens is the campaign to deny automatic citizenship to children born in the United States to undocumented immigrant parents.[17] Although most countries do not apply the *jus soli* rule, this expectation has always been part of the culture and tradition of the United States for whites, and it has been the universal law for over a century.[18] "Birthright citizenship" is guaranteed by the Fourteenth Amendment to the United States Constitution, which provides that "all persons born or naturalized in the United States, and subject to the jurisdiction thereof, are citizens of the United States." Stripping second-generation immigrants of birthright citizenship, therefore, would require amending the Constitution.

The Fourteenth Amendment provision was enacted to ensure the citizenship rights of freed black slaves, overruling the Supreme Court's infamous *Dred Scott* decision.[19] Its elimination of blacks' second-class status has broad implications for the meaning of U.S. citizenship: by guaranteeing full citizenship rights to the native-born, the Fourteenth Amendment established a new national citizenship that prevents "the reemergence of a hereditary caste of subordinated denizens." [20] Indeed, a delegate to Louisiana's Constitutional Convention in 1868, Oscar J. Dunn, identified the absence of "privileges founded upon birth-right" as the essence of America's political heritage.[21] Thus, birthright citizenship has been interpreted to extend to all children born in the United States whose parents are within its jurisdiction.[22]

Despite their constitutional implications, proposals to restrict birthright citizenship have gained national attention. Pete Wilson included this issue in his immigration reform platform that swept him into office.[23] Republican representative Brian Bilbray introduced in Congress the "Citizenship Reform Act of 1995" to amend the Immigration and Nationality Act to achieve this end.[24] Bilbray noted that his state of California had allowed 96,000 babies born to illegal immigrants to become U.S. citizens. Democratic Senator Harry Reid of Nevada and Republican Representative Elton Gallegly of California have also introduced immigration reform bills containing provisions that strip the children of illegal aliens of birthright citizenship. Representative Gallegly explained to Congress that the measure was designed to "discourag[e] pregnant aliens from entering this country illegally in order to have their babies delivered free of charge and become U.S. citizens eligible for an array of benefits." [25]

The rejection of the *jus soli* principle finds academic support in *Citizenship without Consent: Illegal Aliens in the American Polity,* written by Yale law professors Peter Schuck and Rogers Smith.[26] The authors criticize birthright citizenship for ascribing membership in the American polity without the consent of the polity or the citizen herself. But the ascription of citizenship is no different from the ascription of inalienable rights, "which rest solely on one's humanity, not on any network of mutual consent." [27]

II. PRESERVING A WHITE NATIONAL IDENTITY

These restrictions on the birth of citizens raise a fundamental question about the national identity: Who is an American citizen? In theory, America subscribes to the ideal of civic nationalism, which defines citizenship according to shared political institutions and values rather than racial descent. But in practice American national identity has revolved around questions of race. From the founding of the nation, the meaning of American citizenship has rested on the denial of citizenship to nonwhites living within its borders. Initially the definition of citizenship had to distinguish between white masters and their African slaves. As Eric Foner observed, "Slavery helped to shape the identity of all Americans, giving nationhood from the outset a powerful exclusionary dimension." [28] The development of a republican conception of citizenship corresponded with the founders' insistence on a white national identity. Whites rationalized blacks' exclusion from citizenship by claiming that blacks lacked the capacity for rational thought, independence, and self-control that were essential for self-governance.[29]

The nation's founders soon extended this racialized definition of citizenship to their immigration policy. America's first naturalization law, passed in 1790, reserved citizenship for whites only: in order to qualify to become a citizen an alien had to be "a free white person."[30] Thomas Jefferson recommended expelling blacks, whom he believed were incapable of acting as citizens, and importing an equal number of whites to complete the American population.[31] Even after the Fourteenth Amendment guaranteed formal citizenship rights to freed black slaves, Jim Crow laws and official segregation, followed by systemic *de facto* discrimination, ensured that blacks remained a subordinate caste.

America's changing demographics threaten this white national identity. Despite the alarm sounded about the recent rise in immigration, the level of immigration has not surpassed the numbers America absorbed in the past. The relative rate of immigration today is lower than the previous high of 9 million at the turn of the century because the current population is three times as large.[32] In 1910, about 15 percent of America's total population was foreign born—still higher than the new postwar peak of 8.7 percent reached in 1994.[33]

But there are two critical differences. First, the new immigrants are no longer predominantly white: between 1968 and 1993, 80 percent came from Latin America, the Caribbean, and Asia.[34] The 1965 Immigration and Nationality Act Amendments, which replaced the national origins quota system with one allowing family reunification, changed the complexion of the renewed mass immigration.[35] Whereas the majority of America's first immigrants were British, for example, by the middle 1980s Great Britain ranked twelfth as a country of origin behind Third World nations such as Mexico, the Philippines, Haiti, South Korea, India, Jamaica, and Cuba.[36] In addition, most of the over 3 million undocumented aliens living in the United States crossed the border from Mexico.[37]

Second, the new immigrants are more visible because of their higher geographic concentration in a handful of metropolitan areas.[38] There is also evidence of a new white flight from cities such as New York, Chicago, and Los Angeles—this time a flight from immigrants rather than from the migrating descendants of African slaves. William Frey and Jonathan Tilove report that "[i]n the last half of the 80's, for every 10 immigrants who arrived, 9 residents left for points elsewhere," places that were whiter, such as Tampa, Seattle, and Phoenix.[39] This concentration of minority immigrants, coupled with white exodus, raises the specter for some white Americans of hordes of people of color taking over America's largest cities.

Proposition 187 was a response to California's changing demographics.

California's population is currently 29 percent Latino and predicted to be predominantly comprised of ethnic minorities by the year 2000.[40] These figures reflect a national trend: the Census Bureau projects that the Latino population will grow from 9 percent to 21 percent of the U.S. population by 2050.[41] The rallying slogan "Save Our State" meant for many Californians an effort to rescue the state from this cultural and demographic transformation. One author interpreted the passage of Proposition 187 as "the last gasp of a segment of white Americans who are trying to preserve a universal Anglo and European culture and return national demographics to the 1950s."[42]

While most politicians tiptoe around the racial subtext animating immigration policy, some commentators have bluntly proclaimed their objective of maintaining a white population. In *Alien Nation,* for example, journalist Peter Brimelow expresses the threat many see in minority immigration: "Race and ethnicity are destiny in American politics. The racial and ethnic balance of America is being radically altered through public policy. This can only have the most profound effects. *Is this what Americans want?*"[43] Brimelow's answer is no. Since America has always had a white "ethnic core,"[44] Brimelow argues, white Americans "have a right to insist [the racial balance] be shifted back."[45]

Other anti-immigration activists have articulated this fear of racial imbalance. John H. Tanton, the founder and former chairman of Federation for American Immigration Reform (FAIR), warned in a private memo of a "Latin onslaught" and the inevitable white backlash: "Will the present majority peaceably hand over its political power to a group that is simply more fertile? . . . As whites see their power and control over their lives declining, will they simply go quietly into the night? Or will there be an explosion?"[46] In *The Path to National Suicide,* Lawrence Auster similarly predicted that the multiculturalism emerging from America's openness to Third World immigration portends "not some utopian, 'equal' society, but simply the end of American civilization."[47]

Proponents of anti-immigration measures explain their position on the basis of culture rather than race. A common theme is the threat that the new immigration poses for national unity. Political columnist George Will, for example, noted that "America is not just an economy. . . . It is a culture. The high rate of immigration since 1960, combined with the high fertility rate of immigrants relative to that of native-born Americans, is producing a rapid change in the nation's ethnic and cultural balance."[48] Conservative presidential candidate Pat Buchanan similarly proposed "a timeout from illegal immigration so that we can become one nation and one culture. So we can all learn the same customs and traditions."[49]

These advocates blame Third World immigrants for refusing to assimilate into American culture, which they define as necessarily white. A *Boston Herald* columnist recently asserted this rationale, adding a concern about the new immigrants' qualification for affirmative action:

New immigrants are altering America's racial/ethnic composition. . . . Blacks from the Caribbean and browns from Latin America immediately qualify for affirmative-action preferences, as will their children and grandchildren. No beautiful mosaic this, but a multicultural fraying of the social fabric. By 2020, whites will comprise less than 60 percent of the population of the nine largest states. . . . Riots, cultural separatism, a racialized justice system . . . and demands for reparations will be among the more pleasant aspects of our growing Balkanization.[50]

Many whites fear a loss of cultural, as well as numerical, preeminence. While whites have demanded that nonwhites assimilate to an Anglo-American way of life, the possibility that whites should assimilate to nonwhite culture seems downright un-American. This thinking assumes that American culture is synonymous with the culture of white people and that the cultures of the new immigrants are inconsistent with a national identity. It also assumes that one-way assimilation is the only model that generates a truly American identity, precluding more inclusive, plural, and accurate notions of American identity. Moreover, some whites interpret demands for political equality as cultural separatism. So embedded is this underlying norm of whiteness that it has become transparent: many view the racialized meaning of national identity as natural and remain oblivious to the racism that maintains it. Thus, concern about immigrants' threat to national cohesion is actually a form of racial prejudice and domination.[51]

Brimelow buttresses his position with America's history of exclusionary immigration policies: he notes that the 1790 naturalization law applied only to whites, that Thomas Paine's enthusiasm for asylum extended only to "every European Christian," and that nineteenth-century Asians were virtually barred from entry.[52] While these policies reflect America's history of racism, they ignore America's heritage of demographic diversity and cultural pluralism.[53] Brimelow dismisses the early nation's black and Indian populations by pointing out that the collectivity that made political decisions was "wholly white."[54] Under this view, America was created as a white nation, and government policy should reverse the recent influx of Third World immigrants that jeopardizes the nation's white identity. Of course, Brimelow's embrace of the racism that resulted in the exclusion of the nonwhite people who helped to build the nation in no way justifies the perpetuation of racism in current immigration policy.

III. EUGENICS AND THE HISTORY OF IMMIGRATION IN AMERICA

Policies directed at the children of racially undesirable immigrants have invidious roots in America's eugenic past. Modern-day advocates of these anti-immigration policies may not espouse eugenic theory, but, like the former eugenicists, they fear "not only the immigrants themselves but also their descendants."[55] Eugenicists opposed open-door immigration because they viewed the children of certain immigrants as "our home-grown foreigners," who remained "foreign stock" despite their birth on U.S. soil.[56] As Francis A. Walker, superintendent of the censuses of 1870 and 1880, explained:

Although born among us, our general instinctive feeling testifies that they are not wholly of us. So separate has been their social life, due alike to their clannishness and to our reserve; so strong have been the ties of race and blood and religion with them; so acute has been the jealousy of their spiritual teachers to our institutions—that we think of them, and speak of them, as foreigners.[57]

These nativist sentiments were inseparably intertwined with eugenic doctrine that held foreigners to be genetically inferior as well as culturally distinct.

During the first half of the twentieth century, the eugenics movement embraced the theory that intelligence and other personality traits are genetically determined and therefore inherited.[58] This hereditarian belief, coupled with the reform approach of the progressive era, fueled a campaign to remedy America's social problems by stemming biological degeneracy. Eugenicists advocated compulsory sterilization to prevent reproduction by people who were likely to produce allegedly defective offspring. Many states around the turn of the century enacted involuntary sterilization laws directed at those deemed burdens on society, including the mentally retarded, mentally ill, epileptics, and criminals.[59]

The U.S. Supreme Court validated eugenic sterilization in its 1927 decision *Buck v. Bell,* which upheld the constitutionality of a Virginia involuntary sterilization law.[60] The Court approved an order that Carrie Buck, described in the opinion as "a feeble minded white woman" who had been committed to a state mental institution, undergo sterilization. Justice Holmes, himself an ardent eugenicist, gave eugenic theory the imprimatur of constitutional law in his infamous declaration: "Three generations of imbeciles are enough."[61]

American eugenicists advocated restrictions on the immigration of "inferior races" as another means of protecting the nation from genetic contamination. While the first wave of mass immigration, beginning in the 1840s, initially emanated from northern and western Europe, the numbers arriving from southern and eastern Europe were increasing. In *A Study of American*

Intelligence, published in 1923, Princeton psychology professor Carl C. Brigham reported that northern Europeans scored higher on intelligence tests than blacks and immigrants from Italy, Poland, Greece, and Russia.[62] Professor Brigham decried the degeneration of the American population through "racial admixture" with inferior immigrants and urged more selective immigration policies that would prevent the influx of less-intelligent groups.

The same year that Brigham's book was published, a new edition of the bestseller *The Passing of the Great Race,* by the New York eugenicist Madison Grant, appeared.[63] Grant extolled the superior qualities of the Nordic race, a people of "rulers, organizers, and aristocrats" whom he claimed were responsible for every great civilization that ever existed. These civilizations had declined, Grant argued, because of the deterioration of the Nordic population through warfare and intermixture with other races of people. *The Passing of the Great Race* warned that the Nordic stock in America was similarly threatened by racial intermixture with blacks and inferior immigrant groups which inevitably produced children of the "lower" type.

Claims about immigrants' high fertility levels fanned hostility toward the foreign born. Studies purporting to show that immigrants were reproducing faster than native, Anglo-Saxon Americans generated hysterical predictions of imminent "race suicide."[64] At the same time, eugenicists used William Rossiter's 1909 study *A Century of Population Growth* to claim that the majority of white Americans of the 1920s were descendants of the original colonial stock.[65] Their goal became to preserve the Nordic race's predominance in the American population.

Nativists recommended that Congress adopt an immigration quota based on a census that predated the increase in the numbers of southern- and eastern-European immigrants.[66] As Harvard professor Robert Ward explained, ending this undesirable influx was necessary "[i]f we want the American race to continue to be predominantly Anglo-Saxon-Germanic, of the same stock as that which originally settled the United States, wrote our Constitution, and established our democratic institutions."[67] Influenced by testimony of eugenic lobbyists, Congress passed the National Origins Act of 1924, which imposed national quotas based on the 1890 census and effectively cut off immigration of Poles, Italians, Slavs, and eastern-European Jews.[68] The law also explicitly prohibited Japanese immigration. Meanwhile, the U.S. Supreme Court upheld the ban on citizenship for Asian immigrants, reasoning that the Naturalization Act of 1790 was intended "to confer the privilege of citizenship upon that class of persons whom the fathers knew as white, and to deny it to all who could not be so classified."[69]

Like the turn-of-the-century eugenicists, some current opponents of immigration espouse the theory that immigration from the Third World is a form of "race suicide": it threatens the numerical predominance of the white race.[70] Some anti-immigrant organizations have close ties with population control organizations that espouse a eugenics philosophy. FAIR, the Federation for American Immigration Reform, for example, is supported by the Pioneer Fund, a foundation established in 1937 and dedicated to "human race betterment."[71] [For further discussion of the relationship between these organizations, see chapter 7 in this volume—*Ed.*]

Moreover, conservatives today, as during the eugenics movement, propose policies to limit immigrants' reproduction in tandem with policies designed to discourage dispossessed, predominantly minority citizens from having children. These measures include "family cap" legislation that denies additional benefits for children born to women already on welfare[72] and proposed cash bonuses to encourage these women to use Norplant, a long-acting contraceptive.[73] The House Republicans' proposed Personal Responsibility Act includes provisions cutting off AFDC benefits for children born to unwed teenagers and mothers already receiving benefits, as well as to certain categories of immigrants.[74] The impact of these restrictions on reproduction and citizenship extends beyond the numbers of children born to immigrants.

IV. WHOSE CHILDREN MAY BE AMERICA'S FUTURE CITIZENS?

The immigration policies I have discussed regulate the identity of America's future citizens. The 1990 census counted 5 million children who were either foreign born or born in this country to first-generation immigrants; it is estimated that this number will rise to 9 million by 2010.[75] Much of the new nativism targets these children for exclusion. Peter Brimelow's most passionate claims, for example, revolve around his son, Alexander, to whom *Alien Nation* is dedicated.[76] Brimelow feels that America's future citizens should look like his son, a "white male with blue eyes and blond hair," rather than the dark-skinned children of immigrants.[77] He wants to guarantee that the next generation will remain predominantly white: "If only for my son, Alexander's sake, I'd like it to stay that way."[78] It is clear that Brimelow believes that he, as a white man, is entitled to contribute his offspring to the next generation of Americans, even though Brimelow himself is an immigrant. But he resents that his son must share that inheritance with children of color.

Several years ago I described government restrictions on reproduction as a form of dehumanization:

The right to bear children goes to the heart of what it means to be human. The value we place on individuals determines whether we see them as entitled to perpetuate themselves in their children. Denying someone the right to bear children—or punishing her for exercising that right—deprives her of a basic part of her humanity. When this denial is based on race, it also functions to preserve a racial hierarchy that essentially disregards black humanity.[79]

One of the tests of privileges of inclusion in a community is the ability to contribute one's children to the next generation of citizens. The measures I have discussed treat the new undocumented immigrants as unworthy, on the basis of their race, of adding their children to the national community.

Eugenicists acknowledged the connection between their control of reproduction and their definition of citizenship. They premised the citizenship of many social outcasts on their inability to procreate. A 1928 Wisconsin study of women who were discharged after being sterilized in institutions for the feebleminded found: "Many mentally deficient persons by consenting to the operation are permitted to return, under supervision, to society where they become self-supporting social units and *acceptable citizens*."[80] The social engineers who administered this program made allegedly "feebleminded" women's citizenship contingent on their consent to sterilization. But by imposing this condition, they treated the women as less than citizens: they were considered unworthy of contributing to the future generation of citizens.

Policies that devalue dark-skinned immigrants by excluding their children from the community of citizens help to resolve the paradox of American immigration policy. The federal government has opened the nation's borders to immigrants, even facilitating the entry of illegals, in order to meet employers' demands for cheap labor.[81] Yet, many white Americans see the resulting demographic shift as a threat to their sense of national identity. Americans complain about the economic drain perpetrated by undocumented aliens, while employing them at low wages to clean their homes and offices, mow their lawns, take care of their children, pick their crops, and perform other undesirable jobs.[82] As a U.S. senator, Pete Wilson backed provisions in the 1986 Immigration Reform and Control Act that allowed "guest workers" temporarily into the country to harvest crops.[83] At a more global level, Americans enjoy cheap crops and products produced abroad by the exploited work forces that migrate to this country in search of better working conditions.[84]

Denying these immigrants the privileges of citizenship—especially the right to give birth to citizens—is a way of maintaining an exclusive meaning of citizenship while continuing to exploit immigrants' economic contribution. Although these laws have a very concrete impact on the health and status of immigrant children, they send an equally powerful message about their humanity and inclusion. Denying dark-skinned immigrants the right to give birth to citizens perpetuates the racist ideal of a white American identity. Instead, our policy should be to make every effort to embrace these children and to include them in a pluralistic redefinition of American citizenship.

NOTES

I am indebted to Juan Perea for sharing with me his insights on the new nativism, to Eric Foner for his comments on an earlier draft of this chapter, and to Edward Paulino for his excellent research assistance.

1. Linda S. Bosniak, *Exclusion and Membership: The Dual Identity of the Undocumented Worker under United States Law,* 1988 *Wis. L. Rev.* 955, 963. See, e.g., Peter Schuck and Rogers Smith, *Citizenship without Consent: Illegal Aliens in the American Polity* 99 (1985); Michael Walzer, *Spheres of Justice* 31–63 (1983); Bruce Ackerman, *Social Justice in the Liberal State* 88–95 (1980).

2. Carol Sanger, *Immigration Reform and Control of the Undocumented Family,* 2 *Geo. Imm. L.J.* 295, 307–11 (1987).

3. See e.g., Richard Sybert, "Population, Immigration and Growth in California," 31 *San Diego L. Rev.* 945 (1994) (criticizing immigration policy that "poses an enormous financial burden on taxpayers [and] tears at the country's social fabric under the banner of divisive multiculturalism"). Sybert was Director of Planning and Research for the State of California from 1991 to 1993 under Governor Pete Wilson.

4. Robert Reinhold, "A Welcome for Immigrants Turns to Resentment," *New York Times,* Aug. 25, 1993, at A1.

5. James Bornemeier, "Charting Wilson's Transformation on Immigration," *Los Angeles Times,* Nov. 2, 1994, at A3; David S. Broder, "California's Immigration Backlash," *Washington Post,* Oct. 20, 1993, at A29. Governor Wilson may not have realized that legislation denying welfare benefits to undocumented aliens may encourage these immigrants to become naturalized citizens rather than to leave the country. See Laura Keeton, "More Legal Aliens Seeking Citizenship to Keep Benefits," *Wall Street Journal,* Mar. 6, 1995, at B1.

6. Proposition 187, Sec. 1.

7. Bornemeier, supra note 5.

8. Patrick J. McDonnell and Robert J. Lopez, "70,000 March through L.A. against Prop. 187," *Los Angeles Times,* Oct. 17, 1994, at A1.

9. Paul Feldman and Rich Connell, "Wilson Acts to Enforce Parts of Prop. 187; 8 Lawsuits Filed," *Los Angeles Times,* Nov. 10, 1994, at A1.

10. Ron K. Unz, "Immigration or the Welfare State," 70 *Policy Review* 33, 34 (Fall 1994); Leif Jensen, "Patterns of Immigration and Public Assistance Utilization, 1970–1980," 22 *Internat'l Migration Rev.* 51, 80 (1988). See, generally, Julian Simon, *The Economic Consequences of Immigration* (1990) (arguing the immigrants benefit the nation economically).

11. Michael Fix and Jeffrey S. Passel, *Immigration and Immigrants: Setting the Record Straight* (1995). But see Donald L. Huddle, *The Net National Costs of Immigration into the United States: Illegal Immigration Assessed* (1995) (estimating that the national net cost of illegal aliens in 1994 was between $16 billion and $21.6 billion).

12. Frederick Ross, "Muddled Masses: The Growing Backlash against Immigration Includes Many Myths," *Wall Street Journal,* April 16, 1995, at A1.

13. Patrick J. McDonnell and Jack Cheevers, "Immigrant Care Costs Fuel Debate; Finances," *Los Angeles Times,* Oct. 29, 1995, at A25.

14. Paul Feldman and Amy Pyle, "Wilson Acts to Enforce Parts of Prop. 187," *Los Angeles Times,* Nov. 10, 1994, at A1.

15. Geoffrey Cowley and Andrew Murr, "Good Politics, Bad Medicine," *Newsweek,* Dec. 5, 1994, at 31.

16. See Karen Ellsworth and Judith Long, "Physicians Can't Enforce Prop. 187 on Suspected Illegals," *San Francisco Examiner,* Dec. 1, 1994, at A16 (letter to editor); Cowley and Murr, supra note 15.

17. See, generally, Robert J. Shulman, "Comment, Children of a Lesser God: Should the Fourteenth Amendment Be Altered or Repealed to Deny Automatic Citizenship Rights and Privileges to American Born Children of Illegal Aliens?" 22 *Pepp. L. Rev.* 669 (1995). See also Peter H. Schuck and Rogers M. Smith, *Citizenship Without Consent: Illegal Aliens in the American Polity* (1985).

18. Schuck and Smith, supra note 17, at 8.

19. Gerald L. Neuman, "Back to Dred Scott?" 24 *San Diego L. Rev.* 485 (1987).

20. Gerald L. Neuman, "Justifying U.S. Naturalization Policies," 35 *Va. J. Internat'l Law* 237, 248 (1994).

21. Eric Foner, "Rights and the Constitution in Black Life during the Civil War and Reconstruction," 74 *J. Am. Hist.* 863, 873 (1988).

22. See *United States v. Wong Kim Ark,* 169 U.S. 649 (1898).

23. Broder, supra note 5.

24. H.R. 1363, 104th Cong., 1st Sess. (1995).

25. 138 Cong. Rec. E2572–01, E2573 (Sept. 10, 1992).

26. Schuck and Smith, supra note 17.

27. David A. Martin, "The Civic Republican Ideal for Citizenship, and for Our Common Life," 35 *Va. J. Int'l L.* 301, 316 n. 50 (1994). See also David A. Martin, "Membership and Consent: Abstract or Organic?" 11 *Yale J. Int'l L.* 278, 293 (1985) (reviewing Peter Schuck, *Citizenship without Consent*).

28. Eric Foner, "Who Is an American?" 4 *Culture Front,* Winter 1995–1996, at 7.

29. Eric Foner, "The Meaning of Freedom in the Age of Emancipation," 81 *J. Am. Hist.* 435, 444 (1994); Ronald Takaki, *Iron Cages: Race and Culture in 19th-Century America* 1–55 (1990).

30. 1st Cong., Sess. II, Ch. 3 (1790).

31. Ellis Cose, *A Nation of Strangers* 20 (1992).

32. William H. Frey and Jonathan Tilove, "Immigrants In, Native Whites Out," *New York Times Magazine,* August 20, 1995, at 44.

33. U.S. Bureau of the Census, *The Foreign Born Population: 1994* (August 1995); Peter H. Schuck, "The Transformation of Immigration Law," 84 *Colum. L. Rev.* 1, 89 (1984).

34. Frey and Tilove, supra note 32; Peter Brimelow, *Alien Nation* 77 (1995).

35. See Immigration and Nationality Act Amendments of 1965, Pub. L. No. 89–236, 79 Stat. 911; Brimelow, supra note 34, at 74–84.

36. Cose, supra note 31, at 11.

37. Thomas A. Aleinikoff and David A. Martin, *Immigration: Process and Policy* 252 (2d ed. 1991).

38. Frey and Tilove, supra note 32, at 45.

39. Id. at 44.

40. Jim Gogek, "Prop. 187 Will Galvanize 'Hispanic' Activism," *San Diego Union Tribune,* Oct. 30, 1994, at A2.

41. U.S. Bureau of the Census, Current Population Reports, P23–183, *Hispanic Americans Today* 2 (1993).

42. Gogek, supra note 40.

43. Brimelow, supra note 34, at xvii.

44. Brimelow, supra note 34, at 10. Brimelow stated during a television interview that "the U.S. is not remotely a multicultural society. It is actually—and has always been—a society based on European values." Transcript, Charlie Rose, Thirteen/WNET, April 20, 1995 (available at 1995 WL 6126129).

45. Brimelow, supra note 34, at 264.

46. Patrick J. McDonnell and Paul Jacobs, "FAIR at Forefront of Push to Reduce Immigration Population," *Los Angeles Times,* Nov. 24, 1993, at 1.

47. Lawrence Auster, *The Path to National Suicide: An Essay on Immigration and Multiculturalism* 63 (1990).

48. George Will, "Slamming Shut the Golden Door to Immigrants," *Times-Picayune,* July 30, 1993, at B7.

49. Lori Rodriguez, "No Justice in Simpson Trial, Buchanan Tells Black Group," *Houston Chronicle,* Oct. 8, 1995, at 23.

50. Don Feder, "This Melting Pot Is Boiling Over," *Boston Herald,* Oct. 4, 1995, at 33.

51. See, e.g., Mari J. Matsuda, "Voices of America: Accent Antidiscrimination Law," and "A Jurisprudence for the Last Reconstruction," 100 *Yale L.J.* 1329 (1991) (discussing how accent discrimination masks biased cultural judgments); Bill Ong Hing, "Beyond the Rhetoric of Assimilation and Culture Pluralism: Addressing the Tension of Separatism and Conflict in an Immigration-Driven Multiracial Society," 81 *Cal. L. Rev.* 863 (1993) (observing that immigration challenges the definition of American identity); Juan F. Perea, "Ethnicity and Prejudice: Reevaluating 'National Origin' Discrimination under Title VII," 35 *Wm. and Mary L. Rev.* 805 (1994) (criticizing courts' treatment of national origins discrimination under Title VII).

52. Brimelow, supra note 34, at 14–17.

53. See Juan F. Perea, "Demography and Distrust: An Essay on American Languages, Cultural Pluralism, and Official English," 77 *Minn. L. Rev.* 269 (1992) (discussing historical responses to American cultural pluralism).

54. Brimelow, supra note 34, at 18.

55. See Miriam King and Steven Ruggles, "American Immigration, Fertility, and Race Suicide at the Turn of the Century," 30 *J. Interdisciplinary Hist.* 347, 347 (1990).

56. Id. See, generally, John Higham, *Strangers in the Land: Patterns of American Nativism 1860–1925* (2d ed. 1974) (explaining the sources of American nativism).

57. King and Ruggles, supra note 55, at 347.

58. Mark Haller, *Eugenics: Hereditarian Attitudes in American Thought* (1984).

59. Phillip P. Reilly, *The Surgical Solution: A History of Involuntary Sterilization in the United States* 101–2 (1991).

60. 274 U.S. 200 (1927).

61. Id. at 207.

62. C. C. Brigham, *A Study of American Intelligence* (1923).

63. Madison Grant, *The Passing of the Great Race* (1923).

64. King and Ruggles, supra note 55, at 348. King and Ruggles found, however, that the combined fertility of immigrants and their children was actually *lower* than that of native-born women of native parentage: "the much-heralded 'breeding power' of ethnics at the turn of the century was an illusion." Id. at 364.

65. Margo J. Anderson, *The American Census: A Social History* 144–45 (1988).

66. Cose, supra note 31, at 75.

67. Quoted in id., at 75.

68. Immigration Act of 1924, ch. 190, 43 Stat. 153, 155, 159–60. See, generally, Aleinikoff and Martin, supra note 37, at 40–60; E. P. Hutchinson, *Legislative History of American Immigration Policy 1798–1965,* at 470–74 (1981).

69. *Ozawa v. United States,* 260 U.S. 178, 195 (1922).

70. McDonnell and Jacobs, supra note 46.

71. Id. See Jean Stefancic, "Funding the Nativist Agenda," in this volume, chapter 7.

72. See Melinda Henneberger, "Rethinking Welfare: Deterring New Births—A Special Report; State Aid Is Capped, but to What Effect?" *New York Times,* April 11, 1995, at A1; Mike Dorning, "Welfare Caps Try to Put Lid on Size of Families," *Chicago Tribune,* March 12, 1995, at 1.

73. See Kan. H.B. 2089, 74th Leg., 2d Sess. (1991); Tenn. H.B. 1860, 97th Leg., 2d Sess. (1992); La. H.B. 1584, 17th R. Sess. S 1 (a) (1991). In addition, at least two states have proposed legislation to mandate the use of Norplant as a condition of receiving welfare benefits. See H.B. 3207, S.C. (1993); S.B. 2895, Miss. (1992).

74. Personal Responsibility Act, H.R. 4, 104th Cong., 1st Sess., Sec. 405 (a) (3) and (4).

75. Michael Fix and Jeffrey S. Passel, *Immigration and Immigrants: Setting the Record Straight* (1994).

76. See Ira Glasser, "Letter to the Editor," *New York Times,* June 16, 1995, at A26.

77. Brimelow, supra note 34, at 11.

78. Id. at 221.

79. Dorothy E. Roberts, "Punishing Drug Addicts Who Have Babies: Women of Color, Equality, and the Right of Privacy," 104 *Harv. L. Rev.* 1419, 1472 (1991).

80. Quoted in Reilly, supra note 59, at 101–2 (emphasis added).

81. Bosniak, supra note 1; Sanger, supra note 2, at 302–11.

82. See Penny Loeb et al., "To Make a Nation: How Immigrants Are Changing America for Better and Worse," 115 *U.S. News and World Report* 47 (Oct. 4, 1993) (listing immigrants' most common jobs and average income).

83. William J. Bennett, "Immigration: Making Americans," *Washington Post,* Dec. 4, 1994, at C7.

84. Joe Maizlish, "Debate over Immigration," *Los Angeles Times,* Dec. 8, 1993, at part-B, p. B6 (letter to the editor).

V

BORDER CROSSINGS
Critical Views of the Border

Ordinarily we think of the border as a fixed, given geopolitical line: permanent, immutable, timeless. The chapters in this part show how the border is more a powerful, evolving idea than a permanent line. Néstor P. Rodríguez deconstructs the idea and meanings of the border through a thoughtful analysis of the metaphors used in its description and its uses in our politics. Robert S. Chang deconstructs the border in an entirely different, but equally revealing, way. He shows us how the meaning of the border is contingent upon the characteristics of the person seeking to cross it.

The whole concept of the undocumented or illegal alien depends heavily on the assumed permanence and relevance of a national border. One must have such a border before it can be crossed without papers or illegally. Berta Esperanza Hernández-Truyol show us that, regardless of the borders that define nation-states, international norms of human rights constitute a body of law, binding on the United States, that protects the human rights of all persons whether their status is legal or not.

12. THE SOCIAL CONSTRUCTION OF THE U.S.-MEXICO BORDER
Néstor P. Rodríguez

Nation-state boundaries are social constructions. They do not exist independent of our volition. With the exception of insular countries, they usually do not mark any significant topographical change in the surrounding land mass. Nation-state borders exist primarily because state governments agree, voluntarily or through coercion, that they delimit political divisions. Solemn treaties formalize international boundaries, but it is the daily reproduction of ideas and myths that socially construct borders. One idea is that international boundaries are *essential* dividers between areas of different social qualities.

Nation-states, and thus their boundaries, are recent creations in human history.[1] Measured against the earliest evidence of fully modern humans (Homo sapiens sapiens) some 150,000 years ago in Africa, they have existed for less than one percent of modern humankind's existence.[2] In Europe, nation-states emerged in the 1100 to 1600 period. In the latter part of this period European regions coalesced into a capitalist system, with trade and colonial ties to many other world regions.[3] At times the growth of capitalism clashed with the development of European states, but, in general, the medieval consolidation of governmental authority into the state provided a political framework that assisted world capitalist development.[4] Countries that enjoyed strong state structures competed for dominance in the young capitalist world system. European powers also created regional and state boundaries in peripheral areas (such as Africa, Asia, and the Americas) to facilitate the formation of colonial structures.[5] By the nineteenth and twentieth centuries, nation-state boundaries reached a peak of consolidation with nationalism, nativism, and national-security concerns forming strong bases for this development. Indeed, disagreements over the location of international boundaries sometimes led to military confrontations. The present location of the U.S.-Mexico border, for example, was the product of a 1846–48 war fought between the countries, in part, over the location of the border line in southern Texas.[6]

Even in the most formidable border settings, individuals, groups, and whole communities have attempted to cross international boundaries without state authorization for a variety of reasons, such as to escape political persecution, seek economic opportunity, and reunite with family members. Sustained large-scale unauthorized border crossings often result from pressures created by macro-structural forces, such as regional economic restructuring or political transformation, as people struggle to survive through strategies of international migration.

The very global framework of capitalism produces tension for state boundaries. Historically capitalist development has tended to link capital and labor from different countries into a global system either by promoting international divisions of labor or by attracting capital and labor resources across state boundaries.[7] Capitalists thus sometimes have sought to minimize border restrictions at times when government officials have sought to enhance them.[8] This tension has been evident within U.S. government institutions, for example, when the Department of Agriculture promoted the U.S.-Mexico *Bracero* Program on behalf of agribusiness, while the Department of Labor resisted the program on behalf of organized labor.[9] This was also evident in the implementation of the Immigration Reform and Control Act (IRCA) in 1986, where agricultural interests dependent on immigrant labor sought to obtain less-stringent amnesty conditions for undocumented agricultural workers.

Transnational communities also lessen the border's salience. These are communities formed by immigrants who maintain strong interaction between settlement areas in the United States and communities of origin back home.[10] Transnational communities contain social structures (economic, family, political, and other institutions) whose reproduction is dependent on this binational relation. While immigrants have always maintained contact with their communities of origin, the present interaction with communities of origin among immigrants in transnational communities has reached an unprecedented level through high-tech communication, jet travel, and superhighways. In earlier times, Mexican transnational communities in the United States were located mainly in U.S.-Mexican border areas. Today they exist far from the borderlands, most recently in Atlanta and New York City. The constant interaction across the border by transnational residents makes the U.S.-Mexico boundary seem almost irrelevant.

In the last two decades of the twentieth century, industrial countries in

Europe and North America have considered, and initiated, major policies to make their international boundaries less rigid for economic integration. These measures include the Schengen Agreement and the Maastricht Treaty in Europe and the North American Free Trade Agreement (NAFTA) in North America.[11] The Schengen Agreement, proposed in the mid-1980s, calls for common visa policies and an eventually border-free Europe. The Maastricht Treaty, ratified in 1993 by countries of the European Community (EC), provides for common foreign policies, a single currency, and a central regional bank by 1999. The Maastricht Treaty also endorses voting in local elections by nationals of one member country residing in another member country. NAFTA, adopted in 1993, reduces trade restrictions among the three member countries of Canada, Mexico, and the United States, facilitating the movement of capital to Mexico and the movement of commodities to Canada and the United States.

These three treaties do not represent a definite withering away of international borders. While seven European controls have lifted border controls for European travelers, five remaining countries who signed the Schengen Agreement have yet to do the same.[12] Also, some EC members have not approved specific measures (e.g., a common currency) of the Maastricht Treaty.[13] In both treaties, foreign nationals from non-EC countries face possible restrictions. In the case of NAFTA, at the request of the United States no provisions were made to facilitate the transnational movement of workers.[14] Indeed, in the United States NAFTA was enacted alongside measures to restrict crossings at the southern border.

In the late twentieth century, social construction of the border has reached intense levels as various actors (for example, politicians, government personnel, restrictionist groups, appointed commissions, academic researchers, and media agencies) create "knowledge" of an everyday life "reality" that the U.S. southern border is out of control, that immigration is overwhelming U.S. institutions (especially public ones), that present levels of immigration threaten the established social order and underlying U.S. core values and identity, and so on. In a word, according to this social construction, the country is facing a border-control crisis that threatens society's capacity for social integration. The motivations for this crisis ideology are wide ranging. They include eugenic concerns, political opportunism, anxieties about the changing population composition, inter- and intra-ethnic fears and prejudices, conservative desires for fiscal cutbacks in public expenditures, and worries about a reduced job market.

To be sure, the social context does present itself with a relatively large number of new immigrant and transnational communities. The question, however, is whether this constitutes a border breakdown, which can be fixed with new enforcement policy, or a new condition of capitalist global development in which the heightened movement of capital and labor across world regions make international boundaries increasingly irrelevant. In other words, is the "problem" the situation that we do not have enough Border Patrol agents and fences to secure the border, or is it the situation that nation-state boundaries have become greatly incongruous with the economic boundaries of capitalist development? My premise is the latter. From this perspective, the "crisis" of the border is not that "illegal aliens" are swarming across the U.S.-Mexico border, but that global capitalist growth is overwhelming nation-states as units of social-economic development.[15]

Viewing capital as a social relation among economic classes, capitalist development transcends nation-state boundaries not only in terms of transnational transfers of investment moneys and production activities, but also in terms of working-class strategies to overcome global economic stratification through international migration. While in some cases, capital, with state assistance, directs the transfer of labor across state borders, in other cases workers themselves *autonomously* relocate to more prosperous transnational settings of capitalist development.[16] Often this action of workers is an attempt to escape severe economic hardship in peripheral regions of the world economy and resettle, temporarily or permanently, in more secure and higher-income labor markets in advanced industrial countries. This survival strategy has played a major role in the creation of wage labor forces for capitalist development, especially in the United States.

CONSTRUCTING THE U.S.-MEXICO BORDER

The state boundary between the United States and Mexico appears today as an immutable fact. For the generations of U.S. people historically removed from its inception, the border takes on the character of an institution, that is, as "objective reality" and as "self-evident."[17] Perceived as possessing its own reality, the border, as an institution, confronts the individual "as an external and coercive fact."[18] In contrast to other social institutions that are subject to regular review and modification (such as educational and health systems), the U.S. southern border is seen as having an absolute integrity crucial for the security of the United States and U.S. society in general. While some U.S. residents in borderlands may take a neighborly view of their Mexican counterparts, away from the borderlands, in the more general U.S. population, the border is seen as absolute and necessary.[19]

Undoubtedly the perceived absolute character of the border is related to the absolute power that maintains it. At U.S. border sites, this power is manifested through the presence and activities of the Border Patrol, Customs, and other federal agencies. Yet, the "necessary" character of the border is also produced by other processes of social construction, more powerful than enforcement agencies, since these processes affect the very conceptualization of the southern border.

"IN THE INTEREST OF NATIONAL SECURITY"

Ideas of nationalism and limited national resources are central to the social construction of the border, but it is the issue of national security that most elevates the view of state boundaries as crucial and necessary. National security is seen as essential for national sovereignty and the public order, hence governments have the right to control the entry of people from other countries.[20] According to this perspective, unrestrained entry through the U.S. southern border endangers the existence of basic social, cultural, and political institutions, and thus the very "American way of life."[21] In the words of the Select Commission on Immigration and Refugee Policy in 1981, "Our policy—while providing opportunity to a portion of the world's population—must be guided by the basic national interests of the people of the United States."[22] As I will describe later, this conventional view of national interest implies particular characteristics of those seeking entry.

Reacting to higher levels of Spanish-speaking immigrants in the 1970s, some U.S. policy makers cautioned about the implications of this influx for the country's security. In 1978, CIA Director William Colby described Mexican immigration as the single greatest security threat facing the United States, greater even than the threat from the Soviet Union.[23] For Colby, the immigration-assisted growth of the Spanish-speaking population in the U.S. Southwest could result in a *Quebecois*-like separatist movement by the region's Mexican-origin population. Senator Alan Simpson, a long-term proponent of immigration restrictions, warned about potential erosion of national unity and stability due to Spanish-speaking immigrants in an addendum to the Final Report of the U.S. Select Commission on Immigration and Policy Reform appointed by President Carter.[24] In an essay on "Wetbackism," Arthur F. Corwin and Johnny M. McCain saw undocumented Mexican immigrants ("wetbacks") as aiding the growth of Chicano militancy.[25] The two authors, who identify the term "Chicano" as originating in "wetback barrios of the border states," make the following point:

> Chicano nationalism, sprouting in barrios across the country [United States], and reinforced by mass immigration, works for the political "reconquest of the Southwest by the Mexican race," that is, *la raza,* and the spiritual restoration of the mythical Aztlán, or the original homeland of the Aztecs. Characteristically, Chicano leaders call for an open border with Mexico in reparation for the unjust conquest of "Chicano territory," and insist on the ancient and unalienable right of the Indo-Americans . . . to migrate where they please. . . . Naturally liberation also means removing the deportation menace from the *colonias,* and accordingly

Raza leaders have set up court challenges and workshops to implement "Aztlán immigration policy."[26]

Portrayals of ethnic balkanization and diversity overloads continued into the 1980s and 1990s, serving as backdrops to argue for more rigid border enforcement.

It is important to understand that, coming from governmental and social scientific sources, such portrayals are more than just another alternative interpretation, among many, of social change. Coming from established authoritative sources, the portrayals become major forces in the social construction of the border as absolutely essential for national security.

BORDER "CRISIS"

The social construction of the U.S.-Mexico border involves more than promoting ideas of the border's necessity. It also has often involved promoting the idea of the southern border as a hot spot, in a way that is not applied to the U.S.-Canadian border. More than being essential for national security, the southern border is portrayed as being in a state of crisis as an endless wave of "illegal aliens" constantly assaults it.[27] From this perspective, the border should not only be maintained—it must be blockaded. Instead of exploring bilateral arrangements to deal with heightened entry of unauthorized immigrants, the orders of the day include intensified surveillance, the introduction of military technology, more fences, and the amassing of federal agents at border points.[28] Constructing a portrait of an overrun border becomes particularly intense in the preludes to new legislation to restrict immigration.[29]

The representation of a border out of control, and thus a country in imminent danger, is made at various levels. One level consists of border visits by government officials, political candidates, commissions, and so on, in which declarations are made of the border's supposedly crisis situation and of proposals to control the border. In the summer of 1995, for example, Republican presidential candidate Senator Phil Gramm traveled to El Paso to call border control one of the United States' most urgent problems and to discuss his $500 million to $600 million proposal to add 5,000 more Border Patrol agents.[30] This type of representation has softened somewhat from previous decades. It has certainly softened since 1954 when, in a border tour preceding a major round-up of undocumented Mexican immigrants, U.S. Attorney General Herbert Brownell hinted at shooting down undocumented border crossers.[31]

A second level of representation occurs where state and local government officials, as well as restrictionist organizations, create scenarios of fiscal abuse and ensuing crisis, which, according to them, is due to a border, and an immigration policy, out of control. The fiscal abuse supposedly caused by undocumented immigrants, because of a border in crisis, is usually represented with announcements of dramatic actions that will be taken to seek redress. In 1994, for example, Governor Pete Wilson described California as undergoing an "invasion" by undocumented immigrants at a cost of over $10 billion to the state, for which he filed a legal claim against the federal government for reimbursement.[32]

While Governor Pete Wilson has been a major producer of this representation, other local sources exist across the country. In 1994, for instance, school officials at the La Joya school district in the Texas-Mexican border announced that they would screen the district's more than 12,000 students for residency status after fearing that ineligible Mexican students were attending the school, at a substantial educational cost.[33] After an initial screening of over 1,000 students, only a very small number were found to have residency outside the district, these included U.S. students who were fleeing gangs in Houston schools. In another Texas case in 1995, a Harris County fiscal-conservative commissioner proposed sending constables to the homes of the over 100,000 registered users of the county's public health facilities after some Latino foreign visitors were apprehended at a Houston airport with unauthorized cards to use county hospitals.

A third level of social construction involves organizations and think tanks that sponsor conferences and meetings and produce reports to promote the view essentially that the country is being overrun by immigrants, directly or indirectly implying that the border is out of control. Perhaps the most aggressive of these organizations is the Federation for American Immigration Reform (FAIR). With headquarters in Washington, D.C., and regional representatives and membership throughout the country, the organization accomplishes a host of political and technical activities to promote border enforcement and immigration restriction. The activities range from organizing public and congressional briefings to supplying the Immigration and Naturalization Service (INS) with sophisticated, technical manuals on how to physically make the border less penetrable. Some former top INS officials work closely with FAIR.

Think tanks also play a role in creating an image of a crisis immigration situation, which requires immigration reform. In contrast to FAIR and other restrictionist groups, restrictionist think tanks couch their language in social-scientific vernacular. In the publication "Shaping Texas: The Effects of Immigration—1970–2020," the Center for Immigration Studies in Washington, D.C., presents a potentially bleak picture of Texas' population growth propelled by immigration. In several direct and subtle ways, the report from the Washington think tank emphasizes predicaments that may befall the state with continued immigration growth. While the report cites the work of Professor Donald Huddle of Rice University, whose statistical estimates are frequently used by restrictionists, it omits the work of Urban Institute researchers Jeffrey Passel and Michael Fix, who have published an impressive, elaborate report detailing significant weaknesses in the Rice professor's work.[34] The think tank's report seems to be especially concerned with the Hispanic aspect of Texas' immigration-spurred population growth and begins its concluding section with the following:

Unless there are near-term reductions in immigration and fertility, Texas in the twenty-first century will be much more populous than it is today, *and it will be more heterogeneous.* How can Texas deal with negative effects on the quality of life implicit in population growth to 25 or 30 million inhabitants?[35]

In contrast to the report's pessimistic tone, across many Texas localities, community leaders from diverse ethnic and racial groups can be found celebrating Hispanic contributions to the state's social, economic, and cultural growth.

At the end of 1995, as congressional committees moved to finish work on a new, restrictive immigration bill, the INS conducted its third exercise of an "enhanced border control plan" to counter an imagined massive immigration from a collapsed Mexican economy or some other massive failure of the United States' southern NAFTA partner.[36] Practiced in the Arizona desert, and with Pentagon advice, the exercise included cyclone-fence corrals, floodlights, olive-drab Army field tents, water tanks, and portable toilets as a "temporary collection point." According to the plan, immigrants who did not immediately return "voluntarily" to the border would be taken inland to prisons, county jails, and military bases where they would be detained and questioned by intelligence agents. If the immigration overwhelmed INS resources, other law enforcement and military forces would be called.

CONSTRUCTING THE "ALIEN"

Without doubt, a principal aspect of the social construction of the southern border involves promoting the perception that the border is absolutely essential to protect the United States from the potential Latino entrant, who is very different from "Americans," in other words, to protect the United States from "aliens."[37] This perception, of course, omits the fact that Spanish-speaking people have an almost five-hundred-year history in the region that is now the U.S. Southwest and in other parts of the country, a history that predates the arrival of whites (Anglos) by hundreds of years. For indigenous and *mestizo* populations it is a history that predates the arrival of European-origin populations by thousands of years.

Immigration waves have always led to the perception that new immigrant groups are alien and thus substantially different—inferior—vis-à-vis older immigrant groups. For example, during the large influx of eastern- and southern-European immigrants in the late 1800s and early 1900s, restriction-ist movements developed that depicted these new immigrants as vastly infe-rior to assumed superior traits of earlier immigrant groups.[38] When the Immigration Commission established by Congress in 1907 differentiated between "new" and "old" immigrant groups in its forty-one-volume report, it was reflecting a public sentiment that new immigrant "races" were to blame for many social ills, including:

unemployment, female and child labor, the introduction of machinery, unsafe coal mines, lack of organization among wage-earners, congestion in great cities, industrial crisis, inability to gain a controlling interest in stock corporations, pauperism, crime, insanity, race suicide, gambling, the continental Sunday, paro-chial schools, atheism, political corruption, municipal misrule.[39]

The Commission's report, along with eugenic and other restrictionist views, served as a political-ideological preface for the eventual enactment of a national origins system that dramatically reduced immigration from south-eastern Europe in favor of immigration from countries in northwestern Europe.

Negative representations of newcomers as alien and detrimental to the American quality of life have continued into the post-World War II era and into the 1990s. As undocumented immigration rose in the early 1950s, undocumented migrants were seen in government reports and media presen-tations as associated with suffering, exploitation, filth, disease, crime, narcot-ics, soaring welfare costs, and subversive infiltration.[40] More recently, in 1995, the head of the National Immigration Commission, appointed by President Bill Clinton, portrayed undocumented immigrants as not contribut-ing to community development.[41]

By the late 1900s, the term "alien" became a common term in government bureaucracies to refer to foreign-born persons, especially from Mexico and other Latin American countries. Yet, "alien" is hardly a neutral term. Among the definitions and synonyms listed for "alien" in the *Random House Web-ster's College Dictionary* (1991) are found the following: "unlike one's own; strange," and "opposed; hostile." "Alien" comes from the Latin word "*ali-enus,*" which has mainly negative connotations, such as "contrary," "hos-tile," "strange," "unsuitable," "incongruous," "inconsistent," and "inconvenient."[42] Sometimes "alien" is used with other words to produce a negative effect, such as "Alien and Sedition Acts" and "illegal alien."

The recent book *Alien Nation* portrays the United States as a country in imminent collapse due to unregulated immigration policies, and the *Alien* Hollywood movie series shows an extraterrestrial creature slaying and in other ways manacling space explorers from Earth.[43] U.S. government documents also illustrate the use of "alien" with negative effect. In the *Statistical Abstract of the United States,* for example, "immigrants" is used in headings of statistical tables of persons admitted for legal permanent residence in the United States, while "aliens" is reserved mainly for headings in tables of persons committing immigration violations.[44]

Promoting perceptions of Mexicans or other national groups as "aliens," whether residing in the United States or in their own countries, adds to the social construction of the U.S.-Mexico border by reinforcing the idea that these national groups are incompatible with, and even harmful to, U.S. society and culture. It amounts to a process of villainization of the foreign born, which thus must be kept out with strict immigration policies and a strong southern border.

COMPARISON WITH EUROPEAN IMMIGRANTS

Just as immigrants at the turn of the century were considered inferior in comparison with earlier immigrants, today's immigrants, especially Latinos, are described as lacking in positive characteristics in comparison with earlier European immigrants in general. Today's immigrants are portrayed as welfare dependent, unwilling to assimilate, and anti-American, while earlier, European immigrants are seen in very favorable, ancestral terms. Introducing one of the harshest immigration bills in Congress, U.S. Representative Bill Archer illustrates this comparison:

How many jobs that would be held by American citizens are filled by citizens of other countries? How many governmental services paid for by increasingly scarce taxpayer dollars are being used by noncitizens? How long can this continue? . . .
It is true that our country, in its early years, thrived on the many immigrants who arrived here during the western expansion. And we owe thanks to an immigrant labor force that allowed our economy to grow during the Industrial Revolution.[45]

To deal with the new menacing immigration, Representative Archer introduced an ultrarestrictionist bill that would reduce legal immigration by 60 percent. The bill, if approved, would also militarize the U.S.-Mexico border and provide for such actions as massive round-ups of undocumented immigrants and their detention in closed-down military bases.[46]

In many materials and sources, early immigrants—Mexicans and others—who entered through the country's southern border are not accorded the privileged founding status given to European immigrants. Indeed, the recognition of historical European immigration appears to have reached fetishistic proportions in some cases, while remaining silent on southern immigration. One example is the immigrant museum at Ellis Island, which in 1965 was made part of the Statue of Liberty National Monument under the management of the National Park Service.

Ellis Island has become a major semiotic force communicating an official view of the American heritage of European immigration. After passing under a sign describing Ellis Island as "The Gateway to America," visitors entering the museum's souvenir store encounter a large array of items commemorating the country's European immigration (T-shirts, caps, sweaters, pencils, books, dishes, wall posters, wall plaques, mugs, cups, pot holders, key rings, paper weights, letter openers, stickers, patches, and so forth). Commemorations of Latino immigration are almost nonexistent, some Guatemalan and Ecuadoran small coin purses and a few Chilean wooden snakes.[47] Comments in a guide book at the souvenir store relate the following about "the story of Ellis Island": "It is . . . the story of the immigrants' faith and courageous dedication as they sought freedom of speech and religious thought and economic opportunity. The story of their pursuit of happiness is the saga of America."[48]

Needless to say, the immigration history at Ellis Island is central to American heritage and worth commemorating, but so are the immigration experiences of other U.S. areas, especially in the country's Southwest. The lack of official government recognition and commemoration of such areas, similar to Ellis Island, indirectly reinforces the perception that the historical significance of Mexican immigrants and others who entered through the southern border is less valuable and not a part of the American saga. From this perspective, Mexicans and other immigrants who came to America through the southern border remain "aliens" and not "immigrants" as their European counterparts are portrayed.

The social construction of the border described above has a lengthy history, but, at least in Texas, it does not go all the way back to the formation of the U.S.-Mexico boundary in 1848. Fifty years after the creation of this border, many Mexicans still traveled with ease between the two countries, hindered mainly by small border crossing fees. While a number of Immigration Service mounted guards patrolled parts of the U.S.-Mexico border by the early 1920s, it was not until 1924 that the U.S. Border Patrol was formed to enforce border-crossing policies. The context was a growing presence of Mexican immigrants dislodged by Mexico's revolution and continuing political turmoil in the 1920s, and by the attraction of labor-hungry industries in the United States.

In this early period of the twentieth century, U.S. capital entered a phase of rapid expansion, especially in agriculture and manufacturing, which included the development of labor markets that transcended the U.S.-Mexico border into the Mexican hinterland. This social force, and the vigorous response of Mexican labor, initiated an economic deconstruction of the border, which by the latter part of the century had significantly reduced U.S.-Mexican social and cultural boundaries as well.

DECONSTRUCTING THE U.S.-MEXICO BORDER

Since the establishment of the present U.S.-Mexico border through the Treaty of Guadalupe Hidalgo in 1848, various social forces have acted to socially deconstruct the border.[49] To be sure, the U.S.-Mexico border was never fully constructed from the Mexican side. It was a U.S. border, not a Mexican one. For many *mexicanos,* Mexico—the people and their culture—continued north of the Río Bravo (Rio Grande) and other state boundary areas between the two countries. The raids of Juan Cortina to liberate Texas border areas in the 1860s and 1870s, the organizing of railroad Mexican workers by the Unión Federal de Mexicanos in California in the 1900s, the farm labor unionizing in Texas by Mexican organizers in the 1970s, the Zapatista solidarity movement among Mexican immigrants and U.S. supporters in various U.S. cities in the 1990s—all are examples of the many Mexican political movements that have pursued popular interests among *mexicanos* and U.S. partisans north of the border.

A DECLINING ECONOMIC DIVIDE

In the late 1800s and early 1900s, U.S. capitalists shared the perception of many Mexicans who refused to see the U.S.-Mexico border as a hard and fixed barrier to transnational movement. By the early 1900s, U.S. employers were helping to stimulate massive immigration of Mexican immigrants for wage labor in a variety of expanding industries. Thus, within fifty years after the signing of the Treaty of Guadalupe Hidalgo, the U.S.-Mexico border experienced significant economic deconstruction when thousands of Mexican immigrant workers were attracted to U.S. industries.

In the U.S. Southwest, Mexican immigrant workers, many from *campesino* backgrounds, found jobs with wages ranging from $.50 to $1.25 a day in labor-intensive industries, such as agriculture, mining, railroad construction, and ranching.[50] While social turmoil, landlessness, and poverty pressured Mexican workers to migrate north, in many cases U.S. labor recruiters became the conduit for crossing the border and reaching labor markets "on the other side." Commenting on the sharp rise of officially recorded Mexican immigration, from 49,000 in 1901–10 to 459,000 in 1921–30, the noted immigration historian Maldwyn Allen Jones states, "Partly because many Mexicans were unable to fulfil literacy test requirements, but more because of the expense and delay involved in obtaining American visas ... great numbers entered the United States illegally, *a large proportion of these "wet-backs" being smuggled in by American labor contractors.*"[51] While labor recruiters helped give rise to the first wave of undocumented Mexican immigration, the U.S. government also assisted the importation of Mexican immigrant labor through labor contract agreements with Mexico in 1907 and 1917–21.[52] [For an extensive discussion of these agreements, see chapter 10 in this volume—*Ed.*]

By the 1920s, Mexican immigrant workers became concentrated in several Southwest cities as large manufacturers turned to Mexican labor recruitment agencies.[53] The 1930 U.S. Census found large numbers of Mexican men and women in manufacturing jobs, 40,000 in California and 48,000 in Texas.[54] In the Midwest, the 1910s and 1920s also saw the settlement of sizable numbers of Mexican workers as automobile and steel manufacturers turned to Mexican labor agencies in the Southwest.[55]

At the surface, the recruitment of Mexican immigrant labor seems a logical process given the labor demands of an industrializing United States and the availability and proximity of the Mexican labor supply. A closer examination, however, reveals that the logic at play was not based solely on principles of markets and propinquity but also on strategies of class struggle. In some Midwestern factories, for example, Mexican workers were first hired as strikebreakers. Commenting on the use of Mexican labor as "strike insurance" in steel mills, Mark Reisler states, "By keeping the workers of various nationalities numerically balanced, employers believed that workers would not unite and organize and that labor troubles could thereby be avoided."[56]

In the 1930s, labor activism in some U.S. agricultural areas matched the militancy of worker organizing efforts in manufacturing industries. In California, communist and socialist labor organizers could count on the support of thousands of agricultural workers to maintain strikes for weeks at a time.[57] Mexican workers, natives and immigrants alike, waged strikes in the fields of Southern California through the Confederación de Uniones Obreros Mexicanos and the Confederación de Uniones de Campesinos y Obreros Mexicanos.[58] In south Texas, the Asociación de Jornaleros joined with some 1,200 striking farm workers in 1935.[59] With ties to Mexico, these labor organizations of native and immigrant Mexican workers demonstrated that the economic deconstruction of the U.S.-Mexico border included a political, class dimension from the standpoint of Mexican *obrero* attempts to improve working conditions through collective struggles. Nonetheless, in the 1930s, the central concern of many Mexican immigrants in the United States was not unionization but forceful repatriation to Mexico by U.S. federal, state, and local agents. Blaming undocumented Mexicans for the country's high levels of unemployment, government agents rounded up and repatriated over 400,000 Mexican immigrants (and their U.S.-born children) back to Mexico during the Depression years.[60]

While the repatriation movement, and the Depression in general, lessened the mass movement of Mexican workers north of the U.S.-Mexico boundary, it did not mean the economic closure of the border. Indeed, the state-sponsored program to import Mexican labor that followed in 1942 helped create a second wave of undocumented Mexican immigration that reached into the 1950s.

Responding especially to the labor demands of agribusiness, in 1942 the U.S. government sought and obtained a labor contract agreement with the Mexican government to annually import thousands of Mexican workers (*braceros*) for temporary work in agriculture and a few other industries. Started as a wartime measure, the Bracero Program lasted for twenty-two years, importing a total of 4.8 million Mexican contract workers mainly for farm work in California and Texas, with the U.S. government as the official employer.[61] The *Bracero* Program involved only men, not their families, and was highly regimented. U.S. government officials and grower associations supervised the movement and work of the *braceros* from the time they left the recruitment centers in Mexico to the time they returned home after the harvests. The *braceros* were used as "shock troops" in corporate farms and were allowed no opportunity to join collective struggles.[62] It was an ideal workforce for the multibillion-dollar agribusiness sector. One grower commented on this feature of *bracero* labor as follows: "[W]e used to own our slaves, now we rent them from the government."[63] *Braceros* played a significant role in the expansion of the country's agricultural capital, which saw the value of crop marketing rise from $3.5 billion in 1940 to $17.2 billion in 1964, when the contract labor program ended.[64]

SOCIAL EXPANSION INTO "EL OTRO LADO"

The implementation of the *Bracero* Program through labor recruitment centers in Mexico attracted more workers than were requested for contract work. According to some scholars, many of the Mexican workers who were not recruited migrated to U.S. rural labor markets on their own, initiating a second phase of undocumented migration.[65] In some cases, Mexican workers migrated to the United States first as *braceros* and later as undocumented workers in order to have greater freedom to select employers and stay longer in the United States.[66] Undocumented Mexican workers were a special advantage for corporate farmers in Texas, since initially the Mexican government considered Texas to be anti-Mexican and refused to allow *braceros* in the state.[67] With more U.S. agents to enforce immigration violations, undocumented workers usually remained a politically constrained labor force, sometimes working alongside *braceros* in the fields.

While undocumented status kept many Mexican immigrant workers politically restrained, it did not limit their capacity for social and cultural development on the U.S. side of the border, nor did it limit their capacity to travel with some ease between the United States and Mexico.[68] Given their significant degree of autonomy, and the constant demand for their labor, undocumented Mexican workers grew in number in many U.S.-Mexican areas. By the late 1940s and early 1950s, the INS initiated several sweeps to round up undocumented Mexican immigrants. This response of the U.S. state culminated in Operation Wetback in 1954, which coordinated efforts by various federal agencies and local authorities to repatriate over one million Mexican immigrants.[69] While the operation was seen as the end of the undocumented Mexican worker, it actually only ended the second wave of undocumented Mexican immigration, which served as a precursor to a third, record-setting wave beginning in the late 1960s and early 1970s. It was a wave that fueled the growth of transnational immigrant communities, which in turn substantially reduced social, cultural, and economic boundaries between the United States and Mexico.

Undoubtedly affected by rapid agricultural mechanization, in the 1950s and 1960s undocumented Mexican labor shifted significantly from rural to urban destinations. This was a critical change because it brought Mexican immigrant workers and their families to more stable work and residential urban environments—two basic resources for the social reproduction of transnational immigrant communities. Also significant, Mexican settlement in urban areas provided some support from Mexican American legal and political groups. This factor proved crucial in the struggle of undocumented Mexican communities to gain access to public education for undocumented children.

Mexican immigrants have enjoyed social and cultural reproduction in established Mexican settlement in the United States since the early 1900s, but the development of Mexican transnational communities in the third wave of Mexican undocumented immigration has been phenomenal and unprecedented in size and intensity. The large settlement of legal resident immigrants after the 1965 Immigration Act and the presence of traditional Mexican Americans reinforced the large-scale development of Mexican transnational communities. Throughout the Southwest, Midwest, and eventually on the East Coast, Mexican transnational communities enjoyed vigorous growth and in many ways reproduced social, cultural, and economic institutions from back home. Technological advances in transportation, travel, and communication in the 1980s and 1990s strengthened ties between Mexican immigrant settlements in the United States and communities in Mexico. The legalization of over one million Mexican immigrants through IRCA added a critical resource to this development as large numbers of newly legalized residents traveled freely across the border.[70]

Border deconstruction by transnational Mexican communities involves more than the facilitation of travel and the expansion of social and cultural Mexican institutions north of the border. It also involves a conceptual and metaphysical deconstruction of the border. Rather then conceptualizing the border as the boundary of a vastly different world on the other side, for much of the present century many Mexican men and women workers have viewed the border as a gateway to potential economic mobility. Also, rather than perceiving the border as a natural, self-evident divide, Mexican immigrants see the U.S.-Mexico boundary as a human, social artifact, namely, the beginning of a social-political space where their labor power is sought and used by industry but is subject to repression by the U.S. state. This is a critical deconstruction for working-class peoples because it enables their development of survival strategies over ever-wider spatial planes.

The autonomous nature of undocumented immigration has been a major source of transnational community development. And it is precisely this characteristic of much of the history of Mexican immigration that is the target of today's immigration restrictionists. At high official levels, for some the goal of present-day social construction of the border is not to stop immigration (legal and undocumented) but to gain more control of it. Some government officials who are among the staunchest proponents of immigration restrictions propose a return to a *bracero* program, where the work and movement of temporary immigrant laborers are closely monitored by state supervisors and employers. The concern here is to deflate the autonomy characteristic of undocumented immigration. As described above, this autonomy has been the source of the development of large Mexican communities in various U.S. areas. Autonomous migration represents labor out of control of the state and to an extent of employers and collective capital in general. From capital's perspective autonomous migration lessens the value of immigrant labor, especially as immigrant workers are able to develop elaborate survival strategies through transnational structures.

The current social construction of the U.S.-Mexico border, and accompanying nativism, in the United States can be seen as a reaction to the expansion of immigrant communities (especially Latino ones) but also as a reaction to the changing significance of the nation-state, and state borders, in the larger global order. Since the emergence of both nation-states and capitalist development in the Middle Ages, the two systems of global organization have advanced with some degree of conflictive interaction. Specifically, capitalist development has pressured nation-state boundaries through direct and indirect promotion of international labor migration. Capitalist development directly promotes the mass movement of labor across state boundaries when it resorts to segmented workforces in labor-intensive industries. It indirectly stimulates international migration when it introduces the commodity form of goods and labor in remote regions, as well as when it violently suppresses worker movements in these areas. In these scenarios, the forces of global capitalist development become problematic for advanced nation-states, in the absence of effective international policies of labor immigration.

It would be misleading to exclusively relate the present nativistic sentiments to tendencies of capitalist development. Other factors are at play. Perhaps the most salient of these are racial/ethnic differences between new immigrants and established residents. The historical development of the global structure of nation-states clearly reflects an order of race/cultural differences, with mainly white nation-states at the top and mainly Asian, black, and Latino nation-states at the bottom. Mass immigration, undocumented and legal, into the United States from the lower sectors of this global order thus introduces large numbers of peoples historically considered racially and culturally inferior. From this perspective, the present-day reaction to restrict the entry of Asian, black, and Latino immigrants differs little from attempts in the early 1900s to limit the entry of eastern and southern Europeans, as well as of Asian immigrants, all of whom were considered inferior in their day. It is an attempt to maintain a stratified world order where working-class populations face a strong correlation between racial and cultural differences and position (core versus peripheral) in the global capitalist system.

NOTES

1. See Robin Cohen, "Policing the Frontiers: The State and Migrant in the International Division of Labor," in *Global Restructuring and Territorial Development,* ed. Jeffrey Henderson and Manuel Castells (Newbury Park, Calif.: Sage, 1987), 88.

2. Dating the age of *Homo sapiens sapiens* as 150,000 years is given in Richard Leakey and Roger Lewin, *Origins Reconsidered: In Search of What Makes Us Human* (New York: Doubleday, 1992), front flap copy.

3. Immanuel Wallerstein, *The Modern World-System: Capitalist Agriculture and the Origins of the European World-Economy in the Sixteenth Century* (New York: Academic Press, 1974).

4. See Cohen, "Policing the Frontiers"; Joseph R. Strayer, *On the Medieval Origins of the Modern State* (Princeton: Princeton University Press, 1970); and Michael Kearney, "Borders and Boundaries of State and Self at the End of Empire," *Journal of Historical Sociology,* vol. 4, no. 1 (March 1991): 52–74.

5. Harry Magdoff, *Imperialism: From the Colonial Age to the Present* (New York: Monthly Review Press, 1978).

6. John S. D. Eisenhower, *So Far from God: The U.S. War with Mexico 1846–1848* (New York: Doubleday, 1989), chap. 4.

7. Saskia Sassen-Koob, "Issues of Core and Periphery: Labor Migration and Global Restructuring," in Henderson and Castells, eds., *Global Restructuring and Territorial Development*, 60–87.

8. One example of this was the demand for Mexican immigrant labor by agribusiness in the 1950s as the U.S. government implemented Operation Wetback and other measures to control border crossing by undocumented Mexicans.

9. Richard B. Craig, *The Bracero Program,* (Austin: University of Texas Press, 1971), chap. 5.

10. Michael Kearney of the University of California at Riverside is presently conducting some of the leading studies on transnational community development in California; see Kearney, "Borders and Boundaries of State and Self." For another cutting-edge conceptualization of transnational communities, see Luin Goldring, "Blurring Borders: Transnational Community, Status, and Social Change in Mexico-U.S. Migration," paper presented in the 1995 annual meeting of the American Sociological Association, Washington, D.C.

11. Wayne A. Cornelius, Philip L. Martin, and James F. Hollifield, "Introduction: The Ambivalent Quest for Immigration Control," in *Controlling Immigration: A Global Perspective* (Stanford: Stanford University Press, 1994).

12. "Seven European Nations Lift Border Controls," *Houston Chronicle,* 27 March 1995, sec. A, p. 9.

13. Cornelius, Martin, and Hollifield, "Introduction," 33.

14. Ibid.

15. For a somewhat related view, see Manuel Castells and Jeffrey Henderson, "Techno-economic Restructuring, Socio-political Process and Spatial Transformation: A Global Perspective," in Henderson and Castells, eds., *Global Restructuring and Territorial Development*, 1–17.

16. Néstor Rodríguez, "The Real 'New World Order,' " in *The Bubbling Cauldron: Race, Ethnicity, and the Urban Crisis,* ed. Michael Peter Smith and Joe R. Feagin (Minneapolis: University of Minnesota Press, 1995), 211–25.

17. Peter L. Berger and Thomas Luckmann, *The Social Construction of Reality: A Treatise in the Sociology of Knowledge* (Garden City, N.Y.: Doubleday, 1966), 47–128.

18. Ibid., 58.

19. See Oscar J. Martínez, *Border People: Life and Society in the U.S.-Mexico Borderlands* (Tucson: University of Arizona Press, 1994), chap. 1.

20. See Joseph J. Carens, "Aliens and Citizens: The Case for Open Borders," in *Theorizing Citizenship,* ed. Ronald Beiner (Albany: State University of New York Press, 1995), 229; Myron Weiner, "Security, Stability, and International Migration" in *Global Dangers: Changing Dimensions of International Security,* ed. Sean M. Lynn-Jones and Steven E. Miller (Cambridge, Mass.: MIT Press, 1995), 183–218; Warren Zimmerman, "Migrants and Refugees: A Threat to Security?" in *Threatened Peoples, Threatened Borders: World Migration and U.S. Policy,* ed. Michael S. Teitelbaum and Myron Weiner (New York: Norton, 1995), 88–116.

21. See Zimmerman, "Migrants and Refugees," 88–97.

22. Quoted in Carens, "Aliens and Citizens," 251n. 1.

23. See Wayne A. Cornelius, "America in the Era of Limits: Migrants, Nativists,

and the Future of U.S.-Mexican Relations," in *Mexican-U.S. Relations: Conflict and Convergence,* ed. Carlos Vásquez and Manuel García y Griego (Los Angeles: UCLA Chicano Studies Research Center Publications and Latin American Studies Publications, 1983), 389–90.

24. Arthur F. Corwin and Johnny M. McCain, "Wetbackism since 1954," in *Immigrants—and Immigrants: Perspectives on Mexican Labor Migration to the United States,* ed. Arthur F. Corwin (Westport, Conn.: Greenwood Press, 1978), 72.

25. Ibid., 73.

26. Ibid., 73 (italics in original).

27. This became a common theme in television ads used to promote the passage of Proposition 187 in California in 1995.

28. For example, see "Three Lines of Defense to Stop Illegal Aliens," *Migration World,* vol. 22, no. 5 (1994): 17; "Stepped-Up Border Controls," *Migration World,* vol. 23, nos. 1/2 (1995): 13; "200 More Border Patrol Agents for San Diego," *Migration World,* vol. 23, no. 3 (1995): 11.

29. From this perspective, it is possible that the INS's record high number of undocumented immigrant apprehensions in 1986, over one million, may have been partly motivated by the desire to encourage Congress to pass the Immigration Reform and Control Act, which it did in the latter part of the year.

30. "Gramm visits El Paso," *Houston Chronicle,* 16 August 1995, sec. A, p. 27.

31. Rodolfo Acuña, *Occupied America: A History of Chicanos,* 2d ed. (New York: Harper and Row, 1981), 157–58.

32. "Wilson Sues U.S. over Immigrant 'Invasion,' " *Migration World,* vol. 22, no. 5 (1994): 12.

33. "Cracking Down on Mexican Students as a Ploy for Aid," *Migration World,* vol. 22, no. 1 (1994): 7.

34. Michael Fix and Jeffrey S. Passel, *Immigration and Immigrants: Setting the Record Straight* (Washington, D.C.: Urban Institute, 1994).

35. Leon F. Bouvier and John L. Martin, "Shaping Texas: The Effects of Immigration—1970–2020," Center for Immigration Studies, Washington, D.C., n.d., 15 (italics mine).

36. Sam Dillon, "U.S. Tests Border Plan in Event of Mexico Crisis," *The New York Times,* 8 December 1995, sec. A, p. 16.

37. Zimmerman, "Migrants and Refugees," 93.

38. Maldwyn Allen Jones, *American Immigration* (Chicago: University of Chicago Press, 1960), chap. 9.

39. Isaac A. Hourwich, *Immigration and Labor,* 2d ed. (New York: B. W. Huebsch, 1922), 40, 55.

40. Craig, *The Bracero Program,* 126.

41. Against the views of immigrant rights groups, the U.S. Commission on Immigration Reform recommended a national registry to keep track of all persons authorized to work in the United States; see "In the Spotlight: Barbara Jordan," *Migration World,* vol. 22, no. 5 (1994): 43–44.

42. John C. Traupman, *The Bantam New College Latin and English Dictionary,* revised and enlarged (New York: Bantam Books, 1995), 52.

43. Peter Brimelow, *Alien Nation: Common Sense about America's Immigration Disaster* (New York: Random House, 1995).

44. For example, see Table 6, "Immigrants Admitted by Class of Admissions: 1980

to 1991" and Table 319, "Aliens Expelled and Immigration Violations: 1980 to 1991" in U.S. Bureau of the Census, *Statistical Abstract of the United States: 1993* (Washington, D.C.: U.S. Government Printing Office, 1993).

45. Bill Archer, "Just Can't Take So Many Immigrants," *Houston Chronicle,* 8 August 1994, sec. E, pp. 1, 5.

46. Ibid., 5.

47. Personal observation, August 10, 1995.

48. Mark K. Mullins, *Ellis Island and Statue of Liberty: Historical Highlights, The Immigrant Journey,* 5th ed. (San Francisco: American Park Network, 1995), 5.

49. After 1848, the U.S.-Mexico boundary line was affected by the Gadsen Purchase of 1853 and the Chamizal Treaty of 1963; see Stanley R. Ross, "Introduction," in *Views across the Border: The United States and Mexico* (Albuquerque: University of New Mexico Press, 1978), 1–22. For a brief description of the ratification of the Treaty of Guadalupe Hidalgo, see Eisenhower, *So Far from God,* 365–68.

50. Lawrence A. Cordoso, *Mexican Emigration to the United States, 1897–1931* (Tucson: University of Arizona Press, 1980), 17; Mark Reisler, *By the Sweat of Their Brow: Mexican Immigrant Labor in the United States, 1900–1940* (Westport, Conn.: Greenwood Press, 1976), 4.

51. Jones, *American Immigration,* 291 (italics mine).

52. Manuel Garcia y Griego, "The Importation of Mexican Contract Laborers to the United States, 1942–1964," Working Paper in U.S.-Mexico Studies, no. 11, Program in United States-Mexico Studies, University of California, San Diego, 1970.

53. Reisler, *By the Sweat of Their Brow,* 96.

54. Ibid., 98.

55. Ibid., 100–104.

56. Ibid., 103.

57. Ramon D. Chacon, "The 1933 San Joaquin Valley Cotton Strike: Strike Breaking Activities in California Agriculture," in *Work, Family, Sex Roles, Language,* ed. Mario Barrera, Alberto Camarillo, and Alberto Hernandez (Berkeley: Tonatiuh-Quinto Sol International, 1980), 34.

58. Joshua Freeman, Nelson Liechtenstein, Stephen Brier, David Bensman, Susan Porter Benson, David Brundage, Bret Eynon, Bruce Levine, and Bryan Palmer, *Who Built America? Working People and the Nation's Economy, Politics, Culture, and Society,* vol. 2, *From the Gilded Age to the Present* (New York: Pantheon Books, 1992), 357–59.

59. Acuña, *Occupied America,* 233.

60. Abraham Hoffman, *Unwanted Mexican Americans in the Great Depression* (Tucson: University of Arizona Press, 1974), ix.

61. Mario Barrera, *Race and Class in the Southwest: A Theory of Racial Inequality* (Notre Dame: Notre Dame University Press, 1979), 117.

62. Ernesto Galarza, *Merchants of Labor: The Mexican Bracero Story* (Santa Barbara, Calif.: McNally and Loftin, 1964), 55.

63. Quoted in Wayne Moquin with Charles Van Doren, *A Documentary History of the Mexican Americans* (New York: Praeger, 1971), 334.

64. U.S. Bureau of the Census, *Statistical Abstract of the United States: 1969* (Washington, D.C.: U.S. Government Printing Office, 1969), table 914.

65. Barrera, *Race and Class in the Southwest,* 122.

66. I have met Mexican immigrant men in Houston and other Texas localities who have recounted this to me.

67. Garcia y Griego, "The Importation of Mexican Contract Laborers to the United States," 15.

68. By this I mean that large numbers of undocumented immigrants were able to cross the border without being apprehended by the INS. I do not mean that the actual border crossing is an easy task.

69. Craig, *The Bracero Program,* 127–29.

70. Rogelio Saenz and Clyde S. Greenlees, "The Demography of Chicanos," in *Chicanas and Chicanos in Contemporary Society,* ed. Roberto M. De Anda (Boston: Allyn and Bacon, 1996), 11.

13. A MEDITATION ON BORDERS
Robert S. Chang

The poet Robert Frost wrote that good fences make good neighbors.[1] It pains me to see that the United States is taking this advice literally vis-à-vis our southern neighbor. But while good fences may make good neighbors, it's not clear to me that they make good nation-states.

I should probably emphasize here that I am not necessarily against borders. What I am against is an uncritical approach to the construction and operation of our borders which has permitted an unreflective nationalism with dire consequences for us as a nation.

As a nation, we are undergoing many changes. Externally, there's the much-touted New World Order, which Noam Chomsky reminds us was announced by President George Bush "[a]s bombs were raining on Baghdad, Basra, and miserable conscripts hiding in holes in the sands of southern Iraq."[2] The bombing of Iraq was consistent with the premises of this new world order: "unless international boundaries between sovereign nation states are respected, the alternative is chaos."[3] We see echoes of this concern for borders in our domestic sphere. Internally, changes in demography have created the specter of a coming majority of color which threatens to eclipse the numerical white majority. Anxiety engendered by these changes has led to a renewed policing of national and institutional boundaries. With the coming immigration restrictions and the affirmative action rollbacks, borders are closing and doors are shutting on people of color. Increasingly, in order for a justice claim to be heard, you must be able to assert membership in the national community.[4] Insofar as you are perceived as foreign, your claim to membership in the national community is weakened, and accordingly, your justice claim may be ignored. This attitude gives rise to the response, "If you don't like it here, go back where you came from." But many of us don't have a place to go back to. For many, that place exists only as an "imaginary homeland."[5]

This sense of in-between-ness, of being not quite part of the (imagined) national community yet not belonging to an imaginary homeland, leads me to introduce myself sometimes as a recovering Oriental.[6] This phrase is very rich, full of multiple meanings. One might ask: What is it that I am recovering from? What am I trying to recover? This phrase recognizes that people who look like me exist in the American imaginary as "Orientals," as the objects of American orientalism.[7]

American orientalism is marked by a pathology that I term nativistic racism which regulates the lives of Asian Americans and which helps to demarcate the boundaries of the American national community and its national identity. Asian Americans present a crisis point for America's discourse of national identity which "incessantly negotiates the two poles of, on the one hand, solid foundations or grand narratives and, on the other, the ever-present threat of the collapse of absolutes."[8] This essay explores the interaction of nativistic racism and concepts of the border, worked through the problematic of Asian Americans.

NATIVISTIC RACISM

Nativistic racism is the name I give to one facet of the oppression of Asian Americans.[9] Many commentators discuss racism and nativism as part of a laundry list of "-isms" that are plaguing the nation. Thus, we are beset by a "resurgence of racism, anti-semitism and nativism";[10] or patriotism is described as "the vehicle for racist or nativist policies."[11] But as Kimberlé Crenshaw has pointed out in the context of racism and sexism, intersections must be explored—otherwise, people fall through the cracks.[12] Here, nativism and racism intersect as nativistic racism targeting Asian Americans. Naming it is crucial in helping us to recognize its operation and to combat its effects.

Some of the effects of nativistic racism can be seen in the rise of English-Only and in such legislation as Proposition 187 in California which would deny education, healthcare, and other social services to illegal aliens.[13] In addition to a federal version embodied in the Personal Responsibility Act, Proposition 187 has spawned copycat legislation and initiatives in other states.[14] These events bear a striking resemblance to what happened in the early 1900s with the Alien Land Laws which prevented land ownership by those ineligible for citizenship. California, in 1913, was the first state to institute such a law. Other states soon followed suit.[15] Although these laws targeted Asian immigrants as the only racial group ineligible for citizenship, they were written in race-neutral terms and thus survived constitutional challenge.[16] Alien Land Laws gained new popularity with the advent of

World War II; in 1943, Utah, Wyoming, and Arkansas instituted such laws. This legislation came shortly after the relocation of Japanese Americans to internment camps in these states. Like the earlier Alien Land Laws, they were instituted to discourage settlement of "ineligible aliens." [17]

So those for whom the border is not so mediate, beware. If the history of the Alien Land Laws is any indication, we will begin seeing Prop. 187 clones in the heartland of America, even in such places as Kansas. For example, if a Korean national flies from Seoul and lands in Kansas, the border will be there to greet her. The border is everywhere.

BORDER ANXIETIES

Although the border is everywhere, your perspective may render it invisible. It is through this invisibility that the border gains much of its power.

A friend told me a story about a conversation at a party where a colleague was making fun of someone who actually thought that they needed a passport to visit Canada from the United States. When my friend informed her that passports were often demanded of Asian Americans, the person was irritated. Her funny anecdote, ruined.

This story reminded me of my own encounter with the border. Until then the border had been transparent to me. I thought about the U.S. border guard who stopped me when I tried to return after a brief visit to Canada. My valid Ohio driver's license was not good enough to let me return to my country, even though the guard had just let in a white man with only a driver's license. No passport was asked of him, yet the guard demanded mine. I told him that I didn't have one. We were at an impasse; my day, ruined.

Although these stories operate at many different levels, I tell them here to show how the properties of the border change depending on the contingent features of who or what is trying to get in or out. I might draw an analogy from cell biology, comparing the cell wall or membrane which is vital to the cell's survival with the national border. Although there are obvious differences between a cell and a nation, the importance of the national border to the nation's survival can be seen in the Supreme Court's border jurisprudence. Congress must be able to exercise plenary power because a sovereign nation must exercise control over its borders—that's what it means to be a sovereign entity. This relationship between a sovereign nation and its borders is made clear in the 1892 case of *Nishimura Ekiu v. United States*:

It is an accepted maxim of international law, that every sovereign nation has the power, as inherent in sovereignty, and essential to self-preservation, to forbid the entrance of foreigners within its dominions, or to admit them only such cases and upon such conditions as it may see fit to prescribe. [18]

To hold otherwise would mean the end or death of the nation as a sovereign entity.

In the same way, then, that the cell wall or membrane serves a screening function, the border operates to keep out that which is dangerous, unwanted, undesirable. In the *Chinese Exclusion Case,* which established the plenary power doctrine, the Supreme Court held that "[if Congress] considers the presence of foreigners of a different race in this country, who will not assimilate with us, to be dangerous to its peace and security . . . its determination is conclusive upon the judiciary."[19]

I want to push on this sentence, to tease out some of its meanings and unstated assumptions. The Court begins by stating that the Chinese are foreigners of a different race, or what Neil Gotanda terms, racialized foreigners.[20] These racialized foreigners "will not assimilate with us." Implicit in this is a notion of *us* or of the *we* in "We the People." The *us* the Court is talking about is the national community. *They,* the Chinese, are not *us.* Further, *they* will not assimilate with *us.* This slides into *they* cannot become *us.* And therefore, we will not let them become us. This is justified because *they* are dangerous to *our* peace and security. They are the Yellow Peril, threatening our sense of the national community. Therefore, Congress must exclude them at the border. The Court went one step further in the citizenship cases, holding in essence that Asian immigrants could not become naturalized; they could not become full members of the national community, even if they wanted to become citizens.[21] Then World War II taught us the tragic lesson that even citizenship was not enough. The Nisei, second generation Japanese Americans and United States citizens by birth, were denied their place in the national community.

These restrictions were based on a sense of who properly belonged in the national community. These restrictions also solidified or helped to construct the country's sense of the national community. They reinforced each other. The stronger the sense of the national community, the more natural the restrictions were, and vice versa. It is in part through the figure of Asian immigrants and their descendants as perpetual internal foreigners that the national community has been able to identify itself. Without Asian Americans, they (the "real" Americans) would not have known who they were.[22]

James Baldwin makes a similar point in the inverse: "If I'm not who you say I am, then you're not who you think you are."[23] Today, new social movements comprising Asian Americans, African Americans, Latinos, Native Americans, women, and gays and lesbians are all resisting the dominant majoritarian constructions that have been imposed upon them. These subordinated, previously silenced groups are saying, "We're not who you say we are," thus destabilizing America's national identity. The result, crisis.

NATIONAL IDENTITY CRISIS

Earlier, I stated that changes in demography have created the specter of a coming majority of color. These changing demographics have created a national identity crisis which is evident in the debate over multiculturalism. Arthur Schlesinger, Jr., observes astutely that

a struggle to redefine the national identity is taking place . . . in many arenas—in our politics, our voluntary organizations, our churches, our language—and in no arena more crucial than our system of education. . . . The debate about the curriculum is a debate about what it means to be an American. What is ultimately at stake is the shape of the American future.[24]

I part company, though, with his conclusion that "the American synthesis has an inevitable Anglo-Saxon coloration" which must be preserved through proper education if we are to avoid "disintegration of the national community, apartheid, Balkanization, tribalization."[25] An unstated subtext to Schlesinger's fear of the disintegrating national community is taken up by Peter Brimelow who locates the passage of the 1965 Immigration Act as the beginning of the end of "America."[26] While Schlesinger would instill the Anglo-Saxon tradition in all immigrants and minorities, Brimelow would stop the problem at the border. Both solutions, though, are motivated by a real sense of crisis.

Within this broader national identity crisis, Asian Americans present a special problem. On the one hand, we are constructed as a model minority, and certain discourses try to incorporate Asian Americans into the American allegory of hard work and perseverance.[27] Poor whites and other racial minorities are scolded for not being more like Asian Americans. On the other hand, our purported successes are turned upon us and we are told that there are "too many" of us.[28] We don't quite fit the mold of the American success story because we remain, on the surface, un-American. A real tension exists because Asian Americans are, to an extent, incorporated into the narrative of the American dream; yet our successes threaten the collapse of that dream for "real" Americans. At present, this tension is mediated through the nativistic racism that regulates the lives of Asian Americans, keeping us from transgressing too far.

POLICING NATIONAL AND INSTITUTIONAL BOUNDARIES

Let me return to my story about the U.S. border guard. When the white man presented his state driver's license, he was immediately recognized as belonging to the national community. When I presented my state driver's license, I was recognized as foreign. I required further investigation. As such, my place in the national community is less certain.

This has repercussions beyond the geopolitical border, because one problem is that the border is imperfect. It does not operate perfectly in excluding that which does not belong. Some slip through, managing to escape detection. Mistakes are made. As a result, the geopolitical border is supplemented by internal policing mechanisms, formal and informal.

Sometimes, the foreign element has to be isolated so that it can be monitored, controlled. The early Chinatowns, which were used to demonstrate the unwillingness of the Chinese to assimilate, were often the result of residential segregation. At other times, the foreign element has to be driven out, expelled for the good of society.

In both cases, though, the foreign is seen as a threat, dangerous to peace and security. Anxiety over this threat becomes exacerbated during times of economic uncertainty. Efforts then are made to further restrict membership in the national community.

Measures such as Proposition 187 are directed against illegal immigrants. Illegal immigrants are colored as the problem. They take jobs away from those who belong here. They use public services so that there's less for everyone else. Blaming illegal immigrants slides quickly into blaming all immigrants. Welfare reform measures have been proposed that cut off aid to even legal immigrants.[29] Although these measures focus on immigration status, problems arise because that status is not evident on an individual's features. Foreign-ness then becomes a proxy for questionable immigration status. Foreign-ness triggers further scrutiny.

This presents a special problem for Asian Americans (and other perpetual foreigners). Because of the way the national community is constructed, Asian Americans are discursively produced as foreign. Foreign-ness is inscribed upon our bodies in such a way that Asian Americans carry a figurative border with us. This figurative border, in addition to confirming the belonging-ness of the "real" Americans, marks Asian Americans as targets of nativistic racism. It renders them suspect, subject to the violence of heightened scrutiny at the border, in the workplace, in hospitals, and elsewhere.

Then there's the different intrusion of physical violence. Nativistic racism directed against those of Asian descent in America has historically expressed itself in violent attacks. The killing of Vincent Chin in Detroit is one variation on this theme. Vincent Chin was the Chinese American killed in 1982 by Detroit autoworkers Ronald Ebens and Michael Nitz. Ebens, according to one witness, said "that it was because of people like Chin"—Ebens apparently mistook him for a Japanese—"that he and his fellow employees were losing their jobs."[30] Ebens and Nitz pleaded guilty to manslaughter and were given no prison time. Instead, they were each given three years' probation and fines of $3,780.[31]

Another variation on the theme of nativistic racism targeting Asian Americans is the killing of Navroze Mody. Mody was an Asian Indian who was beaten to death in 1987 in Jersey City by a gang of eleven youths. The gang did not harm Mody's white friend. No murder or bias charges were brought; three of the assailants were convicted of assault while one was convicted of aggravated assault.[32] To understand the significance of this attack, it must be placed in context. Asian Indians were the fastest-growing immigrant group in New Jersey; many settled in Jersey City. Racially motivated hostilities increased with the growth of the Asian Indian community and the transformation of Jersey City as Asian Indians opened shops and restaurants. Earlier in the month that Navroze Mody was killed, a Jersey City gang called the Dotbusters (a reference to the bindi, the dot that Indian women often wear as a sign of marital fidelity) had published a letter in the *Jersey Journal* saying that they "would 'go to any extreme' to drive Indians from Jersey City."[33] Violence against the Indian community began the next day.

These recent events read in some ways like a page from the book of history. They resemble other racially motivated incidents of the past, such as what happened in 1877 in Chico, California. While attempting to burn down all of Chico's Chinatown, white arsonists murdered four Chinese by tying them up, dousing them with kerosene, and setting them on fire. The arsonists were members of a labor union associated with the Order of Caucasians, a white supremacist organization that was active throughout California. The Order of Caucasians blamed the Chinese for the economic woes suffered by all workers.[34]

The Chinese Massacre of 1885 also took place in the context of a struggling economy and a growing nativist movement. In Rock Springs, Wyoming, a mob of white miners, angered by the Chinese miners' refusal to join their strike (it should be remembered that unions did not permit Chinese members), killed twenty-eight Chinese laborers, wounded fifteen, and chased several hundred out of town. A grand jury failed to indict a single person.[35]

I tell these stories not to point out failures of justice but to show how violence operates to regulate boundaries. This violence is spurred on by certain narratives of America that permit the pathological impulse toward nativistic racism. This violence is not confined to the geopolitical periphery; it may explode anywhere that there is a border (and remember: the border is everywhere). This has serious consequences for those who carry a figurative border on their bodies. Asian Americans, as perpetual internal foreigners, are made available for "real" Americans who need to reassure themselves that the national community begins and ends with themselves, ensuring, at least momentarily, a stable notion of the national community and the fiction of a homogeneous American identity. This is a shabby foundation on which to build any nation.

A POSTSCRIPT IN LIEU OF A CONCLUSION

In my thinking about nation, Benedict Anderson's work has been very influential. He talks about nations as imagined communities.[36] It saddens me to think that we have imagined our community in this way. We have allowed our imaginations to be bounded so that we are left with a nation full of borders, borders that too easily become fault lines.[37] We are left with people who live in transit, between their imaginary homelands and the mythic America. But let us not forget the power of imagination. Let us imagine, then, a better community.

NOTES

Versions of this essay were presented at the Critical Networks Conference hosted by American and Georgetown Universities in March 1995, the Second Asian Pacific American Law Professors Conference hosted by John Marshall Law School in September 1995, and the Latina/o Law Professors Colloquium held in conjunction with the Hispanic National Bar Association Meeting in October 1995. I'd like to thank the participants at those conferences for their comments. Special thanks go to Linda Bosniak for her careful reading and comments on an earlier draft. Thanks also go to Adrienne Davis, Todd Hughes, and Juan Perea who listened to paragraphs read over the phone as they were being written.

A version of this chapter also appears in Robert S. Chang, *Dis-Oriented: Asian Americans, Law, and the Nation-State* (New York University Press, forthcoming 1996) where the ideas treated here appear in expanded form.

1. Robert Frost, "The Mending Wall," in *Robert Frost's Poems* 94 (New York: Washington Square Press, 1971).

2. Noam Chomsky, *World Orders Old and New* 7 (New York: Columbia University Press, 1994).

3. Thomas Friedman, *New York Times Week in Review,* June 2, 1992, quoted in Chomsky, *supra* note 2, at 7.

4. Yasemin Nuhoglu Soysal, writing in the context of contemporary European nation-states, takes the opposite view, stating that "[a] new and more universal concept of citizenship has unfolded in the postwar era, one whose organizing and legitimating principles are based on universal personhood rather than national belonging." Yasemin Nuhoglu Soysal, *Limits of Citizenship: Migrants and Postnational Membership in Europe* 1 (Chicago: University of Chicago Press, 1994). Without commenting on the validity of her thesis in the European context, I would argue that the recent proposals in the United States to limit welfare to citizens demonstrates the renewed importance of national belonging in the United States context.

5. Salman Rushdie, "Imaginary Homelands," in *Imaginary Homelands: Essays and Criticism 1981–1991*, at 9 (London: Granta, 1991).

6. The assertion that the national community is largely an imagined one is drawn from Benedict Anderson, *Imagined Communities: Reflections on the Origin and Spread of Nationalism* (New York: Verso, 2d ed., 1991).

7. As pointed out by Lisa Lowe, orientalisms have their own specificities such that orientalism does not "*monolithically* construct the Orient as the Other of the Occident." Lisa Lowe, *Critical Terrains: French and British Orientalisms,* at ix (Ithaca, NY: Cornell University Press, 1991). Edward Said concedes that Americans will have a different relationship with the Orient, "which for them is much more likely to be associated very differently with the Far East (China and Japan, mainly)." Edward Said, *Orientalism* 1 (New York: Vintage Books, 1978).

8. Frederick M. Dolan, *Allegories of America: Narratives, Metaphysics, Politics* 2–3 (Ithaca, NY: Cornell University Press, 1994).

9. I discuss this phenomenon in Robert Chang, "Toward an Asian American Legal Scholarship: Critical Race Theory, Post-Structuralism, and Narrative Space," 81 *Cal. L. Rev.* 1241, 1255–58 (1993). Nativistic racism also targets Latinos but it has a different history and different specificities which are beyond the scope of this chapter. It is a fruitful area for further research.

10. Lynne Henderson, "Authoritarianism and the Rule of Law," 66 *Ind. L.J.* 379, 380 (1991).

11. David A. Martin, "Due Process and Membership in the National Community: Political Asylum and Beyond," 44 *U. Pitt. L. Rev.* 165, 204 (1983).

12. Kimberlé Crenshaw, "Demarginalizing the Intersection of Race and Sex: A Black Feminist Critique of Antidiscrimination Doctrine, Feminist Theory and Antiracist Politics," 1989 *U. Chi. L. Forum* 139.

13. On English-Only, see Antonio J. Califa, "Declaring English the Official Language: Prejudice Spoken Here," 24 *Harv. C.R.—C.L. L. Rev.* 293 (1989); Juan F. Perea, "Demography and Distrust: An Essay on American Languages, Cultural Pluralism, and Official English," 77 *Minn. L. Rev.* 269 (1992). On Proposition 187, see Linda Bosniak, "Membership, Equality, and the Difference that Alienage Makes," 69 *N.Y.U. L. Rev.* 1047, 1052n. 12 (1994).

14. According to one news report near the beginning of 1995, Colorado, Florida, Illinois, Louisiana, Minnesota, Missouri, Nebraska, Nevada, New York, Texas, Vermont, Washington, Wisconsin, and Wyoming were considering Prop. 187 style laws. Lourdes Medrano Leslie, "Group Seeks to Give State a Prop. 187 Wants Coast-Style Law on Illegals," *Ariz. Republic,* Jan. 23, 1995, at B1.

15. Dudley O. McGovney, "The Anti-Japanese Land Laws of California and Ten Other States," 35 *Cal. L. Rev.* 7 (1947).

16. See, e.g., *Terrace v. Thompson,* 263 U.S. 197 (1923) (upholding Washington's Alien Land Law); *Porterfield v. Webb,* 263 U.S. 225 (1923) (upholding California's Alien Land Law).

17. McGovney, *supra* note 15, at 9. He also comments on the small number of Japanese aliens residing in states other than California that have Alien Land Laws: "These states may, however, be retaining their 'ineligible alien' land laws out of fear that some of the Japanese aliens now residing in other states may move into them." Id at 17.

18. *Nishimura Ekiu v. United States,* 142 U.S. 651, 659 (1892).

19. *Chae Chan Ping v. United States,* 130 U.S. 581, 606 (1889).

20. Neil Gotanda, *Towards Repeal of Asian Exclusion: The Magnuson Act of 1943, the Act of July 2, 1946, the Presidential Proclamation of July 4, 1946, the Act of August 9, 1946 and the Act of August 19, 1950,* in *Asian Americans and Congress: A Documentary History* (Hyung-chan Kim ed., New York: Greenwood Press, 1995).

21. *Ozawa v. United States,* 260 U.S. 178 (1922) (denying naturalization rights to Japanese immigrants); *United States v. Thind,* 261 U.S. 204 (1923) (denying naturalization rights to Asian Indian immigrants).

22. Cf. Keith Aoki, " 'Foreign-ness' and Asian American Identities: Yellowface, Propaganda and Bifurcated Racial Stereotypes," *UCLA Asian Pacific American L.J.* (1995) ("everything they are, we are not, and vice versa").

23. Interview with James Baldwin, CBS News (CBS television broadcast, Oct. 1967), quoted in Adeno Addis, " 'Hell Man, They Did Invent Us': The Mass Media, Law, and African Americans," 41 *Buff. L. Rev.* 523, 528 (1993) (citation omitted).

24. Arthur M. Schlesinger, Jr., *The Disuniting of America: Reflections on a Multicultural Society* (Knoxville, TN: Whittle Direct Books, 1991).

25. Id. at 67. For a cogent critique of Schlesinger, see Stanley Fish, "Bad Company," 56 *Transition* 60 (1992).

26. Peter Brimelow, *Alien Nation: Common Sense about America's Immigration Disaster* 58–73 (New York: Random House, 1995).

27. See, e.g., "Success Story of One Minority Group in U.S.," *U.S. News and World Rep.,* Dec. 26, 1966, at 73, reprinted in *Roots: An Asian American Reader* 6 (Amy Tachiki et al. eds., Los Angeles: UCLA Asian American Studies Center, 1971). For critiques of the Asian American model minority thesis, see Ronald Takaki, *Strangers from a Different Shore: A History of Asian Americans* (New York: Penguin Books, 1989); Chang, *supra* note 9, at 1258–65.

28. See, e.g., Selena Dong, Note, " 'Too Many Asians': The Challenge of Fighting Discrimination against Asian-Americans and Preserving Affirmative Action," 47 *Stan. L. Rev.* 1027 (1995).

29. See Bosniak, *supra* note 13, at 1050–51n. 7.

30. Sucheng Chan, *Asian Americans: An Interpretive History* 177 (Boston: Twayne, 1991). The men were indiscriminate in their use of epithets, also calling him a "Chink." American Citizens for Justice, Confidential Report on the Vincent Chin Case to the U.S. Dep't of Justice, Civil Rights Division, 3 (June 28, 1983) (copy on file with author).

31. U.S. Commission on Civil Rights, *Civil Rights Issues Facing Asian Americans in the 1990s,* at 25 (1992).

32. Id. at 29.

33. Al Kamen, "When Hostility Follows Immigration: Racial Violence Sows Fear in New Jersey's Indian Community," *Washington Post,* Nov. 16, 1992, at A1, A6.

34. Chan, *supra* note 30, at 49.

35. Paul Crane and Alfred Larson, *The Chinese Massacre,* 12 Annals of Wyoming 47, 47–49 (1940).

36. Anderson, *supra* note 6.

37. I take the phrase "fault lines" from Tomas Almaguer, *Racial Fault Lines: The Historical Origins of White Supremacy in California* (Los Angeles: University of California Press, 1994).

14. RECONCILING RIGHTS IN COLLISION

An International Human Rights Strategy
Berta Esperanza Hernández-Truyol

I. INTRODUCTION

Currently, the United States is in the midst of an alarming nativistic movement plainly reflected in federal and state immigration reform bills, the most prominent of which (to date) is California's now infamous Proposition 187.[1] This initiative, patently capitalizing on the tight economic climate to promote hostility, prejudice and xenophobia—a basic fear of "others/outsiders"—in the name of protecting red-blooded, law abiding, *real* Americans, seeks to deny health, education, and welfare benefits to persons—young and old alike—who illegally enter the United States.[2] Proposition 187 blames undocumented persons, revealingly called "illegal aliens," for all that ails California, specifically, the depressed economic environment and crimes against persons and property. In response to the mischief such illegals are said to cause in California, Proposition 187 aims to rid the state of these undesirables by not educating them, not taking care of their health, and generally running them out of the state.

The unproven, unfounded premise underlying these actions and attitudes, which are rather unbecoming to a land of opportunity, is that illegal aliens are a drain on the system and a burden to the hardworking, taxpaying citizens who support them. These negative perceptions of "others/outsiders" are wholly contrary to the facts—most come here to work and would like to become citizens; many take the menial, low-paying jobs *real* Americans won't; and all have a dream of making a better life for themselves and their families. Yet the nativistic initiatives make it clear that these trouble making, law breaking, social services-taking people are not welcome here, despite the fact that evidence shows they "contribute more to national, state and local economies than they take out in assistance." [3]

The choice of labelling certain immigrants as "illegal" and "alien" itself facially exposes the animus against the persons at whom it is aimed and the intent to create yet another category to reinforce the "us" versus "them" mentality that is infecting (and destroying) our society. It cannot be disputed that the persons *themselves* are neither illegal as there is no such thing as an illegal person (although their presence within the U.S. borders may well be) nor extraterrestrial. They are, rather simply, subjects of a foreign sovereign who have come within the jurisdiction of the United States without proper documentation, papers that, by the way, are not even necessary for some to obtain *legal* entry. For instance, the visa waiver program allows persons who are residents of twenty-two selected countries, largely from Western Europe, to stay in the United States for up to ninety days simply by purchasing a round-trip ticket.[4] Some of the persons coming from these "select" visa-waiver countries, which include France, Sweden, and Italy, are "significant abusers of the system," with the Immigration and Naturalization Service (INS) estimating that they constitute between five and ten percent of the "illegal immigrants who overstayed their visas." [5]

The tendency to condemn and vilify immigrants, particularly those identifiable as "others/outsiders" continues in Proposition 187 and related legislation. Proposition 187's thinly veiled targeting of Mexicans as unwelcome illegals drew ire from Mexico—presenting yet another foreign relations problem. Then-President Carlos Salinas de Gortari called the measure "racist" and "a disgrace for U.S.-Mexican relations." [6] Similarly, the Mexican Ambassador to the United States condemned the measure noting that "[t]here is an equation now in California that goes: Illegal immigrants equal to Mexicans, equal to criminals, equal to one who wants social services." [7]

Unfortunately, this new nativism is not *only* a domestic problem but a global one. The recently reunified Germany with its increasing non-European immigrant population is experiencing a corresponding rise in hate crimes and race-based violence and protest.[8] Similarly, the European Union (EU) has expressed concern that non-EU citizens, particularly gypsies and others, will abuse the open borders and travel unchecked within the Union. International human rights norms are a powerful resource to combat such xenophobia and discrimination against immigrants in the United States.

II. INTERNATIONAL HUMAN RIGHTS LAWS

A. Sources of International Law

International human rights law is part of the general field of international law. As such, the Statute of the International Court of Justice provides that there are two primary sources of international law—treaties and custom—and two secondary sources—general principles recognized by civilized nations and "judicial decisions and the teachings of the most highly qualified publicists of the various nations."[9]

Treaties are "international agreement[s] concluded between States in written form and governed by international law, whether embodied in a single instrument or in two or more related instruments and whatever its particular designation."[10] They comprise a major, and certainly are the most voluminous, source of international obligations.[11] "International agreements—the *lex scripta* of the society of states—have proliferated since the end of World War Two. More than 30,000 treaties have been registered with the United Nations since 1945.... Virtually every aspect of social life affecting transnational relations and intercourse is dealt with in treaties."[12]

Custom, the other primary source, is coequal with treaties as international legal authority. Customary law results from a general and consistent state practice followed from a sense of legal obligation.[13] A customary international law of human rights has developed and continues to grow with the International Court of Justice (I.C.J.) and the International Law Commission having recognized it.[14] The secondary sources are widely used by courts, mostly to establish custom or to explain, expand, and transform custom and/or conventional law.[15]

B. Human Rights as Legal Rights

The initial inquiry when considering international human rights norms is whether they are merely aspirational statements of moral goals or legally enforceable rights and obligations.[16] A centuries-old debate questioning whether international law is *real* law persists. There are some who insist that international law is a mere statement of moral goals and that without an enforcement or legislative mechanism or an executive body cannot be law.

International human rights, specifically, are those vital to individuals' existence—they are fundamental and inalienable rights, predicates to life as human beings.[17] These norms are moral, social, and political rights that concern the respect and dignity associated with our lives as individuals and have their origin in "natural law [and] in contemporary moral values."[18] Central to this articulation of international human rights law is that every individual has rights in society not only with which the state cannot interfere but which the state must affirmatively recognize, respect, and protect.[19] Thus, the human rights obligations of states transcend not only nationality but geographic borders. As such, human rights are subject to the protection of and the control by international law.[20]

One of the complexities in acknowledging the existence of legally enforceable human rights is the concession that there exists a limitation on the

power of government: a crack in states' sacrosanct sovereignty[21] armor—
with the obligation to respect inalienable human rights becoming a limitation
on a state's sovereign power. If international human rights norms are indeed
law, states are accountable for breaches of these norms to individuals and to
other states, even when their own citizens are involved.

In this view, it can hardly be disputed that international human rights law
is *real* law and that it *does* constitute a limitation on state sovereignty. The
primary example, of course, is the universal condemnation of the atrocities
committed by the Nazi regime which included, although they were not
limited to, the killing of German Jews on German soil by Germans. In fact,
modern conventional international human rights law dates to the conclusion
of World War II when, in the aftermath of Nazi atrocities, a shift in philosophy resulted in a marked departure from the positivists' doctrinal view that
only states can be subjects of international law.[22] This contemporary view
recognizes not only that persons have to be protected from states notwithstanding existing principles of sovereignty,[23] but also that "crimes against
international law are committed by men, not by abstract entities, and only
by punishing individuals who commit such crimes can the provisions of
international law be enforced."[24] In reaction to this global disaster, the
nations of the world joined to form the United Nations for the purpose of
"promoting and encouraging respect for human rights and for fundamental
freedoms for all."[25]

The unique and powerful lesson on human rights that emerged from this
tragic event in history, and preserved in *The Nuremberg Trial*, was the
placement of fundamental human rights—rights from which no state may
derogate, even vis-à-vis its own citizens and within its own geographic borders—at the heart of international law.[26] These trials not only defined the
relationship of individuals to international law but also conclusively established that the rules of public international law should, and do, apply to
individuals.[27] In this regard, international human rights agreements have
created obligations and responsibilities for states in respect of all individuals
subject to their jurisdiction, including their own nationals.[28]

III. HUMAN RIGHTS NORMS AS U.S. LAW

A. General Principles

The U.S. Constitution, statutes, and American jurisprudence recognize that
international law is *real* law.[29] In the United States, as in the international
sphere, treaties are one of the sources of international law. Treaties are
defined as agreements between two or among more states or international
organizations that are "intended to be legally binding and governed by

international law,"[30] a definition virtually identical to that of the I.C.J. Statute. The Constitution, by expressly recognizing the existence of international law and articulating the role of the different branches, makes it clear that international law is part of the domestic law of the United States. For example, the Constitution provides that Congress has the power to "define and punish . . . [o]ffenses against the Law of Nations."[31] Similarly, the Constitution defines the relationship between international law and domestic law by designating treaties, which are the province of the executive to be passed with the advice and consent of two-thirds of the Senate,[32] as the supreme law of the land.[33]

In addition to the constitutionally mandated acceptance of treaty law as domestic law, it is well settled that U.S. law recognizes the binding nature of custom as a source of international law, including human rights norms.[34] Custom "may be ascertained by consulting the works of jurists, writing professedly on public law; or by the general usage and practice of nations; or by judicial decisions recognising and enforcing that law."[35] Significantly, although customary law's binding nature is not predicated upon an express constitutional provision, commentators as well as case law recognize that it is binding on all nations.[36]

Almost a century ago, in *The Paquete Habana,* the Supreme Court for the first time ruled that customary law is the law of our land.[37] The Court declared:

international law is part of our law, and must be ascertained by the courts of justice of appropriate jurisdiction as often as questions of right depending upon it are duly presented for their determination. For this purpose, where there is no treaty and no controlling executive or legislative act or judicial decision, resort must be had to the customs and usages of civilized nations.[38]

Much more recently, the Second Circuit reiterated this notion in *Filartiga v. Peña-Irala* when it found that:

In light of the universal condemnation of torture in numerous international agreements, and the renunciation of torture as an instrument of official policy by virtually all of the nations of the world (in principle if not in practice), . . . an act of torture committed by a state official against one held in detention violates the *established norms of the international law of human rights, and hence the law of nations.*[39]

In *Filartiga,* the court plainly explained customary law and general principles as sources of international law in our domestic system:

where there is no treaty, and no controlling executive or legislative act or judicial decision, resort must be had to the customs and usage of civilized nations; and, as evidence of these, to the works of jurists and commentators who by years of labor, research and experience, have made themselves peculiarly well acquainted with the subject of which they treat. Such works are resorted to by judicial tribunals, not for the speculations of their authors concerning what the law ought to be, but for trustworthy evidence of what the law really is.[40]

Finally, strengthening the reality that international human rights norms are binding law, many federal statutes refer to "internationally recognized human rights" and have legislated national policy toward governments guilty of "consistent patterns of violations" of such rights.[41] Thus, human rights obligations assumed by the United States under treaties as well as those that arise pursuant to custom, as evidenced by or derived from treaties or secondary sources, are legally enforceable within the United States by states as well as individuals.

B. United States' Obligations

Of particular importance to domestic law challenges are those provisions of international law that because of the United States' actions—either accession to customary practices or adoption of treaties—must be followed as the supreme law of the land. Significantly, the United States has only signed and ratified several international human rights agreements:[42] the Charter of the United Nations (U.N. Charter);[43] the Charter of the Organization of American States (OAS Charter);[44] the International Covenant on Civil and Political Rights (ICCPR);[45] the Protocol Relating to the Status of Refugees;[46] and the Convention on the Elimination of All Forms of Racial Discrimination (Race Convention).[47]

Ratification is a significant factor in domestic enforcement. The United States becomes internationally accountable for treaty obligations upon signing by the President or her/his plenipotentiary. However, the United States does not become domestically accountable until there is ratification that includes the constitutionally mandated advice and consent function of the Senate.[48] Thus, the United States is internationally but not domestically accountable with respect to documents it has signed such as the International Covenant on Economic, Social, and Cultural Rights (Economic Covenant),[49] the Convention on the Rights of the Child (Child Convention),[50] and the Convention on the Elimination of All Forms of Discrimination against Women (Women's Convention).[51] The United States has expressly declared, however, that even the ratified treaties are non-self-executing,[52] rendering them not domestically enforceable until passage of the requisite enabling legislation.[53]

It is noteworthy that the first time ever the U.S. human rights record was subject to international review (pursuant to the requisite yearly report to the

Human Rights Commission [HRC] under Article 40 of the ICCPR) the Commission severely criticized the United States for not accepting the covenant as domestic law.[54] For its part, the United States defended its stance stating a preference not to use the unicameral treaty power of the Constitution to effect direct charges in domestic law. Additionally, the United States contended that almost all of the rights enumerated in the Covenant were already protected under U.S. law and did not require special enabling legislation. The HRC criticized and rejected these excuses, noting that if the United States was not obligated to comply with the Covenant, ratification of the Covenant delivered no new rights and U.S. courts would not heed the Covenant at all—a fear that is well founded in precedent.[55]

Regardless of whether a treaty is non-self-executing or signed but not ratified, the rights contained therein can create domestically enforceable legal rights if they constitute customary international law as *Paquete Habana* and, more recently, *Filartiga* plainly concluded.[56] Indeed, U.S. Courts have consistently referred to international instruments as a means to define, or assist with the application and interpretation of, domestic law.[57] For example, one document that indisputably has created internationally binding obligations, as recognized by both domestic and international courts and other adjudicative bodies, is the Universal Declaration of Human Rights (Declaration or Universal Declaration)[58]—the cornerstone for the ICCPR and the Economic Covenant which, along with other human rights documents, essentially replicates the Declaration's human rights foundation. Thus, those sections of the Declaration that are custom create independent domestically enforceable private rights—even if the identical rights might not be enforceable as conventional law because they are contained in documents that have not been ratified or have been declared to be non-self-executing.

In addition to the limitations placed on domestic enforcement of treaties by the notion of non-self-execution, the concept of reservations or conditions also can result in shielding the state from liability. Reservations are "unilateral statement[s] . . . made by a state when signing, ratifying, accepting, approving or acceding to a treaty whereby it purports to exclude or modify the legal effect of certain provisions of the treaty in their application to that state."[59] Any unilateral statement of a state that "purports to exclude, limit, or modify the state's legal obligation" under the treaty is deemed a reservation regardless of whether it is labeled a reservation or a "declarations" or "understanding" as the United States did in the ICCPR.[60]

There are limitations, however, as to what a state can take as reservations to an international convention. Both the Vienna Convention on the Law of Treaties and the Restatement prohibit reservations that are incompatible with "the purpose and object of a treaty."[61] It is clear that a reservation designed to enable a state to suspend a nonderogable fundamental right will be deemed ineffectual. Thus any reservation against a right that is *jus cogens*—a peremptory norm—is void.

This notion of reservations is particularly important when contained in human rights treaties. Such reservations may be designed to excuse parties from obligations that might nevertheless be binding *erga omnes*—because such obligations are basic to the concern of all persons. If the reservation seeks to avoid the recognition or enforcement of a nonderogable right, such as a prohibition against racial discrimination or genocide, the reservation itself will fail and the state remains bound to respect the protected right and obey the law.[62]

Notwithstanding the apparent advantages the international human rights construct provides to further the universal protection of individuals, it is important to note that this system is far from perfect. One example is the problem of reservations discussed above. Another is the access of individuals to fora where their rights can be adjudicated. Yet another is the important role the power, real or perceived, of the various states plays in obtaining rights in fact and the related problem of enforcement and implementation of rules against the powerful states.[63] Thus, although I urge expanding the domestic use of this precious body of laws, I also urge working within the international system to rectify its deficiencies.

IV. INDECENT PROPOSITIONS

A. Overview of Domestic Legal Challenges

It is beyond the scope of this chapter to review the numerous substantive constitutional challenges to this initiative and others like it. However, a brief mention of the arguments is instructive to crystallize the benefits of including international human rights arguments in the challenge of nativistic laws. The domestic challenges available include a federal preemption argument contending that as the federal government is charged with the implementation and enforcement of immigration laws, state statutes affecting immigration such as California's Proposition 187 must fail under the Supremacy Clause.[64] Unfortunately, such challenge will be "full of sound and fury, signifying nothing" if the federal government adopts the local principles as the basis of federal law. Other challenges include one based on the Equal Protection Clause; a Due Process challenge premised upon the denial of services and requirement of deportation prior to a deportation proceeding; [65] and, finally, a contention that the law is contrary to *Plyler v. Doe*[66] which, at present, is controlling precedent.[67]

As will be shown in the review of established human rights norms that follows, these norms provide significantly broader grounds upon which to challenge xenophobic initiatives, be they state or federal laws. This analysis is particularly interesting in view of the U.S. position, as presented to the HRC, that it is irrelevant that the ICCPR is a non-self-executing treaty because first, issues of implementation are simply a matter of domestic law and, second, the rights guaranteed in the covenant are already protected under U.S. law and consequently do not require special legislation. As an international human rights analysis reveals, the U.S. position is, at best, a misunderstanding of the law; at worst, it is a blatant misrepresentation of the role of international law in domestic law and the state of civil rights protections in this country. In fact, human rights norms afford substantial and significant protections beyond those provided by the purely domestic rights construct. Once established to be domestically enforceable, these rights could have a dramatic transformative effect on domestic civil rights laws.

B. Protected International Human Rights

Of particular importance for a critical analysis of Proposition 187 are those norms that prohibit discrimination and those that affirmatively create individual rights such as the rights to health, education, and welfare. Significantly, the agreements listed in Part III, as well as numerous other documents, provide protections on all the grounds upon which the new nativistic initiatives seek to deny rights.

As discussed earlier, a threshold issue concerning international human rights based challenges to domestic laws is the notion that sovereignty gives the government the unfettered power to legislate. Were such the case, Proposition 187 and its clones would have to be deemed a legitimate exercise of sovereign power. Although at first glance the sovereignty argument is attractive and appears to create an insurmountable obstacle to any challenge of the law, its fatal flaw is that in dealing with human rights norms the focus is on individuals whose rights are nonderogable and thus suprasovereign.

A state can use the principle of sovereignty neither as a shield from accountability for the way it treats individuals and from the implementation and enforcement of those norms nor as a sword to eviscerate the very human rights norms (or at least the application of the norms) to which it is bound. The Nuremberg Trials proved that there is no such thing as a state's unfettered sovereign existence. Professor Louis Henkin, international human rights scholar, recognizing the tension between sovereignty principles and humanitarian "impulse to aid" in refugee law, suggested that "[t]he international community should reject by its refugee law, as it has by its humanitarian law generally, the notion that states maintain exclusive power over entry and presence in their territory as the very essence of their national sovereignty."[68] This view should hold for all human rights norms: domestic laws enacted under the guise of unfettered sovereignty cannot absolve discrimination and inequality that derogates from human rights of individuals simply because it is done in the name of law.

One of the centerpieces of human rights documents is the proposition that existing rights are to be enjoyed by all persons equally. International human rights documents protect the rights of "persons," not the narrower class of citizens. Indeed, a stated purpose of the United Nations was "to achieve international co-operation . . . in promoting and encouraging respect for human rights and fundamental freedoms for *all persons*" and to ensure equality without distinction as to "race, color, sex, language, religion, political or other opinion, national or social origin, property, birth or other status."[69] This vision of equality is at the root of and echoed by every single international and regional human rights convention.[70] In fact, it is deemed so important that the ICCPR does not allow states to discriminate on the proscribed grounds even in times of officially proclaimed public emergencies "which threaten . . . the life of the nation."[71]

It was clearly the intent of the drafters of these documents to protect "persons" rather than the smaller class of "citizens."[72] The ICCPR's "travaux preparatoires" reveal that an amendment was proposed, and rejected, to substitute the word "citizens" for the word "persons."[73] According to the Comments of the ICCPR's Human Rights Committee, "the rights set forth in the Covenant apply to everyone, irrespective of his or her nationality or statelessness."[74] The Human Rights Committee has stated that "the general rule is that each one of the rights of the Covenant must be guaranteed without discrimination between citizens and aliens. Aliens receive the benefit of the general requirement of nondiscrimination in respect of the rights guaranteed in the Covenant, as provided in Article 2 thereof. This guarantee applies to aliens and citizens alike."[75] Thus, the "travaux preparatoires," the language of international human rights instruments, as well as general comments of the Human Rights Committee confirm that the categories of individuals entitled to international human rights include noncitizens.

Beyond conventional norms, the Universal Declaration's statement that "*[e]veryone* is entitled to all the rights and freedoms set forth in this Declaration, without distinction of any kind, such as race, colour, sex, language, religion, political or other opinion, national or social origin, property, birth, or other status"[76] grounds the principle of nondiscrimination on custom. Given the United States' ratification of the ICCPR (with the only explanatory note being one that indicates distinctions could be made if rationally related to a *legitimate* governmental objective), the U.N. Charter and the Race Convention, and that the Universal Declaration is customary law, the United States undeniably is bound by these notions of equality and nondiscrimination.

There are also specific rights that serve to invalidate the intrusions of the initiatives in question. The various instruments protect the international human rights to mental and physical health,[77] to education,[78] to freedom from interference with privacy and family,[79] to liberty and security of the person,[80] to travel,[81] to information,[82] and to freedom of association.[83] Article 24 of the ICCPR provides a special protection for children mandating that "[e]very child shall have, without any discrimination as to race, colour, sex, language, religion, national or social origin, property or birth, the right to such measures of protection as are required by his status as a minor, on the part of his family, society, and the State." And finally, Article 27 provides that "[i]n those States in which ethnic, religious or linguistic minorities exist, *persons* belonging to such minorities shall not be denied the right, in community with the other members of their group, to enjoy their own culture, to profess and practice their own religion, or to use their language." The Child Convention, at Article 30, replicates this provision with respect to the rights of children belonging to "ethnic, religious or linguistic minorities or . . . of indigenous origin." These sources of specific rights, as incorporated into our domestic discourse, provide ample and powerful bases to condemn xenophobic initiatives such as Proposition 187.

With this background, following is an analysis of Proposition 187 vis-à-vis such established human rights norms. To be sure, the equality/nondiscrimination provisions alone provide at least six obvious bases upon which the proposition could be challenged: race, color, language, national or social origin, and birth.[84] The analysis also suggests challenges to the initiative based upon less obvious categories as well as challenges based upon other established human rights as further means to develop, expand, and transform domestic law.

C. Proposition 187: Human Rights Violations

On November 8, 1994, the voters of California approved *Proposition 187: "Initiative Statute—Illegal Aliens—Public Services, Verification, and Reporting"* an initiative aimed at correcting ills the people of California were deemed to be suffering based on the presence of "illegal aliens"—mostly of latinas/os from Mexico, El Salvador, and Guatemala[85]—in the state. One of the ills, the economic burden the "illegals" place on the state's economy, can be exposed as nothing but a myth, as there is ample evidence that the targeted immigrants every year give more to national, state, and local economies than they receive in services.[86] Indeed, such immigrants often fill low-skilled, low-cost jobs—as recognized in *Plyler v. Doe*—that good old red-blooded Americans will not even consider taking.[87]

The initiative's preambular section also asserts that Californians have suffered personal injury and damage by the criminal conduct of these "illegal aliens." This statement is not supported by any proof. However, it appears to be accepted as *true* fact simply because people assume that since their *presence* is not lawful "they" *are* (or clearly must be) criminals.

Ignoring the basic flaws in its foundation, Proposition 187 designs a methodology for correcting these myriad ills: eliminate the targeted class—the "illegal aliens"—from eligibility to receive certain social public services such as health care,[88] public elementary and secondary school education,[89] and public postsecondary education.[90] To achieve these goals the Proposition requires that "any public entity . . . to whom a person has applied for public social services determines or *reasonably suspects,* based upon the information provided to it, that the person is an alien in the United States in violation of federal law . . . shall not provide the person with benefits or services . . . [shall] notify the person of his or her apparent illegal immigration status and notify the State Director of Social Services, the Attorney General of California, and the United States Immigration and Naturalization Service of the apparent illegal status, and shall provide any additional information that may be requested by any other public entity."[91] This mandate runs to reporting with respect to any attempt by these *aliens* to obtain access to health care,[92] public elementary and secondary school,[93] or postsecondary education.[94] Elementary and secondary school districts are required to verify the legal status of each enrolled student/child. Educational services may continue for ninety days without verification, but this *grace period* "shall be utilized to accomplish an orderly transition to a school in the child's country of origin."[95] California's many public postsecondary educational institutions must also verify/document the legal status of each student enrolled or in attendance.[96]

The proposition identifies those ineligible to receive the public social benefits by designating three categories of persons eligible to receive benefits: "(1) [a] citizen of the United States[;] (2) [a]n alien lawfully admitted as a permanent resident[;] (3) [a]n alien lawfully admitted for a temporary period of time."[97] While the proposition purports to exclude "illegal aliens" because of the economic and psychological damage their criminal ways cause and because of the drain on resources their mere illegal presence effects, on its face, the initiative glaringly fails to address, let alone exclude, those who were lawfully admitted but overstay their welcome. This is significant in light of statistics: in 1994 it was estimated that of the total "illegal immigrant" population in the United States 1,909,000 *entered* illegally—consequently being subject to the harsh provisions of Proposition 187; but that 2,070,000 *entered* legally and *stayed illegally,* thus not subject to the immigration reform measures imposed on others similarly situated.

The underinclusiveness of such provision reveals its true racist and mean-spirited nature; as drafted its rational objectives and justifications are but a smoke screen for legislating hate. These classifications are ripe for an international law-based challenge on the bases of equality and nondiscrimination principles. Certainly it should be illegal *presence,* not manner of entry, to which a state objects, were that at all proven to be a cause of crime or shortage of resources. Nonetheless, state and federal authorities alike focus their efforts to curb illegal immigration on mode of entry by substantially funding increased border patrols but not aiming much at increasing visa overstay enforcement.[98] This approach has the effect of impermissibly discriminating between/among similarly situated persons—those *illegally* present—based on the prohibited grounds of color, race, and national origin.

The standard establishing the threshold for denial of services also is subject to challenge based on nondiscrimination/equality norms. The initiative requires the denial of social services if the providers—school teachers, hospital administrators, welfare clerks—"reasonably suspect" that the applicant is an "illegal alien." The factors that might arouse suspicion are, by their nature, purely subjective and prone to biased judgments. For example, suspicion may be based upon a person's "look"—physical appearance, including complexion, height, hair color and texture, as well as manner of dress. These bases for denying benefits are but a thinly veiled denial of benefits on the impermissible bases of the race, color, national or social origin, and birth of the "suspect." Similarly, foreign-accented English and/or poor, "broken," or imperfect English, or the speaking of a language other than English may trigger the requisite suspicion, this time on the impermissible grounds of language, national or social origin, property, birth or other status. Significantly, the grounds upon which enforcers will base their "suspicions"—color, language, national or social origin, ethnicity—are all protected under the ICCPR, the Race Convention, the U.N. Charter, and the Universal Declaration to name but four documents to which the United States is, indisputably, bound.

In addition, the provisions that deny social services are also insupportable based on a broader human rights analysis—one that can help expand and transform the analysis of individuals' civil rights in our domestic forum. The attempt to deny health services on its face is in contravention of the internationally protected right to health. Moreover, the denial of such services could arguably interfere with the right to travel—by interfering with the international flow of persons—and the right to privacy—by invading, among other things, familial relations—both rights guaranteed by every human rights covenant as well as the Universal Declaration.

It is noteworthy that the federal law proposed in the Senate, the Immigration Control and Financial Responsibility Act of 1995, contains various provisions that plainly fly in the face of the international right of privacy. For example, Section 111 of this Act proposes a national database containing information on all Americans and immigrants eligible to work; without one's name in the database, one cannot work. Section 111 also proposes a pilot project to establish whether all persons should be required to carry a national identity card. Section 115 would require all children to register with the Social Security Administration by age 16 and, upon registration, to provide "fingerprint or other biometric data" that will be placed on the child's birth certificate, supposedly to make it tamper-proof.

Particularly egregious are the attempts to deny educational benefits. First, *Plyler v. Doe* is controlling domestic precedent proscribing such denial. Second, "[e]ducation is a human right and an essential tool for achieving the goals of equality, development and peace."[99] The Universal Declaration, the OAS Charter, the Race Convention, and the Refugee Convention, all indisputably binding on the United States, either as customary law or as ratified conventional law, are emphatic about the right to education. Such right is further reinforced by the ICCPR's Article 27 mandate to states to ensure the needs of children are met. Thus, the initiative's attempt to deny children the right to education is not only illegal it is hateful against children who themselves are not only defenseless in the legal maze but very strongly protected by human rights norms.

Further, this denial of education and the concomitant reporting requirements both interfere with the internationally recognized and respected rights to privacy and family life. Significantly, the bases for these denials of services are the above-discussed subjectivities which are independently violative of established nondiscrimination norms. The denial of education also deprives the students (and their parents) of their right to obtain and impart information by being denied access to the educational forum. Moreover, the denial of the right to go to school interferes with the protected freedom of association not only of the children wrongfully kept out of school but also of those who are allowed to remain but deprived of the presence of their "illegal" counterparts and of the learning to which they could contribute.

Finally, the issue of sex discrimination—although perhaps not so evident— presents a serious challenge to the initiative. The issue of gender, moreover, crystallizes the indivisibility of rights. For example, denial of health services to women raises issues of maternal health, maternal and infant mortality (thus also implicating the right to life),[100] and infant health—all issues that have been at the center of the international human rights discourse in recent years with the strongest of endorsements by the United States.[101] Similarly, denial of education, because of historic denial of equality to girls, results in further marginalization based on sex, subjecting the education provisions to challenge on gender grounds.[102]

International human rights norms provide ample grounds to fight nativistic aspects of proposed immigration reform laws proliferating at both the state and federal level. Notwithstanding the apparent advantages of such norms, it is important to note that the system is far from perfect as the notions of sovereignty, reservations, non-self-executing treaties, and the problems of lack of ready access for individuals to adjudicatory fora, implementation, and enforcement make patently clear.

Nevertheless, these norms provide substantive foundations to challenge and invalidate initiatives such as Proposition 187. To be sure, equality and nondiscrimination provisions and rights such as health, education, and equality are directly applicable in such a challenge. International human rights norms afford broader protections than do our domestic laws. For example, domestic norms do not protect language or health to the extent the international norms do. Thus, international laws provide a vehicle to strike the use of sovereignty as a tool of oppression.

These international principles provide grounds, different from and perhaps more efficient than local law, to eradicate invidious distinctions based on race, color, language, national or social origin. They are a wealth of rules that when brought home may bring the notion of equality closer to being a reality. They also provide a framework for positive and constructive discourse on rights as we approach the twenty-first century.

NOTES

Many thanks to my wonderful research assistant, Alison N. Stewart (St. John's Law '96) who provided invaluable assistance in the preparation of this chapter.

1. This chapter uses California's Proposition 187, aimed predominantly at immigrants from Mexico, as a concrete example of such a bill. It is not the only initiative of its kind. For instance, Florida is working on its own version (Florida Proposition 187) and a federal version has been introduced in the Senate—The Immigration Control and Financial Responsibility Act of 1995 (S 269) [hereinafter ICFRA].

2. This is not a new phenomenon. In fact, this country historically has resorted to scapegoating certain groups for the nation's ills during less than favorable times. See Gordon W. Allport, *The Nature of Prejudice* 236–38 (abridged ed., Anchor Books, 1958) (analyzing the blaming of immigrant and other minorities for economic downturns).

3. Peter L. Reich, "Public Benefits for Undocumented Aliens: State Law into the Breach Once More," 21 *N.M. L. Rev.* 219, 244 (1991); see also Michael Olivas, "Preempting Preemption: Foreign Affairs, State Rights and Alienage Classifications," 35 *Va. J. Int'l L.* 217 (1994) at 227–34 (figures cited conclude that immigrants contribute $90 billion in taxes while taking only $5 billion in social services); Michael Fix and Jeffrey Passell, *Immigration and Immigrants: Setting the Record Straight* 6 (1994) (noting that immigration may result in a net gain for the federal government, but impact at state level varies).

4. Immigration and Nationality Act, 217.

5. Ashley Dunn, "Greeted at Nation's Front Door, Many Visitors Stay on Illegally," *N.Y. Times,* January 3, 1995, at A1, B2.

6. Mark Fineman, "Mexico Assails State's Passage of Prop 187," *L.A. Times,* Nov. 10, 1994, at A28.

7. Marc Sandalow, "Mexican Envoy Berates State on Immigration," *S.F. Chron.,* July 6, 1994, at A1.

8. See Daniel Kanstroom, "Wer Sind Wir Wieder? Laws of Asylum, Immigration, and Citizenship in the Struggle for the Soul of the New Germany," 18 *Yale J. Int'l L.* 155, 155–61 (1993).

9. Statute of the International Court of Justice, annexed to the U.N. Charter June 26, 1945, entered into force October 24, 1945, art. 38 [hereinafter Statute of I.C.J.] (The I.C.J. shall apply (a) recognized international covenants, (b) international custom as evidence of general practice, (c) "the general principles of law recognized by civilized nations," (d) judicial decisions and "teachings of the most highly qualified publicists of the various nations").

10. Vienna Convention on the Law of Treaties, U.N. Doc. A/CONF. 39/27, May 23, 1969, entered into force January 27, 1990, art. 2(a) [hereinafter Vienna Convention]. In the international arena, all international agreements are labelled "treaties." However, pursuant to U.S. law, only some international agreements are designated as treaties—those concluded by the president with the advice and consent of two-thirds of the Senate. U.S. Const. art. II, §2. For a discussion of international agreements in U.S. law, as well as the different forms these may take, see *infra* notes 30–33, 42–63, 69–80, and accompanying text.

11. Louis Henkin et al., *International Law: Cases and Materials* 416 (3d ed. 1993) [hereinafter Henkin]("That treaties govern much of international relations is evidenced by the [numbers] of such treaties and their wide scope"); Mark W. Janis, *An Introduction to International Law* 9 (2d ed. 1993) at 9 [hereinafter Janis]; Gerhard von Glahn, *Law among Nations* 17 (4th ed. 1981). See also *Rest. 3rd, Restatement of the Foreign Relations Law of the United States* Pt. I, Ch.1, Introductory Note [hereinafter Restatement] ("In our day, treaties have become the principal vehicle for making law for the international system").

12. Henkin, *supra* note 11 at 95–96.

13. Custom has two identifiable elements, general practice and acceptance as law. Statute of I.C.J., *supra* note 27 at art. 38(1)(b); See Henkin, *supra* note 11 at ch. 2, sec. 2; Frank Newman and David Weissbrodt, *International Human Rights: Law, Policy, and Process* at ch. XII, sec. 1 (1990) [hereinafter Newman and Weissbrodt]; Janis, *supra* note 11 at ch. 3.

14. See *Barcelona Traction, Light and Power Co., Ltd. (Belg. v. Spain),* 1970 I.C.J. 32. See also Restatement *supra* note 11 at §702 (setting out the customary international law of human rights), pt. VII, Introductory Note.

15. See, e.g., *United States v. Smith,* 18 U.S. (5 Wheat.) 153, 160–61 (1820) (Supreme Court looked to the work of learned writers in holding piracy to be a basis for a death sentence).

16. See Henkin, *supra* note 11 at 10–26 (commentary of key figures and discussion of principles and doctrines in the debate over the legitimacy of international law).

17. Rebecca M. Wallace, *International Law* 176 (1986) [hereinafter Wallace].

18. Restatement, *supra* note 11 pt. VII, ch. 1, comment b; Henkin, *supra* note 11 at ch. 8. See, generally, Newman and Weissbrodt, *supra* note 13.

19. Restatement, *supra* note 11 at pt. VII, introductory note. See, e.g., Vienna

Declaration and Programme of Action, A/Conf.157/23, July 12, 1993, para. 1 ("Human rights and fundamental freedoms are the birthright of all human beings; their protection and promotion is the first responsibility of Governments"); International Covenant on Civil and Political Rights, art. 2, sec. 1, 999 U.N.T.S. 171, adopted by the U.N. General Assembly on Dec. 16, 1966, G.A.Res. 2200, entered into force Mar. 23, 1976, ratified by the United States June 8, 1992 [hereinafter ICCPR]("Each State Party to the present Covenant undertakes to respect and to ensure to all individuals within its territory and subject to its jurisdiction the rights recognized in the present Covenant").

20. Fernández v. Wilkinson, 505 F. Supp. 787, 795 (D. Kan. 1980), *aff'd sub nom.* Rodriguez-Fernández v. Wilkinson, 654 F.2d. 1382 10th Cir. 1981); see Janis, *supra* note 11 at 176.

21. Sovereignty is defined as "[t]he supreme, absolute, and uncontrollable power by which any independent state is governed; . . . the international independence of a state, combined with the right and power of regulating its internal affairs without foreign dictation." Black's Law Dictionary 1396 (6th ed. 1990).

22. A full history of the development of international human rights laws is beyond the scope of this chapter. For comprehensive coverage of the subject, see Louis Henkin, *The Rights of Man Today* (1968); Myres McDougal et al., *Human Rights and World Public Order: The Basic Policies of an International Law of Human Dignity* (1980); Louis Sohn and Thomas Buergenthal, *The International Protection of Human Rights* (1973).

23. See, generally, Newman and Weissbrodt, *supra* note 13 at 1.

24. The Nuremberg Trial, 6 F.R.D. 69, 110 (1946).

25. Charter of the United Nations, 59 Stat. 1031, T.S. No. 993, 3 Bevans 1153, arts. 55, 56, entered into force Oct. 24, 1945 [hereinafter U.N. Charter] at art. 1(3); see, generally, Nuremberg Trial, 6 F.R.D. 69.

26. 6 F.R.D. 69.

27. Nuremberg Trial, 6 F.R.D. at 110.

28. U.N. Charter, *supra* note 25 at arts. 55, 56. See, e.g., ICCPR *supra* note 19 at art. 2 §1 ("Each State Party to the present Covenant undertakes to respect and to ensure to all individuals within its territory and subject to its jurisdiction the rights recognized in the present Covenant").

29. See, e.g., Alien Tort Claims Act, 28 U.S.C. §1350 (1980)("The district courts shall have original jurisdiction of any civil action by an alien for a tort only, committed *in violation of the law of nations* or a treaty of the United States") [emphasis added].

30. Restatement, *supra* note 11 at §301(1). Technically, these agreements create obligations that are binding only between or among the contracting states and, thus, are a source of law only with respect to such parties. However, multilateral agreements open to all states are increasingly viewed as statements of generally accepted principles of international norms. These agreements also are used for developing and codifying customary law as in the Vienna Convention on the Law of Treaties. *Id.* at §102, comment f. In the international field, as in this chapter, the terms treaty, convention, and agreement are used interchangeably.

31. U.S. Const. art. I, §8, cl. 10.

32. *Id.* at art. II, §2.

33. *Id.* at art. VI, §2 ("This Constitution, and the Laws of the United States which

shall be made in Pursuance thereof; and all Treaties made, or which shall be made, under the Authority of the United States, shall be the supreme Law of the Land").

34. Filartiga v. Peña-Irala, 630 F. 2d 879, 880 (2d Cir. 1980)("In light of the universal condemnation of torture in numerous international agreements, and the renunciation of torture as an instrument of official policy by virtually all of the nations of the world (in principle if not in practice), . . . an act of torture committed by a state official against one held in detention violates the established norms of the international law of human rights, and hence the law of nations."); *id.* at 889 ("Having examined the sources from which customary international law is derived . . . the usage of nations . . . we conclude that official torture is now prohibited by the law of nations."); *Fernández v. Wilkinson*, 505 F. Supp. 787, 795–800 (D. Kan. 1980), *aff'd sub nom., Rodriguez-Fernández v. Wilkinson*, 654 F. 2d 1382 (10th Cir. 1981) (court cites to various conventions as well as the Universal Declaration as authority and/or principal sources of human rights law evidencing the custom and usage of nations and concluded that international law secured a prisoner the right to be free from arbitrary detention). See also Restatement *supra* note 11 at pt. I, Introductory Note, Pt. VII, Introductory Note, §702, Reporter's Note 1 (listing, in addition to torture and arbitrary detention, prohibitions against slavery, murder or causing disappearance of individuals, and racial discrimination as rules of customary international law). Much of the established customary law has been codified by international legal agreements. Even once codified, however, customary law remains an enforceable source of law. This is significant because custom then becomes the basis for the enforceability of the obligation vis-à-vis states that have not become signatories to the treaties. For a discussion of custom as a source of international law, see *supra* notes 13, 14, and accompanying text.

35. *United States v. Smith,* 18 U.S. (5 Wheat.) 153, 160–61 (1820) (holding, by looking at the work of learned writers, that a statute proscribing piracy as defined by the Law of Nations was sufficiently clear to afford the basis for a death sentence).

36. See Louis Henkin, "The Constitution and United States Sovereignty: A Century of Chinese Exclusion and Its Progeny," 100 *Harv. L. Rev.* 853, 859 (1987); *Banco Nacional de Cuba v. Sabbatino,* 376 U.S. 398, 435 (1964).

37. 175 U.S. 677 (1899).

38. *Paquete Habana,* 175 U.S. at 700.

39. *Filartiga* at 884 (emphasis added). The Circuit Court stated, "having examined the sources from which customary international law is derived—usage of nations, judicial opinions and the works of jurists—we conclude that official torture is now prohibited by the law of nations").

40. *Filartiga* at 880–81, *quoting* Paquete Habana. See also *Lopes v. Reederei Richard Schroeder,* 225 F. Supp. 292, 295 (E.D. Pa. 1963); *Banco Nacional de Cuba v. Sabbatino,* 376 U.S. 398, 435 (1964). Similarly, in *Fernández v. Wilkinson,* 505 F. Supp. 787, 795–800 (D. Kan. 1980), *aff'd sub nom., Rodriguez-Fernández v. Wilkinson,* 654 F. 2d 1382 (10th Cir. 1981), various conventions and the Universal Declaration were cited as authority and/or principal sources of human rights law evidencing the custom and usage of nations concerning a prisoner's right to be free from arbitrary detention. See also, Restatement at pt. VII, introductory note, 702, reporter's note 1.

41. Alien Tort Claims Act, *supra* note 29. This particular statute is the basis for the action maintained in Filartiga. Another example of federal legislation concerning

international human rights is the United States Foreign Assistance Act of 1961, 22 U.S.C. §2151n(a) (1988), as amended which states that "no assistance may be provided . . . to the government of any country which engages in a consistent pattern of gross violations of internationally recognized human rights, including torture or cruel, inhuman, or degrading treatment or punishment, prolonged detention without charges, . . . or other flagrant denial of the right to life, liberty and the security of the person").

42. In addition to those listed, the United States also is a party to various other human rights agreements including the Slavery Convention of 1926, 60 L.N.T.S. 253, 46 Stat. 2183, 2 Bevans 607, T.S. 778 (1929)(and 1953 Protocol amending Convention, 7 U.S.T. 479, 479 T.I.A.S. No. 3532, 182 U.N.T.S. 51, but not to other amendments); Inter-American Convention on the Granting of Political Rights to Women, O.A.S.T.S. No. 3, 27 U.S.T. 3301, T.I.A.S. No. 8365 (1976); Convention on the Political Rights of Women, 193 U.N.T.S. 135 (1954), 27 U.S.T. 1909, T.I.A.S. No. 8289; Supplementary Convention on the Abolition of Slavery, the Slave Trade, and Institutions and Practices Similar to Slavery, 266 U.N.T.S. 3 (1957), 18 U.S.T. 3201, T.I.A.S. No. 6418; and the four Geneva Conventions: Geneva I, 6 U.S.T. 3114, T.I.A.S. No. 3362, 75 U.N.T.S. 31 (1956); Geneva II, 6 U.S.T. 3217, T.I.A.S. No. 3363, 75 U.N.T.S. 85 (1956); Geneva III, 6 U.S.T. 3316, T.I.A.S. No. 3364, 75 U.N.T.S. 135 (1956); Geneva IV, 6 U.S.T. 3516, T.I.A.S. N. 3365, 75 U.N.T.S. 287 (1956); the Convention against Genocide, 78 U.N.T.S 277, adopted by the U.N. General Assembly on Dec. 9, 1948, U.N.G.A. Res. 2670, entered into force, Jan. 12, 1951, ratified by the United States Nov. 25, 1988.

43. See *supra* note 25.

44. 119 U.N.T.S. 3, entered into force Dec. 13, 1951, for the United States, 2 U.S.T. 2394, T.I.A.S. No. 2361, Protocol of Amendment, O.A.S.T.S. No. 1–A, 21 U.S.T. 607, T.I.A.S. No. 6847, entered into force Feb. 27, 1970.

45. See *supra* note 19.

46. 606 U.N.T.S. 267 (1967), 19 U.S.T. 6223, T.I.A.S. No. 6577.

47. 660 U.N.T.S. 195, entered into force Jan. 4, 1969, ratified by the United States June 24, 1994.

48. Restatement *supra* note 11 at §312 comment d.

49. 993 U.N.T.S. 3, adopted by the U.N. General Assembly on Dec. 16, 1966, Annex to U.N.G.A. Res. 2200, entered into force on Jan. 3, 1976.

50. Adopted Nov. 20, 1989, G.A. Res 44/25, 44 U.N. GAOR Supp. No. 49 at 166, U.N. Doc. A/44/736 (1989), *reprinted in* 28 I.L.M. 1448 (1989).

51. Adopted by the General Assembly of the United Nation on Dec. 18, 1979, U.N.G.A. Res. 280, entered into force Sept. 3, 1981.

52. See Convention on the Prevention and Punishment of The Crime of Genocide, U.S. Reservations and Understandings, 28 I.L.M. 782 (1989); Letter of Submittal, Dept. of State, Dec. 17, 1977, re: International Covenant on Civil and Political Rights ("The United States declares that the provisions of Articles 1 through 27 of the Covenant are not self-executing"); re: International Convention on the Elimination of All Forms of Racial Discrimination: ("The United States declares that the provisions of Articles 1 through 7 of this convention are not self-executing").

53. *Foster v. Neilson*, 27 U.S. (2 Pet.) 253 (1829); *Dreyfus v. Von Firck*, 534 F. 2d 24, 30 (2d Cir. 1976) ("It is only when a treaty is self-executing, when it provides rules by which private rights may be determined, that it may be relied upon for the enforcement of such rights").

54. At the March 29, 1995, meeting of the HRC, Conrad K. Harper, Legal Advisor to the U.S. State Department, noted that Articles 1–27, the substantive provisions of the ICCPR, had been declared non-self-executing under U.S. domestic law, therefore unenforceable in U.S. courts *sans* enabling legislation. He maintained that this decision in no way affected the United States' obligations under the Covenant. Some Commissioners criticized this approach as evidence of an unwillingness to conform U.S. laws to the demands of the Covenant.

55. See, e.g., *Hitai v. Immigration and Naturalization Service,* 343 F. 2d 466, 468 (2d Cir.) *certiorari denied,* 382 U.S. 816 (1965) (U.N. Charter provision held not self-executing and thus unable to invalidate immigration law provision); *Sei Fujii v. California,* 217 P. 2d 481, *reh denied,* 218 P. 2d 595 (Cal. Dist. Ct. App. 1950) (U.N. Charter held not self-executing and thus unable to invalidate state statute, although statute ultimately held unconstitutional under Fourteenth Amendment).

56. See also, *Fernández-Roque v. Smith,* 622 F. Supp. 887 (N.D. Ga. 1985), *aff'd sub nom*; *García-Mir v. Meese,* 788 F. 2d 1446 (11th Cir. 1986), *certiorari denied,* 479 U.S. 889, 107 S.Ct. 289 (1986) (Circuit Court held long term detention of Cuban refugees to be a violation of international law, but failed to enjoin actions committed under authority of Attorney General).

57. *Paquete Habana,* 175 U.S. 677 (1900); *Filartiga v. Peña-Irala,* 630 F. 2d 879; *Rodriguez-Fernández v. Wilkinson,* 505 F. Supp. 787 (D.Kan. 1980), *affirmed,* 654 F. 2d 1382 (10th Cir. 1981) (court takes into account principles of international and Constitutional law and interprets relevant statute as not authorizing indefinite detention of alien); *Fernández-Roque v. Smith,* 622 F. Supp. 887 (N.D.Ga. 1985), *affirmed sub nom. García-Mir v. Meese,* 788 F. 2d 1446 (11th Cir. 1986), *certiorari denied,* 479 U.S. 889, 107 S.Ct. 289 (1986)(long term detention of Cubans violative of international law but courts failed to enjoin violation committed under authority of Attorney General).

58. U.N.G.A. Res 217, Dec. 10, 1948.

59. Vienna Convention, *supra* note 10 at art. 2(1)(d); see also Restatement *supra* note 11 at §313, comment g.

60. Restatement, *supra* note 11 at §313, comment g.

61. Vienna Convention, *supra* note 28 at art. 19(c); Restatement, *supra* note 11 at §313(1)(c). Whether a reservation contravenes the object and purpose is an issue that is resolved by judicial decision.

62. It is not yet clear whether the same conclusion would be reached regarding sex discrimination, although it should be as the human rights conventions list sex as a protected right along with race, color, religion, national origin, etc.

63. See, e.g., *Case concerning Military and Paramilitary Activities in and against Nicaragua* (Nic. vs. U.S.A.), 1984 I.C.J. Rep. 392 (Jurisdiction), 1986 I.C.J. Rep. 14 (Judgment).

64. See *Gregorio T. v. Wilson,* No. 94–7652 (D.Cal. 1994) (using preemption argument to challenge Proposition 187); see also *Chy Lung v. Reeman,* 92 U.S. 275 (1876) (Supreme Court finds that federal immigration law preempts state legislation); see, generally, Hiroshi Motomura, "Immigration and Alienage, Federalism and Proposition 187," 35 *Va. J. Int'l L.* 201 (1994); Michael Olivas, "Preempting Preemption: Foreign Affairs, State Rights and Alienage Classifications," 35 *Va. J. Int'l L.* 217 (1994) (noting that constitutional bases of preemption include not only the Foreign Relations Power Clause but also the Supremacy Clause [which implicates treaty power], the Commerce Clause, the Necessary and Proper

Clause, the Uniform Rule of Naturalization Clause, and the Naturalization Clause).

65. *Gregorio T. v. Wilson,* No. 94–7652 (D.Cal. 1994).

66. 457 U.S. 202 (1981).

67. *League of United American Citizens v. Wilson,* No. 94–7569 (D.Cal. 1994).

68. See Louis Henkin, "An Agenda for the Next Century: The Myth and Mantra of State Sovereignty," 35 *Va. J. Int'l L.* 115, 116, 118 (1994).

69. U.N. Charter, *supra* note 25 at arts. 1(3), 55, 56.

70. ICCPR, *supra* note 19 at arts. 2(1), 26 ("All persons are equal before the law and are entitled without any discrimination to the equal protection of the law"); Economic Covenant, *supra* note 49 at art. 2; European Convention for the Protection of Human Rights and Fundamental Freedoms, 312 U.N.T.S. 221, E.T.S. 5, as amended by Protocol No. 3, E.T.S. 45, Protocol No. 5, E.T.S. 55, and Protocol No. 8, E.T.S. 118, November 4, 1950, entered into force on September 3, 1957, at art. 14 [hereinafter European Convention]; American Convention on Human Rights, 9 I.L.M. 673 (1970), entered into force on July 18, 1978 at art. 1 [hereinafter American Convention]; Race Convention, *supra* note 47 at pmbl. (race, sex, language, or religion), but see *id.* at art. 1(2) (Race Convention does not apply to distinctions between citizens and noncitizens); OAS Charter, *supra* note 44 at art. 3 (race, nationality, creed, or sex), art. 15 (states with equal jurisdiction over nationals and aliens).

71. ICCPR, *supra* note 11 at art. 4.

72. See, e.g., ICCPR Arts 2(1), 26; American Convention, art. 1.

73. See UN Doc. A/C.3/SR.1103 Section 38 (1961). During the drafting of Article 27 of the ICCPR, India proposed such an amendment.

74. General Comments of the Human Rights Committee, General Comment 15, par. 1 (Twenty-seventh session, 1986). See also M. Cherif Bassiouni, The Protection of Human Rights in the Administration of Criminal Justice (Transnational Publishers, Inc. 1994).

75. General Comments of the Human Rights Committee, par. 2.

76. Universal Declaration, *supra* note 58 at art. 2; see also *id.* at art. 7 (all are equal before the law).

77. Economic Covenant, *supra* note 49 at art. 12 ("right of everyone to the enjoyment of the highest attainable standard of physical and metal health"); Universal Declaration, *supra* note 58 at art. 25; Women's Convention, *supra* note 51 at art. 12; Child Convention, *supra* note 50 at art. 24; African Charter on Human and Peoples' Rights, art. 16, OAU Doc. CAB/LEG/67/3/Rev. 5 (1981), *reprinted in* 21 I.L.M. 58 (1982)[hereinafter African Charter].

78. Universal Declaration, *supra* note 58 at art. 26 ("Everyone has the right to education"); Economic Covenant, *supra* note 49 at art. 13; Women's Convention, *supra* note 51 at art. 10; OAS Charter, *supra* note 44 at art. 47 (states have to ensure effective exercise of right to elementary education for school age children); Child Convention, *supra* note 50 at art. 28; African Charter, *supra* note 73 at art. 17; Race Convention, *supra* note 47 at art. 5; Convention Relating to the Status of Refugees, 189 U.N.T.S. 150, April 22, 1954, at art. 22 (refugees to be given same treatment as nationals regarding elementary education).

79. Universal Declaration, *supra* note 58 at art. 12; ICCPR *supra* note 19 at art. 17; Child Convention, *supra* note 50 at art. 16; American Convention, *supra* note 70 at art. 11; European Convention, *supra* note 70 at art. 8.

80. Universal Declaration, *supra* note 58 at art. 3; ICCPR, *supra* note 19 at art 9

("Everyone has the right to liberty and security of the person. . . . No one shall be deprived of his[/her] liberty except on such grounds and in accordance with such procedure as are established by law"); Race Convention, *supra* note 47 at art. 5; African Charter, *supra* note 73 at art. 6; American Convention, *supra* note 70 at art. 7; European Convention, *supra* note 70 at art. 5.

81. Universal Declaration, *supra* note 58 at art. 13; ICCPR, *supra* note 19 at art. 13 (limited to those "lawfully within the territory of a State"); Race Convention, *supra* note 47 at art. 5; American Convention, *supra* note 70 at art. 22 (limited to "person lawfully in the territory").

82. Universal Declaration *supra* note 58 at art. 19; ICCPR, *supra* note 19 at art. 19; Race Convention, *supra* note 47 at art.5; Child Convention, *supra* note 50 at art. 13; African Charter, *supra* note 73 at art. 9; American Convention, *supra* note 70 at art. 13; European Covenant, *supra* note 70 at art. 10.

83. Universal Declaration *supra* note 58 at art. 20; ICCPR, *supra* note 19 at art. 21; Race Convention, *supra* note 47 at art. 5; Child Convention, *supra* note 50 at art. 15; African Charter, *supra* note 73 at art. 10; American Convention, *supra* note 70 at art. 16; European Covenant, *supra* note 88 at art. 11.

84. It is important to recall that such international human rights norms, once adopted, are enforceable as a matter of constitutional law based upon the supremacy clause.

85. Ashley Dunn, "Greeted at Nation's Front Door, Many Visitors Stay on Illegally," *N.Y. Times,* January 3, 1995, A1. See also Kevin Johnson, "Public Benefits and Immigration: The Intersection of Immigration Status, Ethnicity, Gender, and Class," 42 *UCLA L.Rev.* 1509, 1544–49 (1995) (for discussion of demographics of immigrants).

86. See *supra* note 3 and accompanying text.

87. *Plyler v. Doe,* 457 U.S. at 227 (no credible evidence supporting argument that children are burden on economy; recognizing that what attracts immigrants is availability of employment which results in labor being provided to the local economy and tax money to the state).

88. CA Health & S §130(c) (emergency services excluded).

89. CA Educ §48215(e).

90. CA Educ §66010.8.

91. CA Wel & Inst §10001.5 (emphasis added).

92. CA Health & S. §130(c).

93. CA Educ §48215(e). In addition, any notice provided must also be provided to the parent of the enrolee or pupil. This section also requires verification by school districts of the legal status of each child enrolled and in attendance in the school district. Id. §(c). Finally, this section provides that for students whose legal status in the United States cannot be verified, there is a ninety day period during which educational services will continue to be delivered. In fact, the statute expressly provides that "[s]uch ninety day period shall be utilized to accomplish an orderly transition to a school in the child's country of origin." Id. §(f).

94. CA Educ. §66010.8. This section requires that public postsecondary educational institutions to verify the status of each person enrolled or in attendance at the institution.

95. CA Educ. §48215(c), (f).

96. CA Educ. §66010.8.

97. CA Wel. & Inst. §10001.5.

98. IFCRA *supra* note 1 at §§101, 102.

99. United Nations Fourth World Conference on Women, Declaration and Platform for Action, A/CONF. 177l.5 [hereinafter Beijing Platform] at para. 71.

100. Universal Declaration, *supra* note 58 at art. 3; ICCPR *supra* note 19 at art. 6; Child Convention, *supra* note 50 at art. 6; African Charter *supra* note 73 at art. 4; American Convention, *supra* note 70 at art. 4; European Convention, *supra* note 70 at art. 2.

101. Speech by Hillary Clinton, First Lady of the United States of America, on September 5, 1995, at the United Nations Fourth World Conference on Women, Beijing, China, September 4–15, 1995. ("If there is one message that echoes forth from this conference, it is that human rights are women's rights. . . . And women's rights are human rights." She specifically notes that girls and women are lacking health and education services.) (Copy on file with author.) See, e.g., Beijing Platform *supra* note 95 at decl. par. 17 (right of all women to control all aspects of their health, in particular their own fertility, is basic to their empowerment), par. 91 ("Women have the right to the enjoyment of the highest attainable standard of physical and mental health. The enjoyment of this right is vital to their life and well-being and their ability to participate in all areas of public and private life. Health is a state of complete physical, mental and social well-being and not merely the absence of disease or infirmity. Women's health involves their emotional, social and physical well-being and is determined by the social, political and economic context of their lives, as well as by biology. However, health and well-being elude the majority of women"); *Id., passim,* Ch. IV. Sec. C (on women's health). United Nations Human Development Programme, Human Development Report 75 (1995) ("a widespread pattern of inequality between women and men—in their access to education, health and nutrition").

102. See, e.g. Beijing Platform, *supra* note 95 at decl. par. 27 (promote provision of basic education, life-long education, literacy and training, and primary health care for girls and women); par. 71 ("Education is a human right and an essential tool for achieving the goals of equality, development and peace. . . . Literacy of women is an important key to improving health, nutrition and education in the family") *id. passim,* Ch. IV, Sec. B (on women's education).

Analyzing the Discourse of Immigration and Citizenship

The chapters in this part probe the evolving meanings and implications of many of the terms whose meanings we take for granted in discussions of nativism, immigration, and citizenship. Linda S. Bosniak's chapter focuses on exactly what we mean when we use the term "nativism." One of the term's important functions is to define boundaries of propriety (and impropriety) in our discourse on immigration. Daniel Kanstroom compares the anti-immigrant discourse of Peter Brimelow with the writings of Oswald Spengler, whose work laid foundations for the National Socialist Party in Germany of the early 1930s. He finds haunting parallels between the two, and harrowing possibilities, already realized in World War II Germany, when nations adopt an underinclusive racial and ethnic definition of membership in the polity. Richard Delgado's chapter on citizenship assesses recent proposals to deny citizenship to the United States-born children of undocumented persons and concludes that these proposals, based on a dangerous conception of communitarian philosophy, represent a serious regression in our legal and constitutional discourse. T. Alexander Aleinikoff concludes this part with an essay describing his perception of a tightening circle of membership in the political community of the United States. He urges that we not go too far in tightening the circle.

15. "NATIVISM" THE CONCEPT

Some Reflections

Linda S. Bosniak

Talking about nativism usually means talking about a set of phenomena in the social world to which the word "nativism" can be said to correspond or which it can be said to describe. Contributors to this volume have in various ways addressed themselves to the *new* nativism, by which they mean, roughly, the climate of immigration-related anxiety currently sweeping this country and the various restrictionist practices that have followed. Here, as elsewhere, addressing nativism means addressing the referent of "nativism," the thing in the world designated by the word.

In this brief essay, however, I want to examine "nativism" the word, or the concept, itself. By doing so, I believe we can learn something more both about the set of social phenomena the word is used to characterize and also about our understandings of it. It seems to me that in discussions on the subject, the term "nativism" is often employed as if its meaning and significance were self-evident, yet I would like to suggest that these are far more complex and contested than they may first appear. In addition, I want to suggest that the word "nativism" does not exist entirely independently of its referent; while the word certainly seeks to describe an aspect of social reality, it is, at the same time, partially constitutive of it. My purpose, therefore, is to offer some thoughts on the role and significance of the concept of "nativism" in the current debates over immigration policy in an effort to cast further light on the phenomenon we call nativism itself.

My reflections here are informed by a linguistic approach to politics—one that views political language as a key site, or arena, of political practice.[1] In this view, certain powerful political concepts—such as "nativism"—are inextricably bound up with the political phenomena they are meant to represent. The concepts not only reflect conventional understandings of these phenomena but also serve to shape the understandings we maintain of them.

Political language, in other words, is not merely constituted by politics but constitutes politics as well; as one group of social theorists has recently written, "map and terrain vary together."[2] In examining the concept of "nativism," therefore, I am mindful of its intimate interplay with the phenomenon it seeks to describe. My goal is to help to illuminate nativism's terrain by reflecting upon the map.

Just a few years ago, the word "nativism" was languishing in relative linguistic obscurity in this country. As recently as 1991, the word was rarely spoken or printed, except to refer to the anti-immigrant sentiment of bygone eras: those, for example, of the Know-Nothing Party of the mid-nineteenth century, or the Chinese exclusion era at the turn of the century, or the so-called Red Scare of the post-World War I era. The term had a distinctly anachronistic ring; although immigration has periodically been the subject of sharp political contention in this country, the kind of mob-driven, antiforeign mentality the term evokes seemed to have little contemporary relevance.[3]

Today, however, the word "nativism" is back. Policy makers and citizens' groups and the media now employ the term with great frequency to characterize the current proponents of immigration restriction and the various policies they promote. Scholars have also resurrected the word for contemporary usage, as the essays in the present volume make clear.

The timing of the dramatic comeback of "nativism" is hardly mysterious. It seems clear enough that the word has reemerged alongside a virulent discourse of anti-immigration hostility in this country the likes of which have not been seen, or heard, for several decades. Many Americans have come to blame immigrants for a variety of the country's social ills in recent years; and dramatic restrictions on both the admission of prospective immigrants and the rights of those already here are now at the top of the policy agenda. "Nativism," the word, has been increasingly invoked by critics to both characterize and condemn these developments.[4]

Renewed preoccupation with nativism, however, is not unique to the critics. Many immigration restrictionists themselves have recently invoked the threats posed by nativism in support of their preferred restrictionist policies; they warn that a "nativist backlash" will shortly be upon us if the country does *not* get serious about immigration control.[5] Most restrictionists, moreover, expend substantial energy in defending themselves against charges of "nativism," while they also bitterly attack their critics for leveling the charge in the first place.

By now, it seems, Americans are nearly as preoccupied with nativism and its dangers as they are with immigration itself—and they are nearly as divided over it. But the reasons for this renewed concern may not be entirely self-evident. What is it about the concept of "nativism" that has engendered such anxiety and disagreement? When we argue about "nativism," precisely what are we arguing about?

At one level, the recent controversies over "nativism" can be understood as a straightforward debate over the correspondence of word to world. The question over which many Americans disagree, often quite viscerally, is whether the current moment of immigration-related anxiety in this country can be appropriately characterized in these terms. Is the word "nativism" properly applied to the kinds of restrictionist discourses and practices currently prevailing in this country? Can the current wave of immigration restrictionism reasonably and fairly be characterized as nativist?

This question, however, turns out to be far more complex and loaded than it may at first appear. First of all, in order to answer it, one needs a working understanding of what the word "nativism" means. Yet such an understanding is not easy to come by, for conventional understandings of the word's meaning are extremely diverse and often inconsistent. Even appealing to the scholarly community is ultimately not much help. Since "nativism" is a word used in the social sciences, one might expect that scholars would share some relatively fixed, common understanding of the term, but even in this context its meaning remains elusive.

Scholars differ, first of all, in their understanding of the term's scope. Some analysts have defined the term "nativism" quite broadly to denote "strong attachment to a reference group to which one has, so to speak, 'been born.' "[6] In this formulation, the racism of the Ku Klux Klan represents a form of nativism, as did the anticommunism of the McCarthy era.[7] Others employ the term to refer to the adverse response of cultural majorities to "outsider" racial and ethnic groups; in this understanding, the dominant culture's treatment of American-born blacks or Jews are both exemplary forms of nativism.[8]

Most analysts, however, more narrowly associate the term "nativism" with negative sentiment of various kinds toward foreigners—with "antiforeign" feeling.[9] At times, the term is employed to refer to the expression of antipathy toward foreigners abroad; for example, during the campaign for the Republican primary nomination in 1992, Patrick Buchanan's "America First" crusade against foreign imports and foreign policy entanglements was described in the press as "nativist" in character.[10] This use of the term suggests nationalist chauvinism or isolationism, sometimes with racial overtones.[11] More commonly, however, "nativism" is associated with an exclusionary impulse directed toward the foreigner within; it suggests animosity or bias, in other words, toward *immigrants,* or toward aspiring immigrants.[12] In historian John Higham's well-known formulation, nativism "should be defined as intense opposition to an internal minority on the ground of its foreign (i.e., 'un-American') connections."[13]

But even assuming, as many scholars do, that "nativism" denotes negative attitudes toward internal foreigners, or immigrants, defining the term this way still leaves the question of its application—or its reference—unanswered. Some historians, for example, have described "nativism" as signifying "hostility to foreigners" (by which they mean territorially present foreigners, or immigrants).[14] This definition seems at first glance clear and unobjectionable; but on closer examination, we see that it is severely question-begging, since it tells us nothing about which sorts of policies and positions regarding immigration qualify as "hostile." Is it "hostile," for example, to increase the border patrol presence at the U.S.-Mexican border, or to deny citizens the right to sponsor their foreign-born siblings or adult children for immigration, or to deny welfare benefits to noncitizens—all of which the federal government is currently poised to do? Nothing in this definition of nativism can help us to answer these questions.

Of course, there is one particular form of "hostility to foreigners" that is consistently associated with nativism in both the scholarly literature and in colloquial usage: I refer to race- or ethnicity-based animus toward immigrants.[15] In fact, nativism as ethnonational bias against immigrants is unquestionably the most common understanding of the term today. In this usage, nativism is treated as closely analogous to racism; the suggestion is often that nativism is a species of racism, except that the objects of prejudice are foreigners or particular classes of foreigners rather than "native" minorities.[16] But this usage of the term, while very widespread, is far from universal. And one wonders whether this understanding of nativism is meant to be an exclusive one or whether ethnonational bias should be viewed as but one expression of a larger antiforeign phenomenon. In other words, can anti-immigrant sentiment that is *not* specifically motivated by racial bias nevertheless be considered nativist?[17]

My point is that to the extent we seek to resolve the question of whether current restrictionist politics are "nativist" by looking to standard understandings of the term—scholarly or otherwise—we are likely to be disappointed. We are likely, in fact, to be embroiled in endless disputes either about which definition applies, or, even if we agree upon a definition, about its applicability to any given set of facts.[18] The meaning of "nativism" is in important respects indeterminate to us, and we will often find ourselves unable to agree on whether any particular set of conditions in the world can appropriately be described in these terms.

But when we argue about whether the current wave of immigration restrictionism should or should not be characterized as "nativist," we are not merely engaged in a dispute over social classification. For quite beyond the empirical "correctness" of the label (even if we could determine such a thing) in any given situation, the designation of a statement or policy as "nativist" is laden with enormous normative significance. Simply put, "nativism" is a term of intensely negative appraisal. The evaluative content of "nativism" is so strong, in fact, that historian John Higham—whose own work on historical American nativism did much to popularize the term—has more recently asserted that the word is of limited use to historians as an analytical concept because it is indelibly associated with "subjective irrationality" and "prejudice."[19] In other words, Higham submits, to call a thing "nativist" serves less to explain or describe it than to condemn it.

What Higham's remark suggests is that a core aspect of nativism's meaning resides in what the word *does*, in the "speech act" that it performs (or, more accurately, the speech act that it can be used to perform).[20] And what the word "nativism" does, almost invariably, is to register enormous social disapproval and disapprobation. It is a term of unmitigated political censure. This is one reason why advocates for immigrants are eager to characterize the current climate of immigration restrictionism in these terms: to claim that current anti-immigration discourse and policy are "nativist" is to say that they are beyond the normative pale and unworthy of either consideration or toleration.

This is also why restrictionists are so eager to avoid the charge of "nativism," and why they engage in a variety of rhetorical strategies to avoid the designation. As I stated earlier, sometimes restrictionists themselves invoke the dangers of nativism *on behalf of* their restrictive immigration projects; as they tell it, nativism may not be upon us now but it surely will be in the absence of stern and sober-minded reform (the theory being that Americans will take matters into their own hands if the government fails to get tough).[21] Additionally, some of the more moderate restrictionists contrast what they characterize as their own "pragmatic" restrictionist agenda with the more extreme mindset of the "true" nativists; by this means, they seek to reclaim at least some restrictionist ground from its association with nativism and thereby render it normatively permissible.[22] At the same time, many hard-core restrictionists furiously repudiate the charge; as they characterize it, calling anti-immigration views "nativist" (or "xenophobic" or "racist") is a form of "intimidation" by politically correct liberal zealots which serves to suppress real substantive debate. These restrictionists speak bitterly of the "motive assassination" and "liberal McCarthyite" assaults they have had to endure for airing their views; they complain that their views have been "stigmatized, stereotyped, and stifled," and urge restrictionists to smash the taboo against anti-immigration opinion that the threatened charge of "nativism" imposes by refusing to be silenced.[23]

Despite the disagreement and confusion in our political culture over precisely what nativism *is*, therefore, there appears to be virtual unanimity about what the charge of "nativism" does: To call discourse or policy "nativist" represents an effort to disable it through social opprobrium. And if the charge sticks, delegitimization is usually successful. It is no wonder that nobody wants to be called a "nativist."

Or almost nobody does, I should say, for every rule has exceptions. Restrictionist Peter Brimelow, for instance, author of the by-now notorious *Alien Nation*,[24] specifically complains that the term "nativism" has long gotten a bum rap. While the word, he writes, serves as an "exorcist's spell always cast against anyone who dares question current immigration policy," the original nativists were, in fact, "far from an ignorant mob," and they *never actually proposed restricting immigration*."[25] The nativists were simply ardent nationalists in both political and cultural terms; "[t]hey saw their American national identity as inextricably involved with . . . 'the survival and success of liberty.' "[26] In light of this "corrected" history,[27] Brimelow suggests that "nativism" the term should be rehabilitated and perhaps even embraced—and he concludes his discussion by all but proclaiming himself a nativist.

It is certainly possible that, over time, the normative content of "nativism" will shift from bad to good—and that being called a nativist will become a source of pride rather than iniquity. In the history of language, shifts like this have happened many times.[28] Meanwhile, however, "nativism" remains a marker of unacceptability in our debates over immigration, and most restrictionists will continue to assiduously avoid the association.

When we ask, therefore, what it is that we are arguing about when we argue about nativism, perhaps the best answer is that we are arguing about legitimacy. I mean that we are arguing about the normative status of our arguments about immigration; we are engaged in a self-reflexive, second-order debate about the legitimacy of our first-order immigration-related discourse and practice. And there is a lot at stake in this debate, for to call a statement or policy "nativist" is to designate it as normatively out of bounds. The word signals a zone of normative impropriety that most Americans—however restrictive their views on immigration—make every effort to avoid.

Yet we have also seen that there is important disagreement in our political culture about which sorts of discourses or policies do and do not fall within nativism's forbidden domain. Americans are not entirely sure what "nativism" means; but even if we were to broadly agree on a definition—even if we took it to mean "hostility to foreigners," let's say—we would not necessarily agree about what sorts of discourse and policy in fact qualify as hostile; we would not necessarily concur about whether "the agreed criteria for applying the word . . . are present in a given set of circumstances."[29] While nativism is indisputably "bad," in other words, its boundaries remain uncertain.

Still, I do not wish to suggest that nativism's meaning is entirely up for grabs. We know that "nativism" signifies that which is out-of-bounds in our immigration-related discourse; and while our understandings of the boundaries of permissibility and impermissibility in the immigration arena are highly contested, they are not entirely indeterminate. At the margins, at least, we can still make out certain patterns of rough agreement, or relative consensus, as to what is and is not legitimate vis-à-vis immigration.[30] If, let's suppose, we were to place various arguments for immigration restriction along a kind of hypothetical "legitimacy spectrum," we would find that some of these arguments would be conventionally understood to fall closer to the forbidden end—the "nativist" end—whereas others would be regarded as entirely appropriate and defensible—as anything but "nativist." At every point along the spectrum, there would be dispute and disagreement, but clustered at either end, we would find certain arguments located with some consistency. We might describe the arguments on either end of this spectrum as legitimacy benchmarks; they embody certain shared (though never unanimous) understandings of right and wrong in this arena, and they serve to structure the way we argue about immigration more generally.

These benchmarks, I would like to suggest, broadly frame our conventional understandings of where nativism begins and ends. We have seen that the concept of "nativism" serves to demarcate the boundaries of permissibility and impermissibility in our immigration discourse; but these same boundaries also shape conventional understandings of what nativism is. It seems to me that we can identify two legitimacy benchmarks in the immigration debates in particular—one on either end of the spectrum—which shape common understandings of nativism's scope. Their status *as* benchmarks has structured the way Americans argue about immigration.

While advocates for immigration restriction advance a broad variety of arguments in support of their anti-immigration project, the most normatively suspect, by far, are those that charge that American national well-being is threatened by the racial or ethnic identity of the immigrants who come here. Race-based arguments for immigration restriction are nothing new, of course; they have a long and miserable pedigree in the history of American political thought. But our current immigration regime bears the stamp of the civil rights legacy, with its formal commitment against race- and ethnicity-based discrimination.[31] National origins quotas were abandoned by Congress in 1965, and the corresponding advent of race- and nationality-neutral criteria for admission has been widely and consistently celebrated in this country.[32] In such a climate, racially exclusionary arguments for immigration restriction have come to be regarded as highly illegitimate.

This is why, when Patrick Buchanan stated during the 1992 Republican presidential primary campaign that the state of Virginia would be far better able to assimilate a million Englishmen than a million Zulus, public reaction was fairly explosive.[33] Buchanan was widely condemned for the statement in the press, and most immigration restrictionists themselves seemed to find the remark a terrible embarrassment. As a general matter, many restrictionists have made careful efforts to distance themselves from racialist immigration discourse: according to one prominent restrictionist, "[u]nder no circumstances should a prospective immigrant's race, ethnic background or religious preference be a factor in determining if that person should be admitted."[34] This is not to say that Buchanan was alone in his views, for they were clearly compelling to many people. But they were also commonly considered extreme and outlandish in mainstream political discourse. I think it is fair to say that if anything has been understood to be nativist in our contemporary political culture, this is clearly it.

Yet, it is also true that the common presumption against explicit race- and ethnicity-based arguments for immigration restriction has recently come in for serious challenge. Perhaps the clearest articulation of this challenge can be found in Peter Brimelow's book *Alien Nation,* which takes direct aim at these normative conventions. Brimelow baldly asserts that "the American nation has always had a specific ethnic core [a]nd that core has been white."[35] The difficulty, he argues, is that today's immigrants are, "for the first time, virtually all . . . racially distinct 'visible minorities.' . . . [T]hese new immigrants are from completely different and arguably incompatible cultural traditions. And . . . they are coming in such numbers that their impact on America is enormous—inevitably within the foreseeable future, they will transform it."[36] To forestall a national "shipwreck," and safeguard "American identity," Brimelow proposes that we begin to "shift back" the country's racial balance to its white European core by, among other things, repealing the 1965 Immigration Act and ensuring that future immigrants (if any) do not further disturb "that interlacing of ethnicity and culture that now constitutes the American nation."[37]

Brimelow's tract is notable for its unabashed—indeed, its defiant—embrace of heretofore marginalized forms of racial discourse. He is quite self-conscious about the political transgression his book represents; he anticipates his critics' legitimacy objections, and while he tries to meet some of them with substantive argument, he also ridicules their concerns as little more than knee-jerk liberal orthodoxy.[38] He reserves some of his most biting criticism for conservatives who, he complains, have capitulated to the prevailing orthodoxy and go "scattering for cover like hightailing rabbits" whenever race is mentioned.[39]

Alien Nation has been highly influential, among other reasons because Brimelow is not regarded as a fringe political actor in the way that Buchanan has often been. He is, instead, an establishment conservative with "insider" credentials.[40] And while many proponents of immigration restriction have sought to distance themselves from the book,[41] and although Brimelow has been criticized for it, one could sense a collective sigh of relief on the part of at least some restrictionists after its publication.[42] For these restrictionists, *Alien Nation* has opened up a space for expression on this highly volatile subject and has perhaps served to diminish somewhat the power the threatened charge of "nativism" possesses in immigration-related discourse. Still, I suspect that the weight and history of the taboo against expressly racialist immigration discourse will continue to impel most restrictionists to express their sentiments in other terms.

Of course, cultural or identity-based arguments for immigration restriction need not necessarily be expressed in explicitly racial terms. Many restrictionists voice apprehension, in nominally race-neutral terms, about immigrants' alleged unwillingness to assimilate to fundamental American values and institutions and, in particular, their alleged unwillingness to master the English language.[43] These restrictionists make no reference to the merits or demerits of particular national groups or to the color of anyone's skin: their fear, rather, is that the American national culture cannot survive the massive influx of foreigners who stubbornly insist on retaining their own tongues and traditions. The concern is not any particular cultural difference but the persistence of difference itself.

The perceived normative status of this "cultural assimilationist" position is far less problematic than the express racial exclusionism espoused by Brimelow and others. For however controversial assimilationist views may be, it is by no means politically *verbotten* in this country to promote the ideal of a unitary national culture in the same way that it has been to defend the idea of a racially pure America. This has meant that debates over the legitimacy of assimilationist discourse often take the form of a debate over the boundaries of racism. Many immigrants' rights advocates have charged that the cultural assimilationist position is cut from the same Eurocentrist cloth as the racial exclusionist stance, despite their apparent differences, and that the former is therefore as repugnant—and racist—as the latter.[44] Defenders of the cultural assimilationist position, in contrast, have tended to argue that Buchanan et al. are the real racists and that they themselves are simply concerned to prevent the fabric of a cohesive American society from being torn asunder.

If, as I have suggested, express race and national identity arguments for immigration restriction lie at one end of the hypothetical legitimacy spectrum, then arguments that invoke the asserted material costs of immigration lie at the other. Cost arguments—which usually stress immigrants' allegedly negative economic and environmental impact on this country—are certainly subject to vigorous debate, but I want to suggest that however controverted these arguments may be on other grounds, they are rarely treated as normatively suspect—or "nativist"—per se. One rarely hears immigrants' rights advocates arguing that it is intrinsically illegitimate for a national society to restrict immigration in order to safeguard the economic or environmental well-being of its members.[45]

Instead, cost arguments for immigration restriction are usually met with *empirical* refutation: Immigration advocates argue, for example, that contrary to the claims of restrictionists, immigrants do not, in fact, take jobs from Americans, nor do they deplete the public purse. Rather, they argue, immigrants help to create jobs and to prevent other jobs from being transferred abroad; and immigrants contribute more in taxes than they receive in public services—at least on a net national basis. Parties on both sides of this debate invoke economic studies in support of their positions, producing the by-now notorious battle of the experts in the field.[46] But neither side challenges the legitimacy of cost arguments themselves.

I should note that the empirical debate can itself give rise to normative critique: on the theory that the cost arguments are factually wrong, the critics claim that immigrants are being unfairly scapegoated for economic and social conditions that they have nothing to do with.[47] But the real dispute here is still about the facts, for restrictionists themselves would presumably agree that to blame a person for something she is not responsible for is indeed indefensible. They simply believe that given the facts, the blame is appropriately placed.[48]

What I wish to emphasize about the debate over costs is its unspoken normative backdrop: it presumes that determining who is right in empirical terms on the cost question is dispositive of the immigration policy issue. It presumes, in other words, that if immigrants could somehow be definitively determined to cost more than they contribute, then restrictionists' efforts to curtail immigration would be basically unassailable on normative grounds. One is unlikely to hear the argument (except in the refugee context, where the structure of normative argument is different) that it is illegitimate to cut back on immigration if immigration is, in fact, shown to materially disadvantage the nation.

But why should this be? Why isn't this assumption, like so many others in the immigration arena, up for normative debate? The reason is that we live in a world in which it is ordinarily presumed that "compatriots take priority," in philosopher Henry Shue's phrase;[49] it is presumed that national immigration policy should promote the welfare, first and foremost, of the national society's members. This is, after all, the normative heart of the principle of national sovereignty: the sovereignty principle "affirms the priority of particular peoples—the citizens of particular states—over any universalizing claims to humanity as such."[50] Even liberal theorists, who urge recognition of moral duties to humanity in general, still usually concede that protecting the interests of current members of a national society can sometimes justify the distinctly *illiberal* exclusion of foreigners from admission and membership.[51]

One might well respond that the "national priority thesis" runs counter to a powerful tradition in American political consciousness—the tradition of American identity as "a nation of immigrants." This national self-conception presupposes a basic openness to outsiders who wish to become members of the national society; and it would seem to entail a corresponding disapproval of efforts to selfishly draw the gates closed around us. Yet even this "cosmopolitan" strain in American national thought, as John Higham has called it,[52] presumes that American openness to immigrants serves American material interests. If the "tired and poor" whom Americans sometimes profess to welcome turn out to cost more than they contribute, the imperative to openness is ordinarily ignored.

The point is that cost arguments for immigration restriction presume that what counts in determining immigration policy is the health and well-being of Americans. And as such, they are unlikely to be regarded as illegitimate— or "nativist"—forms of argument, since their underlying premise is treated as almost beyond question in our political culture. Cost arguments may be wrong on the facts—and I think they often are—but they are certainly not intrinsically "bad."

Unless, of course, they are "bad" for other reasons. In fact, critics of restrictionism quite frequently claim that they *are* bad; specifically, they charge that despite their more pragmatic appearance, cost arguments are really proxies for arguments about race—and, to this extent, are nativist. Opponents of California's Proposition 187, for example, commonly advanced such a critique, arguing that the fiscal-drain arguments invoked by the initiative's supporters as justification for denying education and medical care to undocumented immigrants masked their true motivation—namely, antipathy to ethnic minorities—Mexicans in particular.[53] To the extent that the critics are successful in these characterizations, they are, of course, able to shift cost arguments over to the impermissible side of the legitimacy divide.

There is not much question that the illegitimacy of race-based immigration arguments has driven much of the racial animus in the immigration debates underground and that cost arguments sometimes possess an unmistakable racial subtext. The presumptive normative legitimacy of cost arguments surely make them an attractive means of communicating the restrictionist message without falling afoul of the general proscription against race-based arguments—and such subterfuge clearly needs to be exposed. But it is also true that not all arguments for immigration restriction based on costs can be reduced to covert expressions of racial or ethnic hostility. Many people who support more limits on immigration, including growing numbers of people of color in this country,[54] are genuinely concerned about the effects of immigration on what they perceive to be a shrinking national pie; they really are worried about jobs, overpopulation, and the public purse. They are not demanding that America be preserved for the ethnically and racially domi-nant, but that America be preserved for those who are already Americans—for the current members of the national society.

Once again, critics of restrictionism can and do dispute these characteriza-tions of the national economy and the immigrants' role within it on the facts. But if they have doubts about the underlying legitimacy of opposing immigration based on arguments like these, they tend to keep it to them-selves.[55] For anyone who publicly argues that American interests should not be the only relevant interests at stake in formulating national immigration policy—anyone who dares to contend that Americans' normative obligations extend beyond the national community's formal members and that the inter-ests of immigrants or would-be immigrants should also be taken into ac-count—will not merely be dismissed as a soft-headed utopian but will inevi-tably be charged with "supporting open borders"—a charge whose pejorative weight begins to rival that of "nativism" itself.[56]

Nationalist particularism, then, marks the permissible end of the legitimacy spectrum, at least as things stand now. Although Patrick Buchanan's "America First" platform was widely regarded as an exemplary form of nativism, the assumption that immigration policy should be shaped by a commitment to *Americans* first is not ordinarily viewed in such terms at all. Far from being illegitimate, in fact, the assumed priority of citizens over foreigners, of nationals over strangers, lies at the absolute core of contempo-rary political thought. Whatever else we conventionally understand "nativ-ism" to be, this clearly isn't it.

The concept of "nativism" is of real interest only because nativism the phenomenon has become an increasingly pressing national preoccupation. But once we attend to the concept, we begin to see the phenomenon itself more clearly. We see, first of all, the uncertainty of its boundaries: nativism's scope and character are far more elusive and contested than they may initially appear. We see also that understanding what nativism is requires understand-ing what the word does—or what is done with it—in public debates over immigration. To call an argument or policy "nativist" is, fundamentally, an effort to disable it through condemnation; it is, perhaps more than anything, a statement of normative repudiation. And we see, as well, that "nativism" the concept is an integral part of the political landscape that it purports to characterize, for its delegitimizing power serves to shape the ways in which Americans argue about immigration.

But if "nativism" represents that which is normatively out of bounds in our immigration debates, what sorts of discourses and practices can be properly designated in these terms? The question of where nativism begins and ends, I have argued, is often subject to bitter dispute in our society. But I have also suggested that the legitimacy debates associated with nativism do seem to be framed by certain broad normative themes or landmarks; and these, in turn, give content to our conventional understandings of what nativism is. I have focused here on common understandings about race-based exclusion, on the one hand, and the prerogatives of national sovereignty, on the other, but there are surely others. I also do not mean to suggest that there is anything intrinsically necessary about our current understandings of these questions; our sense of what is legitimate and illegitimate in this arena will surely shift over time as it has before. Still, whatever "nativism" means or comes to mean, the current pervasiveness of the concept in the national debates over immigration makes clear how preoccupied Americans are with the legitimacy of their immigration-related discourse and practice. In this deeply ambivalent "nation of immigrants," these concerns will no doubt plague us for some time to come.

NOTES

In this essay, I have drawn on work first published in the Proceedings of the American Society of International Law, April 1994. See Linda Bosniak, "Immigration Crisis, 'Nativism,' and Legitimacy," 88 *Proc. A.S.I.L.* 440–46 (1994). For extremely helpful comments on earlier drafts of this essay, I wish to thank Andrew Bush, Karen Engle, David Frankford, Rand Rosenblatt, and Robert Gordon.

1. I draw, in particular, upon the methodology both theorized and exemplified in Terrence Ball, James Farr, and Russell L. Hanson, eds., *Political Innovation and Conceptual Change* (Cambridge: Cambridge University Press, 1989), at 2, especially the essays by James Farr and Quentin Skinner. See also Raymond Williams, *Keywords: A Vocabulary of Culture and Society,* rev. ed. (New York: Oxford University Press, 1983).

2. Ball, Farr, and Hanson, *supra,* at 2. See, generally, James Farr, "Understanding Conceptual Change Politically," in Ball, Farr, and Hanson, *supra,* at 24, 32:

A political theory of conceptual change . . . must take its point of departure from the political constitution of language and the linguistic constitution of politics. That is to say, its premises must acknowledge that in acting politically actors do things for strategic and partisan purposes in and through language; and they can do such things because the concepts in language partially constitute political beliefs, actions, and practices. Consequently, political change and conceptual change must be understood as one complex and interrelated process.

See also Quentin Skinner, "Language and Political Change," in Ball, Farr, and Hanson, *supra,* at 22:

It is a "mistake to portray the relationship between our social vocabulary and our social world as a purely external and contingent one. It is true that our social practices help to bestow meaning on our social vocabulary. But it is equally true that our social vocabulary helps to constitute the character of those practices. . . . As Charles Taylor . . . has remarked, 'we can speak of mutual dependence if we like, but what this really points up is the artificiality of the distinction between social reality and the language of description of that social reality.' "

(quoting Charles Taylor, "Interpretation and the Sciences of Man," 25 *Review of Metaphysics* 3, 24 [1971]). See also Murray Edelman, *Constructing the Political Spectacle* (Chicago: University of Chicago Press, 1988), at 112 ("There is an important sense in which language constructs the people who use it, a view manifestly in contrast with the common sensical assumption that people construct the language they use").

3. According to a 1988 work on the history of American nativism, "nativism was no longer viable by 1950" in the United States. David H. Bennett, *The Party of Fear: From Nativist Movements to the New Right in American History* (Chapel Hill: University of North Carolina Press, 1988). See also James Hollifield, *Immigrants, Markets, and States* (Cambridge: Harvard University Press, 1992), at 172 ("nativist politics have receded in the post-war period . . . in the wake of the civil rights revolution, which laid the groundwork for a new ethnic pluralism").

4. See, e.g., Ann Davis, "The Return of the Nativists," *National Law Journal,* June 19, 1995, at A1; Frank Sharry, "The Rise of Nativism in the United States and How to Respond to It," *National Immigration Forum,* Washington, D.C., Spring, 1994; Laarni C. Almendrala, "Proposition 187 Update: The Return of the Nativists," *Filipinas Magazine,* January 31, 1995, at 19; "The War on Immigration," *Detroit News* (editorial), June 25, 1995 ("The nativist dogma permeating the reform proposals poses a greater threat to the nation than any supposed immigration crisis"); "Learning the Value of Citizenship," *Chicago Tribune* (editorial), March 24, 1995, at N28 ("Many Americans are uneasy with the sound, if not always with the substance, of our current national debate on immigration. It has at times an intolerant, nativist tone that is deeply disturbing").

5. For example, *Newsweek* reported that support in Congress for restrictionist policy reform reflects a "scrambling to neutralize nativist backlash." *Newsweek,* August 9, 1993, at 19.

6. See Seymour Martin Lipset and Earl Raab, *The Politics of Unreason: Right-Wing Extremism in America: 1790–1970* (New York: Harper and Row, 1970), at 488. See also Bennett, *supra.*

7. *Supra,* note 6.

8. See e.g., Kenneth L. Karst, "Paths to Belonging: The Constitution and Cultural Identity," 64 *N.C. L. Rev.* 303, 320–21 (1986) ("Jim Crow illustrates the main technique of nativist domination").

9. See, generally, John Higham, *Strangers in the Land: Patterns of American Nativism 1860–1925* 4–5 (New York: Atheneum, 1970).

10. See, e.g., Stephen L. Carter, "Nativism and Its Discontents," *New York Times,* March 8, 1992, at Sec. 4, p. 15; Norman J. Ornstein, "Foreign Policy and the 1992

Election," *Foreign Affairs,* Summer 1992. See also Ben Wildavksy, "Going Nativist?" *National Journal,* May 27, 1995 (using the term "nativism" to refer to anti-free trade positions and isolationism).

11. See, e.g., Robert Reno, "Why All the NAFTA Fuss?" *Plain Dealer,* November 19, 1993, at B7 ("the Mexico-as-monster theory was certain to pick up the votes of those nativists always disposed to believe that nothing good comes from closer association with foreigners, especially when they are a darker skinned people"); Harold Meyerson, "The New American Liberal: Guilt-Ridden and Nativist," *Los Angeles Times,* September 19, 1993, at M2 (describing "nativist component" of the "populist attack on free trade").

This use of the term "nativism" is reflected in the definition of the term provided by *The Encyclopedic Dictionary of Sociology:* "Nativism is a movement by members of a society to improve their way of life by eliminating foreign persons, objects, customs and ideas." (Guilford, Conn.: Dushkin, 1986).

12. "Xenophobia" is another term often associated with hostility to foreigners or to immigrants. Xenophobia has been described as "dislike of the stranger, the outsider, and reluctance to admit him into one's own group." Elie Kedourie, *Nationalism* (New York: Praeger, 1960), at 74. Some analysts of American immigration history use the word to convey the antipathy of "native" Americans to foreigners. See, e.g., Thomas J. Curran, *Xenophobia and Immigration: 1820–1930* (Boston: Twayne Publishers, 1975). However, the word "nativism" is far more commonly used to describe such sentiments.

13. Higham, *supra* note 9, at 4.

14. Leonard Dinnerstein, Roger L. Nichols, and David M. Reimers, *Natives and Strangers, Blacks, Indians and Immigrants in America,* 2d ed. (New York: Oxford University Press, 1990), at 62.

15. One reference source formally defines the word in these terms. According to *The Dictionary of Immigration History,* "The nativist sentiment is one of ethnic prejudice, racism, and anti-immigration." Francesco Cordasco, ed., *Dictionary of American Immigration History* (Mutuchen, N.J.: Scarecrow Press, 1990).

16. See, e.g., Rogers Smith, " 'The American Creed' and American Identity: The Limits of Liberal Citizenship in the United States," 41 *Western Political Quarterly* 225, 228 (1988) (describing "nativism" as "ethnocultural Americanism . . . at its extreme"); Juan F. Perea, "Demography and Distrust," 77 *Minn. L. Rev.* 269, 278 (1992) ("At times of national stress, American nativism has often come to the fore, labelling American cultures, American traits different from those of the core Anglo-Saxon culture as 'foreign' or 'un-American' "); Kenneth L. Karst, "Paths to Belonging: The Constitution and Cultural Identity," 64 *N.C. L. Rev.* 303, 304 (1986) ("throughout the nation's history, differences in race, language, religion, and ethnicity have produced waves of nativist hostility to the members of cultural minorities").

17. One scholar recently criticized use of the term "nativism" to characterize anti-immigration animus that is not specifically motivated by ethnocultural bias:

Some of the discussion regarding U.S. immigration policy seems to suggest that the immigration law reform efforts of the last two decades, especially those that seek more effective enforcement of laws against unauthorized migration, represent a new form of nativism. This is a discouraging misreading of recent efforts to deal with growing migration pressures. If we are beset with nativism, where are the mass roundups of people who look foreign? Where are the scientists proving that foreign stock is polluting native blood, that sloping craniums reveal inferior mentality? How could multiculturalism become such a powerful mantra? How could anti-discrimination have been a key element in the new enforcement package [IRCA] adopted in 1986?

See David A. Martin, "Commentary: Disentangling the Strands of Immigration Policy Reform," in *Controlling Immigration: A Global Perspective,* ed. Wayne A. Cornelius, Philip L. Martin, and James F. Hollifield (Stanford: Stanford University Press, 1994), at 101.

Nevertheless, historian John Higham characterizes ethnocentrism as but one possible form of nativism. His historical account of American nativist thought identifies "several nativisms," including not merely ethnocentrism but also anti-Catholicism and antiradicalism. Nativism is "[g]enerically a defensive type of nationalism," he writes, "but the defense varied as the nativist lashed out sometimes against a religious peril, sometimes against a revolutionary peril, sometimes against a racial peril." Higham, *Strangers in the Land,* preface to the Second Edition, n.p.

The association of nativism with religious intolerance has all but disappeared from the scene. However, the linkage of "nativism" with hostility to foreign-born radicals, although far less common today than several decades ago, has recently reemerged in response to the current widespread association of Arab immigrants with terrorist violence. See David Cole, "The Scapegoats," *Nation,* July 26–August 2, 1993 (describing widespread association of Arab immigrants with terrorism as "nativist paranoia").

I should note that Higham himself has expressed his belief that not all forms of immigration restrictionism can properly be described as nativist. See Higham, *supra* (preface to the Second Edition) ("I would also, if I were writing today, take more account of aspects of the immigration restriction movement that cannot be sufficiently explained in terms of nativism").

18. According to Skinner, when people disagree about a word's meaning, they may be disagreeing, among other things, about "the criteria for applying the word" or about "whether the agreed criteria are present in a given set of circumstances"— and possibly both. Skinner, *supra,* at 11.

19. John Higham, "Another Look at Nativism," in Higham, *Send These to Me: Jews and Other Immigrants in Urban America* (New York: Atheneum, 1975), at 102, 103–4. Higham published this essay twenty years after his earlier work, *Strangers in the Land: Patterns of American Nativism, 1865–1925,* which is widely considered the classic study of early American nativism. In "Another Look at Nativism," Higham argued that because "the intellect and the conscience of America have been in revolt against what is called prejudice" since the 1930s, the term serves more as a marker for "irrationality" than a description of a social phenomenon. *Send These to Me,* at 103–5. Moreover, the term evokes the image of the outsider as victim, and the "native" as perpetrator, thereby limiting the term's usefulness in apprehending structural relations between ethnic groups and classes, which are inevitably more complex than the term would seem to allow. *Id.* at 108, 115.

Thus, Higham pronounced in 1975 that the "nativist theme" is "imaginatively exhausted," *id.* at 103, because it cannot sufficiently aid in "clarify[ing] the structure of society" and accounting for "why certain ideas emerge when and where they do and how those ideas pass into action." It can shed little light, he argues, on "the objective realities of ethnic relations." *Id.* at 105.

Intriguingly, in the revised edition of *Send These to Me*, which was published in 1984, Higham *omits* the essay "Another Look at Nativism," entirely without explanation. See John Higham, *Send These to Me: Jews and Other Immigrants in Urban America*, rev. ed. (Baltimore: Johns Hopkins University Press, 1984).

20. See, generally, J. L. Austin, *How to Do Things with Words*, 2d ed. (Cambridge: Harvard University Press, 1962). See also Skinner, *supra* note 2, at 10 (to fully understand an appraisitive political term, one must understand not merely "its sense and its reference" but also "what exact range of attitudes the term can standardly be used to express").

21. See Austin, *supra* note 20. See also Morton Kondracke, "Immigration to Be Demagogues' Next Issue after NAFTA," *Roll Call*, November 18, 1993 ("unless Clinton reacts more forcefully to [increasing anti-immigrant sentiment] by tightening border security, the political vacuum could be filled by nativist demagogues"); *U.S. News and World Report*, June 21, 1993, at 34 (according to a White House source, the President is concerned that " 'unless the administration gets out front, you'll see what you did in Germany: a violent reaction against immigration.' ")

22. This strategy could be characterized as one of "splitting": Its adherents divide anti-immigration sentiment into two domains, one of which is established as out of bounds (the "nativist" domain) and the other of which is thereby rendered permissible. What the pragmatists object to in particular about the "nativist" domain is its explicitly racialized anti-immigrant character. In contrast, the pragmatists portray themselves as part of a new, responsible social movement espousing reasoned immigration limits and control in the interests of national well-being. Many of its spokespersons bear liberal credentials. Environmental groups increasingly include immigration restriction among their generally "green" objectives; population control groups have begun to target immigration; and some advocates for domestic minorities have likewise come out in favor of immigration restriction on grounds that immigrants threaten minorities' jobs and other benefits. These restrictionists are concerned not about identity but about material limits; in their view, Americans—whatever their identities—are entitled to take care of their own first. For a sampling of literature espousing immigration restrictionism with a pragmatist flavor, see Garrett Hardin, *Living within Limits* (Oxford: Oxford University Press, 1993); Jack Miles, "Black vs. Brown: Immigration and the New American Dilemma," *Atlantic Monthly*, October 1992; Michael Lind, *The Next American Nation: The New Nationalism and the Fourth American Revolution* (New York: Free Press, 1995).

Perhaps the most consistent pragmatist strategy in the recent immigration debates is one of splitting undocumented from legal immigration and condemning the former in the interests of safeguarding the latter. As the U.S. Commission on Immigration Reform put it, "The United States must have a more credible immigration policy that deters unlawful immigration while supporting our national interest in legal immigration." U.S. Commission on Immigration Reform, U.S. Immigration Policy: Restoring Credibility: A Report To Congress (1994 Executive Summary).

23. The quoted words and phrases in this paragraph appear in Roy Beck, "Challenging Immigration Fatalism," *The Social Contract*, Vol. II, No. 2, (Winter 1991–92); and Otis L. Graham, Jr., "The Wind Has Shifted: A New Agenda for Immigration Reformers," *Social Contract*, Vol. II, No. 2 (Winter 1991–92), at 93. For other critiques of the alleged "liberal orthodoxy" in American immigration discourse, see Peter Brimelow, "Time to Rethink Immigration?" *National Review*, June 22, 1992; Lawrence Auster, *The Path to National Suicide: An Essay on Immigration and*

Multiculturalism (Washington, D.C.: American Immigration Control Foundation, 1990).

Some restrictionists have more recently noted—with clear satisfaction—that this "liberal orthodoxy" has begun to give way to a conservative consensus as the American public gets increasingly fed up with immigration. See, e.g., Richard D. Lamm, "Immigration: The Shifting Paradigm," *The Social Contract,* Vol. V, No. 1 (Fall 1994).

24. Peter Brimelow, *Alien Nation: Common Sense about America's Immigration Disaster* (New York: Random House, 1995).

25. *Id.* at 12 (italics in the original) (referring to the American Know-Nothing Party of the mid-nineteenth century).

26. *Id.* at 13. According to Brimelow, the nativists "may well have been overzealous. But their descendants need not feel ashamed of them." *Id.*

27. Brimelow's characterization is actually misleading. According to John Higham, the word "nativism" first emerged to characterize the "anti-foreign" parties of the mid-nineteenth century, in particular, the Know-Nothing Party. The Know-Nothings themselves, however, "preferred another designation. At first they called their organizations Native American parties, then simply the American party. Their philosophy they described as Americanism. 'The grand work of the American party,' proclaimed one of the Know-Nothing journals in 1855, 'is the principle of nationality . . . we must do something to protect and vindicate it. If we do not it will be destroyed.' " Higham, *supra,* at 4. While it may be true that the Know-Nothings did not specifically call for government restrictions on the admission of immigrants to the United States, their ideology was firmly antiforeign and anti-immigrant. As Thomas Curran has written, the organization and others like it "wanted to maintain America as they thought it had been before the arrival of the immigrant, that symbol of many unwanted changes." They sought to preserve " 'America for Americans.' " According to Curran, the Know-Nothings "emphasized the importance of continuing the unity of the American nation and the superiority of the native-born over the foreign born." Curran, *supra* note 12, at 44, 47, 49–50.

28. Farr, *supra* note 2, at 35–36; Skinner, *supra* note 2, at 18–19.

29. Skinner, *supra* note 2, at 11.

30. When I speak of "broad patterns of agreement," I draw to some degree on the methodology of political theorist Michael Walzer, who has argued that we can identify "shared understandings" or "shared meanings" in our political culture about what justice requires. See, generally, Michael Walzer, *Interpretation and Social Criticism* (Cambridge: Harvard University Press, 1987); Michael Walzer, *Spheres of Justice* (New York: Basic Books, 1983). However, I do not mean to claim that uniform agreement exists on this or any other matter, for conventional understandings are ordinarily both partial and contested and are subject to constant shifts and transformations.

31. The current family-based immigration regime was instituted in large part through the Immigration and Nationality Act of 1965, whose signal achievement was abolishing the national origins quotas that had prevailed for decades in our immigration system. The story of this Act is in important respects the story of the penetration of civil rights norms that had gained power and authority elsewhere in our society into the immigration domain. For discussions of the origin and political antecedents of the 1965 Act, see, generally, Select Commission on Immigration and Refugee Policy, "U.S. Immigration Policy and the National Interest," Staff Report, 1981.

32. See, e.g., Nathan Glazer, Introduction, in Nathan Glazer, ed., *Clamor at the Gates: The New American Immigration* (San Francisco: Institute for Contemporary Studies, 1985), at 6–7 ("Thus, in the atmosphere of 1964 and 1965, when America's unfinished business in regard to race, poverty and prejudice was attacked with determination, immigration was not left out . . . the matter of immigration was to be settled, this time in the liberal and open spirit of 1965, rather than the cabbed and xenophobic one of 1924").

33. *This Week with David Brinkley* (ABC News Television Broadcast, December 8, 1991): "I think God made all people good, but if we had to take a million immigrants in, say Zulus, next year, or Englishmen, and put them in Virginia, which group would be easier to assimilate and which would cause less problems for the people of Virginia? There is nothing wrong with us sitting down and arguing that issue, that we are a European country." Likewise, when Buchanan took to calling Mexicans "Jose" during his 1996 bid for the Republican presidential nomination, he faced substantial criticism for "rhetorically wink[ing] and nod[ding] to bigots." See James Bennet, "Politics: Patrick J. Buchanan: Candidate's Speech Is Called Code for Controversy," *New York Times*, February 25, 1996, at Sec. 1, p. 22.

34. Leon Bouvier, *Peaceful Invasions* (Washington, D.C.: University Press of America, 1992), at 7.

35. Brimelow, *supra* note 24, at 10. According to Brimelow, when that core is denied (as it routinely is), "Americans . . . are being tricked out of their own identity." *Id.* at 15.

36. *Id.* at 56. According to Brimelow, "America will become a freak among the world's nations because of the unprecedented demographic mutation that it is inflicting upon itself." *Id.* at xix.

37. *Id.* at 257–68.

38. E.g., "*[A]nyone who says anything critical of immigration is going to be accused of racism.* This is simply a law of modern American political life. . . . Because the term 'racist' is now so debased, I usually shrug such smears off by pointing to its new definition: *anyone who is winning an argument with a liberal.*" *Id.* at 9–11 (original emphases).

39. *Id.* at 116. See also *id.* at 107–8.

40. Brimelow is a senior editor at both *Forbes* magazine and the *National Review.* I should also note that the timing of the book's publication was clearly central to its success. Had *Alien Nation* been published even two years earlier, before immigration-related anxiety had seized the nation to the extent that it since has, it—and its author—would surely have garnered far less public attention.

41. See, e.g., Michael Lind, "American by Invitation: A Conservative Call to Arms on a Coming Issue," *New Yorker*, April 24, 1995, at 107 (reviewing *Alien Nation*).

42. See, e.g. Ira Mehlman, "Brimelow Drops 'The Big One,' " *Social Contract*, Vol. V, No. 4 (Summer 1995), at 275–77.

43. E.g., Arthur M. Schlesinger, Jr., *Disuniting of America: Reflections on a Multicultural Society* (New York: W. W. Norton, 1992).

44. See, e.g., Bill Ong Hing, "Beyond the Rhetoric of Assimilation and Cultural Pluralism: Addressing the Tension of Separatism and Conflict in an Immigration-Driven Multiracial Society," 81 *Cal. L. Rev.* 863, 871 (1993).

45. The exception is the refugee context, where the structure of normative debate is different. Here, cost arguments are often understood to be overcome by humanitarian commitments to people fleeing persecution and other violence.

46. For a comprehensive recent study which concludes that the presence of immigrants fundamentally advantages the American economy, see, e.g., Michael Fix and Jeffrey S. Passel, *Immigration and Immigrants: Setting the Record Straight* (Washington, D.C.: Urban Institute, 1994); see also Julian Simon, *Economic Consequences of Immigration* (New York: Basil Blackwell, 1989). For opposing views, see Donald Huddle, "Immigration and Jobs: The Process of Displacement," *NPG Forum*, Vol. 6 (May 1992); Donald Huddle, "The Cost of Immigration," *Carrying Capacity Network*, Washington, D.C., revised July 1993. See also George Borjas, *Friends or Strangers: The Impact of Immigrants on the United States Economy*, vol. 1 (New York: Basic Books, 1990).

47. See, e.g., Gustav Niebuhr, "Catholic Bishops Condemn Hostility to Immigrants," *Washington Post*, November 17, 1993, at A3 (a committee of Roman Catholic Bishops warned against " 'a new wave of nativism' in the United States," pursuant to which "immigrants are being made scapegoats for a weak economy").

48. Some restrictionists, on the other hand, make a specific point of not "blaming" immigrants themselves for the problems they believe immigration causes for this country. For example, one commentator noted that those who seek to control undocumented immigration do not necessarily believe that "all of our social and economic problems can or should be blamed on . . . immigrants. . . . The fault for the crisis lies not with the poor immigrant but with the politicians who have encouraged illegal immigration for their own political gain." Ron Maggiano, "It's Time to Say the Lifeboat Is Full," *San Diego Tribune*, June 16, 1993 at B7.

49. Henry Shue, *Basic Rights: Subsistence, Affluence, and U.S. Foreign Policy* (Princeton: Princeton University Press, 1980), at 131–32.

50. R. B. J. Walker and Saul H. Mendlovitz, "Interrogating State Sovereignty," in Walker and Mendlovitz, eds., *Contending Sovereignties: Redefining Political Community* (Boulder, Colo.: Lynne Rienner Publishers, 1990), at 4.

51. In some contexts, the "national priority thesis" has been subject to dispute. On questions of international resource distribution, for example, liberal theorists have often criticized it, arguing that people have duties not merely to their own particular national communities but to humanity in general. Yet, despite their usual universalist commitments, most liberals still allow that the protection of the interests of current members of a liberal national society can sometimes justify the distinctly illiberal exclusion of foreigners. Denial of admission and membership to national outsiders can be justified, as one theorist has argued, where it is necessary to preserve the nation's "liberal conversation." Bruce Ackerman, *Social Justice in the Liberal State* (New Haven: Yale University Press, 1980), at 95. See also Joseph Carens, "Migration and Morality: A Liberal Egalitarian Perspective," in Brian Barry and Robert E. Goodin, eds., *Free Movement: Ethical Issues in the Transnational Migration of People and Money* (University Park: Pennsylvania State University Press, 1992), at 25, 28–31, 36–38.

52. Higham, *Strangers in the Land*, at 20 (describing "a type of [American] nationalism that had long offset and outweighed the defensive spirit of nativism. A cosmopolitan and democratic ideal of nationality made assimilation plausible to Americans").

53. As just one example, organizations opposed to Prop. 187 repeatedly emphasized that "the people behind Prop. 187 [namely, the Federation for American Immigration Reform, or FAIR] have close ties to a white Supremacist group, the Pioneer Fund," which is "a secretive group that believes in the genetic superiority of

the white race." See Taxpayers against 187, Memo to Opponents of Prop. 187 Re: Press Coverage of Prop. 187 Promoters (Campaign Literature, undated, on file with author). See also Jean Stefancic, "Funding the Nativist Agenda," chapter 7 in this volume.

54. As just one measure of growing minority concern about immigration, 56 percent of African American voters and 57 percent of Asian American voters voted in favor of California's Proposition 187, as did 31 percent of the state's Hispanic voters. See "After Prop. 187: Heading North," *The Economist,* November 19, 1994, at 29.

55. For an argument that the presumptive legitimacy of such arguments ought, perhaps, to be subject to challenge, see Linda S. Bosniak, "Opposing Prop. 187: Undocumented Immigrants and the National Imagination," 28 *Connecticut Law Review* (forthcoming 1996).

56. See, generally, *id.*

16. DANGEROUS UNDERTONES OF THE NEW NATIVISM

Peter Brimelow and the Decline of the West
Daniel Kanstroom

O Oswald, O Spengler, this is very sad to find
— John Ashbery, "The Decline of the West"

I. INTRODUCTION

Much of the current debate in the United States over immigration policy inspires a revision of Alexis de Tocqueville's famous observation that every political question in this country eventually becomes a legal one.[1] As recent legal events relating to Proposition 187 in California demonstrate,[2] Tocqueville remains right but only partially so. Certain immigration policy questions about state-restricted access to medical care and public benefits will indeed likely be resolved in courts.[3] Ultimately, though, even if a specific legal question is framed as one of federalism, due process, or equal protection doctrine, government policies relating to aliens also embody deep questions about the nature of our nation-state. Moreover, many fundamental immigration policy questions remain outside the legal system. For example, equal protection doctrine does not yet provide a legal framework for debates over what criteria we should use in selecting immigrants. Congress, due to the survival of the so-called plenary power doctrine, has virtually unreviewable authority to base such decisions on race, ethnicity, national origin, or any other factor it chooses.[4]

Once we recognize that immigration policy debates in the United States tend to involve not just practical aspects of our immigration system but also an assessment of the nature of our nation-state,[5] we are obliged to examine very carefully the way in which that debate is conducted. My purpose in this short essay is therefore not so much to explain why our present national discussion has such importance, but to start from the premise that it does and then to consider where certain solutions to, and certain types of discourse about, immediate immigration dilemmas could lead us.

There is no better contemporary starting point for such a discussion than the widely disseminated words of Peter Brimelow, author of the cleverly titled book *Alien Nation*.[6] Though an immigrant himself, Brimelow is a leading proponent of highly restrictive U.S. immigration policy. Largely because of its extremely populist and polemical tone, his book has struck a deep chord. Much of the resonance of that chord, however, has to do with Brimelow's willingness—indeed his eagerness—to "touch on some issues of race and ethnicity that in American debate nowadays are usually taboo."[7] He does substantially more than "touch" on these issues. They form the substratum for his entire argument. One need not read long to find this theme made quite clear: "Race and ethnicity are destiny in American politics."[8] If the reader had any doubt about the underpinning of such a prophesy it is resolved by the tenth page of *Alien Nation*: "The American nation has always had a specific ethnic core. And that core has been white."[9]

Brimelow builds his immigration policy argument around a racially and ethnically charged assessment of the problem: "There is no precedent for a sovereign country undergoing such a rapid and radical transformation of its ethnic character in the entire history of the world."[10] The primary demons in Brimelow's narrative are the 1965 Amendments which eliminated the so-called National Origins Quotas from U.S. Immigration and Nationality law. Though he (grudgingly) accepts the need for the 1964 Civil Rights Act and the 1965 Voting Rights Act, Brimelow describes the elimination of the na-tional-origins immigration formula as "like shooting the wounded" after the battle for civil rights was over.[11] The book is essentially three hundred pages of highly contestable but breezily written polemic. (Though it is beyond the scope of this essay to undertake the full debunking that much of Brimelow's work demands, one example that struck me as especially astounding was his assertion that, at the time of the U.S. Civil War, "[M]ost Northerners simply never saw a black . . . [and] [o]ther minorities, of course, did not exist.")[12]

Posturing as a latter-day Tom Paine, Brimelow culminates his work with as explicit a call for race-based immigration law as has been heard in this country since the last great U.S. nativist wave of the 1920s: "It is simply common sense that Americans have a legitimate interest in their country's racial balance. It is common sense that they have a right that their govern-ment stop shifting it. Indeed, it seems to me that they have a right to insist that it be shifted back."[13] Though reviewers have (rightly in my view) criticized Brimelow's call for a "shift back" to the pre-1965 ethnic and racial composition of the United States as "pernicious nonsense,"[14] his book's wide circulation and apparent acceptance demand a more detailed analysis. Brimelow, ironically perhaps, helps us to recognize the racially charged high stakes in the immigration debate that often remain hidden beneath more polite or subtle discourse. *Alien Nation* forces us to think hard about the possible consequences of different ways of framing the immigration debate. The most inflammatory approach—and, I shall argue, the most dangerous— is one that combines an apocalyptic vision of the decline of "our" civilization with a race-based diagnosis (whether implicit or explicit) and a race-based solution.

Immigration specialists will immediately recognize aspects of this form of discourse as characteristic of some of the most shameful and most vigorously repudiated periods in our national legal history. In the infamous so-called *Chinese Exclusion Case,*[15] for example, Justice Field described at painful length how Chinese immigrants came into competition with "our" laborers and artisans, competed with "our" people and how their immigration had "the character of an Oriental invasion."[16] In 1921, as the national debate over immigration policy was culminating in the first National Origins laws, then-Vice President Calvin Coolidge added a measure of eugenics to this mixture: "America must be kept American. Biological laws show . . . that Nordics deteriorate when mixed with other races."[17]

There was always a clear link between immigration policies and race-consciousness in this country when the issue concerned non-Europeans. But a more systematic form of race thought developed in the late nineteenth century. As John Higham has noted, "Hardly any aspect of American xenophobia over its course from the eighteenth to the twentieth century is more striking than the monotony of its ideological refrain. . . . But in one major respect the pattern of nativist thought changed fundamentally . . . it veered toward racism."[18] Nineteenth-century race theorists extended to European nationalities "that sense of absolute difference which already divided white Americans from people of other colors."[19] More generally, we can define two types of race thinking that were ascendant in the nineteenth century. One may be characterized as romantic or proto-nationalistic. Often grounded in literature and Nietzschean philosophy, this variant of racism is defined by its lack of a physiological or biological basis. It is essentially a cultural idea.

Another variant, however, was rooted in the natural sciences. This school associated cultural characteristics with physiological attributes such as skin color, height, and head shape or size. Throughout the late nineteenth and early twentieth centuries the distinctions between these two schools of thought became less and less clear. In the United States, this convergence resulted in the conversion of what John Higham has called the "vague Anglo-

Saxon tradition" into a "sharp-cutting nativist weapon and, ultimately, into a completely racist philosophy."[20] In many ways, Peter Brimelow seeks to exemplify Higham's classic "Anglo-Saxon" variant of North American nativism. Most significantly, he focuses most of his attention on the "in-group," arguing that the United States belongs in some special sense to the Anglo-Saxon "race" and that it is that race that is the source of our national greatness.[21] However one may evaluate this philosophy in the context of the time in which it arose, it seems extremely doubtful that it now can be separated from the more malignant, racist strains of nativism into which its older form evolved.

It should hardly be necessary to explain the dangers of blurring this distinction as U.S. soldiers are deployed to Bosnia in the aftermath of ethnic cleansing. It is not just explicit racism that is dangerous in immigration policy and "national character" debate. Veiled racism may be just as dangerous. Brimelow, for example, quotes the first part of Calvin Coolidge's statement ("America must be kept American") while ominously alluding to the second (biological) part: "Everyone knew what he meant."[22] What, exactly, shall we presume that "everyone" now knows? And who is "everyone"? I do not, of course, mean to suggest that the subjects of race and ethnicity should be completely taboo in immigration or any other social-policy debates. But there is an obvious and important difference between recognizing an "ethno-cultural" component[23] in the imagined community of a "nation"[24] and (even implicitly) asserting that this is a "white" nation.

The history of the twentieth century reveals the potential dangers of another aspect of Brimelow's rhetorical style. Extreme pessimism,[25] even if unaccompanied by racist undertones, can be a volatile catalyst for radical social-policy proposals. Apocalyptic rhetoric about the decline of our culture therefore should generally be held to the highest burden of proof. Holmes's classic First Amendment exception for shouting fire in a crowded theater surely requires a fire of some magnitude.[26] Brimelow's fire, however, threatens to burn only his idealized conception of a white America.

When such rhetoric is explicitly combined with the argument that a particular race of people is responsible for the decline of "our" civilization or culture, the potential danger of apocalyptic historical pessimism is greatly magnified. This, sadly, seems to be where Brimelow and others want to take the U.S. immigration debate. The reach of such discourse naturally extends beyond immigration policy. Brimelow, for example, asserts that, "Inevitably, therefore, certain ethnic cultures are more crime prone than others. . . . For example, Blacks make up only 12 percent of the American population but 64 percent of all violent-crime arrests."[27]

Reasonable people can surely reasonably question whether too much immigration may unduly strain the cultural cohesion of the United States.

Debate among the proponents of the melting pot,[28] the rainbow, the mosaic, and the kaleidoscope[29] is undoubtedly healthy and important. There is, in fact, no inherent reason why immigration restrictionism must be linked to racial politics at all. Theoretically, at least, it is possible to base anti-immigration arguments solely on economics or ostensibly value-neutral demographics such as "the environment" or overcrowding. Such arguments, however, often seem to lack critical "bite." The empirical data supporting them are contestable, their statistical methods debatable, their conclusions variable. Nonspecialists often find it impossible to evaluate the claims of Brimelow's favorite economist George Borjas,[30] for example, versus those of Julian Simon.[31] Moreover, even if we were to conclude that immigration has a somewhat negative economic consequence, this does not necessarily override political/ cultural arguments in favor of, say, diversity, multiculturalism, or, at the least, a nonracial, nonethnic definition of our nation-state. A careful recognition (with a careful definition) of racial or ethnic factors may therefore be an inevitable component of real-world immigration policy debate. This does not mean, however, that all forms of such discourse are the same or equally legitimate.

Immigration restrictionists such as Peter Brimelow are not alone in their tendency to engage in rhetorical excesses. But that tendency varies greatly across the political spectrum. The excesses of the supporters of open immigration, for example, are generally accusatory. There is a tendency among immigration supporters to suspect disingenuousness or, worse, a hidden "racial" agenda of some sort on the part of the restrictionists. Brimelow's book is thus read by his opponents as a confirmation and as an embarrassment by his more careful fellow restrictionists.

Proponents of "melting pot" assimilation and cultural cohesion, though generally more moderate in their immigration policy proposals, are also given to rhetorical excess if not occasional historical revisionism. Arthur Schlesinger, Jr., for example, tends to overstate the ease with which "ethnic differences" melted away in the American pot: "The United States had a brilliant solution for the inherent fragility of a multiethnic society: the creation of a brand-new national identity, carried forward by individuals who, in forsaking old loyalties and joining to make new lives, melted away ethnic differences. . . . The point of America was not to preserve old cultures, but to forge a new *American* culture."[32] Brimelow's excesses, however, are of an entirely different cast. What is one to think when he analogizes an Immigration and Naturalization Service waiting room to the New York City subway system by noting that each is "an underworld that is not just teeming but also is almost entirely colored"?[33]

What are the characteristics of Brimelow's book that permit him to engage in such inflammatory discourse with so little public condemnation? Part of the answer seems simply to be that the times have changed. Yesterday's radical, marginalized race talk is increasingly part of today's mainstream debate.[34] But another important reason for the success of Brimelow's book has been his clever ability to combine a polemical writing style with always-popular apocalyptic historical pessimism and an undercurrent of (only partially) hidden racism.[35] Unfortunately, this volatile combination has been seen before. Although I feel impelled strenuously to emphasize my desire not to overstate the parallels, it is illuminating to revisit the most infamous historical example where such discourse appeared in the past. I felt virtually compelled to do so, in fact, by the very first sentence in Brimelow's book: "There is a sense in which current immigration policy is Adolf Hitler's posthumous revenge on America."[36]

It is important to consider how the German National Socialists are invoked throughout *Alien Nation.* Brimelow uses National Socialism not, as one might have hoped, as the limiting extreme example of where majoritarian race-consciousness can lead even a modern democratic society. Rather, the Nazis are used to distinguish (and thereby legitimize) American nativists of the late nineteenth and early twentieth century: "*The nativists were not Nazis: they were nationalists.*"[37] Though literally true, this generous assessment of U.S. nativism overlooks many disturbing similarities between its biological racist variant and German National Socialism.

Alien Nation also contains other loose invocations of Nazi theory and history. Perhaps most astounding to anyone with even a passing familiarity with modern European history is Brimelow's bald assertion that it was the "diversity" of the Austro-Hungarian Empire "where the Germans were a minority exposed to Slavs, Magyars and Jews from the shtetls of Galicia" that caused anti-Semitism and formed the consciousness of Adolf Hitler.[38]

There clearly are many substantial differences between American nativism past and present and German National Socialism. Likewise, contemporary U.S. civic culture is far from that of the Germany of the 1920s and 1930s in which Hitler ascended. But there are also important historical parallels which it is foolish and possibly perilous to overlook. In response to Brimelow's ironic invocation of Hitler as the force behind the current U.S. immigration debate, I will therefore sketch the outlines of two historical transformations in Germany. The first was the transformation of a rather mainstream, conservative form of historical pessimism with only implicit racist undertones into the virulent doctrines of Nazi theorists. As an exemplar of this development I will focus on a relatively obscure[39] German historian—Oswald Spengler—and his grandly (and, in light of recent events in California, relevantly) titled work, *The Decline of the West.* The second transformation involved what were initially minor changes in German citizenship laws into the ultimate political and legal structures of genocide. I propose that we draw two related conclusions from this brief review of history. First, to reiterate, we should be very careful about the manner in which we debate matters concerning the racial and ethnic constitution of our nation-state. Nonracist nationalism is still a very fragile idea. Second, because of that fragility, the creation of two classes of citizenship or of a large "illegal" or "unassimilable" ethnic minority with (more or less) distinct ethnic or racial characteristics is a formula for predictable social disaster.

II. THE DECLINE OF THE WEST

In the late summer of 1918, with the final defeat of the German empire only a few months away, the first volume of a work that later became known in English as *The Decline of the West* began to appear in Germany and Austria.[40] Written by a then unknown German historian named Oswald Spengler, the book was soon to become a sensation with a profound impact on intellectual debate and German politics for two critical decades.

Though originally conceived as a political critique of the "folly" and "criminal and suicidal optimism" of pre-World War I German foreign policy, the work grew substantially beyond that modest goal.[41] According to Spengler, the book was begun with an assessment of both the imminence and the inevitability of World War I, which he saw as "the inevitable outward manifestation of the historical crisis." The war, Spengler wrote, was not "a momentary constellation of casual facts due to national sentiments, personal influences or economic tendencies . . . but the type of a historical change of phase occurring within a great historical organism of definable compass at the point preordained for it."[42]

The basic character of *The Decline of the West*, as one leading critic has put it, is that of a "somber, murky vision of the doom of our civilization."[43] Its structure was a comparative analysis of the modern world and certain selected aspects of the later ancient world. Spengler's goal, however, was substantially more than to be an expositor of previously underdeveloped historical themes. With Hegelian flourish, he defined his project also to be to predict, "the spiritual form, duration, rhythm, meaning, and product of the still unaccomplished stages of our western history."[44] Beyond Santayana's pedestrian observation that those who do not understand the past are destined to repeat it,[45] Spengler adhered to the deterministic belief that he had discovered eternal, extracultural, inevitable truths about historical development.

There has been some debate over whether Spengler may accurately be called a historical pessimist. In fact, years after the publication of *The Decline of the West*, Spengler went to some trouble to try to distance himself from the "pessimist" label. In an essay written in response to critiques of *The Decline of the West*, Spengler sought to distinguish long-term from short-term pessimism: "In what concerns the 'goal of mankind,' I am a decided pessimist. . . . I see no progress, no goal, no path for humanity."[46] In the same essay, however, Spengler also wrote, "No, I am not a pessimist. Pessimism means to see no more tasks. I see so many still unaccomplished that I fear we shall lack the time and men they demand."[47] Based upon the provocative nature of his title (which is even more provocative in German than English as the German word "*Untergang*" connotes not just decline but ruin and destruction), and the nature of his ultimate conclusions, it seems fair to characterize Spengler as part of a school of pessimistic thought originally linked with the Swiss historian Jacob Burckhardt and most famously continued by the work of Arnold Toynbee.[48] One of Spengler's distinct contributions was his rejection of what he disparaged as the "myopic" linear historical method of his predecessors in favor of a more comparative approach. His comparisons included not just the standard Babylonian, Egyptian, Greek, and Roman civilizations and cultures,[49] but a culture that he claimed to have discovered and that he alternately called Arabian and "Magian." His comparison yielded a belief in what Spengler called "universal symbolism." History, on this view, "ceased to be a casual succession of events . . . and became the majestic unfolding of the implications contained in a limited number of awe-inspiring symbols."[50] Unsurprisingly, given the time and place in which he wrote, there was also a distinctly biological aspect to Spengler's method. He adopted an "organic" view of culture, analogizing it to a living organism, with a concomitant analogy of birth, growth, decline, and death.[51]

At least as interesting as Spengler's historical work is the way that work was understood by nonspecialists.[52] As one observer noted, "Never had a thick philosophical work had such a success—and in all reading circles, learned and uneducated, serious and snobbish."[53] Copies of the book were widely disseminated, including one that made its way to Oliver Wendell Holmes, Jr., who described it as "a stimulating humbug of a book."[54] The year 1919, perhaps best recalled in the United States as the year of the Palmer Raids, has been called the "Spengler year" in the German-speaking world. That year also witnessed the formation of a small, radical, and obscure political party called the German Workers' Party, which evolved into the German Nazi Party.

The catastrophic ascendance of National Socialism in Germany compels a reading of Spengler in light of events that he neither championed nor predicted but to which he surely contributed. Spengler was clearly not a Nazi. Indeed, he expressed a fairly consistent revulsion for many of the central tenets of Adolf Hitler's political philosophy. Yet it is more than Spengler's nationality that has caused some historians to consider him at least an inadvertent philosophical brush-clearer for the Third Reich.

Part of the difficulty was that Spengler appreciated much of the message of Nazi doctrine, while expressing discomfort with certain attributes of the messengers. He had specifically opposed the National Socialists as early as 1924. His opposition, however, seems to have been as much tactical and pragmatic as principled. He found Hitler's followers to be rough and immature. Yet he had specifically lauded the Fascists of Italy for their emphasis on "results" rather than "programs and parades."[55] Nevertheless, Spengler actively promoted many of the same ideals as Hitler. He had written of the "Third Reich" as a "Germanic ideal" in *The Decline of the West*[56] though his meaning was "vague and unpolitical."[57]

Although decidedly not a racist in the biological, Hitlerian sense, Spengler was hardly a consistent antiracist either. He had criticized the idea of a *Volk* in *The Decline*, adopting instead a Nietzschean conception of race that was beyond blood or genetics. Race, on this view, was more akin to what others might call character. It was linked more to geography and common history than to biology. It was not manifested in bodily characteristics but in intangible essences.[58] Thus, in *The Decline*, Spengler viewed the so-called Jewish question mostly as a cultural clash, in sharp contrast to Hitler's views of Semitic versus "Aryan" blood.[59] Spengler's racial theories, however, were not entirely consistent over time. In *Man and Technics*,[60] a small book published in 1931, for example, Spengler asserted that "the group of nations of Nordic blood" was losing control of the world. Among the reasons he gave for this was the fact that the "colored races" had been given access to technology which, Spengler believed, they would soon turn against the "Nordic" peoples. One might reasonably think that such a conclusion would hardly have been controversial in the following years in Nazi Germany. Owing in part to the Nazi regime's need to maintain its alliance with Japan, however, Spengler's particular brand of racial thought actually contributed to his being viewed at least as an outcast and possibly as a potential enemy.

Thus, as H. Stuart Hughes has noted:

On the racial question . . . as on nearly every subject, Spengler clung tenaciously to an eccentric position of his own. And, like his other theories, his racial doctrines offered a curious mixture of fantasy and good sense . . . the theories closest to the Nazis' hearts were manifest absurdities . . . [but] he was unwilling to combat them in the name of universal humanitarianism, he would not be so untrue to his own ideas as to fight one delusion with the slogans of what he believed to be another.[61]

In the end, Spengler was publicly condemned by the Nazis for having failed to recognize "his own children."[62] The main problem for the Nazis, however, was not so much Spengler's vagueness on race theory as it was his failure to embrace the National Socialists as the appropriate leaders of the revolution "for which he, like them, had been working for fifteen years." [63] He stands in history as a tragically ironic figure—one who purported to predict the grand movement of Western civilization only to fail to foresee or prevent the terrible transformation of ideas he had so vigorously propagated. Spengler, despite his reservations, served as an important precursor to the Nazi regime. Hitler himself adopted much of the apocalyptic tone of *The Decline of the West,* while adding a racist component: "On [Aryans] depends the existence of this whole culture. If they perish, the beauty of this earth will sink into the grave with them." [64] As Hughes writes, "Spengler had played with fire. . . . Personally, he might advocate the rule of a cultivated aristocracy. But once he had helped to launch the forces of violence, he was powerless to keep them within the bounds of 'form' and 'style.' " [65]

Alien Nation, to be sure, is hardly *The Decline of the West.* The United States is not Germany, and Peter Brimelow is not Oswald Spengler. Like Spengler, however, Brimelow plays with a fire that, once kindled, may be very hard to control. Nor should one take comfort in the thought that racist immigration discourse will be confined to a limited realm. In this regard, some of the early legal history of Nazi Germany is instructive.

III. CITIZENSHIP AND DEPORTATION UNDER NATIONAL SOCIALISM

By the time of its ascendance to state power on January 20, 1933, the German Nationalist Socialist Party had a fairly well-developed theory of immigration and citizenship. In *Mein Kampf,* [66] begun in 1924 and completed in 1927, Adolf Hitler wrote,

The institution which today is wrongly named "the State" knows of only two kinds of individual: State citizens and foreigners. State citizens are all those who either by birth or naturalization enjoy the rights of State citizenship; foreigners are those who enjoy similar rights under other States. Nowadays these rights are acquired in the first place by the fact of being born within the frontiers of the State. Race and nationality play no part in it. The child of a Negro, who once lived in a German protectorate and now is domiciled in Germany, is automatically a citizen of the German State. [67]

Leaving aside the fact that Hitler was wrong about the legal underpinnings of German citizenship law (it was [and still is] based primarily upon the *jus sanguinis* principle of blood transmission of citizenship), [68] his views on the matter were quite clear. The ideal, race-based "national State" should divide its inhabitants into three classes: "State citizens, State subjects, and foreigners." [69] Birth should give no more than the status of subject, which would not include the right to vote or to hold political office. Citizenship, however, would have to be earned, and "race and nationality" would have to be "proved" as a prerequisite.[70] These qualities, as Hitler earlier had made plain, were matters of "blood," not language or upbringing.[71]

Particularly in light of Peter Brimelow's opening salvo invoking the "posthumous revenge" of Adolf Hitler, it is worth recalling that Hitler actually knew something about U.S. immigration and citizenship law. In fact, he held the U.S. immigration laws of the 1920s in rather high regard. As Hitler put it in *Mein Kampf:*

There is at least one state in which feeble attempts to achieve a better arrangement are apparent . . . the United States of America, where . . . [t]hey refuse to allow immigration of elements which are bad from the health point of view, and absolutely forbid naturalization of certain defined races, and are thus making a modest start in the direction of something not unlike the conception of the national State.[72]

Thus, it seems that if Hitler is to be placed in our current debate about immigration at all it should be as an opponent of the Fourteenth Amendment and the Civil Rights Acts of the 1960s and as a supporter of a return to the national-origins quotas and racist naturalization laws that he embraced in *Mein Kampf.*

Those who support such laws should consider the full historical program of which similar laws were a part in Germany. The Nazi positions on immigration and citizenship were absolutely central to their beliefs about the idealized *Volk*-based nation-state.[73] Changes in these laws were among the first legal steps taken by the new regime. The 1913 German Citizenship Law[74] was amended by decree in 1934 to create the category of "Reich citizens" as "the only" German citizenship.[75] A statute passed in 1935 then distinguished, as Hitler had suggested, "Reich citizens" *(Reichsbürger)* from "state citizens" *(Staatsangehörige).*[76] These laws were crucial components of the so-called Nuremberg Laws which excluded Jews from German society in ways ranging from the highly abstract, such as citizenship, to the extremely specific, such as forbidding Jewish families from having Christian servants.[77]

Beyond their *Volkisch* reordering of Germany's citizenship laws and their use of those laws to justify and develop separate classes of German citizens with sharply different rights, Nazi leaders were also strong supporters of Jewish emigration. This doctrine, like many Nazi ideas, evolved substantially over time, from encouragement of emigration to forced deportation and ultimately to concentration camps and extermination. Early Nazi writers, such as Alfred Rosenberg, purported to accept the fact of a substantial Jewish population in Germany for the foreseeable future. The key, however, was to find the "proper balance" so that *Volkisch* German culture would predominate. Despite talk of balance, though, his highly charged rhetoric was a harbinger of the horrors to come:

Thus, we are obliged to accept the Jews among us as a necessary evil, for who knows how many thousands of years to come. But just as the body would be stunted if the bacteria increased beyond a salutary number, our nation too . . . would gradually succumb to a spiritual malady if the Jew were to become too much for it.[78]

It is, of course, a great tragedy of modern history that these portents did not yield any effective, timely response. An important, if often forgotten, reason for this was the very "legality" of the first steps taken by the Nazi regime and the marginality of many of its first victims. Thus, as Hannah Arendt has noted, emigration of Jews in the early years of the Nazi regime "proceeded in a not unduly accelerated and generally orderly fashion."[79] The first forced Jewish emigrants were mostly young people who perceived that there was no future for them in Germany.[80]

Within a very short period of time, several events demonstrated the links between early Nazi citizenship and immigration laws and the Final Solution. By 1937 it was becoming clear to the Nazi leadership that voluntary emigration was insufficient to achieve the goal of recreating the nation-state. The Nuremberg Laws, in short, had not succeeded. Jews had been deprived of political rights by the gradation of citizenship, but they retained important civil rights especially regarding employment and property in the private sector. Also, because German Jews had been second-class citizens in many respects since 1933, the Jewish community itself began to accept that such a situation was stable and could continue.[81] As further laws were passed that deprived Jews of property, social benefits, and the possibility of earning a living, however, deportation measures also became increasingly harsh. The first group to feel the brunt of this policy and to be deported were those non-German Jewish residents who were formally stateless because they had never applied for German citizenship. In effect, they had now become *illegal aliens,* though that specific term was not used to describe them.

Following the *Anschluss* (the incorporation of Austria into the *Reich*) in March 1938, the use of deportation there became increasingly well organized and efficient. Adolf Eichmann had been assigned the task of deporting all the Jews from Austria. His success was "spectacular."[82] In eight months some forty-five thousand Jews left Austria. In less than eighteen months, the number of "legal" expulsions was close to one hundred and fifty thousand, roughly 60 percent of the entire Jewish population.[83]

When the Polish government announced that as of October 29, 1938, all Polish Jews residing in Germany would lose their Polish citizenship, the orderly use of deportation laws began to seem particularly cumbersome to the Nazi leaders.[84] A group of some fifteen thousand Polish Jews were rounded up and forced by the Gestapo and the Polish government to undergo a macabre back and forth dance between Germany and Poland until the latter state finally agreed to accept them.[85]

A criminal act provided the spark to justify the Nazis' acceleration of anti-Jewish measures in Germany. In November 1938, German councilor Ernst vom Rath was assassinated in Paris by Herschel Grynszpan, the Jewish son of two expelled Polish Jews. Although the full truth about this incident is still unknown (speculation has ranged from the political to the highly personal to the possibility of Gestapo instigation)[86] the assassination led immediately to Joseph Goebbels's orchestration of *Kristallnacht*, the nationwide attack on Jewish places of worship which revealed the full intentions of the Nazi regime. Soon the relationship between the emigration policy and the concentration camps became only too apparent. By January 30, 1939, Hitler was sufficiently confident to speak plainly: "if international Jewish capitalism . . . should succeed once more in plunging the nations into war, then the result will . . . be . . . the destruction of the Jewish race in Europe."[87]

Observers of current anti-immigration rhetoric in the United States have expressed concern about much of its tone and possible direction. Undocumented immigrants are seen by some commentators to be "doubly unpopular." They occupy a "caste-like status."[88] Moreover, beyond their inherent "illegality," they are blamed for sapping public benefits and bankrupting state and local governments.[89] Others have begun to worry more broadly about the apparent movement toward a "smaller concentric circle" of membership in which distinctions between naturalized and native-born citizens could be the next step.[90] History tragically supports this concern.

Among the most fascinating aspects of the Nazis' use of deportation to produce their ideal nation-state was their understanding of how a group of people could be progressively transformed. One starts with an overgeneralized accusation and then turns it into reality. A November 1938 letter from the German Ministry of Foreign Affairs to all German authorities abroad made this point explicitly:

The emigration movement of only about 100,000 Jews has already sufficed to awaken the interest of many countries in the Jewish danger . . . the influx of Jews in all parts of the world invokes the opposition of the native population and thereby forms the best propaganda for the German Jewish policy. . . . *The poorer and therefore more burdensome the immigrating Jew is to the country absorbing him, the stronger the country will react.*[91]

Much of the virulence of this quotation derives from the specific genocidal nature of German National Socialism. But there are lessons to be learned from it that go beyond that. We in the United States must be aware that we have the capacity through incremental laws to "manufacture" an underclass. Each step taken on that road may seem innocuous and even justifiable. First there is the definition of a particular group of people as "illegal aliens," with little recognition of the widely varying circumstances that lead to such a status.[92] Some are refugees, some have overstayed visas, some are in proceedings, some have relatives here, and so forth. The epithet of illegality, however, overshadows such fine distinctions. What is worse is the widespread understanding, supported by Peter Brimelow and others, of the racial and ethnic similarities among members of this group. Once the group is defined in such ways, as both illegal and nonwhite, there are attempts to deprive "them" of the opportunity to work, to educate their children, to obtain medical care, and at least the minimal "safety net" of public benefits. Each of these legal steps is accompanied by a reasonable, ostensibly nonracist justification. But these types of laws—whatever their fiscal or other justification—also have the inevitable effect of transforming this minority group into the very thing they have wrongfully been called: an uneducated, disease-bearing, criminally inclined threat to "our" people and civilization. At this point, they begin to appear even to many "melting pot" supporters as Jews once did to Nazis— they have become an unassimilable group.[93] For those of a somewhat racist disposition already, the new social reality only confirms and strengthens their views. David Duke, it should be recalled, throughout the late 1980s called for a complete end to all "Third World" immigration in conjunction with the racial division of the United States.[94] Now comes Peter Brimelow with a similar program in better garb. It is not easy to pierce the veil of Brimelow's engaging style to see the core of his philosophy. But, as Tom Paine put it in *Common Sense,* "Those who expect to reap the benefits of freedom must . . . undergo the fatigue of supporting it."[95] Even if we cannot perfectly seal our borders and fully enforce our immigration laws, we must avoid the transformation of one serious social problem into one that is potentially much worse.

NOTES

A short essay such as this normally does not include so substantial a "thank-you" note. This essay, however, arose out of an otherwise purely social lunch with Juan Perea, whom I want to thank for encouraging me to participate, despite my inevitable anxieties about time, in this wonderful project. I also thank my father, Richard Kanstroom, not only for everything I ever accomplish (for which he deserves most of the credit) but specifically for his research assistance. Special thanks also to Aviam Soifer, Dean Hashimoto, and Anthony Farley, who generously read and commented on drafts.

1. Alexis de Tocqueville, *Democracy in America,* 280 (New York, 1953).

2. See, e.g., *League of United Latin American Citizens et al. v. Wilson et al.,* 1995 U.S. Dist. *Lexis* 17720 (1995); *Gregorio T. et al. v. Wilson et al.,* 59 F. 3d 1002 (9th Cir. 1995).

3. Such questions might arguably be seen as part of the law of "alienage" rather than "immigration," with the latter category limited to questions relating to the admission and expulsion of noncitizens. See Stephen H. Legomsky, "Immigration Law and the Principle of Plenary Congressional Power," 1984 *Sup. Ct. Rev.* 255–56 (1984). As many commentators have recognized, however, this distinction is extremely elusive. See, e.g., Hiroshi Motomura, "Comment: Immigration and Alienage, Federalism and Proposition 187," 35 *Va. J. Int'l L.* 201–3 (1995) (arguing that it is better to define a spectrum with shades of gray than to try to maintain a rigid categorical distinction); see also, Linda S. Bosniak, "Membership, Equality, and the Difference that Alienage Makes," 69 *N.Y.U. L. Rev.* 1047 (1994).

4. See, generally, Legomsky, *supra* note 3.

5. This aspect of immigration debate is true for other nation-states as well. See, e.g., Daniel Kanstroom, "Wer Sind Wir Wieder: Laws of Asylum, Immigration, and Citizenship in the Struggle for the Soul of the New Germany," 18 *Yale J. Int'l L.* 155 (1993).

6. Peter Brimelow, *Alien Nation: Common Sense about America's Immigration Disaster* (New York, 1995).

7. *Id.* at xvii.

8. *Id.*

9. *Id.* at 10.

10. *Id.* at 57, 129. See also variation of this theme on page 117.

11. *Id.* at 103

12. *Id.* at 69

13. *Id.* at 265.

14. Jack Miles, "The Coming Immigration Debate," *Atlantic Monthly,* April 1995, p. 130.

15. *Chae Chan Ping v. United States,* 130 U.S. 581 (1889).

16. *Id.* at 594–95

17. Calvin Coolidge, "Whose Country Is This?" *Good Housekeeping,* LXXII (February 1921).

18. John Higham, *Strangers in the Land: Patterns of American Nativism 1860–1925* (New York, 1981) p. 131.

19. *Id.*

20. *Id.* at 134

21. *Id.* at 9–11.

22. Brimelow, *supra* note 6, at 211.

23. *Id.* at 203.

24. See Benedict Anderson, *Imagined Communities: Reflections on the Origin and Spread of Nationalism* (New York, 1983).

25. Brimelow's pessimism runs deeper than race, ethnicity, and immigration: "The lesson of history is simply this: *human beings like war. They will always find an excuse for it.*" Brimelow, *supra,* note 6, at 229 (italics in original). Later, he opines, "In fact, there is no solution to the problem of human pain." *Id.* at 248.

26. *Schenck v. United States,* 249 U.S. 47, 52 (1919). Cf. *Gitlow v. People of New York,* 268 U.S. 652, 668 (1925) ("A single revolutionary spark may kindle a fire"). I

do not, of course, mean to suggest that apocalyptic speech should be outlawed, simply that it should be recognized and critiqued.

27. Brimelow, *supra* note 6, at 184.

28. See Arthur M. Schlesinger, Jr., *The Disuniting of America: Reflections on a Multicultural Society* (New York, 1992).

29. See Lawrence H. Fuchs, *The American Kaleidoscope: Race, Ethnicity, and the Civic Culture* (Hanover, N.H., 1990).

30. See, e.g., Brimelow *supra* note 6, at 85, 108, 112, 142–44, 147–48, 150–55, 160–62, 188.

31. See, e.g., *Id.* at 109–11, 115–16, 128–29, 138, 140–41.

32. *Id.* at 13

33. Brimelow, *supra* note 6, at 28.

34. See, e.g., Richard J. Herrnstein and Charles Murray, *The Bell Curve: Intelligence and Class Structure in American Life* (New York, 1995) (arguing for a racial difference in intelligence).

35. Brimelow has made his personal views rather clear in interviews. An interview in *New York Newsday,* for example, contained his assessment of African Americans as "a separate nation, sort of like a fetal nation" and the argument that America should remain largely white because "It has historically been a white nation." "We've Been on an 'Immigrant Binge,' " *New York Newsday,* July 10, 1995, p. A21.

36. Brimelow, *supra* note 6, at xv.

37. Brimelow, *supra* note 6, at 13 (italics in original).

38. *Id.* at 120. It is interesting that Brimelow cites no authority for this proposition. So far as I am aware, the only other writer to view the development of modern European anti-Semitism in precisely this way was Hitler himself in *Mein Kampf.* For an analysis less inclined to blame the victims of racism than its perpetrators, see Hannah Arendt, *The Origins of Totalitarianism* (New York, 1951).

39. But see Henry Kissinger, "The Meaning of History: Reflections on Spengler, Toynbee, and Kant" (unpublished undergraduate thesis, Widener Library, Harvard University, 1951).

40. H. Stuart Hughes, *Oswald Spengler: A Critical Estimate* (New York, 1962) p. 1.

41. Oswald Spengler, *Politische Shriften* (Munich, 1932) p. vi; See also Hughes, *supra* note 40, at 6.

42. Oswald Spengler, *Der Untergang Des Abendlandes: Umrisse Einer Morphologie der Weltgeschichte; I: Gestalt und Wirklichkeit* (Munich, 1923) pp. 46–47 (quoted in Hughes, *supra* note 40, at 6).

43. Hughes, *supra* note 40, at 7.

44. *The Decline of the West,* vol. I, at 112–13.

45. George Santayana, *The Life of Reason* (New York, 1905) vol. 1, ch. xii ("Those who cannot remember the past are condemned to fulfil it").

46. Oswald Spengler, "Pessimismus" in *Reden und Aufsätze* (Munich, 1937) (quoted in Hughes, *supra* note 40, at 87).

47. *Id.*

48. Jacob Burckhardt once wrote, "I have no hope at all for the future," in "Briefe: Zur Erkenntnis Seiner Geistigen Gestalt," Fritz Kaphahn, ed. (Leipzig, 1935) *Zweiter Teil* p. 185 (quoted in Hughes, *supra* note 40, at 17). For an American variant of this school, see Brooks Adams, *The Law of Civilization and Decay: An Essay on History* (New York, 1896).

49. Spengler, like Nietzsche and Thomas Mann, distinguished the concept of culture from that of civilization. The former is the early explosive period of creative activity that distinguishes a particular society. The latter merely refers to material stability. See Hughes, *supra* note 40, at 72.

50. Hughes, *supra* note 40, at 11.

51. Hughes, *supra* note 40, at 10.

52. Indeed, among historians his work has been fairly consistently disparaged if not condemned. See, generally, Hughes, *supra* note 40.

53. Quoted from W. Wolfradt in *Manfred Schroeter, Der Streit um Spengler: Kritik Seiner Kritiker* (Munich, 1922) by Hughes, *supra* note 40, at 89.

54. Letter from Oliver W. Holmes to Dr. John C. H. Wu, January 27, 1925, in *Justice Holmes to Doctor Wu: An Intimate Correspondence, 1921–1932* (1947), at 25–26.

55. Hughes, *supra* note 40, at 125.

56. *The Decline of the West*, vol. I, p. 363

57. Hughes, *supra* note 40, at 123.

58. Hughes, *supra* note 40, at 125.

59. Spengler believed that Christian civilization, since the Enlightenment, had gradually broken down the barriers between Christians and Jews to the point where we would witness the dissolution of Christian and Jewish nationality. The only possibility he foresaw for Jews in the West was complete assimilation. Hughes at 126. *The Decline of the West*, vol. II, pp. 315–23.

60. Oswald Spengler, *Der Mensch und die Technik: Beitrag zu einer Philosophie des Lebens* (Munich, 1931); translated by Charles Francis Atkinson as *Man and Technics: A Contribution to a Philosophy of Life* (New York, 1932).

61. *Id.* at 126.

62. Arthur Zweiniger, *Spengler im Dritten Reich: Eine Antwort auf Oswald Spenglers, "Jahre der Entscheidung"* (Oldenburg i.O., 1933) p. 12 (quoted in Hughes, *supra* note 40, at 131).

63. *Id.* at 132.

64. Adolf Hitler, *Mein Kampf* (Boston, 1971) p. 288.

65. *Id.* at 134.

66. Adolf Hitler, *Mein Kampf* (first English edition, Cambridge, 1933).

67. *Id.* at 181.

68. See, generally, Kanstroom, *Wer Sind Wir Wieder, supra* note 5.

69. *Mein Kampf, supra* note 64, at 182.

70. *Id.*

71. "It is hardly imaginable that anyone should think that a German could be made out of, say, a Negro or a Chinaman because he has learned German and is ready to talk it for the rest of his life and to vote for some German political party . . . nationality, or rather race, is not a matter of language, but of blood." *Id.* at 158.

72. *Id.* at 182.

73. See, e.g., Carl Schmitt, *Staat, Bewegung, Volk* 42 (Munich, 1933).

74. "Reichs und Staatsangehörigkeitsgesetz," July 22, 1913, *RGBL.* 583.

75. "Verordnung über die Deutsche Staatsangehörigkeit," 1934 *RGBL.* 85 §1.

76. "Reichsbürgergesetz," Sept. 15, 1935, *RGBL.* I 1146.

77. See, generally, George L. Mosse, *Nazi Culture* (New York, 1966) p. 320.

78. *Dietrich Eckhart ein Vermächtnis*, ed. Alfred Rosenberg (Munich, 1928) pp. 214–19.

79. Hannah Arendt, *Eichmann in Jerusalem: A Report on the Banality of Evil* (New York, 1966 [revised edition]) p. 38.

80. *Id.* at 39. In fact, during this period of what Arendt terms a "fool's paradise," the immigration laws were sufficiently flexible that some Jews even managed to return to Germany when they discovered that their prospects elsewhere were no better.

81. As the German national Jewish organization of the time saw it, "the intention of the Nuremberg Laws was to establish a level on which a bearable relationship between the German and the Jewish people [became] possible." Arendt *supra* note 79, at 40.

82. Arendt (Eichmann) *supra* note 79, at 44.

83. *Id.* at 44.

84. See, e.g., Arendt (Eichmann) *supra* note 79, at 228.

85. See, generally, George L. Mosse, *Toward the Final Solution* (Madison, 1985) pp. 210–14.

86. See, e.g., Arendt (Eichmann) *supra* note 79, at 228.

87. Quoted in Mosse, *supra* note 85, at 213.

88. Linda S. Bosniak, "Immigrants, Preemption, and Equality," 35 *Va. J. Int'l L.* 179, 187 (1994).

89. See Kevin R. Johnson, "Public Benefits and Immigration: The Intersection of Immigration Status, Ethnicity, Gender, and Class," 42 *UCLA L. Rev.* 1509, 1512 (1995).

90. T. Alexander Aleinikoff, "The Tightening Circle of Membership," *Hastings Const. L.Q.* 915, 923–24 (Summer 1995).

91. *Nazi Conspiracy and Aggression,* Washington, 1946, published by the U.S. Government, VI, 87 ff. (quoted in Arendt, *Origins,* at 269n. 2) (italics added).

92. See, generally, Gerald L. Neuman, "Aliens as Outlaws: Government Services, Proposition 187, and the Structure of Equal Protection Doctrine," 42 *UCLA L. Rev.* 1425, 1441–42 (1995).

93. See, generally, Nicholas Goodrick-Clark, *The Occult Roots of Nazism: The Ariosophists of Austria and Germany 1890–1935* (Wellingsborough, Northamptonshire, 1985).

94. Lance Hill, "Nazi Race Doctrine in the Political Thought of David Duke," Douglas D. Rose, ed., *The Emergence of David Duke and the Politics of Race* (Chapel Hill, 1992).

95. Thomas Paine, "Common Sense," IV, p. 58 in *The Great Works of Thomas Paine* (New York, n.d.).

17. CITIZENSHIP
Richard Delgado

NATIVISM, THEN AND NOW

History teaches that nativist movements tend to flourish when the country's social and economic situation is unsettled and then to take one of two broad forms.[1] Society enacts restrictive immigration laws and policies to keep foreigners—usually ones of darker coloration—out.[2] And it enacts measures aimed at making things difficult for those who are already here.[3] In the late nineteenth and early twentieth centuries, for example, early immigration from Southeastern Europe prompted proposals for the first literacy tests for immigrants.[4] It took nearly thirty years to get the tests enacted because successive presidents vetoed them on the grounds that they were contrary to the American tradition of open immigration. In 1917, a literacy requirement was finally enacted over President Wilson's veto.[5]

To the surprise of the test's proponents, many of the immigrants from southeastern Europe passed the new test. As a result, the proponents shifted ground, urging restrictive national-origins quotas. These quotas, which were aimed at maintaining America's ethnic makeup (namely, dominantly white) were enacted in 1924 and remained in place for over forty years.[6] During the height of hysteria over postwar communism, English literacy was made a condition of naturalized citizenship for the first time.[7]

Measures such as these, aimed at making immigration or naturalization difficult, have generally been coupled with round-ups, restrictive labor and business laws, and other repressive measures aimed at making life difficult for immigrant groups once they are here.[8] In our time, English-only laws extend the linguistic jingoism inherent in literacy requirements. In earlier times, labor laws were used to discourage Chinese laundries.[9] The campaign against affirmative action and in favor of eliminating social services for immigrants illustrates more contemporary forms of legal treatment designed to disadvantage the foreign born.[10]

MEASURES TO NARROW THE CONSTITUTIONAL GRANT OF CITIZENSHIP

One measure, new to our time, would narrow the constitutional grant of citizenship. Previous measures conditioned the grant of citizenship, or the right to immigrate, for example, denying it to foreigners who had committed a felony, were communists, or could not speak English.[11] The new measures are different—they would change the definition of citizenship itself. As such, they advance both types of nativist objective.[12] They send an emphatic message to would-be immigrants in other parts of the world. And they burden those who are already here by making acquisition of U.S. citizenship more difficult for many who wish to do so.

One such measure is California's Joint Resolution 49. Introduced by Assembly members Mountjoy, Haynes, Morrow, and Rainey on August 23, 1993, the measure urged that the U.S. Congress propose "appropriate amendments to the United States Constitution limiting United States citizenship to persons born in the United States of mothers who are citizens, legal residents of the United States, and of naturalized United States citizens."[13] The measure "would also propose that the constitutional amendments repeal the first sentence of Section 1 of the Fourteenth Amendment to the United States Constitution, among other things."[14] The text of the resolution declares that its purpose is to decrease the incentive for illegal immigration and thus reduce the demand for public services. A few days later, Governor Pete Wilson of California echoed the assembly proposal, calling for congressional action or a constitutional amendment to change the rule under which children born in the United States are automatically granted citizenship.[15]

Slightly less than one year later, four U.S. congressmen introduced 1994 House Joint Resolution 396.[16] Echoing the language of the California version, the resolution proposed "an amendment to the Constitution of the United States to provide that no person born in the United States will be a United States citizen on account of birth in the United States unless a parent is a United States citizen at the time of the birth." The resolution builds on an earlier resolution put forward in March of the same year. The earlier resolution would have denied citizenship "on account of birth in the United States unless the mother or father of the person is a citizen . . . is lawfully in the United States, or has a lawful status under the immigration laws."[17] A third version (H.J. Res. 129) likewise would limit citizenship by birth; at the time of writing it had attracted over forty cosponsors, including four Democrats.[18] All such proposals were pending at the time of writing.

HOW SHOULD WE SEE THESE PROPOSALS?

The reader's first reaction may be to dismiss these proposals to change the constitutional grant of citizenship on the grounds that they are unlikely to be enacted into law. It is true that the Fourteenth Amendment, the Constitution's basic guarantee of equal citizenship, has never been amended in its entire history.[19] It is also true that the U.S. Constitution makes the process of amendment relatively difficult.[20] Yet, most state constitutions also make their own amendment difficult; they make enactment of legislation by popular referendum costly and time-consuming as well. But this has not stopped a host of sponsors from enacting antigay or anti-immigrant measures in California and Colorado, or proposing similar ones in several other states.[21] Given the current climate, one cannot be certain that a national measure limiting the grant of citizenship does not lie ahead.

Such a measure would be consistent and continuous with numerous other nativist laws and policies that have been adopted or proposed. (See, e.g., chapters 4, 5, and 6 in this volume.) Moreover, the resolutions come at a propitious time. As was mentioned earlier, nativist sentiment increases during times of socioeconomic upheaval, like our own.[22] Changes in the job market, and the challenge from overseas competition for markets, mean that many Americans are today less secure of their jobs and status than in former years. At the same time, the conditions that produced the civil rights decade of the sixties are missing. Unlike then, we are not competing with the Soviet Union for the loyalties of the uncommitted Third World, most of which is black, brown, or yellow. Then, racism, lynching, and mean-spirited treatment of domestic minorities and foreign visitors were embarrassments which our competitors seized on as evidence of their system's superiority. Now there is less need to demonstrate that our system is better than godless communism. Derrick Bell's interest-convergence formula (which explains *Brown v. Board of Education* and other Cold War-era advances for blacks in terms of the interests of elite whites) would predict an era of rapid rollback in gains for ethnic minorities, foreigners, and other outsider groups.[23] Finally, we should recall that earlier nativist measures, like literacy tests, were first viewed with outrage but later enacted.[24] The same may happen with citizenship.

THE SCHUCK-SMITH ARGUMENT: CITIZENSHIP BY CONSENT

In addition, today's efforts to limit immigration and citizenship are aided by an elegant and influential argument from national autonomy. First propounded by two moderate liberals, Peter Schuck and Rogers Smith,[25] the argument has been appropriated by conservative forces across the nation. In a nutshell, the Schuck-Smith position holds that a nation ought to have unlimited discretion in deciding whom it shall admit. Communities should be able to determine their own membership; this is an important aspect of national autonomy. If large numbers of outsiders were free to settle, bringing with them new values, languages, and patterns of behavior, they would in effect have the right to force the nation to become something it is not. This state of affairs is inconsistent with the idea of a community of self-defining citizens; any nation is free to resist it.

The argument draws on the premises of communitarianism, a moderate-liberal school of jurisprudence that sprang up in the 1980s, perhaps as an antidote to the unfettered individualism of the early Reagan-Bush years.[26] But the argument struck a chord as well with conservatives, offering them a principled argument for accomplishing what many of them wanted to achieve—the promotion of an America-first philosophy—but for a much less noble reason, namely a dislike of foreigners and immigrants.

How shall we see the Schuck-Smith argument? In an ideal world, it would deserve serious consideration. But we do not live in an ideal world. In the United States, the current community—the institution to which the argument would hand unfettered discretion regarding immigration policy—is deeply affected by racism and exclusionary practices.[27] For much of our history, a national-origin quota system and, before that, anti-Asian and anti-Mexican laws, kept the numbers of immigrants of color low. We denied immigration and travel visas to communists and others espousing ideologies deemed dangerous. Literacy and English-speaking requirements cut down the number of immigrants from areas other than northern Europe. And round-ups, *Bracero* programs, English-only laws, and the panoply of nativist measures detailed in other chapters of this book made things difficult for immigrants from disfavored countries once they were here. For much of our history, women and blacks were denied the right to vote or hold office. Higher education was virtually closed to both until about 1960, and in Southern states, Black Codes made it a crime to teach a black to read.

"The community," then, is deeply shaped by racism, sexism, and xenophobia. This is so not only in terms of its demography and makeup but also its preferences and values. Handing such a community the keys to determine immigration policy is a recipe for self-replication and stasis. The community would (perhaps without knowing it) opt for the familiar—itself. In similar fashion, but even more blatantly, limiting the grant of citizenship to those who can prove blood descent would simply perpetuate the racist past.

BACK TO *DRED SCOTT V. SANDFORD?*

In *Dred Scott v. Sandford,*[28] decided by the U.S. Supreme Court in 1856, the U.S. judicial system dealt with the question of runaway slaves. At the time

Dred Scott was decided, the country was divided into two regions, the South, where slavery was legal and widely practiced, and the free North. The issue before the Court was whether Dred Scott, previously a slave, had become free by virtue of a period of time spent in the free North. The Court rejected his plea, holding that African Americans have "no rights which the white man was bound to respect."[29] The claim of such a person to citizenship was untenable, historically and legally: Blacks could not be citizens because they had not been so from the beginning; and the Framers of the Constitution, "great men," never regarded them that way. Justice Taney's opinion regards blacks as subhumans, a status that was only little improved by enactment of the Civil Rights Amendments a decade later. If blacks had any doubts on that score, *Plessy v. Ferguson,*[30] the "separate but equal" case decided in 1896, should have dispelled them. *Plessy,* which remained the law of the land until *Brown v. Board of Education,*[31] did little to improve society's view of blacks as citizens deserving full equality. Separate facilities served as constant reminders that blacks were a separate, and lower, order of humanity from whites, deserving poorer treatment simply on the ground of who they were.

The argument, structure, and rhetoric of present-day nativism contain overtones of *Dred Scott*-type reasoning—particularly so proposals to limit citizenship under the Fourteenth Amendment.[32] The Schuck-national autonomy argument echoes Taney's by reasoning from preexisting attitudes and enshrining them in law. The rhetoric, like Taney's, has overtones of scorn and condescension—foreigners are treated as pollution, as threats to national values of thrift and hard work. The study of nativist movements, past and present, brings into focus these and other alarming parallels and alerts us to what we may expect in the future. Like Taney's opinion, efforts to limit citizenship are efforts to maintain a system of white supremacy and to give that system the veneer of fairness and principle.

NOTES

1. See Thomas Muller, "Nativism in the Mid-1990s: Why Now?" chapter 6 in this volume, discussing the economic causation of much nativism.

2. The *Bracero* (temporary farmworker) program and national-origin quota system for allocating immigration permits are prominent examples. See introduction, *supra,* and Dorothy E. Roberts, "Who May Give Birth to Citizens? Reproduction, Eugenics and Immigration," chapter 11, and Gilbert Paul Carrasco, "Latinos in the United States: Invitation and Exile," chapter 10, both included in this volume.

3. See *Id.*

4. See Juan F. Perea, "Demography and Distrust: An Essay on American Languages, Cultural Pluralism, and Official English," 77 *Minn. L. Rev.* 269, 332–36 (1992).

5. *Id.* at 333–35.

6. *Id.* at 335–36.

7. *Id.* at 337–39.

8. See Michael Olivas, "The Chronicles, My Grandfather's Stories, and Immigration Law: The Slave Traders Chronicle as Racial History," in *Critical Race Theory: The Cutting Edge* 9 (R. Delgado ed., 1995).

9. *Id.* at 13–14.

10. See Leo R. Chavez, "Immigration Reform and Nativism: The Nationalist Response to the Transnationalist Challenge," chapter 4, and Jean Stefancic, "Funding the Nativist Agenda," chapter 7, both in this volume. See also Jean Stefancic, *No Mercy: How Conservative Think Tanks and Foundations Changed America's Social Agenda* (Temple University Press, 1996).

11. See, generally, T. Alexander Aleinikoff, *Immigration: Process and Policy,* (2nd ed. 1991) (on the many grounds for denying immigration or naturalization).

12. See text and notes 2–10, immediately *supra*.

13. On file with author; see Alan C. Nelson, "Alien Immigration Tide: California Governor's Idea to Deny Benefits Is Logical," *Dallas Morning News,* Aug. 29, 1993, at 5-J (discussing similar proposal).

14. Source cited *supra* note 13.

15. Nelson, "Tide," *supra* note 13.

16. On file with author.

17. On file with author.

18. On file with author.

19. The Fourteenth Amendment, which guarantees equal protection and due process of law, also provides for citizenship to "all persons born or naturalized in the United States and subject to the jurisdiction thereof."

20. See U.S. Const. art. V, setting out the method for amendment (on application of two-thirds of the states' legislatures; two-thirds of both Houses; a Convention; further ratification, etc.).

21. Generally, the proponent must gather a large number of signatures within a relatively brief time and have them verified by a state official, such as the Secretary of State.

22. See editor's introduction, *supra* this volume.

23. Derrick Bell, "*Brown v. Board of Education* and the Interest-Convergence Dilemma," 93 *Harv. L. Rev.* 518 (1980).

24. Text and notes 4–5 *supra*.

25. Peter Schuck and Rogers Smith, *Citizenship without Consent* (Yale University Press, 1985).

26. On communitarianism, see, generally, Richard Delgado, "Rodrigo's Fifth Chronicle: *Civitas,* Civil Wrongs, and the Politics of Denial," 45 *Stan. L. Rev.* 1581 (1993).

27. See Dorothy E. Roberts, "Who May Give Birth to Citizens? Reproduction, Eugenics, and Immigration," chapter 11, and Daniel Kanstroom, "Dangerous Undertones of the New Nativism: Peter Brimelow and the Decline of the West," chapter 16, both in this volume.

28. 60 U.S. 393 (1856).

29. *Id.* at 407.

30. 163 U.S. 537 (1896).

31. 347 U.S. 483 (1954).

32. See Gerald L. Neuman, "Back to Dred Scott," 24 *San Diego L. Rev.* 485 (1987).

18. THE TIGHTENING CIRCLE OF MEMBERSHIP
T. Alexander Aleinikoff

In a justly celebrated essay entitled the "Transformation of the Statue of Liberty," historian John Higham elaborates on a little known fact: that Emma Lazarus's famous tribute to "A mighty woman with a torch"—a "Mother of Exiles"—went virtually unnoticed when composed in 1883 (Lazarus died in 1887). It was not inscribed on the interior wall of the Statue's pedestal until 1903; and, in Higham's words, "the poem rested there for another thirty years without attracting any publicity at all." [1]

The Statue, as all schoolchildren know, was the inspiration of French sculptor Frederic Auguste Bartholdi and a gift from the French people, symbolizing the friendship of the two republics. It was to have been an exhibit at the Philadelphia Exposition of 1876, marking the centennial of American independence, but only the arm and the torch were completed by that time. At the inaugural ceremonies, the theme of immigration received no mention. Rather, again in Higham's words, "President Grover Cleveland discoursed grandiloquently on the stream of light that would radiate outward into 'the darkness and ignorance and man's oppression until Liberty enlightens the world.' . . . The rhetoric . . . concentrated almost exclusively on two subjects: the beneficent effect on other countries of American ideas, and the desirability of international friendship and peace." [2]

The torch that at first represented shining American ideals that would light the world, of course, eventually took on the gloss of the Lazarus poem—as a beacon of welcome, lighting the way to a free and democratic land. But this transformation occurred much later; indeed, *after* the great migrations of the early part of the century had ceased. By the 1930s, America could begin to recognize "the contributions of the newer ethnic groups" to celebrate its multicultural origins and attributes. [3] By then, the sons and daughters of the immigrants of earlier years *were* Americans—speaking English, graduating from institutions of higher learning, voting. During the 1940s, Higham reports, "the words of the poem became a familiar litany in mass circulation magazines, children's stories, and highschool history texts."[4] And in 1945, the tablet on which it had been inscribed in 1903 was moved to the main entrance of the Statue. Higham concludes: "Because few Americans now were immigrants, all could think of themselves as having been immigrants. ... [T]he new meaning engrafted on the Statue of Liberty in the second quarter of the twentieth century worked to close the rift that mass immigration had opened in American society."[5]

In this essay, I would like to consider whether the meaning of the Statue is again undergoing transformation—and whether that new meaning is widening rather than closing the new rift that the new mass immigration to the United States has opened in our day. I start with the front page of the *Detroit Free Press* on election day 1992. Covering the entire page was a large cartoon of the Statue of Liberty, with the heading (and here I rely on memory): "if you do not vote today, she stands for nothing." This is hardly a message about immigrants; it is, in fact, a statement about *citizenship*. Putting to the side for a moment current legislative proposals to cut legal immigrants off from federal benefits, the franchise remains the single most important distinction between the status of lawful permanent resident and citizen. The editors of the *Free Press* were equating the Statue not with the welcome of new arrivals but rather with the community of already-arrived full members (citizens): if you (citizens) do not vote today, she (a symbol of liberty, democracy—liberal democracy) means nothing. It is not obvious to me why the Statue was used in this manner. Interestingly, a Canadian law professor has suggested to me that it echoes the use of a replica of the Statue by Chinese students martyred in their protests for democracy in Tienanmen Square.

For the Statue to take on this new meaning—a celebration of citizenship—does, to some extent, return it to its roots. [For an extended exploration of the meanings of the Statue of Liberty, see chapter 2 in this volume—*Ed.*] The political liberty it initially memorialized—the liberty of the American and French revolutions—was freedom from monarchy and subjecthood, the establishment of the equal democratic liberty of *"citoyen."* And, of course, there is a natural link between immigrants and citizens. A Statue symbolizing citizenship may also celebrate immigration as the welcoming of persons intent on becoming citizens. It may lead us to put great efforts into naturalization, to encourage all here to become full members. But today I see a darker side of the emphasis on citizenship—a circling of the wagons more than an invitation to climb on board.

This is a new we/theyness. In earlier years, academics had suggested that the line between legal and illegal immigrants was artificial because it failed to recognize the invitation the United States had historically extended—at least de facto—to undocumented workers and also did not appreciate the rather full integration of "illegal" aliens into American society.[6] To these scholars— to many of us—"illegal" was a status, a name, a designation by the law that did not mirror the social reality. The legalization programs of the 1986 immigration legislation explicitly sought to resolve the tension between the legal categories and social reality; and *Plyler v. Doe* represented the (somewhat startling) judicial declaration of a constitutional effacing of the line between "legal" and "illegal."[7]

But times have changed. Although perhaps four million aliens in unlawful status reside in the United States, there is no mood to legalize any portion of them. Proposition 187 could not be clearer in its declaration of nonmembership; the governor and electorate of California have demanded reconsideration of *Plyler*.

So liberals have retreated a bit, choosing a smaller concentric circle: illegals are outside, but legal immigrants and citizens are inside. In words that few would have predicted a year or two ago, immigrant and ethnic advocacy groups are recognizing that enforcement of the border is a legitimate and significant public-policy goal. There is less support among these groups for increased interior enforcement. Laws providing sanctions against employers who hire undocumented workers are criticized for increasing discrimination against "foreign-looking" U.S. citizens and lawful immigrants. And deportations of undocumented long-term residents are criticized for disrupting families and communities. But once the line is drawn between legal and illegal aliens, logic does not limit enforcement to the border. Indeed, there appears to be a growing consensus that enforcement of employer sanctions must be stepped up and that state-of-the-art verification systems must be developed and deployed to ensure that illegal aliens already in the United States receive neither jobs nor benefits. So, too, it is now generally believed that the integrity of the immigration process demands that aliens determined to be living here illegally be removed effectively and expeditiously. So long as fundamental principles of due process are respected, it is unlikely that such efforts will be opposed.

Will the illegal/legal line hold? Here, I return to my opening comments on the Statue of Liberty. There is increasing evidence that yet a smaller circle is taking on primary salience: that of citizen.

As a constitutional matter, we are presented with differing views of the importance of the concept of citizenship in our fundamental law. Alexander Bickel (himself a refugee) opined that "[r]emarkably enough . . . the concept of citizenship plays only the most minimal role in the American constitutional scheme."[8] He finds this a happy fact: "A relationship between government and the governed that turns on citizenship can always be dissolved or denied.

. . . It has always been easier, it always will be easier, to think of someone as a noncitizen than to decide that he is a nonperson." [9] Chief Justice Rehnquist, on the other hand, has concluded that "the Constitution . . . recognizes a basic difference between citizens and aliens," finding that "[t]hat distinction is constitutionally important in no less than 11 instances in a political document noted for its brevity." [10] Most noteworthy for Rehnquist is the fact that the Fourteenth Amendment specifically defines citizenship; in placing a definition in the Constitution, Rehnquist argues, "Congress obviously thought it was doing something, and something important. Citizenship meant something, a status in and relationship with a society which is continuing and more basic than mere presence or residence." [11] Our constitutional tradition pays homage to both views. It is well established that aliens in the United States possess virtually all the constitutional rights with which citizens are endowed. Yet, it has never been doubted that, for some purposes, states and the federal government may distinguish citizens and aliens. [12] It is clearly constitutional, for example, to require that voters, jurors, and candidates for high office be U.S. citizens. And the Supreme Court has upheld state laws imposing citizenship requirements for occupations it concludes involve exercises of sovereign power: teachers, [13] police officers, [14] and probation officers. [15]

For years, Congress has taken Bickel's approach when defining eligibility for most federal benefits and opportunities. [16] That is, permanent resident aliens and citizens have been treated alike. The Supreme Court has applied similar rules under the Fourteenth Amendment to the states. [17]

But recent legislative proposals "reforming" the welfare system represent a dramatic shift in national policy. Under legislation adopted by the House of Representatives, lawful permanent residents would be fully excluded from five major "safety net" entitlement programs—cash assistance, food stamps, supplemental security income, Medicaid, and social services under title XX of the Social Security Act—whether or not they had previously worked in the United States and paid taxes. There would be some exceptions, for immigrants over seventy-five, veterans and their immediate relatives; but for the vast majority of permanent resident aliens, the bar would last until citizenship. According to its sponsors, the exclusion of immigrants from these programs will save over $20 billion a year.

What justifications are offered in support of this rending of the safety net? One justification might be the need to save funds in order to pay for other parts of welfare reform (or for tax cuts). But this justification appears impermissible.

Under general principles of constitutional law, a class of persons may not be carved out from protection or specially burdened without a rational basis. Indeed, when the burdened group is one that cannot protect itself in the political process, it might be argued that a more substantial justification is required.[18] The simple desire to save money cannot be an adequate justification for the exclusion of permanent resident aliens—either in constitutional or public policy terms.[19]

A more tenable justification would be to link the bar to exercise of the federal immigration power: Congress has the power to determine classes of admissible aliens; and for many years, aliens who are "likely to become a public charge" have been excludable. From this perspective, the ban on benefits can be viewed as enforcement of the public-charge exclusion ground. During the floor debate, Congresswoman Roukema expressed it this way:

> While the exclusion for legal aliens has received quite a bit of criticism, I want to make sure that everyone realizes an often-overlooked, but essential component of our immigration laws. For decades, our immigration laws have required immigrants to stipulate that they will be self-sufficient once they arrive in America, as a condition of their being allowed to immigrate in the first place. Consequently, receiving welfare has been grounds for deportation for these very same immigrants for generations.[20]

This is not quite right. The deportation ground for welfare usage mandates removal of an alien who "within five years after the date of entry, has become a public charge *from causes not affirmatively shown to have arisen since entry.*"[21] That is, the deportation ground enforces the exclusion ground. Importantly, it does not provide that any immigrant who goes on welfare is deportable. This theory underlying the existing law is consistent with a view of immigrants as "members-becoming"; it recognizes that they, like citizens, may fall on hard times and need assistance.

These considerations support the conclusion that the actual justification for the exclusion of immigrants from major entitlement programs turns on a narrowing conception of membership. In the words of Congressman Riggs, "the message that we are sending here, and we are clearly stating to our fellow citizens, [is] that we really are going to put the rights and needs of American citizens first."[22]

Of course the needs of American citizens come first. But does that necessarily mean that the needs of lawful permanent residents should count not at all? The problem with drawing a hard-and-fast legal immigrant/citizen line is that the transition from immigrant to citizen is a process, a maturation, an evolution—not an on/off switch. Many immigrants live in families with, and support, U.S. citizens. The majority of immigrants seek and attain citizenship. The vast majority of adult immigrants are gainfully employed, paying taxes to support the benefit programs. Immigrants, to my mind, are appropriately characterized not as outsiders or nonmembers, but as "citizens-in-training."

Heretofore, public policy has generally viewed immigrants this way,[23] recognizing that citizenship-building is a sound investment.[24]

This perspective suggests a different approach to the benefits issue—one proposed by the minority in the House and supported by the Clinton Administration—that offers a more direct link to the public-charge exclusion ground. An intending immigrant can overcome the public-charge test by demonstrating either that he or she has a job in the United States (and is therefore self-supporting) or by submitting an affidavit of support from a U.S. sponsor. The problem has been that courts have found the affidavits of support unenforceable. The minority proposal had two aspects: to make the affidavits of support judicially enforceable and to deem the sponsor's income to an immigrant who applies for needs-based benefits. Unlike the full-scale cut-off, these provisions are more carefully tailored to the manner by which an alien seeks to overcome the public-charge exclusion, and they avoid sending the binary message (citizens 1, legal immigrants 0) of the House-passed measure.

To be troubled by a hardening of the legal immigrant/citizen line may lead us not only to resist new measures but also to give closer scrutiny to lines existing in our current law. Consider, for example, the different treatment afforded citizens and permanent resident aliens under the preference system. Immediate relatives of U.S. citizens (parents, minor unmarried children, and spouses) are not subject to a numerical quota and therefore immigrate to the United States in relatively short order. However, spouses and minor children of permanent resident aliens (who were not related at the time of the permanent resident's entry) are subject to the numerical limits of the second preference. Parents of permanent residents are not covered by any entry category; they may join a child living in the United States only after the child naturalizes. To see the difference, consider two unmarried adults—Fred, a citizen at birth, and Lazlo, a permanent resident alien who came to the United States two years ago. Suppose that both spend some time overseas, fall in love and marry a non-U.S. citizen. Not surprisingly, Fred and Lazlo choose to petition for their spouse's entry to the United States. Fred's spouse will be granted permission to enter in a year or less; Lazlo will wait four to five years.

What sustains this distinction, trenching, as it does, on a fundamental constitutional interest protecting family? Perhaps the thinking is that we are more sure that Fred is likely to be with us for the long haul, but Lazlo—just as he has once changed his permanent residence—might decide to leave. Or maybe we recognize that "unification" can occur over there as well as here and that Lazlo would face less of a hardship than Fred in moving to where his spouse currently resides. Or perhaps the distinction is intended to provide an incentive to naturalization.

The rather straightforward answers to these possible justifications should be apparent, and I will not run through them here. The underlying theme to all is that the classification is woefully under- and over-inclusive, true for some but not all citizens and some but not all aliens.

But there is one justification that fits perfectly—the same one that seems to be at work in the benefits debate. It is the argument that we may, plain and simple, favor citizens over permanent resident aliens.

While the justifications suggested are probably strong enough to withstand the toothless constitutional scrutiny afforded regulations of immigration, Congress is free to go beyond the constitutional minimum.[25] I would think that a good case can be made for treating citizens and permanent resident aliens more alike in this regard. The interest here—living with close family members—is undeniably substantial.[26] Furthermore, as is frequently noted, permanent resident aliens pay taxes and are liable to military service to the same degree as citizens.

An obvious argument against a change in policy is the numbers. More than one million aliens are currently on the waiting list. Offering equal treatment to citizens and immigrants would render those on the waiting list immediately eligible for entry to the United States as permanent residents. Such a swell in admissions is not likely to be politically acceptable. One answer would be to take numbers from elsewhere—either reducing or eliminating the "diversity" category or crafting the INA to reflect a tighter definition of immediate family by allocating fourth-preference numbers to the second preference.[27] Or perhaps equality could be established over time by slowing increasing admissions until the backlog is cleared.

No doubt there are other proposals to consider here, and I am not recommending—at this point—a particular choice. What I am suggesting is that we should examine more closely what I believe to be the underlying rationale for disparate treatment: the permanent resident/citizen line.

Are we moving toward the smaller concentric circle? Consider the words of Justice White in the 1982 case of *Cabell v. Chavez-Salido,* which upheld a citizenship requirement for the job of probation officer:

The exclusion of aliens from basic governmental processes is not a deficiency but a necessary consequence of the community's process of political self-definition. Self-government, whether direct or through representatives, begins by defining the scope of the community of the governed and thus of the governors as well; aliens are by definition outside this community.[28]

This seems plainly wrong. Resident aliens are not outside the scope of the community of the governed; and they have, as I have mentioned, well-established constitutional rights. But White's language appears to realize Bickel's worst fears: exclusion by definition.

Without sounding too alarmist, let me suggest that the immigrant/citizen distinction may not be the final resting place in the definition of membership. Suppose that Congress determines that legislation cutting off benefits to immigrants has produced a rush to naturalization, and further suppose (1) that this effect means that the requisite dollar savings do not accrue and (2) that members of Congress conclude that the desire to get on the dole is not an appropriate motivation for becoming a U.S. citizen. Is it not conceivable that legislation would be introduced distinguishing naturalized citizens from native-born citizens for purposes of eligibility for federal benefits?[29] Might not some be inclined to make a naturalized citizen's immediate receipt of federal benefits grounds for denaturalization?

We have been proudest of our political history when it has been inclusive: the Fourteenth Amendment rectified the deplorable exclusivity of the *Dred Scott* opinion; the 1965 Immigration Act (belatedly) removed the ignominious National Origin Quota system—eliminating such ugly phrases as "the Asian Barred Zone"; the 1990 Immigration Act deleted outdated cold-war exclusion grounds.

As this nation pursues the crucial task of restoring credibility to immigration enforcement efforts, it must continue to celebrate legal immigration. The Statue of Liberty need not—and ought not—be redefined by narrowing the circle of "we." It should remain an inclusive symbol, extending to the newest Americans—citizens-in-training—an invitation to join in our experiment in democracy.

NOTES

Executive Associate Commissioner, Immigration and Naturalization Service, U.S. Department of Justice. The views expressed here are the author's and do not necessarily reflect the views of the INS or the Department of Justice.

1. John Higham, *Send These to Me* 81 (1975).
2. *Id.*
3. *Id.* at 85.
4. *Id.*
5. *Id.* at 87.
6. E.g., Linda S. Bosniak, "Exclusion and Membership: The Dual Identity of the Undocumented Worker under United States Law," 1988 *Wis. L. Rev.* 955; Gerald P. Lopez, "Undocumented Mexican Migration: In Search of a Just Immigration Law and Policy," 28 *UCLA L. Rev.* 615 (1981).
7. 457 U.S. 202 (1982).
8. Alexander M. Bickel, *The Morality of Consent* 33 (1975).

9. *Id.* at 53.

10. *Sugarman v. Dougall*, 413 U.S. 634, 651 (1973) (Rehnquist, J., dissenting).

11. *Id.* at 652. In *United States v. Verdugo-Urquidez,* 494 U.S. 259 (1990) (plurality opinion), Chief Justice Rehnquist shows ambivalence, stating that the Fourth Amendment only applies to "the people" of the United States, which he construes as "a class of persons who are part of a national community or who have otherwise developed sufficient connection with this country to be considered part of that community." 494 U.S. at 265.

12. T. Alexander Aleinikoff, "Federal Regulation of Aliens and the Constitution," 83 *Am. J. Int'l L.* 862 (1989).

13. *Ambach v. Norwich,* 441 U.S. 68 (1979).

14. *Foley v. Connelie,* 435 U.S. 291 (1978).

15. *Cabell v. Chavez-Salido,* 454 U.S. 432 (1982).

16. The one significant exception is eligibility for the federal civil service.

17. Welfare (*Graham v. Richardson,* 403 U.S. 365 [1971]); state civil service (*Sugarman v. Dougall,* 413 U.S. 634 [1973]); higher education financial assistance (*Nyquist v. Mauclet,* 432 U.S. 1 [1977]).

18. Gerald M. Rosberg, "The Protection of Aliens from Discriminatory Treatment by the National Government," 1977 *Sup. Ct. Rev.* 275; John Hart Ely, *Democracy and Distrust: A Theory of Judicial Review* 148 (1980).

19. Cf. *U.S.D.A. v. Moreno,* 413 U.S. 528 (1973).

20. 141 Cong. Rec. H3412 (1995).

21. Immigration and Nationality Act §241(a)(5), 8 U.S.C. §1251(a)(5) (1988 and Supp. V 1993) (emphasis supplied).

22. 141 Cong. Rec. H3412 (1995).

23. Ugly, glaring counterexamples were laws prohibiting Chinese and Japanese from naturalizing.

24. See Roberto Suro, *Remembering the American Dream: Hispanic Immigration and National Policy* 112 (1994) (describing policies of "integration"): "Immigration should be viewed as an enterprise in which both the immigrant and the host nation bring certain assets to the table and both have an interest in seeing that the enterprise succeeds. Both sides must make investments in each other, and both take risks on the assumption that they will each draw returns."

25. See Aleinikoff, *supra* note 12; Stephen H. Legomsky, "Immigration Law and the Principle of Plenary Congressional Power," 1984 *Sup. Ct. Rev.* 255.

26. See John Guendelsberger, "Implementing Family Unification Rights in American Immigration Law: Proposed Amendments," 25 *San Diego L. Rev.* 253 (1988).

27. Unused visa allocations for employment-based immigrants already rollover to the family-based categories the following year.

28. 454 U.S. 432, 439–40 (1982).

29. Cf. Immigration Reform and Control Act §201(h), 8 U.S.C. §1255a(h) (1988 and Supp. V 1993) (disqualifying legalized aliens from most federal benefits for five years, despite the fact that most would be permanent resident aliens for much of that time period).

INDEX

African Americans: Los Angeles riots, 111; rivalries with Hispanics, 89, 111; U.S. oppression of, 16, 52; white fear of in the South, 82. *See also* Blacks

Agriculture: binational system of production and reproduction, 138; migrant workers, 138

Aldrich, Thomas Bailey: "Unguarded Gates," 50–51

Aleinikoff, T. Alexander: identified "good alien/ bad alien" pattern in Supreme Court decisions, 172, 185 n. 47

Alien: connotations of the term, 231; as metaphor, 231; signifying Mexicans and Latinos, 231

Alien Land Laws: and Japanese, 169; as nativistic racism, 245

Alien: movie series, 232

Alien Nation, 284, 301; constructing the "Alien," 232; immigrants taking U.S. jobs, 31; racial anti-immigration arguments, 210, 214, 286

Aliens: images of in legal history, 167–73, 178–80; numbers in the U.S. population, 105; social construction, 230–32; war against, 2. *See also* Legal aliens; Undocumented aliens

Almaguer, Tomas: *Racial Fault Lines: The Historical Origins of White Supremacy in California,* California and racism, 136, 156

"America First": anti-internationalism, 67, 112, 281. *See also* Buchanan, Patrick

American identity: anti-immigration discourse, 62, 66; and Asian Americans, 245; and blacks, 208; and citizenship by birth, 208; and demographic change, 215; and James Baldwin, 247; and *jus soli* rule, 208; and multiculturalism, 248; and race, 208; and racial differences, 249; and racism, 211, 215; and slavery, 208; as white, 205

American Immigration, 234–35, 241 n. 38

American Immigration Control Foundation (AICF): donations from Pioneer Fund, 129

Americanization: Barbara Jordan, 94; Henry Ford, 25; U.S. Commission on Immigration Reform, 95–96

Anderson, Benedict: imaginary homelands, 245, 251; *Imagined Communities: Reflections on the Origin and Spread of Nationalism,* 252 n. 6

Anti-Chinese sentiment, 245; Chinese exclusion laws, 168; expressed in Supreme Court opinions, 167–69, 247. *See also* Chinese

Anti-immigrant sentiment: based on ethnicity, 109, 115; based on new immigration, 109; based on religious diversity, 115; Buchanan, 112; discourse, 61; economic concerns, 108; initiatives, 7, 63; legislation, 6; and multiculturalism, 113; nativism, 13; rhetoric, 66, 312; sentiment, 78, 105, 108. *See also* Immigrants

Anti-Japanese sentiment: and alien land laws, 169–70; *Korematsu v. United States,* 170. *See also* Japanese immigrants

Anti-Latino sentiment: as inspiration for new nativism, 2, 209–10; in Official English movement, 87–88. *See also* Latinos

Anti-Semitism: organizations, 26–27; in U.S., 27. *See also* Jews; Nazi Germany

Asian Americans: and American identity, 245; American Orientalism, 245; assimilation, 247; discursive production as foreign, 249; as foreigners, 180; as a model minority, 248; nativistic racism, 245; as opposite to "real" Americans, 247; as "Oriental," 245; as perpetual internal foreigners, 237; restrictions against community membership, 247; as threat to American dream, 248; and U.S. population growth, 28. *See also* Nativistic racism

Assimilation, 13; as Anglo-conformity, 18, 25, 211; Asian Americans, 247; of immigrants of color, 36, 165–66, 285–86; as one-way process, 211; racialized foreigners, 247; and U.S. English, 35. *See also* Americanization

Baldwin, James: America's national identity, 247
Balibar, Etienne: "neo-racism," 73; *Race, Nation, Class: Ambiguous Identities,* 73, 77
Balkanization: ethnic, 228; multiculturalism, 248
Bartholdi, Auguste: Statue of Liberty, 44, 324
Bell Curve, The: race and immigration, 32; race-IQ theories, 129
Bell, Derrick: interest-convergence theory, 3, 320
Benefits: brought by immigrants, 73; denial of benefits to immigrants, 65, 71; Federal Immigration Legislation, 65
Bennett, Bill: and Proposition 187, 113, 128
Bilingual education: opposition to, 124; debate, 110; criticisms of, 124
Bilingual Education: History, Politics, Theory, and Practice, 89, 101
Binational production and reproduction: agriculture, 138; binational households, 140; families and guest-workers, 72, 140. *See also* Production; Reproduction
Birthright citizenship: and American identity, 208; proposals to deny, 205, 207–8, 319; *Dred Scott* decision, 207; Fourteenth Amendment guarantee, 207, 319; *jus soli* rule, 207, 208. *See also* Citizenship
Blacks: and American identity, 208; and citizenship, 209; immigration and low wage jobs, 107; oppression of, 52; portrayal in *Dred Scott,* 322; and white tensions promoted by multiculturalism, 110. *See also* African Americans
Bo, Saum Song: "A Chinese View of the Statue of Liberty," 52–53, 55
Borders: control crisis, 225, 228–30; early history, 223; jurisprudence, 246; meditations on, 244–53; and national security, 227–28; contingency dependent upon racial features, 246. *See also* Nation-state borders; United States-Mexico border
Bosniak, Linda S.: analysis of usage of "nativism," 279–99
Bracero Program, 224; creation, 72, 138–39, 194, 236; and McCarran-Walter Act, 198; numbers of Mexican workers imported, 139, 203; and production and reproduction, 71; World War I-1922, 193; and World War II effort, 195; after World War II, 196
Brigham, Carl C.: early study of IQ, 22; intellec-
tual inferiority, 22, 213; study used in *The Bell Curve,* 32
Brimelow, Peter: *Alien Nation,* 284, 301; Amendments to Immigration and Nationality Law 1965, 301; American history of racism, 211; extreme pessimism, 303; Adolf Hitler, 305, 310; immigrant children, 214; immigration policy, 301; increasing number of immigrants, 33, 67; multiculturalism, 248; nativism, 284; race and ethnicity, 301; racial anti-immigrant arguments, 31–34, 210, 286; racism, 305. See also *Alien Nation*
Brown v. Board of Education, 322
Buchanan, Patrick: "America First," 67, 112, 281; American culture, 210; Proposition 187, 127; Republican presidential candidate, 35–36, 91; remarks on immigrants of color, 36, 285–86
Buck v. Bell: and Justice Holmes, 212; Supreme Court validated eugenic sterilization, 212
Bush, George: and New World Order, 244

Cabell v. Chavez-Salido: aliens and community membership, 330
California: anti-Chinese sentiment, 168; anti-Japanese sentiment, 169–70; attacks on immigration, 33, 61; border crisis, 229; demographics, 209–10; economy, 137–43; English as official language, 120; English Only, 136; farm workers, 138; history, 136; immigrant use of public services, 108; immigration, poverty, and social conflict in, 136–61; job losses, 138; latinization, 140; Los Angeles riots, 111; military base closures, 138; as "paradise lost," 137; plant closures, 138; population, 210; poverty by ethnic group, 141; Proposition 63, 120; *Racial Fault Lines,* 136; social conflict in, 136–61. *See also* Proposition 187
Camp of the Saints: and the Laurel Foundation, 123
Carrasco, Gilbert Paul: history of *Bracero* programs, 192–99
Charter of the Organization of American States. *See* OAS Charter
Charter of the United Nations. *See* U.N. Charter
Chavez, Leo R.: *Shadowed Lives: Undocumented Immigrants in American Society,* 137, 156
Chavez, Linda: resignation from U.S. English, 88, 123
Chico, California: racism expressed through violence, 250. *See also* Nativistic racism
Chin, Vincent: racism expressed through violence, 249. *See also* Nativistic racism
Chinese: exclusion laws, 168; immigration,

167; immigration restrictions against, 52. *See also* Anti-Chinese sentiment

Chinese Exclusion Case, The (Chae Chan Ping v. United States), 168, 183; based on race, 302; threat to sovereign nation, 247

Chinese Massacre of 1885: racism expressed through violence, 250. *See also* Nativistic racism

"Chinese View of the Statue of Liberty, A," 52–53

Chomsky, Noam: and New World Order, 244

Citizenship: 'citizen,' 326; by consent, 320–21; and the Constitution, 319, 326–27; as control of reproduction, 215; Delgado, Richard, 318–23; and eugenicists, 215; Federal Immigration Legislation, 64; forced repatriation of Mexican workers, 194, 197; law used to create a Jewish underclass in Nazi Germany, 313; law used to create an underclass in the U.S., 313; narrowing conception of membership, 328; Nazi position on, 310; proposals to deny, 2, 64; and racism, 321; restricting birth of citizens, 205; and the Statue of Liberty, 325; distinguished from permanent resident aliens, 329. *See also* Birthright citizenship

Citizenship without Consent: Illegal Aliens in the American Polity: rejection of *jus soli* rule, 208

Clinton, Bill: immigrants as "aliens," 231; legal immigration, 64; and official English legislation, 98; Proposition 187, 127; support of immigration reforms, 97, 99, 114

Cold War: end of, as cause of nativism, 3–4, 67, 119, 320

Communitarianism: citizenship by consent, 321; dislike of foreigners and immigrants, 321; and racism, 321

Community membership, 8, 205; *Cabell v. Chavez-Salido,* 330; and racial differences, 249; restrictions against Asian Americans, 247

Congress, 103rd and 104th: Official English, 91

Conservative think tanks: production of nativism, 119–35

Convention on the Elimination of All Forms of Racial Discrimination. *See* Race Convention

Coolidge, Calvin: eugenics, 302; veiled racism, 303

Corporate downsizing: as cause of economic hardship, 107; and technological change, 107

Crawford, James: *Bilingual Education: History, Politics, Theory, and Practice,* 89, 101; *Hold Your Tongue,* 120; Laurel Foundation's donations, 123; and nativist hypothesis concerning Official English, 89; on Tanton's FAIR and U.S. English, 121

Cubans in South Florida: effect of Republican loyalties on Official English, 86

Cultural "others," 16

Darwinism: concerning races, 20

Decline of the West, The, 305, 306–9. *See also* Spengler, Oswald

Delgado, Richard: on citizenship, 318–23

Demography: attempts to control, 205, 215; and California, 209–10; changing national composition of ethnic groups, 211; current trends, 38, 117, 166; and end of National Origins quotas in 1965, 28–29, 173, 301; effects of nativistic movements, 14; and immigration concentration in metropolitan centers, 209; Latino growth, 142; as threat to American identity, 209

Dillingham Commission, 1911: and Mexican immigration, 72

Discourse: anti-immigrant, 61; nativism, 6, 8

Dole, Robert: and Official English, 91–92, 97, 112

Domestic terrorism: immigration from volatile nations, 111

Dred Scott v. Sandford: and citizenship, 207, 321–22

Duke, David: Republican presidential candidate, 35

Economic conditions: benefits of immigration, 109; in California, 137–43; cause of nativism, 6, 105, 106–9; corporate downsizing, 107; costs of immigration, 109; affected by immigration, 13, 109; global economic restructuring, 137; net public sector "deficit," 108; Urban Institute study, 130, 230

Education: denial to undocumented aliens, 71; reforms and bilingual education, 124

Ellis Island: only European immigration as American heritage, 233

Employers: relationship with immigrant workers, 70, 235

English First: lobbies for legislative reform, 125; Lawrence Pratt, 125; promote English Only agenda, 119–20. *See also* English Only; Official English movement; U.S. English

English Language Advocates (ELA): chair Robert Park, 126; Tanton and WITAN memo, 126

English Only, 35; California's new nativism, 136; California's Proposition 63, 121; immigration reform, 62; linked with racism, 86–88; nativistic racism, 245; promoted by English First, 119–20, 125; promoted by U.S. English, 119–20; success of, 132. *See also* English First; Language; Official English movement; U.S. English

English-only laws: in California, 120; and citizenship, 318; state enactments, 79–80. *See also* Proposition 63

Equality: and liberty in the United States, 46

Ethnocentrism: in early America, 16–23

Eugenics, 7, 205–19; border-control crisis, 225; and citizenship, 215; Calvin Coolidge, 302; history, 129, 135, 212; and history of immigration, 212–14; Pioneer Fund, 129; sterilization, 212; during World War I, 21

Eugenics movement: contemporary parallels, 214

European immigration: Ellis Island, 233; and meanings of Statue of Liberty, 44–55; romanticized, 233

European nativism, 176–77

Federal Immigration Legislation: denial of benefits to naturalized citizens, 65; denial of benefits to noncitizens, 65; proposals, 63; proposed denial of citizenship, 64, 319–20

Federation for American Immigration Reform (FAIR), 31; border crisis, 229; financial contributors to, 88, 123; and legislation, 130; 1990 Immigration Act, 112; and the Pioneer Fund, 129, 130; Proposition 187 funding, 129; and John Tanton, 87, 121, 210

Filartiga v. Pena-Irala: customary international law as U.S. law, 258, 271 nn. 34, 39

Fix, Michael, and Jeffrey Passel: critique of Donald Huddle, 230, 241 n. 34. *See* Urban Institute

Foner, Eric: American identity, 208

Fong Yue Ting v. United States, 168, 183 n. 17

Forced repatriation of Mexican workers: American citizens, 194, 197; Depression era, 193–94; "Operation Wetback," 172, 197, 236–37

Ford, Henry: Americanization, 25

Forked Tongue: The Politics of Bilingual Education, 124

Fourteenth Amendment: proposals to change birthright citizenship, 2, 207, 319

Franklin, Benjamin: assimilation, 18; xenophobia, 165

Galarza, Ernesto: *Merchants of Labor: The Mexican Bracero Story,* 157 n. 14, 242 n. 62

German citizenship law: Adolf Hitler, 309; Nazis, 310

German Jews: deprived of political rights, 311; as second-class citizens and "illegal aliens," 311. *See also* Anti-Semitism; Jews; Nazi Germany

German National Socialism: and U.S. nativism, 305

German-speaking peoples: movement against, 5

Gingrich, Newt: bilingualism and Quebec separation from Canada, 97; immigrant threat to sovereignty, 68; legal immigration, 112

Gotanda, Neil: racialized foreigners, 247

Government services: immigrant demand, 108, 142; Immigration Reform and Control Act, 142

Gramm, Phil: border crisis, 228; conservative Republicans, 91

Grant, Madison: Nordic race, 21; *The Passing of the Great Race,* 213

Guadalupe Hidalgo, Treaty of. *See* Treaty of Guadalupe Hidalgo, 1848

"Guardian of the gates," Statue of Liberty as, 49

Guest-worker program. See *Bracero* Program.

Hardin, Garrett: funded by Pioneer Fund, 129; *Living within Limits: Ecology, Economics, and Population Taboos,* 123–24

Hayakawa, S. I.: Official English legislation, 120; and U.S. English, 87

Health care: denial to undocumented immigrants, 71; prenatal care, 71; Proposition 187, 70–71, 206–7

Herrnstein, Richard. See *Bell Curve, The*

Higham, John: nativism definition, 1, 281, 283; nativism and racism, 302–3; *Strangers in the Land,* 8 n. 1; "Transformation of the Statue of Liberty," 324; views on nativism, 283, 294–95 n. 19, 302

Hirabayashi v. United States, 170, 184 n. 26

Hispanics: anti-immigrant targets, 62; use of government services, 108; Los Angeles riots, 111; feared reconquest of American Southwest, 68, 227–28; rivalries with African Americans, 89, 111. *See also* Latinos

Hitler, Adolf: Brimelow and, 305, 310; *The Decline of the West,* 309; German citizenship law, 309; *Mein Kampf,* 309; on U.S. immigration laws of the 1920s, 310

Hold Your Tongue, 120

Holmes, Justice Oliver Wendell, Jr.: approved eugenic sterilization in *Buck v. Bell,* 212; *The Decline of the West,* 307

Huddle, Donald: study of economics of undocumented migration, 230

Hughes, Stuart H.: *Oswald Spengler: A Critical Estimate,* 306, 315; on Spengler, 308

Illegal Alien: anti-, 61; refers to Mexicans, 171–72. *See also* Undocumented aliens

Images of the Immigrant: affect law and policy, 166; Mexicans as "bad aliens," 67–69, 172; and race, 165–81

Immigrants: benefits from, 73; demand on government services, 108; and the economy, 73, 109, 190; as "enemy," 67; job threats, 29,

30, 108; low wages, 106–7, 113; negative images, 166; net public sector "deficit," 108; population, 105–6; public opinion of, 30; effect of race on perceptions of, 167; reimagined as less deserving community members, 73; as "savages," 17; sociopolitical and cultural concerns about, 110; and taxes, 33; unequal treatment, 181; unskilled worker wages, 106. *See also* Anti-immigrant sentiment; Blacks; Mexican immigrants

Immigration: acts from 1917–24, 15, 310; California attacks on, 33, 61; crises, 13–14, 38; discourse, 6, 8, 61–74, 279–91; economic benefits, 109; economic costs, 109; end of racist quotas, 28; English colonization, 15; effect on jobs, 31; and nativism, 105; Nazi position on, 310; race and immigration policy, 176, 181; reasons for, 14; reform, 93, 97, 99, 114; reform and nativism, 61–77; rise in racial and ethnic diversity, 111. *See also* European immigration; Recent immigration

Immigration Act, 1924, 15, 24; and social discontent, 109

Immigration Act, 1995, 105, 116

Immigration and Nationality law, 1965 amendments: criticized by Brimelow, 301

Immigration Moratorium Act: current immigration reform, 132

Immigration Reform and Control Act of 1986 (IRCA), 36, 224; special status to migrant farmworkers, 142–43, 199

Immigration restriction: arguments, 174–76; arguments analyzed, 279–91

Immigration rhetoric: anti-immigrant, 66, 312; of Peter Brimelow, 8, 67, 301–6; racial subtext, 175

Immigration Time Bomb, The, 66–67, 76 n. 32

Income-transfer programs: use by Latinos, 142

Independence Institute: and Proposition 187, 130–31

Intelligence tests, 22. See also *Bell Curve, The;* Brigham, Carl C.

Interest-Convergence theory, 3, 320

International Covenant on Civil and Political Rights (ICCPR), 259; applies to "persons" within U.S., 263

International Human Rights, 254–76; definition, 256; norms as U.S. law, 257–61; and Proposition 187, 262

International Law: Convention on the Elimination of All Forms of Racial Discrimination, 259; *Filartiga v. Pena-Irala,* 258; International Covenant on Civil and Political Rights, 259; and nativism, 7; OAS Charter, 259; *The Paquete Habana,* 258; Protocol Relating to the Status of Refugees, 259; sources, 255–56; treaties, 257; U.N. Charter, 259; Universal Declaration, 260

International Migration: reasons for, 14, 28–30

Irish Catholic immigrants: targets of nativists, 18

Italian immigrants: targets of nativists, 21

Japanese immigrants: Alien Land Laws, 169; *Korematsu v. United States,* 170. *See also* Anti-Japanese sentiment

Jefferson, Thomas: citizenship and blacks, 209

Jews: immigrant targets of nativists, 22. *See also* Anti-Semitism; German Jews

Jones, Maldwyn Allen: *American Immigration,* 231, 241; rise of illegal Mexican immigration, 235

Jordan, Barbara: Americanization recommendations, 94. *See also* United States Commission on Immigration Reform

Jus soli rule, 207; rejection, 208. *See also* Birthright citizenship

Kanstroom, Daniel: compares Peter Brimelow's rhetoric to that of Oswald Spengler, 300–17

Kemp, Jack: and Proposition 187, 113, 128

Korematsu v. United States: anti-Japanese sentiment, 170

Ku Klux Klan: against southern and eastern European and Asian workers, 23; violence against Jewish and Catholic immigrants, 22, 27

Laboulaye, Edouard de: and Statue of Liberty, 44

Lamm, Richard: *The Immigration Time Bomb,* 66

Language: linguistic politics, 93; middle-class resentment of language difference, 109. *See also* English First; English Only; Official English movement; Spanish language; U.S. English

Latinos: as "aliens," 230, 231; anti-immigrant initiatives, 7; flee political oppression, 29; as foreigners, 180; images of, 192; income-transfer programs, 142; latinization of California, 140; multiculturalism, 68; population of California, 210; use of social services, 142; in U.S., 190–204; U.S. population growth, 28, 137, 142. *See also* Anti-Latino sentiment; Mexican Americans; Mexican immigrants

Laurel Foundation: funded Hardin's *Living within Limits: Ecology, Economics, and Population Taboos,* 123–24; James Crawford examines, 123; reprint of Raspail's *Camp of the Saints,* 123; support of Tanton organizations, 123

Lazarus, Emma: "The New Colossus," 47; and "Transformation of the Statue of Liberty" (John Higham), 324

Legal aliens: reforms proposed to reduce legal
immigrants, 64–65, 328–31; war against, 2.
See also Permanent resident aliens
Liberty: Statute of Liberty as French symbol,
46
Literacy tests of 1917: precursor to immigra-
tion curbs of 1920s, 98, 318; analogy to Of-
ficial English, 98
*Living within Limits: Ecology, Economics, and
Population Taboos,* 123–24; funded by Pio-
neer Fund, 129
Lodge, Henry Cabot, 23
Los Angeles riots: interethnic strife, 111

Maastricht Treaty, 225
*Maidens Meal and Money: Capitalism and the
Domestic Community,* 69, 76 n. 47
Marti, Jose: observations of Statue of Liberty,
48
Meillassoux, Claude: immigration production
and reproduction, 69; *Maidens Meal and
Money: Capitalism and the Domestic Com-
munity,* 69, 76
Mein Kampf, 309
Men: support of Official English, 81
Metaphors of immigration: "aliens," 230–32;
annexation by Mexico, 68; enemy, 67; invasion, 67; objects of lynching and vigilante
mobs, 68; reconquest, 68, 69; territory control, 68; Third World, 67; threat to national
security, 68; threat to sovereignty, 68; war,
67, 68
Mexican Americans: discrimination after World
War II, 196; fighting in World War II, 196.
See also Mexican immigrants
Mexican immigrants: "alien," 231; anti-immigrant initiatives, 7; control of California, 69;
militancy, 227; and national security, 227;
rise of officially recorded Mexican immigration, 235; stereotyped "illegal aliens," 171–
72; unrecognized as part of American heritage, 233. *See also* Latinos; Mexican Americans
Mexican labor: demanded by American employers, 235; migrant workers, 138; as strikebreakers, 235; treatment of, 149; as union-
ized strikers, 235. *See also* Forced
repatriation of Mexican workers; Migrant
workers
Mexican Labor Program: creation, 194. See
also *Bracero* Program
Middle-class: resentment towards immigrants,
109
Migrant workers: agricultural production and
reproduction, 138; Immigration Reform and
Control Act, 199
Migration from Mexico: causes, 139–40. *See
also* International migration

Miller, Alice Duer: Statue of Liberty, 53–54;
"An Unauthorised Interview between the Suf-
fragists and the Statue of Liberty," 54
Minorities: discriminatory treatment of, 3,
320–21; nativism definition, 1; U.S. against,
1; white fear of, 82
Modern nativism, 13, 92; race neutral justifications, 178. *See also* New nativism
Mody, Navroze: racism expressed through violence, 250. *See also* Nativistic racism
Mongrelization, 21
"Mother of Exiles," 47
Muller, Thomas: economic and political factors
causing nativism, 6
Multiculturalism: and American identity, 248;
anti-immigrant, 113; and Balkanization, 248;
and Latinos, 68; promotes black and white
tensions, 110
Murray, Charles: See *Bell Curve, The*
Myths about immigrants, 38; illegal entry,
31

Nation: population shaping, 15
Nationalism: nativism definition, 1; response to
transnational migration, 73
National-origin: immigration bias, 14
National origin quota restrictions of 1924, 5;
history of, 23–25; literacy tests preceded, 98,
318; to preserve white supremacy, 24–25; relation to present nativism, 82–83; return to,
98
National security: borders, 227–28; metaphors,
68
"Nation of Immigrants": United States as, 14
Nation-state borders: as inconsistent with capitalist development, 226; changing significance of, 238; early history of, 223; as social
constructions, 223, 226. *See also* Borders;
United States-Mexico border
Nation-states: racial/ethnic difference in the
structure of, 239
Native Americans: U.S. oppression of, 16
Nativism: anti-immigrant, 13; causation, 105–
9; the concept, 279–99; and conservative
think tanks, 119–35; and cost arguments
against immigration, 287; definition, 1, 167,
279, 281, 283; effects on demography, 14;
discourse on, 6, 8, 279–99; diverse meanings
of concept, 281; and economic uncertainty,
6, 105, 106–9; end of Cold War, 67; and ethnicity, 109; European, 176; and German National Socialism, 305; global economic restructuring, 137; history of, 13–43, 82, 165;
and immigration, 105; and immigration reform, 61–77; as indeterminate concept, 282;
international legal context, 7, 254–68; literacy tests, 98; movements, 1, 14; and Nazis,
305; as normative boundary for immigration

debate, 291; and Official English, 78–102; race-based, 166–67; and racialist immigration discourse, 287; racism, 245, 302–3; restriction of who gives birth to citizens, 205; sentiment, 82; and sciences, 21; and social, ethnic and cultural disparities, 105; as a Southern phenomenon, 83; targets of, 2, 18, 21; as term of condemnation, 283; World War I, 21; and xenophobia, 165. *See also* Modern nativism; Nativistic racism; New nativism

Nativism Reborn? The Official English Language Movement and the American States, 79, 99 n. 2

Nativistic racism, 19–23, 166; and Asian Americans, 245; and Chico, California, 250; Chinese Massacre of 1885, 250; defined, 245, 249; and English Only, 245; expressed through violence, 249–50; and Navroze Mody, 250; and Proposition 187, 245; and Vincent Chin, 249

Naturalized citizens, denial of benefits to, 65, 331

Nazi Germany: citizenship and immigration laws, 310–11; citizenship laws used to create Jewish underclass, 313; construction of Jews as illegal aliens, 311; use of deportation, 312; Final Solution, 311; and nativism, 305; positions on immigration and citizenship, 310

Neo-racism: Etienne Balibar, 73, 77 n. 66; immigration replaces race, 73

"New Colossus, The" (Lazarus), 47

New nativism: combination of influences, 165; as crises, 226–32; described, 61–74; immigrants as less deserving community members, 73; ways of viewing, 119. *See also* Modern nativism

Nishimura Ekiu v. United States: border jurisprudence, 246, 252 n. 18

North American Free Trade Agreement (NAFTA), 225

Nuremberg Laws: voluntary Jewish emigration, 311

Nuremberg Trial, The: international human rights, 257; and national sovereignty, 262

OAS Charter: international law, 259; Proposition 187 and education, 267

Official English movement, 4, 6; development, 78–88; Robert Dole, 91–92, 97, 112; elite driven, 80; explanations, 80; funding, 119; history, 120; laws, 78–80; laws by legislative enactment, 83; laws by referendum, 83; and nativism, 81; nativist backlash, 78–102; nativist hypothesis, 89; political hypothesis, 89; political right, 89; popular support for, by ethnicity, 90; popular support, hypotheses regarding, 88–91; popular support by Republi-

cans, 86; popular support by Republicans, whites, and men, 81, 89; precursor to tightening immigration laws, 98; racial hypothesis, 88; referendum campaign, 85; state enactments, 79; symbolic laws, 79. *See also* Language

Operation Wetback: repatriation, 172, 197, 237; rise of illegal Mexican immigration, 235. *See also* Forced repatriation of Mexican workers

Otherness: racial others, 13, 16. *See also* Cultural "others"; Minorities; Race

Oyama v. California, 169, 183 n. 20

Paquete Habana, The: customary international law as U.S. law, 258, 271 n. 37

Park, Robert: English Language Advocates, 126

Passel, Jeffrey, and Michael Fix: critique of Donald Huddle, 230; immigrants and taxes, 33

Passing of a Great Race, The: eugenics, 213

People of Color: demographics of U.S., 38

Perea, Juan F.: on the Official English movement, 35, 42 n. 71

Permanent resident aliens: legislative proposals, 327; shift in national policy, 327; treatment of, vs. treatment of citizens, 329. *See also* Legal aliens

Pioneer Fund: and FAIR, 129–30; funds American Immigration Control Foundation, 129; funds eugenicists, 129; funds Hardin's *Living within Limits,* 129; history, 129

Plessy v. Ferguson: Justice Taney's conception of blacks, 322

Plyler v. Doe: right to education of children of the undocumented, 4, 10 n. 26, 261, 326

Political oppression: as cause of Latino immigration, 29

Population-Environment Balance (formerly Environmental Fund): contributions to, 123

Porter, Rosalie: director of READ, 124; *Forked Tongue: The Politics of Bilingual Education,* 124

Poverty, in California: Cabanas family case study, 150–52; Green family case study, 152–55; by ethnic group, 141; multiracial poor, 148

Pratt, Lawrence: English First president, 125

Prenatal care of undocumented women, 71, 206–7. *See also* Proposition 187; Undocumented aliens.

Production: agriculture, 138; *Bracero* programs, 71, 190–200, 224, 321; relationship to reproduction, 70, 71. *See also* Binational production and reproduction

Proposition 63, 120; supporters and opponents, 90

Proposition 187, 2, 37, 61, 143, 249, 254; Bennett and Kemp, 113, 128; California's new nativism, 136, 177–81; creation, 126; as declaration of nonmembership, 326; response to demographics, 209; denies reproductive health services, 206–7; domestic legal challenges, 261; drafters' nativist sentiment, 178; FAIR, 129; funding for, 119, 128–29; funding opposing, 128; inconsistency with international human rights, 262; Independence Institute, 130; national effects, 131; nativistic racism, 245; OAS Charter, 267; creates permanent underclass, 107; and Governor Pete Wilson, 92, 127, 178; political significance, 108; political support for, by ethnicity, 63, 93; pregnant women, 207; Race Convention, 266–67; U.N. Charter, 266; undocumented immigrant women, 207; Universal Declaration, 266–67

Protocol Relating to the Status of Refugees: international law, 259

Public assistance: use by immigrants, 142. *See also* Government services

Public opinion: of immigrants in 1993, 30

Pulitzer, Joseph: funding of Statue of Liberty pedestal, 45

Quebec: linguistic comparisons with U.S., 97, 110

Race: and American identity, 208, 249; and Darwinism, 20; of immigrants, and nativist response, 166, 167; effect on immigration policies, 176, 181; inferiority, 13; and recent immigration, 209

Race Convention: international law, 259; nondiscrimination on custom, 263; Proposition 187; denial of services, 266; education, 267

Race, Nation, Class: Ambiguous Identities, 73, 77

"Racial Balance": reason for discriminatory National Origins quotas of 1924, 24

Racial Fault Lines: The Historical Origins of White Supremacy in California: and California racism, 136, 156

Racialized foreigners: Asian Americans, 247; presumed inability to assimilate, 165–76, 247

Racism: and American history, 211; and American identity, 215; and Brimelow, 305; and Chico, California, 250; and communitarianism, 321; in creation of American identity, 211, 215; and English Only, 86; and immigration quotas, 28; and immigration rhetoric, 175; and limiting citizenship, 321; manifested in perception of immigrants, 211; nativism, 19–23; "neo-racism," 73; Official English laws by referendum, 84, 86; shapes "the community," 321

Raspail, Jean: *Camp of the Saints* and the Laurel Foundation, 123

Recent immigration: compared negatively with past European immigrants, 232; demographic concentration in metropolitan centers, 209; ethnicity as a cause of nativism, 109–11

Refugees: use of government services, 108; Haitian policies, 111

Rehnquist, Chief Justice William: and citizenship, 327

Reich, Robert B.: employer sanctions on illegal immigrants, 70

Reisler, Mark: Mexican labor as strike breakers, 235

Reproduction: agriculture, 138; citizenship as control of, 215; costs, 70; eugenics, 7; examining immigration, 69; relationship to production, 70, 71; restrictions as dehumanizing, 214; target for immigrant reform proposals, 70. *See also* Binational production and reproduction.

Reproductive Health Services: denial to undocumented immigrants, 206–7

Republicans: support Official English, 81

Santa Cruz County, 143–50; immigrant labor, 137

"Save Our State" (SOS): creation, 126; immigrants blamed for economic problems, 190; Proposition 187, 136, 177

Schengen Agreement, 225

Schlesinger, Arthur, Jr.: American identity, 304; multiculturalism, 248

Schuck, Peter: citizenship by consent, 320–21; *Citizenship without Consent: Illegal Aliens in the American Polity,* 208

Sciences: used for nativism, 21

Shadowed Lives: Undocumented Immigrants in American Society, 76 n. 46, 156 n. 3

Simpson, Alan: anti-immigrant sentiment, 115; proponent of immigration restrictions, 115, 227

Slavery: abolition of, and liberty ideal, 45; and American identity, 208

Smith, Rogers: citizenship by consent, 320–21; *Citizenship without Consent: Illegal Aliens in the American Polity,* 208

Social Conflict: in California, described, 136–61

Social Services: use by immigrants, 142. *See also* Government services

Spanish language: organizations against Official English legislation, 85; sentiment against, 96, 110

Spengler, Oswald, 305; *The Decline of the*

West, 305; *Man and Technics,* 308; precursor to the Nazi regime, 309
Spengler, Oswald: A Critical Estimate, 306, 315
Statue of Liberty, 44–58; Bartholdi, 44, 324; "A Chinese View of the Statue of Liberty," 53; and citizenship, 325; funding for, 45; "Guardian of the Gates," 49; as an inclusive symbol, 331; Laboulaye, 44; "Mother of Exiles," 47; symbolism, 44, 46; Tienanmen Square, 55; "Transformation of the Statue of Liberty," 324; "An Unauthorised Interview between the Suffragists and the Statue of Liberty," 54. *See also* Lazarus, Emma
Stein, Dan: anti-immigrant advocate, 30–31; FAIR and the Pioneer Fund, 130
Strong, Josiah: *Our Country,* 20
Symbolism: nativism, 6; Official English laws, 79; Official English laws and moving beyond, 91; Statue of Liberty, 44–55

Takahashi v. Fish & Game Comm'n, 169, 183
Taney, Chief Justice Roger: image of blacks, 322
Tanton, John, M.D.: background, 87; English Language Advocates, 126; Federation for American Immigration Reform, 87, 121, 210; Laurel Foundation Support of, 123; U.S. English, 121. *See also* Tanton Memo
Tanton Memo, 87; anti-Latino sentiment, 87–88, 210; English Language Advocates, 126; immigration in California, 122; opponents of U.S. English, 122
Tatalovich, Raymond: *Nativism Reborn? The Official English Language Movement and the American States,* 79, 99; Official English movement development, 6
Third World: as metaphor for recent immigration, 67. *See also* Metaphors of immigration
Tienanmen Square: and Statue of Liberty, 55
"Transformation of the Statue of Liberty": and Emma Lazarus's poem, 324
Transnational communities: defined, 224; across Mexico-U.S. border, 224
Transnational labor, 149
Transnational lives, 158
Transnational migration: definition, 62; challenge to nationalism, 73; treatment of migrants, 149
Treaty of Guadalupe Hidalgo, 1848: ceded California to U.S., 191; established present U.S.-Mexico border, 234

"Unauthorised Interview between the Suffragists and the Statue of Liberty, An," 54
U.N. Charter, 257, 270; international law, 259; nondiscrimination on custom, 263; Proposition 187 and denial of services, 266

Undocumented aliens: denial of education, 71; "invasion" of, 67, 229; refers to Mexicans, 171–72; prenatal care, 71, 207; Proposition 187, 2; war against, 2; women, 207
Undocumented families: as threat to nation, 206
"Unguarded Gates," 50–51
United States: history of immigration and nativism, 13–39
United States Commission on Immigration Reform: and Americanization, 95–96; Clinton support, 114; findings and recommendations, 114; immigration restrictions, 94; legal immigration, 64, 95
United States corporations: responsibility for immigration, 29–30
United States government: responsibility for immigration, 29–30
United States-Mexico Border: constructing, 226–27; social construction of, 223–43; Treaty of Guadalupe Hidalgo, 234. *See also* Borders; Nation-state borders
United States Supreme Court: border jurisprudence, 246; eugenic sterilization, 212; on illegal Mexican immigration, 172
Universal Declaration of Human Rights: international law, 260; Proposition 187 and denial of education, 267; Proposition 187 and denial of services, 266.
Urban Institute: economic impact of undocumented immigrants, 33, 130, 230
U.S. English: assimilation, 35; Chavez, Linda, 88, 123; English-only workplaces, 122; financial contributions to, 88, 123; funding for California's Proposition 63, 121; S. I. Hayakawa, 87; immigrants blamed for economic problems, 190; leading Official English movement, 81, 119; opponents concerning Tanton memo, 122; promotes English Only, 189–20; referendum campaign, 85; response to Tanton memo, 123; Tanton, 87, 121. *See also* Official English
U.S. English Foundation. *See* U.S. English
U.S. Inc., donations to, 123

Watsonville, California: described, 144–46, 150–52; Latino majority, 144
Welfare benefits: denial of benefits to undocumented persons, 63–66, 206–7; Depression era, 193
White, Justice Byron R.: *Cabell v. Chavez-Salido* and community, 330
Whiteness: and American identity, 205; and black tensions promoted by multiculturalism, 110; fear of minorities, 82; population shaping, 15; support of Official English, 81; "white race" origin, 19
Will, George: American culture, 210

Wilson, Pete: border crisis, 229; and guest-
worker program, 71; illegal immigration, 92;
denied prenatal care to undocumented
women, 71; Proposition 187, 92, 127; Proposition 187 and race, 178; undocumented
aliens, 3

WITAN: English Language Advocates, 126;
Tanton memo, 122

Xenophobia: defined, 293 n. 12; history of nativism, 13–43; nativism, 165; reason for immigration reform, 69, 254